THE LIVING LIGHT DIALOGUE

Volume 16

Reproduction of the cover image of the
1972 edition of *The Living Light*

[See the appendix for a discussion of the image's symbolism.]

THE LIVING LIGHT DIALOGUE

Volume 16

※

Through the mediumship of
Richard P. Goodwin

Living Light Books

The Living Light Dialogue Volume 16
Copyright © 2022 Serenity Association
Through the mediumship of Richard P. Goodwin.

All rights reserved. No portion of this book may be reproduced—electronically, mechanically, or via internet transmission—without advance, express written permission of the publisher except in the case of brief quotations embodied in critical articles and reviews. No derivative work—games, supplemental material, video—may be created without advance, express written permission of the publisher. For information address Living Light Books, P.O. Box 4187, San Rafael, CA 94913-4187.

Cover design copyright © 2022 by Serenity Association.
Cover photograph by Serenity Association, 2022; copyright © 2021 by Serenity Association.

www.livinglight.org

Library of Congress Control Number 2007929762
ISBN: 978-1-947199-40-8

FIRST EDITION

This volume of teachings is dedicated to the spirit friends who brought to Earth the Living Light Philosophy. With eternal gratitude, we pray that we may demonstrate these principles and continue to bring to publication these teachings.

CONTENTS

Acknowledgment ix
Preface xi
Introduction xv
A/V Class Private 36 3
A/V Class Private 37 27
A/V Class Private 38 71
A/V Class Private 39 115
A/V Class Private 40 155
A/V Class Private 41 197
A/V Class Private 42 223
A/V Class Private 43 253
A/V Class Private 44 283
A/V Class Private 45 313
A/V Class Private 46 341
A/V Class Private 47 375
A/V Class Private 48 399
A/V Class Private 49 427
A/V Class Private 50 459
Appendix.. 491

ACKNOWLEDGMENT

Grateful acknowledgment is made to the many friends and associates for invaluable aid in compiling this book, for their helpful suggestions, for their loyal interest and encouragement.

Special acknowledgment is due to those who painstakingly and selflessly transcribed and proofread the text.

PREFACE

It was through the mediumship of the Serenity Association founder, Mr. Richard P. Goodwin, that a philosophy known as the Living Light was given in more than 700 classes over a twenty-five-year period.

To be specific, the philosophy was imparted through Mr. Goodwin by a magistrate who had lived on Earth some 8,000 years ago. The former magistrate is known to Living Light students as "the Wise One," and he narrated the journey of his soul on the other side of life, the experiences—especially the difficulties—he encountered in having to face himself, as well as the teachings he earned to help himself through the realms in which he traveled. It was his decision to share the teachings with souls on both sides of "the curtain."

Prior to the advent of the Wise One, Mr. Goodwin had prayed for a teacher from the realms of light. Mr. Goodwin, since age fourteen, had been the instrument through which spirit was able to communicate with those seeking help. But he saw that his mediumship brought only temporary solace, because the people he was trying to help soon became fascinated with the phenomena and ignored the help that spirit was imparting. He prayed for someone who would bring forth teachings that would benefit any soul seeking a path to a greater awareness of himself and of God.

His prayers were answered in 1964 when the Wise One came through for the first time. Mr. Goodwin, at first apprehensive about what this new teacher would impart, was taken into deep trance and not able to control what was being revealed through him. Upon hearing the recorded classes afterward, however, he became convinced of the goodness of the teacher and of the value of the simple, beautiful teachings. This, then, was the beginning of the Living Light Philosophy given to Earth through the mediumship of Richard P. Goodwin.

These classes were held Sunday mornings at the Serenity temple. This particular volume includes fifteen classes, from A/V Class Private 36 through A/V Class Private 50, and cover the period of time from February 23, 1986, until June 8, 1986.

The foundation of the classes—the foundation of the Living Light Philosophy itself—is the Law of Personal Responsibility which states, in part, that we are responsible for all our experiences, and that our experiences are the return of the laws that we have established with our thoughts, acts, and deeds. Through greater awareness of our thoughts and by exercising our divine right of choice, we may choose to establish laws of greater harmony and goodness.

The Living Light Dialogue teaches that we have come to Earth to learn the lessons that are necessary to free us from the dictates and limits of our own thoughts and judgments, which are the mental patterns that we follow through our own lack of awareness and are so very potent, forceful, and limiting. These teachings guide us in making the necessary changes in our thinking in order to free ourselves from those patterns and to express our soul consciousness.

The choice of guiding the direction of our life, as stated by the Wise One when he speaks of being with a person, place, or thing, is, in essence, of being in this world and not a part of this world. He further explains that no matter what experiences we encounter, no matter what we do or do not do, we—our spirit—may view the experience in objectivity from a soul level of consciousness where peace reigns supreme.

The teachings of this volume help us to restore harmony or balance in our life by flooding the consciousness with spiritual affirmations and prayers, a few of which can be found in the appendix. When reason is restored, by balancing our sense functions with our soul faculties, we will consciously experience peace. Without annihilating our ego or our sense functions, we will find a pathway of expression for our soul. Where there was once disturbance, now there is acceptance. Where there was disease, now there is poise. And where there was hopelessness and despair, now there is reason, divine neutrality; and peace shows the way.

If you make the effort to apply these laws, such as, "If man is a law unto himself, what are you doing with the law that you are?", and demonstrate the wisdom of patience, the truth of this philosophy will be your living demonstration.

As the teacher states in CC 130, "My journey of many centuries and much experience has brought me here to Earth to share with you these simple teachings that have come as the effect of a long, long, long journey. Let not your journey be so long in the realms of illusion. For it is not necessary for you. For in your evolution, you have earned an awakening. But it is up to you to do something that is constructive and worthwhile."

INTRODUCTION

[This introduction was written by Mr. Goodwin and originally appeared in *The Living Light,* which were the first teachings of the Living Light Philosophy published in book form. The entire text of The Living Light was republished in *The Living Light Dialogue, Volume 1.*]

"Think, children. Think more often and think more deeply."

The teachings in this book were given as a progressive series of lessons to a group of four students who were sitting for spiritual unfoldment with me beginning in January of 1964. The communications were regular until October of that year, when nearly a seven-year silence ensued, and resumed in 1971 to the present. They were received in three ways by me as a channel. The main text was taped from a direct control of my voice in deep trance at special sittings of our group, during which I had no experience of the voice or what was being transmitted. A few scattered verses were given independently when I was privileged to see and hear our teacher clairvoyantly. I have also been a channel for this communicant when speaking from the podium at church and in answering difficult questions at our public seminars.

Nearly all we know about our teacher is contained in the lectures. He reports that he had tried for sixteen years to break through an interference barrier that the channel had to deep trance. When our conditions were in resonance with his patient wisdom, he came through ready to teach his understanding. I have seen him as an old man dressed in white with long flowing white hair. He has blue eyes, slightly smiling and deeply compassionate. I have always called him the Old Man. The students liked to call him the Wise One. He is surely one of those often called a Teacher of Light. I do not know his country, although he indicated at one time that he was from 6000 B.C., and a form of a judge in his time.

The text is often difficult, but it is complete, having been transcribed word for word from the original tapes recording the trance voice. It is presented with a minimum of punctuation to be freer for the individual interpretation of each reader. The lessons given before the long silence are phrased with many allegories often paradoxical. There are repetitions and renewals of theme, but it is explained that if an understanding is not perceived, compassion dictates that it be said again. Some of the topics have but a simple mention with little development but all are revealed, we are told, according to merit.

The Old Man is a fine teacher. He has in a hundred ways intertwined his allegory, progressive explanations, unfolding exercises, and timely references to reach a multitude of levels of individual understanding. A notable change is his more direct style of presentation beginning in 1971.

There is an endearing intimacy of person that can be felt through his lectures, a meaningful and loving encounter with a wise friend. Like an old man, he makes a mistake and conscientiously corrects himself a few paragraphs later. He listens often and carefully to our earnest discussions of his words. He consults with a group of experts on evolution and cites their learning in his lesson. His use of the direct address "children" or "my children" is not patronizing but infinitely loving and supportive.

A word must be said about the teachings. The Old Man makes clear that his lessons are not dogma, a creed or a narrow way, but simply his own understanding offered to us as a form of instruction to aid us in our own individual progression. When he speaks of Laws, he does not refer to man-made rules or moral traditions but to the cosmic and atomic way-things-are, the natural world of what-is, the universal laws of life, part of the original creative design and through which creation is fulfilled. These laws are beyond the possibility of being changed, suspended, transcended, or destroyed but they are ever a tool of mankind, not his master. First, through our awareness of the universal laws and then slowly through our developed understanding, the powers of creation are accessible to us. Not power over men's minds or circumstances, but power over whatever is selfish and imperfect in ourselves is the way up the eternal ladder of progression. When the Old Man cautions us concerning the Law of Responsibility or gives us a thinking exercise to explore the Law of Identity in a dynamic manner, he prepares us to take another step. And all move in accordance with the Law of What Can Be Borne.

Our teacher shows us how the two worlds are drawn together. In his realm, he describes, there is a great diversity of thought, many schools of understanding; but the Light is always known by the Light. Because of the interdependence of the two realms, listening to our discussions helped to clarify his teaching to others on his side of the curtain. His love and gratitude he humbly equates with ours.

The lessons to be perceived are not new, they are very old, but they are new to certain levels of our being. I would personally advise the reader, after reading this volume of discourses in full, to make a daily habit (or when there is a feeling or need) to sit quietly with the book. Open it at random and be guided to the Light by the passage that is there for the day. This technique is still used by the original students who were given the lessons and by many students after them who have studied in unfolding classes with me through these teachings.

Go beyond the words into feeling, into the immediate meanings for you. Touch into the inspiration that flows into the form of this book. It is from the Divine..

RICHARD P. GOODWIN
San Geronimo, California
June, 1972

A/V Class Private

A/V Class Private 36

[*In A/V Class Private 35, the teacher was seated in the east wing, which was located on the second floor of the temple, while the students were seated in the dining room watching the class on a large monitor, and questions that had been submitted in advance were read by the cameraman. Again, in this class the teacher and the cameraman are in the east wing, while the students were in the dining room. However, in this class, the teacher uses a blackboard to draw various diagrams and images. The words written by the teacher on the blackboard are often spelled phonetically, usually abbreviated, and in uppercase. The images in the first three classes of this volume have been exported from the video frames of the classes, digitally enhanced, and, when necessary, redrawn to match as closely as possible the lines drawn by the teacher. Regarding the images of this volume, when only a portion of the blackboard is depicted, the images do not have a frame; when the images represent the complete blackboard, a frame is used, which signifies that the blackboard is about to be completely erased.*]

Good morning, class. Welcome to our new semester.

Now I expect you all have your notebooks and pens ready this morning for these classes that will be given to you in this way. And so let us get our pens ready. And for today's class, we'll begin this with the question, What are we?

[*The teacher writes "WAT R WE" at the top of the blackboard. He first writes the "W" in the "WE" as a "V", but after he finishes, he corrects the letter. This results in a "W" that is slightly malformed.*]

I'm going to give you a few moments to do your drawing.

[*On the left side of the blackboard the teacher draws a straight, horizontal line and labels it "INF."*]

This is the line of infinity.

[Well past the right endpoint of the line of infinity and well above it, the teacher draws a small circle and adds three lines radiating downward from the circle. He then draws a somewhat larger circle at the right endpoint of the line of infinity so that its lower arc overlaps that endpoint. He subsequently labels that larger circle "ETRN."]

And this is the circle of eternity. So we'll take just a moment so you have an opportunity to draw what is on the blackboard. *[The teacher labels the small circle with the three radiating lines "PRCPN".]*

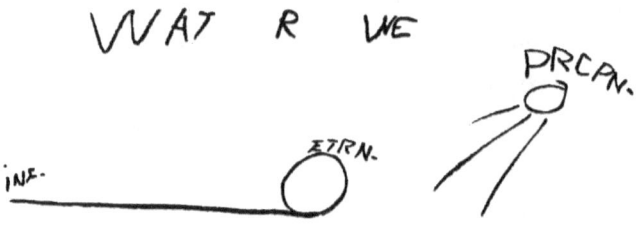

[Figure 36.1]

This is perception. Eternity is our perception of infinity. *[He points to each label as he speaks.]*

Infinity plus eternity equals totality. Totality is understanding. *[As he speaks these sentences, he writes them just below the horizontal line of infinity.]*

We are infinity. *[After first pointing to the word "WE", the teacher then points toward the line of infinity.]* Our perception *[He points to the rays emanating from the circle labeled "PRCPN."]* of what we are, infinity, *[He now points to the line of infinity.]* is eternity. *[He now points to the circle of eternity.]* Infinity and perception thereof, known as eternity, is totality. Totality is understanding. *[As the teacher speaks, he points to the corresponding word of the sentences written on the blackboard.]*

And so you have the mathematical figure of nine, which is known as totality or understanding. *[The teacher draws a nine below the circle of eternity and labels it "TOTA".]*

Now an obscure view of what we are, what life is, infinite or infinity, an obscure view thereof, what you would consider as a lower perspective, is known as conception. *[In the lower right corner of the blackboard, he draws a small circle with three radiating lines and labels it "CONCP."]*

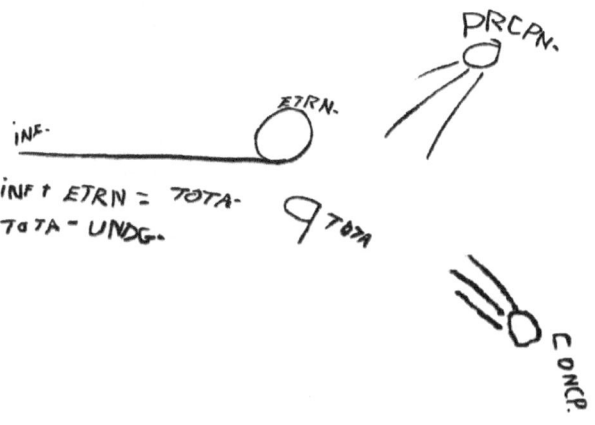

[Figure 36.2]

Therefore, when you look from below *[He points to the circle of conception.]* at what you are, infinity, *[He now points to the line of infinity.]* you conceive from your perspective, *[He again points to the circle of conception.]* instead of perceive *[He now points to the circle of perception.]* what you are. *[He now points toward the circle of eternity.]* By looking from below, *[The teacher again points to the circle of conception.]* you see clearly what you create. *[The teacher points to the area of the blackboard between the circle of conception and the circle of eternity.]* By looking from above, you view what you are and its potential, for that which is below is controlled by the Law of Gravity, which is known as grounded. Therefore, those who look from below conceive, from their advantage point, as some might say, conceive varying forms, *[The teacher draws many curved lines, representing forms, between the rays circle of conception and the circle of eternity.]* which create and cause the viewer, looking through the mist of form, from the vantage point of below, [many obstructions].

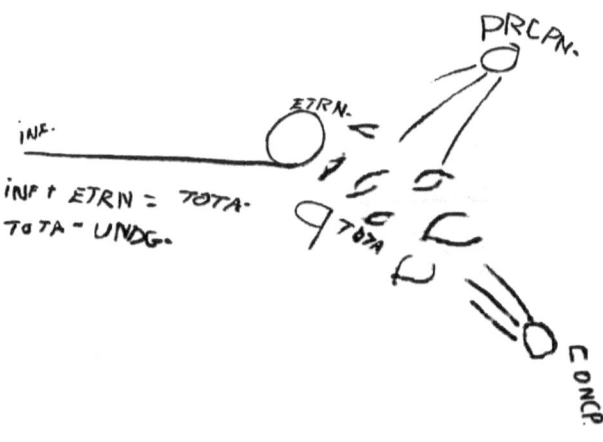

[Figure 36.3]

That which is above, that which is above controls that which is below. *[He writes an "A" at the top of the blackboard, just to the right of the "WE" and a "B" just to the left of the circle of conception.]* The control of that which is below is the sustenance which is drawn from that which is above.

Now kindly take and make your notes that we may move on with these teachings that you are receiving in this new semester. *[The teacher pauses for a moment.]*

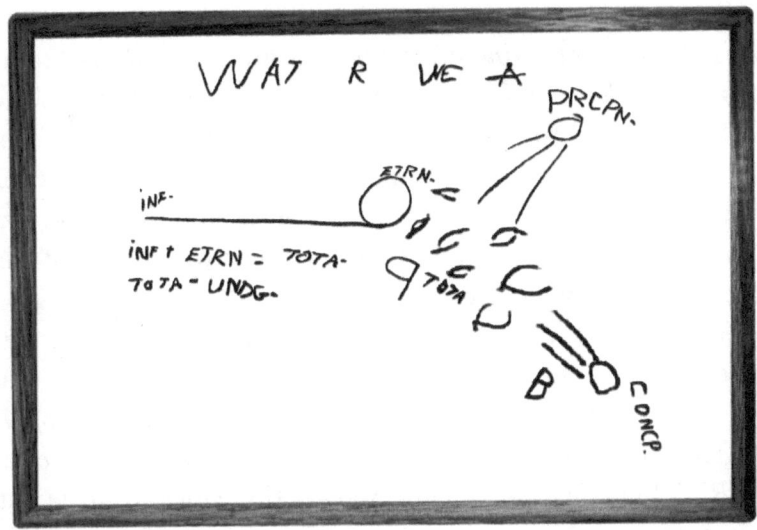

[Figure 36.4]

Now I accept that you all have this copied in your notebooks that we may move on to the next step.

[The teacher erases the entire blackboard. Images with frames are the complete drawings, while images without frames are only a portion of the final image.]

I'm in hopes that in time we'll have our little blackboard well conditioned so that it won't take quite so long to erase. It's much easier to imprint something than to remove it. Even our little blackboard is proof to us of that this morning.

We therefore have what is known as perception, which leads us to, of course, the viewing in its fullness of what we are, which is known as infinity. We also have seen conception, a viewing from a lower vantage point. And being lower, we therefore are controlled by the Law of Gravity, which is necessary for form or limit. Without gravity, the Law of Gravity, form or limit does not exist.

For example, here we have infinity. *[The teacher draws a straight, horizontal line on the blackboard. Just above the left endpoint of the line, he labels it "INF.-"]* A straight line. That is what we are. We are infinity. Life *is* infinity. When we view what we are, we move in a straight line and return unto our self. That is the goodness of life. The awareness and the awakening of moving on a straight line is true to that which is, and that which is, is that which you are.

So you take what is known as infinity and eternity, your perception of it, here, your perception of what you are is eternity. *[The teacher draws a circle so that the lowest arc of the circle overlaps the right endpoint of the line and labels the circle "ETRN".]* That's what you are. You are that which returns unto its source.

If you look at what you are, then your eternity is questionable for you have made it so. As I stated a moment ago, your eternity is dependent upon perception. That which is does not exist without the reaction of what is known as the observer. For example, the straight line of infinity cannot be perceived without the perceiver. So when infinity is perceived, you have the awareness of eternity. For those who do not perceive infinity do not have awareness of eternity, for eternity is perception of infinity.

In time, we will all know beyond all the shadows of doubt, which are conception, forms created by the laws of gravity, what we are. There will then no longer be question of whether there is eternity or there is not eternity, for we have perceived what we are.

All experiences in life are dependent upon conception for experience is the movement of form or limit. Now let's put that down in your notebooks. Experience is the movement of limit. *[Just below the line of infinity, the teacher writes the sentence as he speaks.]* Experience is the movement of limit. The movement of limit is the action of—what? *[As he speaks, he writes that sentence just below the first sentence, but stops at "of".]* Experience is the movement of limit. The movement of limit is the act of? *[After a short pause, he continues.]* Put that in your notebooks. The movement of limit is the action of what? The movement of limit is the action of being. *[He writes "BEING" and then underlines it.]* We'll write that out fully so that you will have no question in your notebooks. *[Most of the words in both sentences were abbreviated, but "BEING" was spelled out completely. Since there were no video frames with sufficient detail, the text in the figure below was almost entirely redrawn.]*

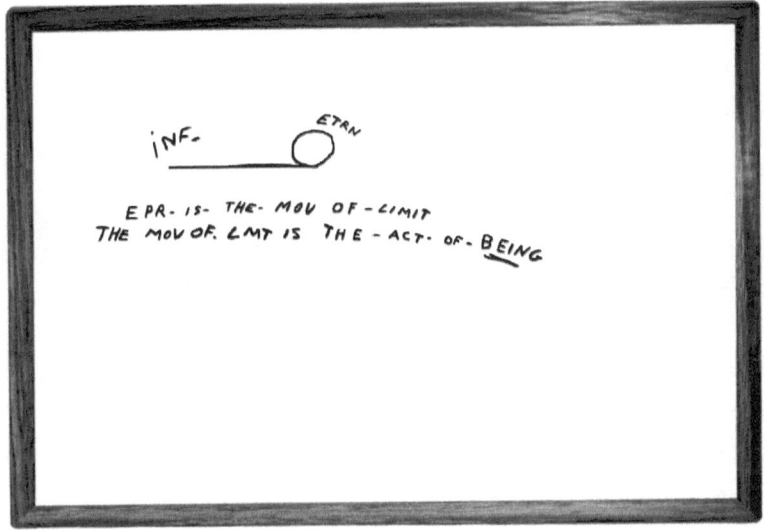

[Figure 36.5]

We'll go on here this morning to our next step. *[The teacher erases the entire blackboard.]*

Now let us not forget in our classes it's much easier to put it on than to take it off, speaking here of the blackboard and this eraser. Experience.

The number of the universe of infinite, eternal goodness is what? The number of responsibility is the number of power. It has already been given to you. *[The teacher writes the numeral nine on the blackboard.]* You call it the number nine. You've got it topsy-turvy. This is the way a nine is. *[He draws a horizontal straight with a circle, the lower arc of which overlaps the right endpoint.]*

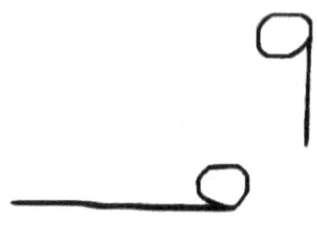

[Figure 36.6]

[The teacher erases the vertical (or topsy-turvy) nine, but leaves the horizontal nine.]

Now, because you are infinity *[He writes "INF-" just above the left endpoint of the horizontal line.]* and because your perception of what you are is eternity, *[He writes "ETRN" just above the circle.]* all experience takes place, all experience *[He writes "EXP-" just below the circle.]* takes place in your perception *[He writes "PRCPN" to the right of the circle.]* of what you are. *[As he speaks the words, the teacher writes "WAT Y R" beneath the line of infinity.]*

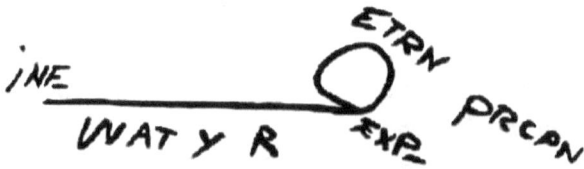

[Figure 36.7]

Now let us take a moment for our notes, and I will repeat this for you. You are infinity. *[Using a pointer, he points to the*

"*INF-*".*]* Your perception of what you are is eternity. *[With his pointer, he retraces the circle of eternity.]* All experience takes place in keeping with your perception *[He points to the "PRCPN".]* of what you are. *[He again retraces the circle with his pointer.]* The basic principle of perceiving infinity, what you are, is eternity. *[He points to the center of the circle.]* From this, *[Using his pointer, he retraces the horizontal line and the circle.]* what you understand as nine or totality (understanding), all numbers have been given birth. There are nine. All others are combinations thereof.

So when you feel that you have had enough experience, when you feel that change, for you, is advisable, then you must, through your perception, remove this. *[The teacher erases the labels "PRCPN", "ETRN", "EXP-" and the circle of eternity.]* And return to what you are. *[With the eraser, he points to the line of infinity.]*

In the moments *[He now erases the label "WAT Y R" below the line of infinity. All that now remains on the blackboard is a horizontal line with "INF-".]* that you remember what you are, in those moments, there is no limit; there is no obstruction, for in those moments, in the moments of what you are, *[Using a pointer, he traces the horizontal line.]* there is no distortion. And being no distortion, there cannot be obstruction. That in life which is not distorted is not obstructed. Let us understand that all obstructions are effects of distorting the basic design of what is. So when you do not tempt yourself to distort the design of the principle of what is, you have no obstructions.

For example, you say that you want to move from five to eight. *[The teacher writes a 5 above the line of infinity and well to the right he writes an 8.]* First of all, to move from five to eight, you must remember what you are. *[He draws a horizontal line to the left of 5.]* By perceiving what you are, remembering there is, you therefore, through that perception *[The teacher draws a circle at the right endpoint on the horizontal line that is to the left of the 5.]* have your totality. Within your totality, which is your understanding, you have accepted number five. *[The teacher writes a 5 within the circle.]* That's what you have created. Having created number five, you desire to move to number eight. *[He adds a dash and an 8, also within the circle.]* For you are under the Law of Gravity and, therefore, must move in keeping with the laws that are in gravity.

[The teacher draws a new line of infinity and circle of eternity below and slightly to the left of the 8 that is not within the circle.]

You have, in order to move from number five to number eight, you must establish the law that governs manifestation.

[Figure 36.8]

The law governing manifestation *[The teacher now draws a large circle below the newest line of infinity and circle of eternity. And inside that circle, he draws a roughly equilateral triangle, the apex of which touches the top of the circle. The lower vertices of the triangle also touch the arc of the circle, below its midpoint.]* is that. This is the symbol *[With his pointer, he points to the large circle with the triangle within.]* of the law governing the laws of gravity. You must therefore, in equal portion, you must therefore establish equal distribution *[In the upper left area within the circle but outside of the triangle, the teacher writes 1. He then writes 2 in the area inside the circle but outside of the triangle below its horizontal line and a 3 in the area on the right corresponding to the location of 1.]* of what you are, *[He retraces the line labeled "INF-".]* infinite, intelligent Energy, into perfect balance of what you have created: being number five. *[He points to the 5 within the circle of eternity on the line of infinity near the 5.]* Being number five *[He writes 5 in the center of the triangle.]* and moving to number eight. *[He now writes 8 outside the lower left quadrant of the circle with the triangle.]*

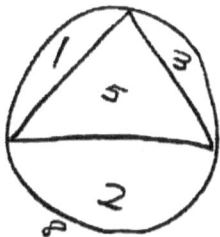

[Figure 36.9]

Now, the difference between five and eight, mathematically, is three. You desire to move, mathematically, to number eight. You must therefore use the power from above, perfectly balanced with the power from below, *[The teacher first draws an equilateral triangle with the apex pointed downward and then another overlapping equilateral triangle with the apex pointed upward.]* which gives to you what I gave you so long ago: a number eleven. *[The teacher writes 11 near the top of the board between the first 5 and the first 8.]*

So you see clearly that the manifestation of what you desire is subject to the power above and the force below. When you have followed the formula of life, you will have the manifestation, and you will also have, as its benefit, if you can call it benefit, you will have as its benefit manifestation of that which you desire, for you have now created it. *[He now draws a circle connecting the two vertical lines of the 11 at the top of the 11 and then another circle connecting the two vertical lines at the bottom of the 11.]* And it is your dual eternity.

We'll take a few moments here because I know it takes time for you to put this information into your little notebooks.

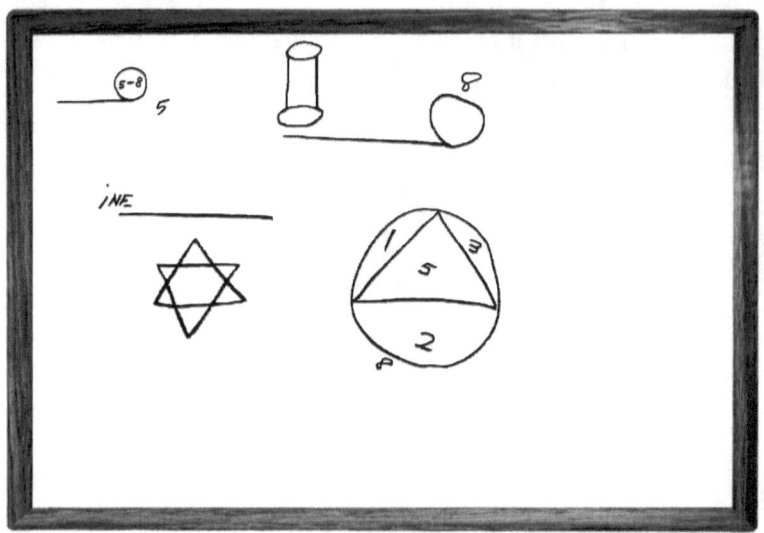

[Figure 36.10]

Now while you are doing so, I will remind you that next class, next Sunday, all questions submitted will be pertinent to that class which has been given, which is today's class. And so this is our new semester. And I'm sure that you already have many questions, but kindly place your attention upon putting it as clearly as possible into your notebooks so that you may do your studies and be qualified to ask questions concerning the class. If I'm going too fast for you, perhaps you could speak up. I think we have a communication system here in this temple. I know we do. But if I'm going too fast, I'm pausing now so that you will have time. *[He pauses for a few moments.]*

Surely that's sufficient time. *[The teacher erases the entire blackboard.]*

Now we'll move on to the next step. Whereas so much of [our] time seems to be spent in dreaming, we should discuss a bit about dreaming. *[As he speaks, he draws a straight, horizontal line with a circle at its right endpoint. The circle extends slightly below the line, instead of resting upon it.]* You will note that the circle of eternity, which is now a little off the line of infinity, which, of course, is created by your perception *[Well to the right of the circle of eternity and just a little higher than the line, he draws a smaller circle with three lines radiating from it and labels it "PRCPN".]* of what you are: infinity. *[He now writes "INF" just above the left endpoint of the horizontal line.]* And because of how you are perceiving what you are, your eternity is off-balance. You see, it has no stabilization of infinity under it. *[Without writing on the blackboard, the teacher retraces the arc of the circle that is below the line of infinity.]*

And so life, experience for you is a very, very delicate, delicate balance. One moment you feel good; the next moment you don't feel so good. For that which you perceive of what you are, your perception is off. You are not off. Your perception of what you are is not quite right, for you have lowered your perception *[He points to the lowest of the three lines radiating from the circle labelled "PRCPN".]* of what you are. Your esteem is lacking energy. *[As he speaks this sentence, he writes "ESTM IS LACK-ENG" on the blackboard between the circle labeled perception and the circle of eternity. He underscores the "ENG" just before he speaks the word "energy."]*

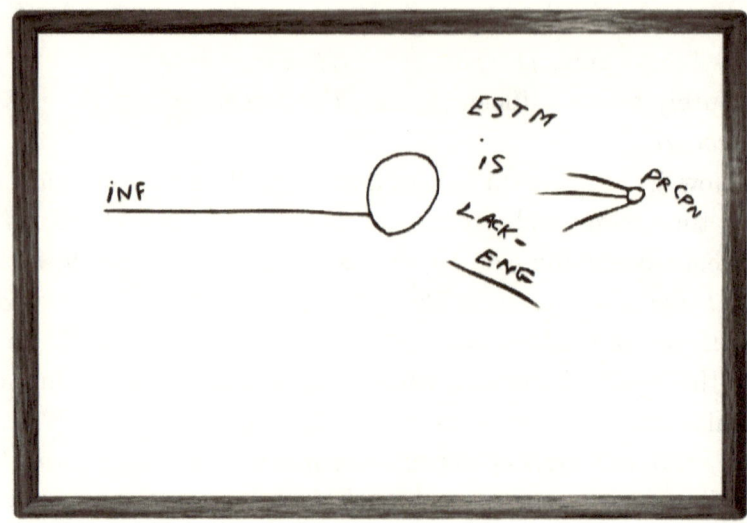

[Figure 36.11]

Now I would like to say a few [words] here to you at this time. It is my preference, and has always been, to give my teachings direct to my students. And I want to assure you, as students, when the day comes—and it shall come—that the balancing percentage, 51, restrain[s] from an off-balance perception, which creates these dreams of so many forms, I will once again bring this little blackboard to you direct. So that I may answer your questions as you raise your hands. That is not only my preference of teaching, it is the way I have always taught. Temporarily, we have had to use monitors, and I've had to be separate from you, in the sense of physically exposing my channel to so much disturbance, in order that he may remain on your planet and be an instrument for you to receive these higher teachings. So as greater effort is made and that change is brought about, which it shall be, then I shall be physically in my channel before you and answer your questions concerning these teachings.

Now you've had plenty of time to put that in your notebooks. And we'll move on to the next step. *[The teacher erases the entire blackboard.]*

One of the sad things in creation is when a person, by lowering their perception, loses, though one never totally loses, loses to an extent their self-esteem. Now there's a vast difference between self-esteem and pride. A vast difference. Self-esteem is an awakening within the consciousness through a proper perspective of what you truly are, and through that awakening, a good feeling takes place within your being. It is the law that all beings, all limits of that which is, experience what you understand as feeling good, for it is the Law of Sustenance.

Now remember, the Law of Sustenance is feeling good. *[The teacher writes that sentence as he speaks it: "LAW O/ SUS. IS FLNG GOD."]* That is the Law of Sustenance. So whenever you permit yourself, through error, not to feel good, you may be rest assured, by not feeling good, you are not being sustained, energy-wise, for you have closed the door to the sustenance of infinite, intelligent Energy and, in so doing, must survive on the reserves that you have mustered up. So a person cannot afford not to feel good. Therefore, a person cannot afford not to make the effort, through a proper perspective, to sustain self-esteem. Self-esteem is an acceptance and a demonstration of gratitude for that which you are: infinite, intelligent Good. That *is* that straight line.

When you have a thought, that is the forming of energy, do not let your thought do this, *[The teacher draws a zigzag line a bit below the sentence.]* for then you pay the price of conception. Do not permit your thought to move in such a direction. When a thought moves *[He now draws a straight, horizontal line just below the zigzag line.]* in a straight line, it carries with it the fullness of what you are. Therefore, carrying with it that which you are in its fullness, it returns unto you, for infinity is a circle of return. *[As he speaks the last few words of this sentence, he draws a circle at the right endpoint of the horizontal line such that the lower arc of the circle overlaps that endpoint.]*

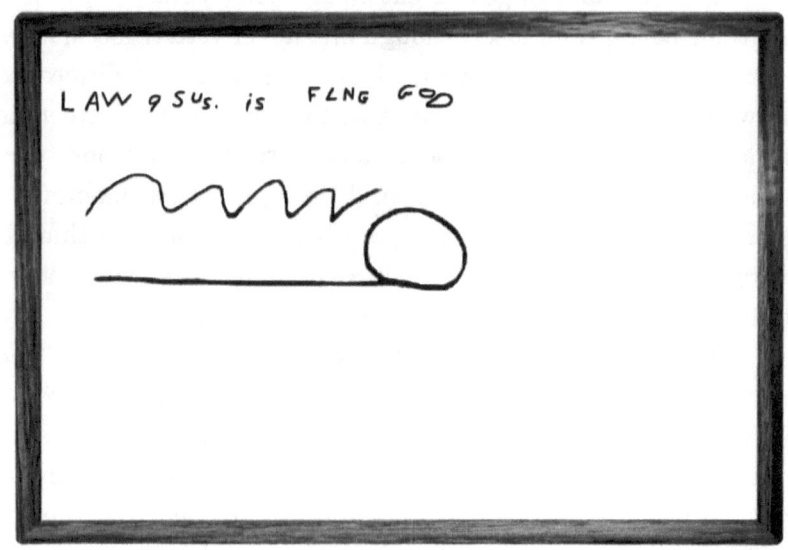

[Figure 36.12]

A straight line is a circle through which, by your perception, you see a portion thereof. Remember, infinity has no beginning and no ending. It is only your perception of infinity that makes your eternity. So depending on your perception of infinity is your eternity in question, in doubt, or acceptance.

[The teacher erases the entire blackboard.]

When you desire, as I spoke a moment ago, to overcome an experience or condition that you do not feel is bringing to you in any way any joy or happiness in life, remember, as long as you permit intelligent Energy (that which you are) *[He draws a straight, horizontal line.]* to be perceived from below (that which you are not), the obstruction will be sustained by the energy that you are directing to it.

Now say, for example, that you have a disturbance in your life, a disturbance in your life. Here we are, once again, *[The teacher draws a circle at the right endpoint of the line so that the lowest arc of the circle just overlaps that endpoint.]* perceiving what we are, our infinity. You experience a disturbance when you lower your perception to what is known as the dream of life. *[As he speaks, he first draws a small circle above and well to the right of the line of infinity and circle of eternity. And then he draws another small circle which is even with the line of infinity and directly below the first small circle. Just before he speaks "dream of life", he moves his hand horizontally from the circle of eternity to the small circle well to the right of that line.]* So in a dream of life, here you are looking *[He now moves his hand horizontally from the small circle even with the line of infinity to the circle of eternity.]* at eternity. *[He points to the right endpoint of the line of infinity.]* By seeing infinity, you are looking at this circle here *[The teacher retraces a small portion of the line of infinity and the entire circle of eternity.]* of eternity.

Now if you continue to look from the vantage point horizontal, *[The teacher draws a straight, horizontal line from near the lower small circle on the right to near the right endpoint of the line of infinity.]* you will, under the very weight of your own view, you will lower your perception, *[He now draws a third small circle in vertical alignment with the other two small circles but well below the line of infinity. The three small circles are approximately equidistant apart.]* where it is grounded and controlled by gravity. Now when you lower your perception to these laws of gravity— *[The teacher draws a straight line from the lowest small circle on the right toward the right endpoint of the line of infinity, but, again, does not touch it.]* Here *[He points to the middle small circle.]* you are parallel *[He retraces the straight, horizontal line between the middle small circle and the right endpoint line of infinity.]* in the dream of life state. Whenever you permit yourself to lower your perception *[He points to the lowest small circle.]* to where you are under the control of gravity, you are bound *[He labels the lowest small circle "BND".]* by the obstruction you have created, which in truth is siphoning and draining the vitality, the energy of what you truly are.

Now you enter the bondage by your believing. *[As he speaks, the teacher labels the middle circle "BLF".]* Your belief is how you enter the bondage. So as you perceive *[He now draws a straight line from near the highest of the three small circles to near the right endpoint of the line of infinity.]* what you are, you are tempted to believe what you are not. *[As he ends this sentence, the teacher first points to the small circle labeled belief and then to the small circle labeled bound.]*

As the rays of the sun *[The teacher draws several lines radiating outward in all directions from the circle of eternity.]* return unto themselves, so everything that you perceive returns unto you.

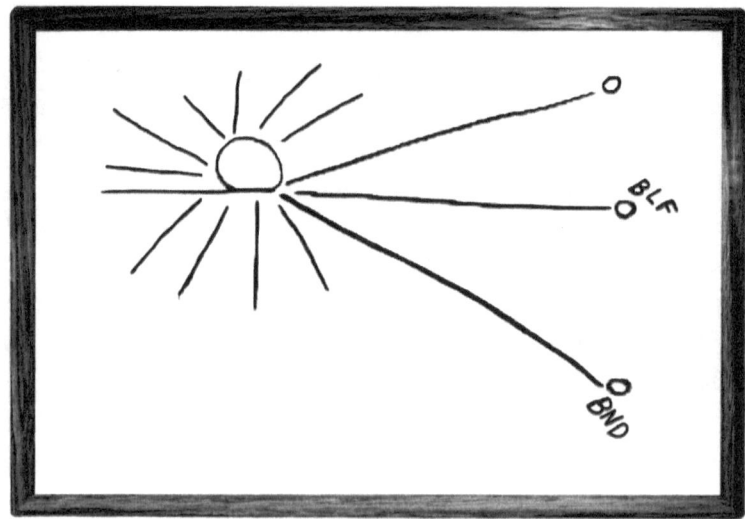

[Figure 36.13]

Now I realize that many people have the type of thinking that the rays of the sun go out. And they do. And the energy goes from it. And they think that someday, *[The teacher begins to erase the blackboard. His microphone picked up the sound of erasing and the sound of erasing makes his words difficult to hear.]* as the sun continues to release—I best stop talking while I'm erasing. *[He stops erasing.]* Go ahead. *[The teacher instructs the cameraman to continue recording the sound, which is often paused as he erases the blackboard.]* And many believe as the sun continues to release this great, vast amount of energy that someday it will be drained; and therefore, it will collapse of its own weight for there is no energy left.

Now we'll pause for just a moment and speak on that as soon as we remove what's on here. *[The teacher completes erasing the entire blackboard.]*

Now, the energy from the sun goes out in what you understand as rays. *[He draws a circle with many rays emanating from it in all directions.]* And it touches many objects. *[He draws many small, curvy lines where the lines of the rays end.]* Wherever it goes, it touches the objects. The objects absorb this energy. And in that absorption, these objects to the rays of the light of the sun, they absorb and they begin their manufacturing process of what they have absorbed. And so we find that the laws of the solar system are the same as the laws of what you believe that your form is. [It] absorbs and begins to manufacture, in its way, from what it has absorbed.

As the absorption and the manufacturing process goes on, like a little factory, it releases that which it has absorbed. And so the rays of the light go out into the universes, out from the sun of your solar system, [and] they reach many objects in the system. Those objects in turn increase their manufacturing process, and they release their rays. Oh, not as high intensity of ray as the sun itself, but they are all manufacturing their own rays of light. Those rays of light go off into the universes. *[He draws short lines emanating from the objects surrounding the rays from the circle.]* And the biggest sponge of all *[The teacher draws another circle around the center circle (or sun) of the diagram.]* absorbs the majority. So that which goes out returns unto us in keeping with the very laws of creation.

So we have this tendency, from an inner thinking and feeling, that bigger is better. That is based upon a basic instinct that that which is the largest receives the most. The most of what is always the question. It is true, *[The teacher taps with his chalk the circle encircling the sun.]* mathematically, that the larger object in the universe shall absorb and receive the most of that which is passing through the universe. However, because it receives the most, it does not always receive the best. This, I am explaining to you in keeping with your thoughts and your views of life.

If you take, for example, a little thought, just a little thought, very, very small thought, *[Below and slightly to the left of the image, he now draws a line with a circle at its right endpoint. The circle is mostly below the line.]* you will find that which is smaller is not so easily polluted with foreign matter in the universe. That which is very, very small *[He taps the center of the newest circle with his chalk.]* is easier to control; it is easier to direct. And why is that so? That which is smaller is not affected by such weight of gravity. And so you find—why, even with your space programs, your so-called shuttles, they're made fairly large, but they're still very small. They are very small for they are tempting and have accomplished overcoming the Law of Gravity, not working through the Law of Gravity. So when you are tempted to overcome something, you must always pay the price of the Law of Gravity, which is known as force. That which goes up is destined to come down.

[Figure 36.14]

Now, take a few moments for your [note]books there. *[The teacher erases the entire blackboard.]*

And once again, *[He draws a large circle near the center of the blackboard.]* we shall consider equal distribution. *[He now draws an equilateral triangle within the circle so that all three vertices touch the circle, with the apex of the triangle at the top of the circle.]* The minds of men want many things. And you notice my equal distribution has a large portion below. *[The area beneath the base of the triangle (and still within the circle) is larger than the other areas that are also outside of the triangle and yet within the circle.]* I have done that purposely; so that you may think and consider what holds the greatest weight: that which is the greater portion. This diagram *[He taps the center of the triangle with his chalk.]* is what you are living in creation. It's quite well weighted down. It's not the true design. Equal portion is the true design. That's not what it is; that isn't what it shows. We find our self weighted, very weighted here. *[With the side of his chalk, he shades in the lower portion of the circle that is beneath the base line of the triangle.]* And so often find it so difficult, so very difficult.

Here we are drowning in a pool of emotion, *[As he speaks, he again shades the lower portion of the circle.]* looking up and seeing how beautiful it is up there. *[He now draws a single vertical line from the base of the triangle to its apex.]* Moments for moments we come up a little bit, only to drop again. *[He draws six short lines from the shaded area below the triangle into the triangle. They transect the base line of the triangle, but they do not reach the other lines of the triangle. Three vertical lines are on either side of the center vertical line.]* We seem to have great difficulty in sustaining the rise. Why does man have great difficulty in sustaining a rise? Man has great difficulty in flying. Therefore, it is understandable he has great difficulty in rising, for man still believes that wings are necessary to fly. The question is, What wings? Not physical wings. The wings that you place on that which you create.

Now there are many thoughts. There are thoughts that crawl. *[The teacher draws a short, zig-zagging line below and to the left of the circle.]* There are thoughts that creep. *[He draws another short, squiggly line just above the zig-zagging one.]* There are thoughts that jog. *[He draws a third short, zigzagging line just above the second line.]* And then there are thoughts that fly. *[As he speaks, the teacher draws a long, smooth line arching over the circle.]*

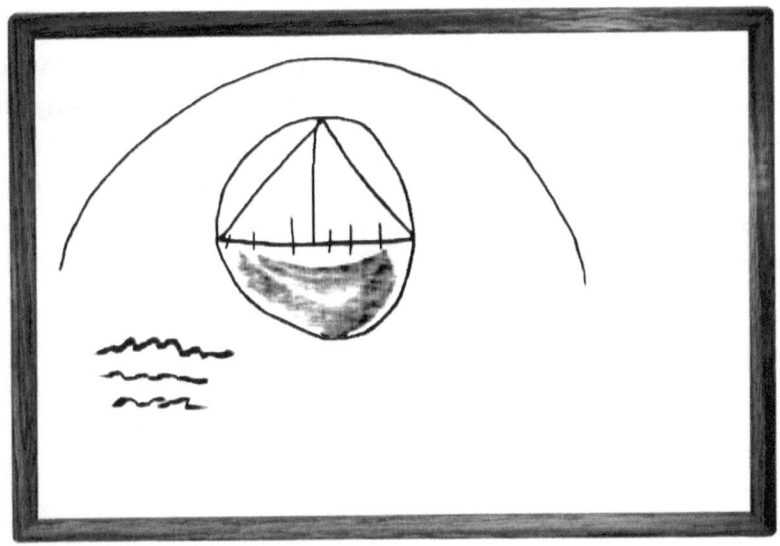

[Figure 36.15]

Now if you want to all enjoy that which you are, then you must learn to fly. Learning to fly is not something of escaping from what is; it is working intelligently with what is. And so let us learn to fly. We learn to fly in the dimension where it is possible for us to do so in our present state of evolution. So we know that in our mind we can do everything. So when you have done what you want to do in your mind, then apply, from that formation, the Law of Manifestation. In other words, everything created is in three parts. Those three parts must have equal distribution of intelligent Energy. What does that mean? That means that you must consciously direct intelligent Energy in equal proportion to all three aspects of whatever it is that you create.

[The teacher erases the entire blackboard.]

And let us not forget that whatever you create, you depend upon. And therefore, you must accept that what you do create depends upon you. And so when you create something and you do not consciously weigh out the responsibility of its dependence upon you, its creator, then you are not distributing equally the energy to the three portions which constitute manifestation.

How quickly the time goes. I expect many questions from you next week to be prepared. And I look forward to the day when I can be there with you and not over the monitor with all these wires and everything.

Thank you and good day.

FEBRUARY 23, 1986

A/V Class Private 37

[For this class, the teacher and the blackboard were set up in the dining room of the temple and his students were seated in a semicircle around him. That is, the teacher was giving this class directly in front the students without the use of video monitors, as was the case in the previous class.]

Good morning, class.

And this morning we'll continue on—are you set there? *[The teacher addresses the cameraman.]*

Yes, sir. All set.

Shall we say "Good morning" again?

It is recording.

Well, good morning. All right. Now we'll continue on with our classes here, and I will get to your questions as soon as we have this next step here for you.

Now we completed here, this little class here on the perception of infinity. *[The teacher draws a straight, horizontal line (a line of infinity) and then draws a circle at the right endpoint so that the lowest arc of the circle overlaps that endpoint.]* Now we'll go through our centers of consciousness. Earth. Fire. Water. Air. Electric. Magnetic. Odic. Ethereal. And celestial. *[As he speaks each center, beginning near the right endpoint and moving counterclockwise around the circle, he writes the first letter of each center of consciousness just outside of the circle.]* I'll give you just a moment to write that down, please.

[Figure 37.1]

Now you all have that down. We also went through our perception. *[The teacher writes "PRCPN" above and well to the right of the horizontal line, and then he draws a straight line descending from that word to near the right endpoint of the horizontal line.]* You all have that written down. And you also have the parallel or horizontal perception. *[He draws a horizontal line to the right of the first horizontal line, which joins the descending line, forming an angle.]* And you also have this perception. *[And he draws a third straight line, ascending from the lower right, which connects with the other two lines of perception.]* Now these perceptions are 45 degrees, these perceptions. *[He writes "45" just above the right endpoint of the horizontal line of perception.]*

Now according to how you perceive what you are, that is the center of consciousness in which you identify and, therefore, become.

Now I'm going to get to the last week's class here and the questions you have prepared. So you kindly raise your hand this morning. Yes, [Student U].

What are three parts of manifestation that must have equal balance of energy in order to manifest?

All right. Now we'll have to go to the three parts of manifestation, which must have equal balance in order to manifest. First of all, that is dependent upon your perception because your perception identifies you with the center of consciousness. So, for example, if you have a parallel perception, *[He retraces the horizontal line of perception.]* which is, of course, the dream state, *[He writes "DS" just above the horizontal line of perception.]* and in the dream state, you wish to manifest something in your physical being, therefore, the dream state, as you will notice here, has placed you in between the centers of consciousness of earth and fire. *[The left endpoint of the horizontal line of perception (and all the vertex of the three converging lines of perception) is located between the E and the F letters on the circle.]* Earth and fire. So in the parallel consciousness of which most people are most of the time on the planet Earth—which, by the way, you should understand that five *[The teacher writes 5 just below the first horizontal line (or line of infinity) near the midpoint.]* is not only the planet Earth and the number of faith—and I don't want to get off of your manifestation, but it is critically important that you understand the number five and what it truly represents. If you'll see, it is two straight lines of infinity with only a half-circle of eternity.

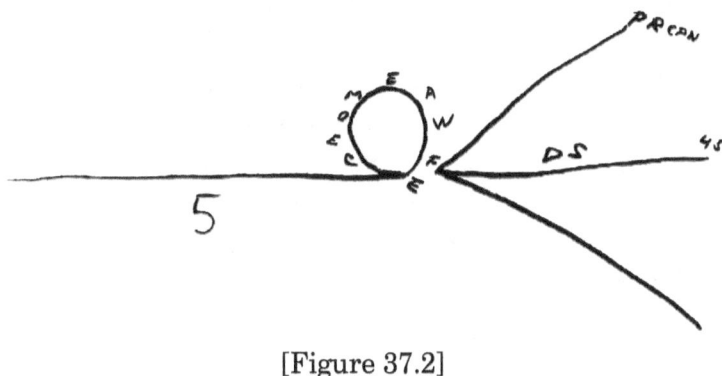

[Figure 37.2]

All right. So you have a perception in the dream state *[He retraces the horizontal line of perception.]* in which you believe that you are, and you wish to manifest something into your physical world. Therefore, you are working through that perception of the earth and fire center. *[With his chalk, he taps each letter as he speaks the center.]* And you must have equal distribution between the triune centers of earth, fire, and water. *[Again, he taps each letter as he speaks the center.]*

Now what is your fire center? That's a question for you, [Student U]. What does it represent to you?

The center through which the energy is expressed.

The center through which the energy is expressed. *[The teacher laughs.]* That is true. Well, [in] all centers energy is expressed; sometimes more abundantly than one would desire, after. However, the fire center, one of the centers in what you would consider the lower consciousness, the fire center is the center of the will, the power of the will. And so you will find that you must balance the will and the water, which is where all things are born. All things are formed in the water center.

And so when you're taking a look here *[With chalk in hand, the teacher points to the vertex of the three lines.]* in your dream state of consciousness, you are looking between earth and fire. *[As he speaks each center of consciousness, he taps the corresponding letter with his chalk.]* You're looking with your will at the physical manifestation that you desire. But it cannot manifest itself, for you have not included, in that perspective, your water center where the formation, where the birth of the form must take place. Birth of all forms take[s] place in the water center, as long as your consciousness is on a parallel view. So in other words, you look at something; you want to have that; you wish to have that manifested for you; you have the view of the earth center that you are viewing it upon, [and] you have the will to desire it, but you have not formed it in the water center. Therefore, you must feel it in order to complete the manifestation of it. You cannot complete the manifestation of something you do not feel. And the feeling is an expression from the water center. Does that help you with your question?

Yes, sir. Thank you.

Any other question on that particular one?

Not at this time, sir.

All right. Yes, [Student B], please.

Does that mean, then, that if you went around the circle and picked any three other centers, you'd have the same principle?

You will have identically the same principle. Now, for example, here you have in the dream state earth, fire, and water. *[With his chalk he taps the letter corresponding to the center as he speaks its name.]* All centers, in order to manifest, must be in a triune expression. They must—the energy—the consciousness must direct energy to all three in order for it to manifest. So here you have earth, fire, and water *[He again points to the three centers as he speaks their names.]* for your physical manifestation. *[Without drawing on the blackboard his hand makes a small circle including those three centers of consciousness and the vertex of the three lines.]* Now what is your next three centers? Air, electric, and magnetic. Now please try to think about this. Here you have your water, your fire, your air—your water, your fire, and your *earth*. *[The teacher draws a three-segment line between the W, F, E letters and the lines forming the vertex.]* Now here you have your air, your electric, and your magnetic. *[He now draws a second three-segment line adjacent to the A, E, and M letters.]*

So you are using now, in the higher consciousness, a manifestation through air, electric, and magnetic. *[Again, with his chalk he taps the letter corresponding to the center as he speaks its name.]* The magnetic, of course, being the water, which you understand; and the electric, of course, being the fire; and the air in keeping with the center of the earth consciousness. *[He again points to the corresponding letter as he speaks the name of the center of consciousness.]* So you have air, electric, and magnetic.

Therefore, people viewing from a different perspective, the next perspective, according upon the degree of the view—these are 45 degrees. *[The teacher retraces the highest of the three lines of perception.]* So if you view what you are, that is, your perspective of what you are, *[He again retraces the highest line of perception.]* then, you see, that will show you in which center of consciousness you are manifesting or forming what is to be in your experiences. Do you understand that, [Student B]?

Yes.

Now we will move from the air, electric, and magnetic *[He taps the corresponding letter as he speaks the names of the centers.]* to the next center of consciousness, which is the odic, the ethereal, and the celestial. Now to get a view of the odic, ethereal, and celestial, your perception must rise considerably in order for you to view the ethereal and the celestial and the odic. *[The teacher draws a straight line from the highest endpoint of the upper line of perception. It just touches the left edge of the circle and ends near the O, which is on the left side of the circle.]*

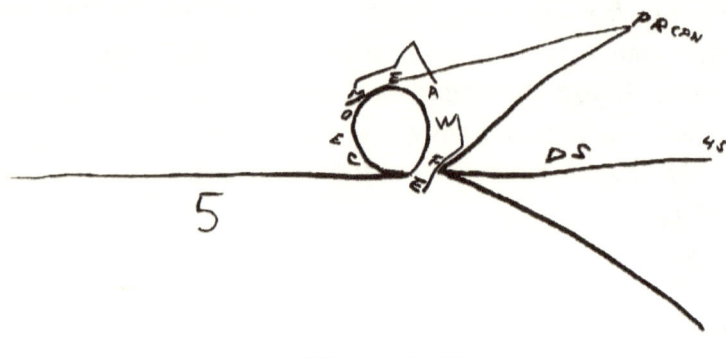

[Figure 37.3]

Now let me put this a little bit, perhaps, a little clearer for you. Here you have earth, fire, and water. *[As he speaks, he writes "E F W" in a row in the upper left corner of the blackboard.]* The centers of which our student, [Student U], was speaking. Now you have air, electric, and magnetic. *[As he speaks the names of the centers, he writes "A E M" in a row just below the previously written letters.]* Now you have odic, ethereal, and celestial. *[He now writes "O E C" in a row just below the row with "A E M". The three rows form a block of letters.]*

Now some time ago I spoke to you that functions are undeveloped faculties, for that's what they are. They are all made possible through direction of infinite, intelligent Energy. So here you have earth, fire, and water in keeping with the lower perspective. Here you have air, electric, and magnetic in keeping with a higher perspective. Here you have odic, ethereal, and celestial with the highest perspective. *[With chalk in hand, the teacher taps the corresponding letter in the block of letters as he speaks the names of all nine centers.]*

This is why I have taught you over these years that a seeming bad experience can produce excellent results; it is ever in keeping with your perspective. For example, say that you have, in an error of ignorance, created something that is, to you, most distasteful and disturbing in the earth, fire, and water center. If you will change your perspective of that which you have created, you can see its manifestation in the air, electric, and magnetic center, for it is also created there. You can also, through a raising of your perspective, see it in the odic, ethereal, and celestial realms of consciousness. As above, so below. So whatever you have created here on the Earth planet is a manifestation of what you have already created in celestial realms of consciousness. Do you understand that? So as above, so below; and as below, so above.

These are the centers of consciousness *[He points to E, A, and O in that order in the block of letters.]* that, through perspective, you experience life as you know it and, therefore, believe that you are the experiences that you have created. That help with your question, [Student B]?

Yes. Thank you.

Yes. Is there another question here? Yes, [Student N], please.

Does the number one correspond with eternity?

Well, if you wish to consider—eternity? Well, now, here is eternity: a circle—right? *[The teacher points to the circle resting on the horizontal line.]*

Right.

That returns unto itself. And that eternity, all eternity, is dependent upon your perspective of infinity. Now you look at infinity as a straight line. Is that correct?

Uh-huh.

Well, the only reason you see infinity as a straight line is because of your perspective. So you view infinity, this straight line; you do not see its continuity as it returns unto itself. Now here we have the line of infinity and we have the circle of eternity. *[The teacher draws a new horizontal, straight line and a circle whose lowest arc overlaps the right endpoint of that line. The new line of infinity and circle of eternity are located just below the first one.]* Hmm?

Uh-huh.

All right. Now that's what you think you see. You don't, however, see the rest of it. *[The teacher adds a circle to the newest line of infinity at the left endpoint so that the top arc of the circle just overlaps the left endpoint of the line.]* See, it all returns unto itself.

[Figure 37.4]

So if you say that number one is infinity, well, in that respect, for you, [it may be] for you've only perceived a single line. It is actually a circle. All things, all forms return unto themselves, for they are all circles. And we see them as forms only because of our perspective. It is the way that we view them.

So would the same earth part, would that be same on the lower circle, too?

Yes. It's the same on all circles because all form is a circle that returns unto itself. All thoughts return unto themselves for they are forms. Everything that has been limited returns unto itself. Yes, [Student S], please.

I'd like to know if that second diagram is leading us to the figure 8 for infinity. And if so, how do we shorten that line so the two circles touch?

Yes, there's no problem whatsoever. It's your perspective. Yes. For you have already suspected that that is the number of infinity, which, of course, it is. All right. Now what does that tell you? What does it tell you when you look at what you understand as the figure 8 and you understand that as the symbol of infinity? What does that tell you? [Student S], for she asked the first question in respect to that.

I'm sorry; I don't understand the question.

What does it tell you that, first of all, you have suspected that this little diagram I just made here for you is in truth a figure 8 and how do you short[en] the line between the two, the two eternities?

Right.

Is that not correct?

Yes.

Of the two circles. Well, I just spoke to you and told you in reference to your perspective, your perspective and your perception. Now what does it mean to you, that symbol of infinity? You see, this here *is* the symbol of infinity. *[The teacher taps the straight, horizontal line with circles at each end.]* You have shortened it in your world and I think you have symbols like this as infinity, don't you? *[He draws two small circles side by side just above the line of infinity and circle of eternity that he drew first.]* Pardon?

Yes.

[Figure 37.5]

You see, you have distorted it. Yes.

It seems that if you were on either circle, looking horizontally at the other, then you wouldn't be aware of the line in between.

That is correct. You are not aware of what you are, for you believe that you are the perception; you believe that you are perceiving what you are instead of understanding what you are. You see, they say that seeing is believing, and that is the control of the mental world. Seeing is not believing, for we see ever in keeping with our perspective and our perception of what we are. Does that help with your question?

Yes. Thank you.

So if you want to say that seeing is believing, remember this: that a person who accepts that seeing is believing is a person who is dependent. And a person who is dependent is a person who is magnetic, out of balance with the electric and the other centers of consciousness. And a person who is out of balance with their other centers of consciousness (being magnetic) is a person who is extremely vulnerable, is a person who is a victim of circumstances and conditions that they believe that they cannot control, for they have denied that which they are, the truth of personal responsibility. Does that help with your question?

Yes. Thank you.

Yes. Yes, the lady here is waiting, please. [Student Y].

Thank you. So the areas that you spoke of, the three equal parts, would that be the triune earth, fire, water in the circle—you drew a circle—

Yes.

—with a triangle. [The student may be referring to Figure 36.10 from the previous class.]

That is correct.

Those are the three equal parts.

That is correct. Because if that is what you perceive and that is what you wish manifested, then, of course, that applies to those centers. That also applies to the odic, to the ethereal, and to the celestial. There must be an equal distribution of energy.

Now what is the difficulty in the equal distribution of energy? A person takes a look and they want to manifest something in the earth consciousness *[The teacher points to the E adjacent to the circle.]* and they have the will to do it, *[He now points to the F near the circle.]* and there is not a balance, an equal distribution of the energy, for they also have their water center.

You see, a person says, "I am going to do this;" a person says, "I am going to attain that." And then they go through all of the various experiences and do not attain it and they end up frustrated. What is the frustration? The frustration is a disturbance of created forms, conflicting, contracting forms in the water center, where, without the magnet, which is a water center, it cannot be attracted unto them. So they have the will and they use it. And they're in the dream state and they believe it, but don't believe it, because they have not created it intelligently. And they have this distortion and separation in consciousness: it's going to happen; it's not going to happen. And all of these doubts and fears and questions rise up.

If my student, [Student E], would like to go to the garage, he may be excused for the rest of class, please. *[Student E was about 18 months old at the time of this class, and he had been expressing himself just before he merited being removed by one of his parents.]*

And do you understand that, [Student Y]?

Yes, I do.

All right. Yes, [Student J], please.

Does that mean, sir, that if we want to accomplish something on the, here, on the earth plane, using the first three centers, and we have to get a—we have to be emotionally involved with it?

Well, you see, that's where your dependence comes. Now, for example, we understand that the magnet is a person who is vulnerable and dependent. You cannot believe something and have it attracted unto you without the use of the magnetic center of consciousness. For example, you've had experiences where you have worked with your fire center and with the power of your will and you have worked in a physical substance, and it has not manifested itself. You must feel its manifestation in order to create the form, for equal distribution, in keeping with the Law of Manifestation. Now by getting emotional over it—if you call it "emotional" that you collapse at that thought that it is not happening, that is not a positive, created form in the water center. Does that help with your question?

Yes, but may I, can I, can I just elaborate—

Well, yes, I think perhaps we can understand it better if you say you're convinced. When you're convinced of something, it happens, doesn't it?

Yes, sir.

I mean, when you're really—you know when you're convinced of something.

Yes, sir.

Is that not true?

Yes, sir.

When you are convinced, it happens.

Yes, sir.

Has that not been your experience?

Yes, sir.

Well, you see, when you are convinced, you have equally distributed the energy into the earth, fire, and water center[s] of consciousness. Do you understand that?

I'm still bothered by the fact that the water center represents emotion.

It does.

And I was always under the impression that we should keep our emotions out of something in order to have it manifest.

That is correct. Because, you see, the water center is not only the center of emotion, it is the center of consciousness where all forms are created, including, of course, one's judgments. This is where life for your planet is created. It's created in the water center. So if you don't have equal distribution of energy into the earth, fire, and water center—you see, you don't have conviction without a form being solidified in the water center. Do you understand that, [Student J]?

Yes, sir. But I'm still—the emotional aspect still perplexes me.

Well, now when you are convinced of something, do you find yourself emotional?

No.

Therefore, you know from experience that you ofttimes are able to convince yourself of something and not be emotional.

Yes.

Is that not correct?

Yes, sir.

Conviction is an expression of a form that is solidified in the water center.

So we don't have to be emotional about it in order to have it manifest.

No, no. It's not a matter of being emotional about it. It's a matter of conviction or feeling, which is a distribution of energy in the water center. You do understand that?

Yes, sir.

You see. Now a person says, well, you know, they are waiting for the manifestation of something; and they have used their fire center, their will power; they have used their earth center; they've made physical effort of its creation, etc., and they are very emotional about whether or not it is going to happen. They're very upset. They're very disturbed. Do you understand that?

Yes, sir.

The only reason that a person is disturbed in the waiting for something to manifest itself, there's only one reason: that tells them immediately that the forms they have created in their water center of consciousness [*Using a pointer, the teacher points to the W on the circle of eternity.*] are forms that are not harmonious to the manifestation of what they desire.

You see, when you have an experience of doubt and fear, that tells you that the forms you have created in your water center of consciousness are contradictory forms. There were moments when you created ones that were solidified and that was going to happen, and it did happen. All right, then you have a new experience in your creating. You're working to create another experience; so you have forms that tell you, "Yes, this is going to happen." Only a moment later, there are other forms that tell you it is not going to happen. That's when you become emotional, for your conviction is moving from one form to another in your own water center. That is because you do not have an equal distribution in order that you may have the manifestation and the control thereof. Yes.

How then do we bring balance between those two, conflicting forms?

Yes. How can you bring balance between those conflicting forms? Now, that tells us right away—you see, in the distribution, the equal distribution of energy, earth, fire, and water, [*With his pointer, the teacher taps the corresponding letters of the centers as he speaks their names.*] that tells you immediately, when you have conflicting forms, that as the energy was being distributed to the earth, fire, and water center, [*He again taps the corresponding letters of the centers as he speaks.*] that forms, that is, shadows that exist there from past creations and past experiences, gobbled up more than their share into the water center. And they created there, in the water center, based upon forms of past experiences, other forms that are contrary to what you are trying to accomplish or to manifest. Therefore, you do not have equal distribution of energy for the manifestation, for when you initially had the thought, the distribution of the energy, more went into the water center than distribution to the fire and earth center.

Now how can you correct that? You correct that with the initial formation. Say that you desire to, to sell something. You're getting something under way to sell. Now when you do that, you must understand you already have past experiences that in principle relate to what you are doing at this moment. All right?

Yes.

You already have shadows there. All right. Now those forms exist in the three centers of consciousness. They exist in the earth, fire, and water center. *[He points to each letter by the circle corresponding to that center.]* You may, however, have removed them from the physical substance. Correct?

Yes, sir.

You have removed them from there. You have removed them, to a great extent, from the fire center, from your desire or will for their continuity. Do you understand that?

Yes, sir.

However, they have not been removed from the water center as long as you have the slightest feeling or emotion concerning that past experience. Do you understand that?

Yes, sir.

So when you go to create and bring about a manifestation *[With his pointer, he circles the lower three centers of consciousness and the vertex of the lines of perception.]* into the physical world, you are working to distribute equal energy to the earth, fire, and water centers. *[He again points to each letter of the circle corresponding to that center.]* The water center gets more than its just share, and you have serious problems, for when it gets more than its share in the distribution of the intelligent energy at the moment of its formation, you understand, then forms of past experiences, related through the Law of Association, are fed and rise up. That's where the emotion and all the conflict is. Did that help with your question?

Yes, sir.

So when you have thoughts, when you are working to create something and you have thoughts in your mind of what has been, you must be on guard not to permit your consciousness to overidentify with any feelings of what has been. For in so doing you once again direct energy to forms that have long, long passed from your physical being. Yes.

Could that work in the opposite? Couldn't we identify and put energy into something that—

Oh, absolutely! It most certainly could. Now if that works—you can use it for the positive. You're creating something and you have here in the water center, *[He points to the W adjacent to the circle.]* you have experiences and you have emotions of a very positive experience from what you'd set into motion years passed. Now when you distribute the energy, you distribute energy to the earth and the fire center. And you also—it is going to the water center. *[He again points to the letters corresponding to the center of consciousness as he speaks their names.]* You be on conscious guard that the feelings involved are positive feelings, though they may be based on a past experience; you have that little army of support. Did that help with that question, [Student J]?

Yes. Thank you, sir.

You're more than welcome. Did someone else have a question? Yes, [Student L], here, has a question.

Yes. Is the river of life infinity?

The river of life? Well, when you take a look at a river and you see that it returns unto its source, and that's what infinity is, yes, in that respect it is. That *is* the river of life. *[As the teacher speaks, he gestures toward the horizonal line with circles at both ends.]*

Thank you.

Yes. You see, you look at a circle and you look at a line and you look at a blackboard, and you do not see its movement. However, there is nothing stationary in the universe. Everything is moving. There is nothing stationary. That's only your perception. You think that the chair you're sitting in is stationary. It is not stationary. It is moving. All the parts within it are moving. Everything is in movement because without movement, it does not exist. It only exists because of movement. That's the only way it can exist. Does that help with your question?

Thank you.

Yes. And [Student D] has a question, please.

In the circle and triangle diagram, could you tell us where the earth, fire, and water points are?

Why, certainly. *[The teacher draws a triangle to the left of the first line of infinity.]* This is the diagram that you are speaking of?

Yes.

[The teacher draws a roundish circle around the triangle so that the line of the circle touches all the vertices of the triangle.] Well, it's not too good a circle for earth, fire, and water, is it? But you know it's a circle. Now I have many students here that have had this teaching, and I want to see some hands to see if you've done your homework over these past twelve or eighteen years. And you tell me where earth, fire, and water is. *[After a short pause, the teacher continues.]* Were you listening, [Student S]?

Yes.

Yes. Well, I'll come to you because I see that you're so busy there with your notes.

Yes.

Earth—now where is earth, fire, and water located here?

OK. Since the fire is the electric, I feel it would be on the lower left.

[On] the lower left [of the triangle] you have electric, is that correct? Is that where you want me to place it? The lower left?

Yes.

You'd like to have the electric on the left? All right. Now I've got a few more students here that have been with me a long time. [Student J] and [Student R], where do you want me to place the electric?

I would place the electric on the lower right. [Student J responds.]

You would place it on the right. You're electric. *[Student J is male.]*

Yes, sir.

[Student S] is magnetic and she'll place it on the left. *[Student S is female.]* Where would [Student R] place it?

On the right. [Student R responds.]

Now [Student R] will place it on the right. [Student J] will place it on the right. And [Student S] is going to place it on the left. Now, yes, I want to respond to your question, [Student S].

I'd like to be refreshed, please. I think that diagram—is that diagram turned around facing us? So if I wrote a diagram on my term . . . [Student S responds.]

Well, if you were the diagram— *[The teacher laughs.]*

Is my left the right on the diagram? [That] is what I want to know.

[The teacher laughs joyfully.] Let's say that this is the right point of the diagram. *[With his chalk the teacher taps the right vertex of the triangle; that is, when one is looking at the triangle on the blackboard, the right point is on the viewer's right.]* And that this is the left point because we're in two dimension[s] here. *[The teacher taps the left vertex.]* And let's say that this is the top. *[He taps the apex.]* This is the right. This is the left. And this is the top. *[Moving clockwise around the triangle, the teacher taps each vertex as he speaks their location.]*

Now where are we going to put this fire center? Where are we going to put this electric center? The fire is electric, you know. Would you say that the right side is magnetic and the left side is electric? That's what you told me earlier. Or would you say that the right side is electric and the left side is magnetic?

I stand corrected. The left side, because we receive, would be the magnetic and the right, the electric. [Student S responds.]

Well, yes, the left side would be magnetic because the magnetic is dependent.

Uh-huh.

Why, certainly. Yes. Now I don't have to give a class on Adam and Eve this morning, do I? *[A few students laugh.]* Now where would you like it placed now?

On the right.

You'd like the fire center on the right.

Right.

Well, it is electric. Yes. *[The teacher writes F just outside the circle next to the right vertex of the triangle.]* That's the fire center.

Right.

All right. Oh, now you students are going to have to do your part. I'm not going to just answer questions that I've answered [for] years and years and years, a thousand times. All right now, where's the rest of this here? We have a fire center here. Now where are we going to put the water and the earth center? [Student D], you asked the question, Where do you want to put the earth center?

Well, I would think the earth center would be on the left, lower left.

Well, would you consider that that would be magnetic? Are you in keeping with that, [Student D]?

Yes.

You would like the earth center on the left?

Oh, no. Not the earth, the water.

You'd like the water center on the left. That sounds more reasonable. How about everybody else? Did I not state over the years that water is magnetic? That is the magnetic. All right, let's put the water center right here then. *[The teacher writes W just outside the circle next to the left vertex of the triangle.]* Right? Now does that help with your question there, [Student D]?

Yes.

Are you missing anything?

The top.

Ah, right here at the top. *[The teacher writes E just outside the circle at the apex of the triangle.]* So we have earth, fire, and water. *[He taps each letter as he speaks the corresponding center.]* Any question there?

So the earth has the view at the top. [Student D observes.]

Ahh...

And the water is the formation on one side—

That's the formation.

Fire is the will.

[Fire] is the will that brings it into being. Absolutely. In everything dealing with that center of consciousness.

[Figure 37.6]

Now what is so important to you as students is to understand your perspective. To make the effort through the power of your will to perceive through the center of consciousness that will bring you the goodness of life. It is your perception. Your perception of what you are. And if you insist on perceiving what you are as something negative and something that's not joyous and happy, then, of course, you're going to have those experiences because you are perceiving through the center of consciousness in a most imbalanced way. Yes, [Student S].

On the perception, you mentioned that they were 45 degrees. And the highest perception there, I'd like to know if it can perceive over that circle into odic, ethereal, and celestial, or do you have to move to a 90 degree?

You have answered the question that you have. You have to have both 45's together in a 90 degree to perceive the celestial realm of consciousness. Yes.

Also, I'd like to know, do those circles on the line of infinity rotate?

Yes. When your dream of life, when your dream of life *[The teacher writes "DL" on the horizontal line of perception near the vertex of those three lines.]* and your belief in what you are, *[He now writes "BWA" on the lower of the three lines of perception, which ascends toward the vertex.]* are united with perception— I'll just put "PR" here *[The teacher writes "PRCN." near the midpoint of the highest of the three lines.]* —when they are harmoniously united, then you will view clearly the celestial consciousness, which you truly are. Yes, [Student O], please.

OK. Would that symbol of infinity, could that also be considered as the two circles that is God above and God below?

Well, yes, you see, for example, that is given in another way. It happens to be what you call, what you call the number eleven, you see. *[The teacher writes 11 at the top of the blackboard, just above the horizontal figure 8.]* That's what you call the number eleven.

Yes, sir.

All right? Hmm? Now that there is this, *[He now points the horizontal figure 8.]* drawn as that. *[The teacher now points to the horizontal line with circles at each end.]* Do you understand?

Yes, sir.

You see, it's all one and the same. It's all one and the same. In fact, I do think that I drew that for you last week. *[The teacher draws one circle at the top and another at the bottom of the eleven. The top circle overlaps both of the upper endpoints and the lower circle overlaps both of the lower endpoints of the parallel lines of the eleven.]* Didn't I draw that for you last week?

Yes.

See there? Do you see there? See, there it is right there. It's the same thing. It's right there.

OK.

Hmm?

Ah—

[Figure 37.7]

Well, can't you see that that there is this here? *[The teacher first points to the figure 11 with circles at the top and bottom, and then he points to the single, horizontal line with circles at both endpoints.]* Or shall I add another line to it? Yes.

I can see that.

Yes, [Student O].

OK. Well. The line of—OK. The previous student's question said the—do the circles move. OK.

Yes, they do.

OK. The circles move. And does the line of infinity lay stationary?

The line of—No. Everything moves. Everything moves. What the student was referring to: do the circles—and I think she will verify that—do the circles move in a clockwise and a counterclockwise position? *[The teacher first draws a circle in a clockwise direction and then draws another circle, which just encircles the first circle, in a counterclockwise direction. Those circles are drawn just below the horizontal line with circles at both ends.]* They do. You see, if you have two circles, one here and one here, *[He first points to the circle on the right endpoint of the horizontal line and then points to the circle at the left endpoint of that line.]* that are moving in a clockwise and a counterclockwise [direction], simultaneously, you want to know what you perceive?

Yes, sir.

[Figure 37.8]

What do you perceive when something is moving at a rapid speed? Clockwise and counterclockwise. When there is a spin clockwise and equally counterclockwise, then you perceive what? What do you—how do you perceive a solid? Yes, [Student L].

Stationary.

Stationary. That's what makes it stationary. When the movement is clockwise and counterclockwise at a revolution that is equal, you perceive a stationary object. Do you understand that? Is there anyone who doesn't understand that? That's how you perceive yourself as a physical, stationary being. You can't perceive yourself as a physical, stationary being unless there is movement both clockwise and counterclockwise at an equal spin or rapidity. It has to be equal in order for you to perceive your being as a solid being, which it in truth is not.

You see, I've spoken to you on the Law of Gravity. And I've spoken to you on perception, and how you move through the Law of Gravity. You move through it—you are presently moving through it by force, by overcoming its reign of control. You see, you are overcoming it by force. And so your space vehicles are moving outside of the Earth's gravitational pull, it's magnetic pull, for that's what gravity is; it is moving beyond it by accelerating a greater force against it to pierce through it. That is a primitive way of overcoming gravity. It certainly is not an evolved way. The way to move through something is to understand it. And so when your world understands what gravity truly is, by understanding it, they will be able to move through it without exerting this extreme force to overcome it.

I'm interested in you moving through the gravitational field that, through perception, you have placed yourself in. Yes, [Student S], please.

If the two spins, being at the same rate, solidifies the object—

That's the only—it gives the appearance of solidification.

OK. Would slowing one end or the other help to get beyond that?

Well, for example, you can't slow one or the other. You have to make a change in the speed of the counterclockwise and the speed or rotation of the clockwise. You see, in order to conquer, you must divide. That law applies to physics as well as everything else. And physics and mathematics is what you are an expression of. Do you understand that? *[After a short pause, the teacher continues.]* There must be a difference between the spin and the retrospin. Do you understand that, [Student R]?

Yes, sir. [Student R responds.]

Pardon?

Yes.

And when you create a difference in the spin and the retrospin, to the degree of difference you create, will you have awareness of something beyond what you think you are in a locked gravitational pull. You see, your perception is controlled by the Law of Gravity. *[The teacher partially retraces the horizontal line of perception, which had been previously labeled "DL" and "DS".]* Yes.

Does this change, then, still end up equal on both ends? Like, do you change both ends of it?

Are you talking about the rotation?

The spin and the retrospin. Do you change them equally?

Yes. They must be changed equally. And they must be changed in their, in their rapidity of their spin.

OK. Thank you.

Do you understand that now?

I'm starting to. I don't understand the whole—

Well, we'll move on then.

Thank you.

[Student J] is waiting on a question. And [then] I'll get to [Student M].

Would the degree of spin and retrospin relate to the length of the line of infinity?

Yes, it does. Yes, it does. Now how long is your line of infinity? That's the question, isn't it?

Yes, sir.

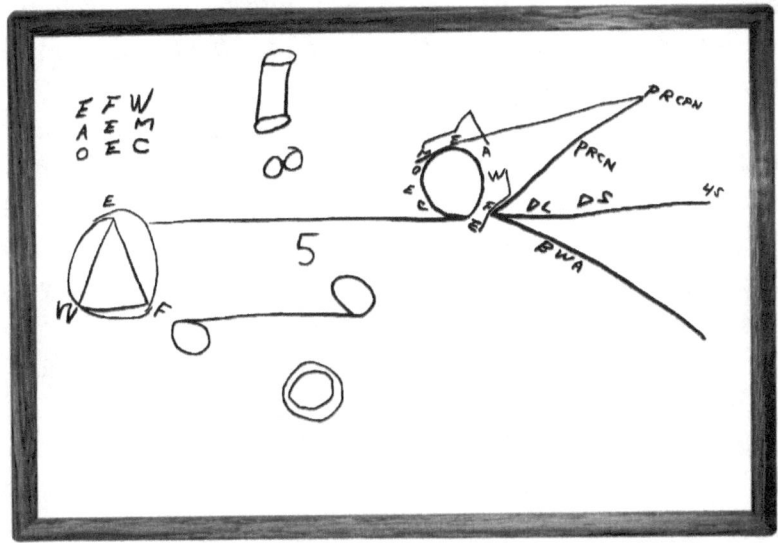

[Figure 37.9]

Let me erase the board. And try, try to remind me not to talk while I'm doing it. Is the cameraman ready here? *[The teacher addresses the cameraman. The microphone is turned down while the teacher is erasing the blackboard to avoid recording the loud erasing sounds. The teacher begins to erase the blackboard, but midway through he begins to speak.]* It's very important, when you start something—I know I told you to remind me not to talk, but it's very important that you start with a clean slate. So often we are tempted, like with a piece of paper or something, "Oh, this will do fine." Well, it only reveals how much value [you have] for what you're putting on, your energy and your effort. So, you see, it's important that you start any endeavor, a class or any endeavor, with a clean slate. Why is it so important to start with a clean slate? *[The teacher returns to erasing.]* You think about that because I want your answer. *[The teacher again returns to erasing.]* Now [Student J], you should have the answer to that.

Well, sir, I would assume the fact that a clean slate would not be contaminated or a prior, old slate would be, would contaminate your new endeavor with the prior forms that were put on the old slate, so to speak.

Absolutely correct. First of all, in order to remove what is on the slate, you must make a conscious decision. You first must make a conscious decision before you can move your hands, pick up the eraser, and remove what's on the slate. When you make that conscious decision, you set the law into motion within your consciousness to begin your new endeavor without any shadows of the past, positive, negative, or otherwise. Do you understand?

Yes, sir.

So a man is much better off, even though there are beneficial things of the past, a man is much better off and in fuller control to clean the slate and begin anew. So no matter what the experience in life is, including the blackboard, clean the slate. Because in consciousness you put yourself into the eternity: in the moment is the eternity. Your perception is changed. Your perspective changes when you clean the slate. So clean the slate. If you have something that you value and you want to get it established, then clean the slate. The slate in consciousness. Because it cleans out all of that in the water center and all of those forms. You've cleaned them out consciously. Now if you're tempted to put them back in, of course—they're created by the mind. But when the effort is made, in that moment you have cleaned them out. You've got a chance. Does that help you with the questions?

Yes, now [Student M] is waiting for a question. Is that it?

Yes.

Time passes quickly, you know, yes—

It was—

—in your world.

It was similar to the diagram with the triangle and talking about dual eternity. Now is dual eternity and the Law of Manifestation one and the same?

Well, yes, you see, everything in life in eternity is dependent on how you are viewing it: from what your perception—from what perspective you've placed yourself. You see, if you insist on perceiving life from a perspective that is not enjoyable, then the more you perceive it from that perspective, the more that you become it. You know, that's in keeping with the teachings you've already had: place your attention upon the—not upon the obstruction. See, the more you place your attention upon the obstruction in your life, that's the more you will create obstruction. Because you are looking from that perspective. Hmm?

Thank you.

You see?

Yes.

You see, if you do not see the whole, then you cannot say all things are possible. To people who perceive from below, they are not only controlled by the Law of Gravity, they do not see the whole; they only see a portion of the whole. You see? That's like a blind man feeling an elephant's trunk and saying, "Oh, well, that's his toe." You see, it's the same type of reasoning. You're looking from a very narrow perspective and [you are] controlled by the Law of Gravity. So, for you, that *is* the whole. And as long as you look from that perspective, for you, it shall continue to be the whole.

Yes.

Hmm?

Thank you.

Now you cannot, you cannot change the spin and retrospin of your consciousness until you change your own perspective, for you have no control over it. You only look at it from a very narrow perspective.

Yes, [does] someone else have a question? [Student L], please.

Does the Law of Gravity govern the first three lower centers of consciousness?

Oh, the Law of Gravity is, as I explained, is controlling the dream state and parallel—and what's the next three centers of consciousness, [Student L]?

Air, electric, and magnetic.

It controls those centers of consciousness.

Oh, it does that, too.

Yes, it does that, too. Because you are not seeing the whole.

I see.

You see, until you see the whole, you will be controlled by the Law of Gravity. Now if you will move to the next three centers of consciousness, then you're going to see the whole, and then you'll be freed from that Law of Gravity. Yes, [Student N], please.

Would that be the fourth dimension, then, the—

Well, you might consider it—I might consider it in your world the fifth dimension. The fourth dimension's almost there. The fifth dimension's when you get there. *[A few students laugh.]*

And by the way, I think we'd better speak on this number five here a moment. *[On the clean blackboard, the teacher writes a large "5" and just above it, he writes a much smaller "F".]* Here you understand that that there—you've had in your teachings—is faith.

Now I'm going to ask you a question. [Student H] hasn't spoken here this morning, and several others, too. [Student H], why is number five the symbol of faith? Why is that? Why isn't it number four or some other number? Why is it number five?

Because when I think of the number five, there's the balance point between two on one side, two on the other side and then if you add it all up, that makes five.

Well, let's draw it properly. *[The teacher writes another large "5" just below the first one, but rotated approximately 80 degrees to the right.]* I told you you've got your numbers all catawampus around here. *[Some of the students laugh.]* That's a little bit better. A little bit. Now why is that the symbol of faith? You already know it's supposed to be a half a circle. Why is that faith? Can you not perceive what five really is? [Student P].

Well—

What is five? Look at it from a different perspective and tell me what five is.

Well, because it has a vertical line, rather than just one horizontal, it goes to a higher perspective where it could view different levels.

Can you not see that the circle is complete in five? Can you not see, in the symbol of five, that the circle is completed? I mean, it is—to your view right now wouldn't you say, [Student B], it's distorted?

Yes. [Student P responds.]

Right. [Student B responds.]

When the five is properly made, you have a half a circle *[With his chalk he taps the lowest arc of the curve of the somewhat horizontal 5.]* and the two lines complete that circle. *[He now gestures to the two lines forming the upper portion of that 5.]* That is why it's the symbol of faith. It is the return unto itself. That's the reason that it is that. I didn't make it that way. Mathematics, the key to the universe, brought that about eons ago. That is the number of faith.

Now take a person—let's take a number eight. *[The teacher writes the number "8" on the blackboard to the left of the upright 5.]* Because I know someone in my class that's a number eight. Their faith in manifestation is insatiable. Wouldn't you say, [Student J]?

Yes, sir.

[The teacher laughs joyfully.] Well, let's erase that. *[The students laugh and the teacher thoroughly erases the blackboard.]* A little difficulty here with the five: it doesn't want to go away.

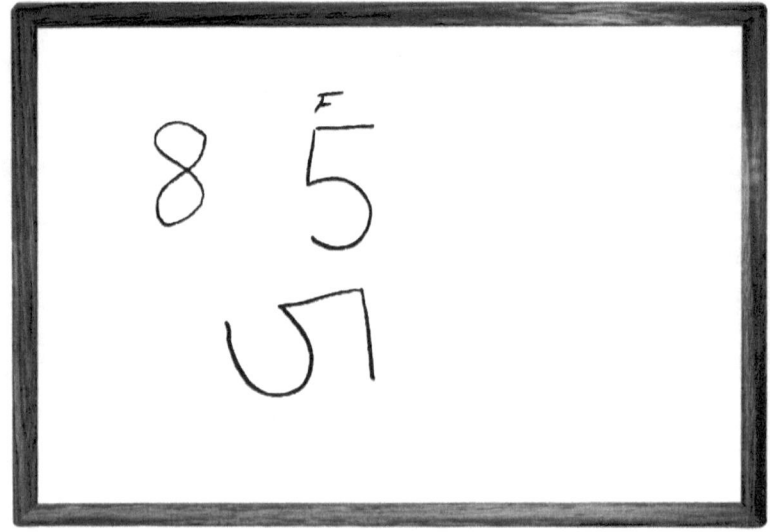

[Figure 37.10]

Now these classes are not too advanced for you. In no way, shape, or form. It's just, perhaps, a little different and you have to study. Would you not agree? Pardon? You're going to have to study, and you're going to have to make some effort, but that's how you're going to grow even more.

Now where's your questions here? Or is my time up? *[The teacher looks at his wristwatch.]* Oh, my, look at the time already. Yes, yes, [Student L].

Do you make a thought fly by moving up to the electric center of consciousness?

Do you make a thought fly by moving to the electric—where do you want it to fly to?

I don't know—

Away or return?

Well, you want it to return, too.

Oh, you do? Well, then you best use equal distribution of energy in all those centers. Why, certainly it takes the will for it to fly. Certainly, it does. But if you want it to return, you best use the other two centers. Yes, [Student B].

When we want to change our perspective, is that when we use the breathing exercise?

Yes. You use the breath to change your perspective. You see, you are working to raise your perspective, and you have to face going through the gravitational pull of what has been.

You understand that changes seem to be so difficult for everyone. Everyone seems to understand changes are difficult, right? You know, it takes effort. Well, then you have to understand that when you go to use your will (the fire center) to make a change in your consciousness, you have to pass through the magnet of the water center. And so when you have an electrical-electric power moving through a water center, you get quite a sensation. Would you not agree? *[After a short pause, the teacher continues.]* Well, put your electric cord in the water and sit in the tub. *[Some of the students laugh.]* I think you will agree that you're going to have a sensation. One, unless you are prepared for, you won't appreciate. But for everything that you want to accomplish, you must move the electric through the water center; you must move through—that is the Law of Gravity—you must move through that law. Yes.

Now you can, kicking and screaming, force yourself through gravity. Yes. And hopefully get beyond the magnetic pull of gravity, for magnetic is what it is. But you must remember that you're going to have that sensation whenever you go to make a change. And unless you prepare yourself for that sensation, then you probably won't make it through to the change because you'll just go back; what the mind says is the easier way.

Well, who tells you it's easier not to make the effort? I will tell you who tells you that: it's the forms when you go to pierce through the magnetic field of your water center. Your emotions, the forms in that water center. That's where conviction is. That's where emotion is. And they tell you, "Oh, no, it's just not worth it." Why, certainly, because they don't want you passing through that. If you pass through that center of consciousness, then you're going to be freed from its control. All right. Some other question? Yes, [Student J].

Sir, would you please elaborate on the prior student's question about the breathing exercise and changing of the perspective?

Yes. In the changing of the perspective, in reference to that, you see, for example, when you do your breathing exercise properly, what you do, you actually are raising your consciousness from the earth center with the fire center into the water center. All right?

Now there are six other centers waiting for you to move into, because you are there also. You see, you *are* there; your perception is not there. Your conscious awareness is not there. You see, what is happening to you in the earth, fire, and water center is happening to you in the air center, in the electric-magnetic center, in the odic center, in the ethereal center, and in the celestial center of consciousness. It is happening to you in all those centers of consciousness. So when you go to accomplish something, it behooves you to make the effort to raise your consciousness to the higher realms, to the higher centers, for in so doing you will gain objectivity, and you will view what is happening in the lower centers in your life. Do you understand? So by viewing it, you have the objectivity; you have the perception; and therefore, you do not have the impact of the activity that is taking place on the earth, fire, and water center[s]. Hmm? Yes, [Student J].

Then any time we're inspired for a new endeavor—
Yes.
—should we then go into a breathing exercise prior to making any conscious effort towards that new endeavor?

Absolutely and positively. Because it will help you to gain perspective. Now, you see, when these things are taking place in the lower centers of consciousness, if you have made the effort to look at them, to look down at them—that which you look down upon you have the possibility of controlling. That which you look up to is controlling you. So when you are on this perception down here, then you are controlled by what's going on here. *[As he speaks, the teacher draws a straight, ascending line from the lower right corner toward the center of the blackboard. And then he draws, at the higher endpoint of that line, a circle, the lowest arc of which just touches that line's endpoint. And then he draws a straight, horizontal line extending to the left at the base of the circle.]* Do you understand? So you are perceiving what you want to accomplish, *[He retraces the ascending line and taps his chalk at the point at which it meets the circle.]* and by that you are bound and you are controlled by those three centers of consciousness. *[He taps the ascending line.]*

When it is brought from a higher center of consciousness, *[Beginning in the upper right corner of the blackboard, the teacher draws a descending line to the top of the circle.]* enters the dream state, *[Beginning at the circle, he now draws a straight, horizontal line from about the middle of the circle.]* you lower your consciousness down here *[He retraces to the ascending line.]* and are controlled by it. You do not return to where it was originally perceived. *[With his chalk, he taps the higher endpoint of the line descending toward the circle.]* You see?

Yes, sir.

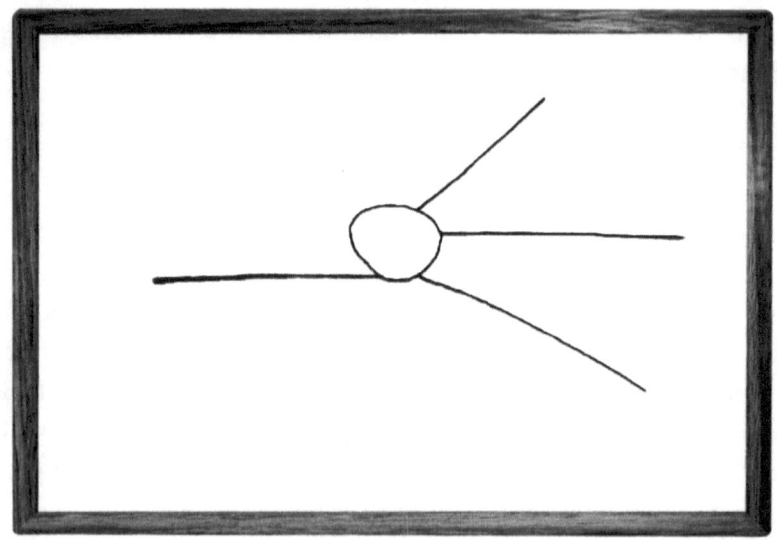

[Figure 37.11]

You see, it's perceived in your higher consciousness. And you lower your consciousness to the dream state and you say, "Oh, I had an idea. I had an inspiration or I had a thought." That is entering your awareness through your perception *[The teacher taps the horizontal line to the right of the circle.]* on that parallel center which you have identified with. Then you lower your perception into the lower centers of consciousness and believe that you are doing it. You see?

Yes, sir.

And by your belief that you are doing it, you are bound and controlled by those laws of gravity, when it came from above, when you were consciously aware in a higher realm of consciousness and brought it through in that dream state, the dream of life state. Does that help with your question?

Indeed. Thank you.

So, you see, when that happens and you're down here, *[The teacher points to the line ascending toward the circle.]* then what you want to do is, through your proper breathing exercises, you will raise your consciousness and in time you will clearly view *[He now gestures towards the line descending toward the circle.]* that's where it originally came from.

In fact, you see, that's where all of these experiences—you see, you have this evolution that you're going through. So up here *[With his pointer, he points to the higher endpoint of the line descending toward the circle.]* are all of these lessons that are waiting down here *[He now points to the line ascending toward the circle.]* for you to continue to evolve. *[He again points toward the higher endpoint of the descending line.]* You see? So you're up here. *[He again points to the higher endpoint of the descending line.]* This is the class we're going to have tomorrow. And then you come down to the dream state. *[He points to the horizontal line to the right of the circle.]* You think you have a—you're inspired. There's something you want to do. You start to do it, you move down here *[He now points to the ascending line.]* because you believe now that it's you. And that's when they [have] got you, you see. *[He taps the lower endpoint of the ascending line.]* When it was simply a little test up here, *[He points again to the higher endpoint of the descending line.]* that in keeping with your evolution and the schooling that you have earned, that was the exam coming the next day. And you went and took that down to the dream state, thought that it was you that got inspired, and down there believed that definitely it is you, and now you're paying the price when it was just a simple, little lesson, a little test that you have to go through. Does that help with your question?

Thank you, sir. Yes.

Certainly. Yes, [Student O]—no. [Student D] has been waiting. Yes, [Student D], please.

When you're piercing through the gravity in the water center, do you talk to those forms? I mean, when you realize that you're being pulled down by gravity, that is the forms that are pulling you down.

Yes, that's what you believe you are. That is correct. Yes. Now I'll sit down on that, on that form, too. *[The teacher sits down.]* Thank you very much. And you go right ahead.

Do you then speak to those forms, you know, and tell them that they are past forms to, to break their hold on you?

Well, certainly, but they won't like it at all. Because, after all, without you, they don't exist.

Right.

So, you see, until you can separate yourself and know beyond a shadow of any doubt what they truly are, well, they'll cause you all kinds of emotional disturbance because they live in that center of consciousness. But that is an early step, of saying, "Now just a moment. This is not me. I'm responsible for those kids, but they are not me. And therefore, you either quiet down or I'll see that I shut you off completely." It's an early step of that. Does that help you, [Student D]?

Yes. Thank you.

Yes. Now [Student O] has a question there. How's your chin, [Student O].

It's fine.

Is it all right? I mean, do you need a rest or do you need a chin rest?

No, I don't think so.

Yes. That's all right.

Do all life experiences and thoughts, do they come from above?

They do. They do.

Well—

That which is below is from above. And that which is above is from below. They absolutely do. You see, say that you're in school. All right? And you have different things to learn. And so the teacher gives to you: "Now these are the lessons you have to learn, and you bring your report back tomorrow." Hmm?

OK.

Now that's what you leave school with. See? Each day. And then you go and after you've left school, you think, "Oh, I had a thought to do this." And so you go do it. And while you're in the process of doing it, you believe that it's you, when all it was, was another little lesson that you had to learn in your evolution. That's all that it ever was. That's all that it can ever be. Hmm? But as long as you insist on looking from below, you're going to believe that that's you and be affected thereby. Yes. Does that help with your question?

Yes, sir. I have one more.

Yes.

So it's, it's almost like they're preplanned or pre—in other words, in the—we have, from moment to moment, to make a choice. And, and we're constantly—these choices are constantly issued or they're constantly coming at us. And I was trying—and I'm wondering about, as to how we view these choices or, or in our making our decision depends on what perspective we are or ... I—

That's right. For example, when you forget that the experiences in your life are in keeping with laws that you have established, that you have left school and believe you are the experiences—you see, these are lessons that you receive each and every moment from higher realms of consciousness in keeping with your own laws of evolution. Now you believe that, in this dream state, *[From his seated position, the teacher moves his right hand along a line parallel to the floor, indicating a straight, horizontal line.]* you convince yourself that that's your thought. All right? And instead of having the objective view of it, that it's the lesson that you have for school today, one of the many lessons, you think, in that dream state, that that's you. Then, as you continue to think that that's you, you lower your perspective: you're absolutely convinced that that is you. And you go through all of these disturbances. And life is not the beautiful thing that it truly is. Do you understand that, [Student O]?

Yes, sir.

You see? Of course, you're responsible. Every child is responsible for the lessons that he earns in school to do his homework. Your experiences are your homework. So many people try to get out of them. Yes. Yes, [Student L] has a question here.

Are the breathing exercises effective—let's say you're in a car and you want to change your perspective and you don't have the tones, obviously, to listen to, is it effective without using that?

Yes, it's effective. It's better to do your exercise before you get in the car, and do it properly and you won't have to worry while in the car—

I see.

—about doing your exercises because you will have done them properly. And they certainly will sustain you the length of time that you're in an automobile.

Thank you.

Yes. Does someone else have a question? [Student U] has a question this morning.

Is there a relationship between dreaming and our self-esteem lacking energy?

Why, certainly. Absolutely. And it's wonderful. I want the questions right direct to the classes. Your self-esteem is absolutely critical because it reveals to you your perception. You see?

See, people with low perception have a terrible self-esteem. They don't feel good about themselves at all. How could they? Look what they're looking through. And believing that they are. You see? So when you're looking through all those forms that have been created, and then you believe that all those forms are you, why, certainly you lose a good self-esteem. And when you lose that, then, really, it seems that life isn't worth living.

When, in a lower perspective, you look at what you truly are, you have to look through all the forms you have created. And when you go to pierce through all those forms, they take a great deal of your energy in order for you to see yourself at all. Does that help you with your question there, [Student U]?

Yes. Thank you.

Yes. Now [Student Y] has a question, please.

When you spoke of the power above and the force below—

Yes.

—does the force below, is that formed in the fire center?

The force below? It takes the water center, the fire, and the earth center to create the forms. It takes the three centers of consciousness to manifest them. So you have a physical form, then you have earth, fire, and water. Hmm? You have a mental form, then what centers do you have?

You have . . .

Air.

Air. Electric.

And magnetic.

And magnetic.

[If] you have a celestial form, what centers do you have?

Odic, ethereal, and celestial.

All right. Now this energy that is flowing through you that you are consciously aware of in an earth, fire, and water center is the same energy that is creating forms in the mental and the celestial realms of consciousness. It's the same energy.

So if it goes for all these other forms into the mental world or the physical, then, of course, it is not available for the forms of the other worlds. That help with your question there, [Student Y]?

Thank you.

Yes. Yes, [Student S], please.

How does sugar relate to the Law of Sustenance, making us feel good?

Well, you mean temporarily?

Right.

I'm sure you mean temporarily. It feeds the forms in the water center. And as long as a person identifies with form, physical, as you know physical form, then they will be affected by the forms that are created and sustained in the water center. Show me the person on your planet without emotion, and I will show you the person completely free from the water center. Yes. Yes, [Student M].

I was trying to understand why the line of infinity in one of these diagrams also is belief. It seems to not—unless my diagram is wrong. We have perception and conception.

Why, certainly. Well, conception and perception—you conceive and you perceive. Correct?

Correct.

Well, when your perception is in the lower centers of consciousness, you conceive.

Right. And—

Did I not give that to you, [Student B], last week?

You did. [Student B responds.]

Yes, go ahead.

And then the middle is feeling. [Student M continues.]

[Student B], did I not—does anybody understand what I gave to you last week? Have you been studying your notes? [Student S] respond to that.

I'm not sure it was given exactly as belief, that line. [Student S responds.]

You see? I am very happy I'm right here in front of you now. But I will let my students answer your question. That's very important.

Thank you. [Student M responds.]

I know what I said. I'm responsible for it.

Yes.

And I'm also responsible that you know what I said.

Yes.

Have you viewed your tape from last class?

Oh, yes.

And what do you have to say? *[After a short pause, the teacher continues.]* [Student L], did you have a response to that?

I have the diagram here. Belief is the dream state. [Student L responds.]

Did [Student M] understand that?

Yes. I do. [Student M responds.]

Is there a problem with that?

No. It is—There is not.

So it's just, temporarily, a misunderstanding from lack of proper study of your class, wouldn't you say?

Yes.

So I want my students all prepared for Sunday to study your classes. Otherwise, you know, there's no sense in me giving them. Show me one dream that you've had that you don't believe is you if it's pleasing to you.

It's true.

Pardon?

That's . . .

Well, know you, life is a dream. We're constantly creating it. If it's something that's pleasing to our mind, we say, "Of course, that's me. Absolutely that's me. Why, certainly." We don't even have to say it. We demonstrate it. Yes, [Student D], do you have a question?

Yes. In the diagram that you made today, you had a line that was the dream state or the dream of life.

Yes.

And then you had a line going down. And you wrote on the line going down "belief."

Yes.

You didn't write it on the line that was the dream of life.

Well, of course, not. Because, you see, you don't have conception without belief.

Right. OK.

So, you see, I'm trying to help you to change your perspective. And when you change your perspective, you're not going to be bound by belief. No one likes to be dependent, do you think, [Student J]?

No, sir!

You see, being dependent is a person who is vulnerable and very weak, very dependent and an easy victim. An easy victim for those realms. So if you want to be an easy victim for the lower realms of consciousness, all you have to do is permit yourself to be dependent. Would you say that a dependent person is one who is fulfilled with what they are? *[After a short pause, the teacher continues.]* No. You can't have dependence without need, and you can't have need without denial.

Now time is passing. What time do we have here? I think our time is up. My goodness. It's past an hour. Are there any questions before we conclude this class today?

I did tell you last Sunday that I would be here with you direct someday. Well, that someday is now.

So let's keep our questions directed directly to what has been given. And I expect you all to study and to present intelligent questions, as you had today, in how to change your perspective. It's all the way you view it. You see?

Now you cannot move to that awareness until you make those change[s] in consciousness. You have a wonderful school and a wonderful opportunity. A hundred thousand times a day in this temple there's some disturbance. That gives you a hundred thousand opportunities a day to say, "Thank you, God. I know that's not me because I know that's not them. I have to first know that it's not me in order to grant to the other that it's not them." Now let us not forget that. *[The teacher begins to erase the blackboard.]* And let us keep a clean slate. *[Many students laugh.]*

You know, so often in life a person says, "Oh, I never want to forget because I never want to go through that experience again." You don't have to worry, if you are making the effort to grow. Because if you're making the effort to grow, your perspective will change and you'll never be tempted again. So you don't have to worry about that. All you have to do is to interest yourself in raising your perspective.

Now I have to get de-wired here. *[The teacher refers to the microphone cable that connects his microphone to the recorder.]* Well, in a moment. I will say good day.

MARCH 2, 1986

A/V Class Private 38

Good morning, class.

This morning, take your notes here. And we'll begin with the question, Why is hell identification with and belief in what you deny? I will expect your answers a little later on in the class.

Now we'll begin here today, continuing on with our understanding of perception and growth and— *[The teacher draws a single vertical line on the blackboard and then draws nine circles on the right side of the line. Each circle just touches any adjacent circles.]* Now I'll give you a few moments to draw that. How many circles do you see there this morning? Pardon? Nine. *[After a pause, the teacher continues.]* Does everyone have that now? Fine.

[Figure 38.1]

Now we spoke to you at our last class on perception. The parallel view here. *[He draws a straight, horizontal line to the right of the column of circles at the middle of the fifth circle from the bottom, but the line does not touch that circle.]* The higher view here. *[Starting near the upper right corner of the blackboard, he draws another straight line descending toward and joining the left endpoint of the horizontal line.]* And the lower view here. *[Starting near the lower right, he draws a third straight line ascending toward and joining the left endpoints of the other two lines. These lines will be described as the upper, middle, and lower lines of perception. For clarity, the count for all numbered circles will begin at the bottom of the column.]*

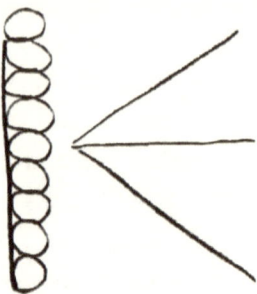

[Figure 38.2]

Whenever you experience desire, which is the divine expression, *[The teacher writes "DE" at the right endpoint of the horizontal line.]* you experience it in what centers of consciousness, [Student S]? Yes. In what centers of consciousness do you experience desire?

The lower three.

No, that's where you *believe* you are the desire; that is not where you experience it. Desire is experienced in what center of consciousness? One, two, three, four, five, six, seven, eight, nine. *[The teacher taps each circle with his chalk as he counts, moving from the bottom to the top of the column of circles.]* What center of consciousness is desire experienced in, which is in truth the divine expression? At what center of consciousness is it pointing to? Can you see? *[After a short pause, the teacher continues.]* Is it the fourth center? The seventh center? The ninth one? Yes.

The fifth.

The fifth center of consciousness. What is the fifth center of consciousness?

The electric.

Is that correct, class? *[After a short pause, the teacher continues.]* The electric. So we now understand, hopefully, that desire, the divine expression, is experienced in the electric center of consciousness. When, [Student S], do you experience the need of its fulfillment? In what center of consciousness? When do you believe that you are the experience?

In the lower three.

In the lower three centers of consciousness. So you must lower your consciousness into the lower three centers *[From the top of the third circle from the bottom, the teacher draws a descending straight line towards the lower endpoint of the lowest line of perception. But just before halfway to that endpoint, he redirects the still descending line back toward the column of circles until it meets about the middle of the right arc of the first circle.]* in order to experience and believe—not to experience, but to believe that you are the desire that you are experiencing in the fifth center of consciousness.

Now in the lower perspective, the perception, *[He writes "PRCPN" at the lower endpoint of the lower line of perception.]* your lower perception, which would place you here *[He places his chalk at the vertex of the lines he just drew and pauses.]* in the lower centers. *[He then draws a line from the vertex of the lines connecting the first and third circles to the lower endpoint of the lowest line of perception.]* You are now bound by that which you believe. Do you understand that, [Student S]?

Yes.

All right. So here we have the fire center of consciousness. *[He now writes "F" inside the fifth circle in the column.]* It either goes to a lower perception into the—what three centers? Yes.

Fire, water, and earth.

Right. Earth, fire, and water center[s] of consciousness. However, if you take the same divine expression, known as desire, and you make the effort to change your perception, to change your perception, *[He writes "PRCPN" at the higher endpoint of the upper line of perception.]* then you are going to experience this divine expression in what center of consciousness? Yes.

The magnetic, the odic...

Would you say—

... and the electric. [A few words of the student are difficult to transcribe.]

Would you say this is earth, fire, water? *[Starting with the first circle, the teacher taps each circle with his chalk as he speaks the name of the center it represents.]* Next.

Air. Electric. Magnetic. Odic. Ethereal. [As the teacher taps each circle with his chalk, the student identifies that center of consciousness.]

Ethereal. *[He writes an "E" in the center of the eighth circle.]* And celestial. *[He writes a "C" in the ninth or top circle.]* And what is this center? *[He points to the seventh circle.]*

Odic.

Odic. *[The teacher writes an "O" in the seventh circle.]* Now in which center of consciousness would you identify with this divine expression, if you changed your perception? *[After a pause, the teacher continues.]* In which center of consciousness do you experience this divine expression *[He points to the vertex of the three lines of perception.]* and believe that you are it? Is it in the earth center, fire center, or water center? *[As he speaks the names of the centers, he writes "E" in the first, "F" in the second, and then "W" in the third circle.]* Or is it all three? And if so, in which center does it originate? Yes.

Would it originate in the water center, where the forms are given birth?

Where the forms are given birth. That is correct. Here in the water center *[He makes a check mark just below the line emerging from the water center.]* is where you believe you are desire, the divine expression, when you permit yourself to believe that you are the dream that you are dreaming. *[He *writes "DREAM" just above the middle line of perception, near the vertex.]*

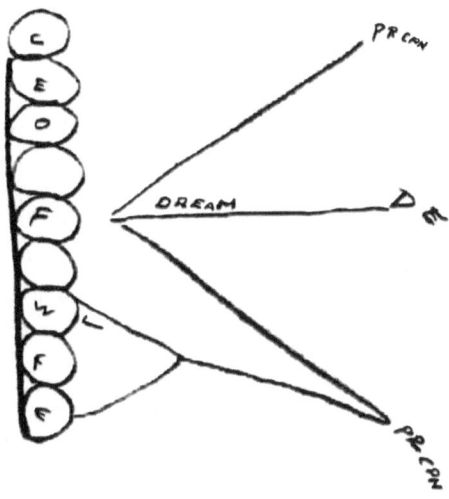

[Figure 38.3]

Now these are the centers of consciousness through which the divine Light flows. Your identification with the center is your bondage to the center, ever in keeping with your own perception. For example, if you, in your dream, your thought, that which you have created, do not make conscious effort through the daily, spiritual exercises that you have been given, then your identification with the divine Light, known as the *prana*, infinite intelligent Energy, is in a center of consciousness *[The teacher points toward the second circle on the column, the fire center.]* of which you are making no effort to control. Therefore, you experience what is known as hell.

Now why do you experience what is known as hell in the centers of consciousness that you believe you are when you dream the dream of life? Yes, [Student S] was answering. Thank you.

Because they're controlled by need, based on denial, in the lower centers there can be no fulfillment of the desire.

Correct. For the fulfillment of the divine expression only exists in the higher realms of consciousness. *[He places a check mark by the eighth circle.]* Now whenever you permit yourself to deny, you guarantee the Law of Need. It is an absolute guarantee. You cannot experience need for the fulfillment of anything until you have first denied it in your consciousness. Is there anyone who doesn't understand that this morning? *[After a short pause, the teacher continues.]*

So when you make little effort to do your spiritual exercises that you have been given over these many years, then you have little results. When you make no effort to do your spiritual exercises and proper breathing and meditations, daily, that you have been given, then you experience the opposite of fulfillment: you experience lack; you experience disturbance and the opposite of a heavenly state of consciousness. You experience the hell which is the effect of the law that you have established. Does anyone not understand that this morning?

So if you do not care to do your spiritual exercises daily, then you must be gracious and willing to pay the price of believing that you are the dream that you are dreaming, the denial of what you are, and experience what you are not.

Now are there any questions on the movement of this Light through your anatomy? If the effort is not made, you remain here, your perception, in the lower centers of consciousness *[The teacher gestures toward the three lower circles.]* for each dream that you dream, *[He now points toward the vertex of the three lines of perception.]* each thought that you entertain.

We'll leave that on there [on the blackboard] for a few moments. And we'll come to the questions that you may have here at this moment on this particular diagram and on questions that you have from the other classes pertinent to last week and the week before. If you have any questions at this time, you please raise your hands. Yes, [Student U], please.

When we see the good in all things, do we rise in perception?

Yes, absolutely! Whenever you permit yourself to make the effort to see the good in all experience, by so doing you identify with this river of life, this intelligent Light that is flowing through your being; you identify in a higher level of consciousness. You change your perception. To see the good in all experiences is to readjust your perception so that your dream that you are dreaming does not become the bondage of your belief. That is correct. Yes. Yes, [Student N], please.

Does the length of our line of infinity affect our, the gravitational pull?

Indeed, it does.

And . . .

Yes.

Would the length of our life of infinity depend on the centers of consciousness we're in, up in the upper realm?

Well, for example, as you're stating, the length of your line of infinity, of course, is dependent on your direction of the energy that is flowing through the nine centers of consciousness. *[The teacher retraces the vertical line adjacent to the column of circles top to bottom.]* So if you have equal distribution *[He again retraces that vertical line.]* through the nine centers of consciousness, then your line of infinity, indeed, in that respect, is lengthened. Yes. For you become—you broaden your horizons and you become more all-encompassing of what you are; therefore, you become what you are, by freeing yourself from what you are not.

If you have a very short perspective, then you are bound to those limited centers that you are identifying with. So you must lengthen your perspective, you must broaden your perspective to include what you are, which is the whole. But each time you permit yourself to dream a dream, known as the divine expression, the desire of life, each time that you permit yourself to dream that dream and do not make the effort to rise in consciousness—for the flow *[Again without touching the blackboard, he traces the vertical line linking all nine circles, but this time his hand ascends from the first to the ninth circle.]* of this energy [is to be] equally distributed throughout all of the centers of consciousness which you are—then you are bound by the laws *[He gestures specifically to the third and then the first circle.]* that control the particular group or centers of consciousness that you have identified with, through lack of effort. Does that help with your question?

Yes. Thank you.

Yes, [Student Y], please.

What—so it would be—would it behoove one to, when the dream, when it starts to form, to do the cleansing breath right at that—

That is the purpose of the cleansing breath. You see, to teach students to put God into it or forget it does not appear to be perceived with many of my students on Earth. Therefore, whenever you have a desire, which is the divine expression, which is rather constant as you identify with the mental world, then, at those moments, that is the time to do your proper breathing exercise so that you will not trap yourself, through identification *[He points to the top of the first circle.]* with the centers of consciousness, only a portion of the nine or the totality that you are. You see, when you declare in your consciousness and you put God in any endeavor, that, of course, is the Principle of Good, the goodness that you are, you receive from anything whatever it is you put into the thing. So if you put good in, then you can only receive good out. If you put limit in, then limit is what is going to return to you. That help with your question? And [Student L] has a question, please.

Yes. The diagram reminds me, somewhat, of the spinal column. And I was wondering—

Well, that's what it is. Thank you. Go ahead.

Oh. I was wondering if that's how the centers relate along the river of life in the body.

Indeed, they do. There are nine. Yes.

Thank you.

You're welcome. Now [Student O] has a question this morning, please.

Yes. Would you explain what is, what is happening in our consciousness when the size of the circle or the spin is increased, when the size of the spin and the retrospin is increased?

Excellent question. I was going to get to it a little later, and I'll get to it right now. The first center *[Without touching the blackboard, the teacher retraces the first circle, moving his hand in a clockwise direction.]* in this particular group, *[He gestures toward the lower three circles.]* of course, is the earth center. It always moves in a clockwise spin. By its process of moving clockwise, *[He again retraces the first circle, moving his hand in a clockwise direction.]* the following center moves counterclockwise. By its process of moving counterclockwise, *[He traces of the second circle in a counterclockwise direction.]* the water center moves clockwise. *[He then traces the third circle in a clockwise direction.]* This is the friction and adhesion process.

And so whenever you permit yourself, for example, to identify here with the earth center, *[He points to the first circle in the column.]* then you set that earth center of your consciousness into an increased acceleration. As that increases in its acceleration, the next center of consciousness, known as the fire center, *[He points to the second circle.]* begins its increase [in] acceleration in the retrospin or counterclockwise. For example, you say that you have an—you permit yourself the dream of life *[The teacher points to the vertex of the three lines of perception.]* and, through lack of effort, you have descended down here, *[From the vertex, he traces the lower line of perception and then moves back toward the lower portion of the column of circles, retracing the lines on the blackboard.]* and your perception is of the earth, fire, and water centers. *[As he speaks the centers, the teacher taps the corresponding circle with his chalk.]* Well, when you do that, you direct the energy into those centers of consciousness. So whenever you have a desire, you believe that that is you down here in the earth center, *[He taps the first circle with his chalk.]* what you are doing is increasing the fire center. And as you are increasing the fire center, you increase your water center or your emotions.

Now a person in those centers of consciousness says that they are in need, for they have registered the divine desire and have lowered their consciousness and experience the lack of that which they believe that they are: their registration of desire. By so doing, you have the expressions of the fire center, for it is born there, by your own direction in the earth center, and you also have the emotions and the turmoil and the impatience that the water center has to offer. Three is a manifestation; it is the law of physics and it controls these three centers. *[The teacher gestures in an elongated circle enclosing the three lower circles.]* Does that help you with your question?

Yes, sir.

So, of course, it is not intelligent, for an intelligent being, not to make the effort to rise the consciousness so that this energy here, *[With chalk in hand, the teacher points to the lower circle and moves his hand upward to the highest circle, and then back down to the lowest.]* through their consciousness, is equally distributed through conscious effort. Whereas all expression of the Divinity flows from the celestial realm of consciousness, *[The teacher traces the letter "C" in the ninth circle.]* it is only intelligent and in our best interest, when we register these desires, *[He taps the vertex of the three lines of perception.]* this dream of life that we are registering on the parallel perception, it is only intelligent that we would make the effort to rise the *prana*

[Gesturing toward the third circle, he moves his hand upwards to the ninth circle.] and the consciousness to the celestial realms where we have received it from. Then, in so doing, having a conscious awareness of from whence it cometh, then we can move it down through these centers *[Beginning at the ninth circle, the teacher moves his hand encircling the entire column of circles.]* and bring about the manifestation of good that we have received it for. That's putting God in it.

To declare that God is in your efforts and your endeavors is simply, through your proper, spiritual, daily exercises, is simply to recognize the source from whence it cometh and, in so doing, to once again gain an intelligent perception. Did that help with your question?

Yes, sir.

Yes. Now [Student M] has a question, please.

That's where, when they say that desire is blind, there is no pausing. There is—therefore, the pause is so, is like one and the same as the cleansing breath, as you pause and you do your . . .

Yes. Thank you. You see, desire is blind to us only because we have stolen it from the Divinity. You see, we steal desire from the—which is the divine expression—we steal it in our error of ignorance for we believe that the desire is ours. That's how we steal the Divinity. And whoever tempts to steal the Divinity must, of course, pay the price. So when you are registering the divine expression here *[With his chalk he taps to the vertex of the three lines of perception.]* in this dream state of this parallel perception—you note, *[He taps the fifth circle several times with his chalk.]* that that is the fifth center of consciousness, don't you?

Yes.

All right. Please make note of these things.

When you do that, you steal the divine expression, or tempt to steal it, by believing that it is yours. You believe—and you can't believe that it's yours until you descend *[The teacher gestures with his hand, first tracing the lower line of perception as it descends away from the fifth circle and then his hand moves back toward the lower three circles of the column.]* in your perception to the earth, fire, and water center. *[With his chalk he taps each circle as he speaks the names of the centers.]* So you believe that it is your desire: special, unique in the universes. It is something that you have received. Your interpretation of that divine expression is, of course, dependent upon your perception. So if you perceive it from a lower vantage point, then you believe that that is yours. And when you believe that that is yours, you separate it: you make the effort to separate it from what it truly is. And when you tempt to separate something from what it is, you go against the law of the purpose of its design. Did that help with your question?

Thank you very much.

Now [Student Y] here has a question, please.

Is it a good idea, when doing the cleansing breath, should you image? What should one image?

Well, one images and, therefore, creates. One images and, therefore, creates. Now, for example, to consciously create is certainly far more intelligent than to be the victim of a creation of which one is not consciously aware. So whereas the Light is, if one permits themselves the acceptance of the Light, then they do not have the need to image anything, do they? You see? For example, you are experiencing the divine expression here. *[The teacher taps his chalk repeatedly at the vertex of the three lines of perception.]* And through this parallel view, *[He moves his hand from the vertex toward the fifth circle.]* it's right there at the center of consciousness, known as faith. So what happens with faith when the mind gets it? Tell me. Yes, here in the back row here. I'm going to move my, my older students up front if they don't speak up. Yes, [Student J], let's hear from you.

I would say the answer would be it turns into belief.

Indeed, it does! And show me one human being in any universe who does not believe, who does not experience fear, doubt, concern, and worry for the fulfillment of that which they believe that they are. Would you not agree?

Yes, sir.

And so because faith, *[The teacher taps the fifth circle and then gestures toward the second circle.]* once entering mental substance is known as fear—it's known as fear by the very bondage of belief. We fear what we believe. We do not fear what we do not believe. Would you not agree?

Yes, sir.

Yes. So that's what's happening with this dream of life through the lack of your daily spiritual exercises and the lack of effort to consistently identify with the centers by conscious choice. They are not receiving equal distribution. One wisely returns to the source that which is loaned to them. Would you not agree, [Student J]?

Yes, sir.

Therefore, if you go to a bank on your Earth planet and they make a loan to you, you, in turn, in time return that to them for it was theirs in the first place. Correct?

Yes, sir.

All right. Now in the process, you pay interest.

Yes, sir.

Usually. Now when you have these desires and these thoughts, *[The teacher taps his chalk several times on the vertex of the lines of perception.]* if you return them to the source from whence they came, *[He taps the ninth circle once with his chalk and then taps the vertex.]* you notice that it's a much shorter interest *[He first points at the vertex of the lines of perception, and then to the ninth circle and then back to the vertex.]* than to go all the way down here *[He taps near the first circle.]* and then try climbing all the way back here. *[He taps his chalk just outside the ninth circle.]* So you pay less interest, you see. When you recognize who has loaned it to you, then you won't have to pay so much interest. It's like a person, as I said, they go to the bank. They get the money that they desire. And they forget that that money belongs to the bank and they take a long time to return it: they pay more interest. Is that not true?

Yes, sir.

Sooner or later they do pay more interest, don't they?

Indeed, they do.

Well, you see, it's the same thing. You see, you have registered within the mental consciousness, *[The teacher taps the vertex of the lines of perception several times.]* you have registered a divine expression that you call desire. When you register that— *[He again points to that vertex.]* I've taught you in other ways, too: you have a desire, give it to God; stop trying to steal it from the Source—you recognize where it came from. *[Again, the teacher first points to that vertex and then to the ninth circle.]* Do you understand? And when you recognize where it comes from, *[He again points to the vertex and then the ninth circle.]* you have less interest to pay than if you insist that it is yours *[He points to the vertex.]* and you have to go all the way down here *[He points near the first circle.]* and then back up again. *[The teacher raises and lowers his hand up and down the column of circles several times.]* Yes.

In keeping with what you're saying, sir, you gave us an affirmation, "Not mine, but thine."

Correct.

When something good happens to us, instead of letting our ego get ahold of it, should we then immediately use that affirmation?

Absolutely. Because that is a recognition of the Source from whence it has come.

Thank you.

You see, whoever recognizes the Source is intelligently sustained by the Source. Our problem here in this world of creation is our refusal to recognize the Source. Now whenever we refuse to recognize something that is, then what we are doing is denying it. And through that Law of Denial, we are experiencing the need of it. You cannot experience the need of anything that is not first denied. When you deny the Source—you deny it by refusing to recognize it—then you must experience a need for it. You cannot experience a need for what you accept. You can only experience a need for what you deny.

So the most important thing here at this class at this time is to look at the many ways that the human mind denies in one's own personal life. We deny ourselves daily and constantly. We deny it by declarations and a refusal to recognize the Source from whence it comes. We pay dearly for denying the Source. And that payment is very heavy, for we believe that we have done it; we believe that we are doing it; we believe that we can change it; we believe we can control it; and that is the high interest that we pay.

You see, a person doesn't feel less goodness by recognizing that they are sustained by an intelligent, infinite Light. They do not experience less goodness; they experience far more. So what is there in truth that one must give in order to experience all of that goodness? All they have to give—if you can call it giving, when it is nothing more than a return of the loan that we have made—all we have to do is to recognize the Source. Now a person says, "Well, I recognize the source of my goodness, but what about these terrible experiences in my life?" Well, we recognize that too. Ever in keeping with our perception have we made it so. Does that help you, [Student J]? Yes, go right ahead.

Thank you, sir.

Certainly.

Yes, [Student H] has a question, please.

A couple of classes ago you mentioned that experience is the movement of limit.

Indeed.

Is this what you are really discussing, then, that the experience would be from a lower perception, having stolen the desire?

Yes, remember this: you have nine centers of consciousness, which are [interrelated in groups of] three [or] triune. You have light, shadow, and darkness. You should mark that down in your notebooks. Light, shadow, and darkness. You will understand that, if you will take a look and see—light, shadow, and darkness— *[As he speaks, the teacher writes an "L" just above the upper line of perception, an "S" just above the middle or horizontal line, and a "D" just above the lower line. All letters are close to the midpoint of the lines.]* If you will take a look and not forget that obstructions do not exist in the Light. It is not possible for obstruction to exist in the Light. Obstructions exist only in shadows and darkness. They are created by our perception. An obstruction to desire is created by our own obstruction. *[The teacher may have intended to say "by our own perception."]* We create the obstruction to the divine expression. How do we create the obstruction to the divine expression? Very simply: through an error of ignorance known as laziness in consciousness. We dream the dream; we make no effort and before the dream is finished, we believe that that is us. Any questions? Yes, [Student N].

Does the—after you've recognized the Source, does that create equal distribution, then, after that or—

It depends on your effort of recognition. You know, it's like a person [who] says, "Well, I [have] got this new job. I recognize that it came from the Divine Source." But do they feel that it came from the Divine Source? For example, one can say many things in a mental realm of consciousness, but do they feel it? Do they sense it? Do they experience it inside of themselves? Because you have nine centers of consciousness to balance out in equal distribution. *[The teacher first points to the first circle then moves his hand straight up the column of circles to the ninth.]* Hmm? So it takes more than a declaration and a statement, "I recognize this goodness in my life has come from the Source that I cannot control, from the Source that is sustaining me. I recognize that." But the question is, Do we feel it? For we have nine centers of consciousness to be considered. Did that help with your question? Yes, [Student B], please.

We've been taught that we remove obstructions through acceptance.

Correct!

What is—is acceptance a number and is it up one of those—

Acceptance is the Light, the movement of the Light. That's what acceptance is. So, you see, obstruction cannot exist in the Light. *[The teacher taps the "L" above the upper line of perception several times with his chalk.]* You see, you cannot have an obstruction when you accept it. You cannot control what you deny. You certainly can control and move whatever you accept, speaking in that sense. Do you understand that, [Student B]? See, for if you accept the right of existence of something, then you are not controlled by it. It is when you deny the right of its existence that you are controlled by it, for you permit it to become an obstruction to the Light that you are.

So acceptance is all those top centers?

Yes! Acceptance—what acceptance is—acceptance is the movement of the divine Principle of Good, known as God. So if you want to see acceptance—because that is what you are. You are acceptance. You are not denial. That is what—perception of what you are. *[The teacher points to the vertex of the lines connecting the first circle and the third circles.]* We convince our self we are denial. Acceptance—this is acceptance. *[To the left of the column of circles, the teacher draws a straight, vertical line, and at its lower endpoint, he then draws one circle, the left arc of which just touches that endpoint.]* Everything is included. Nothing is left out. When you deny, you separate. When you separate, you experience the need for. You cannot experience the need for anything that you accept. You can only experience the need for what you do not accept.

[Figure 38.4]

Thank you.

Now if you will make that effort through—you see, first of all, it is very difficult to accept without the spiritual exercises that all of you students have been given. They're indispensable to the broadening of the horizon and the acceptance of what you are. Because when you accept what you are, you must consciously have equal distribution of intelligent energy through your being.

So if a person makes effort to accept, *[He now points near the vertex of the lines connecting the first and third circle.]* to totally accept while they're in these centers of consciousness, *[He gestures toward the lowest three circles.]* by descending into that realm, *[Beginning at the vertex of the lines of perception, the teacher traces the lines connecting to the first circle.]* then you have what is known as a limited or censored acceptance. And these three centers *[He again gestures toward the lower three circles.]* will certainly receive plenty of energy at the cost and lacking of these other centers of consciousness. *[He points to or taps his chalk at each of the circles that are above the lower three.]* Yes, [Student S].

Do the clockwise and counterclockwise rotation of the centers alternate all the way up or does the pattern repeat itself at every third—

It repeats itself.

May I ask—

In other words—yes, you may ask a question as soon as I answer yours. Earth is clockwise. *[He points to the first circle.]* Fire is counterclockwise. *[He points to the second circle.]* Water is clockwise. *[The teacher now taps the third circle.]* All right? Now you want the question of the next one. What's the next center? *[He taps the fourth circle.]*

Air.

Air. *[As he speaks, he writes the letter "A" in the center of the fourth circle.]* Which is it? Clockwise or counterclockwise? *[As he speaks, he first makes a circle in the air with his hand moving in a clockwise direction and then another circle with his hand moving in a counterclockwise direction.]*

Counter?

No, it is clockwise. You see, each center is a triune expression. *[With his chalk, he taps the lower three circles.]* Earth, fire, and water. And so you must repeat the pattern for the three centers of consciousness. *[Beginning with the first circle, he taps all the circles with this chalk.]* That's what keeps them distinct in their own group. Yes.

So if you were to reverse the spin of one of the centers, it would only affect the other two in that triad.

That is correct. That is correct. But you must also understand [that] would only directly affect that group of three. It would have its indirect effect as you are one being. You see. So it would have its side benefits, so to speak, if you can call it that. It would have an effect, but not a direct effect because they are separate groups, although you are all three of those separate groups.

Thank you.

You see, another thing, too, here that you want to relate to with your notes, and some of you already have, you have the conscious, the subconscious, and the unconscious. Well, here you are. There's conscious. *[The teacher draws a horizontal line perpendicular to and on the left side of the column of circles* between the sixth and seventh circles.] Subconscious. *[He draws a second horizontal line perpendicular to and on the left side of the column of circles between the third and fourth circles.]* And unconscious. *[The teacher draws a third horizontal line perpendicular to and on the left side of the column of circles just beneath the first circle.]*

Yes, now did [Student B] have a question? And I'll get—yes, [Student B].

Between the fourth and the fifth is the power of the will.

That is correct! Between the fourth *[He taps the fourth circle.]* and fifth *[He taps the fifth circle.]* centers of consciousness. *[He draws a horizontal line perpendicular to the column that transects the column between the fourth and fifth circle. He then adds arrows on both ends of that line.]* Pardon?

So then, does that mean that desire comes in on the fifth and it has to drop down to between the fourth or the fifth?

[The teacher laughs joyously.] The will, the lord of our universe, correct?

Yes.

Right. In order to identify—you're absolutely correct—it must drop down from lack of effort. That is true. Now, however, if there's lack of effort, where does this great will go? *[He taps with his chalk the line with the arrows.]* It goes right here, doesn't it? *[He taps the fifth circle with his chalk.]* And starts climbing up *[He taps the six, seventh, eighth, and ninth circles.]* through recognition and acceptance. So, you see, it's when we register this divine expression and if we do not make the effort, it goes right down into our will. *[The teacher makes a short line from the center of the fifth circle down towards the line with the arrows.]* You do see that, don't you, [Student B]?

[Editor's note: In the above paragraph, the teacher may have intended to say "If there's no lack of effort", for it is unlikely that the will would climb as an effect of no effort being made. However, the transcription may be accurate as is.]

Yes.

Because it's a question you brought up. But look what it has to offer down here, *[He draws a large V-shaped line incorporating the four lower circles.]* at the sacrifice of all of this above it, you see. *[He gestures toward the highest circles.]* There's one, two, three, four; there are five centers above it. *[Descending from the top, he taps each circle as he counts.]*

Now that's an excellent question. I'm glad that you asked it. Because when you register a desire for something, *[The teacher retraces the arrow on the line on the right side of the column.]* [Student B] and class, you have two choices: to use your will to attain it, would you not agree?

Yes.

Or to use your faith for that which is in your best interest. Is that not correct?

Right.

So, you see, you stand right here *[The teacher retraces the horizontal line with arrows transecting the column between the fourth and fifth circles.]* between that fourth and fifth, and you are consciously, constantly with choice. You will either use your will to get it or you will use your faith to accept what is best. So if you choose *[He points to center of the fifth circle.]* to move into faith of what is in your best interest, you free it to return to the Source. It's formless and free; you do not have a created form that's been created by the direction of the lord of your universe of your will power. Do you understand?

See, anything from this center of consciousness *[The teacher taps the fifth circle.]* down— *[The teacher draws a vertical line downward on the left of the column from the fifth circle to below the first circle, and as he does so, the chalk breaks.]* pardon me— *[He adds arrows on the lower endpoint of the line he just drew.]* is at great expense, *[He writes "E" at the point of that arrow and he picks up a piece of chalk that had fallen to the floor.]* for it is denial. That's where all struggle and all need and all lack and all discord exist. Anything from this center of consciousness upward is fulfillment. *[Again to the left of the column of circles, he now draws a line from the fifth circle upward and adds arrows at its endpoint. He then writes "FUF" near its point.]* This is fulfillment. *[He points to the "FUF."]* This is all cost. *[He writes "COST" near the point of the arrow pointing downward, adjacent to the E.]* Yes, [Student B].

Isn't the power of will an electric power?

Indeed.

So it's electric—

Indeed.

—power directed—it's the direction of it that's the problem.

It is the direction of it. The moment—you see, when this power descends, do you understand, when it descends—from lack of conscious effort, it descends–when that happens, it steals that which is from the Source. And that's why you can only experience need and all of those problems in these centers of consciousness. *[With his left hand, the teacher first points to the horizontal line transecting the column of circles between fourth and fifth circle, and then gestures toward the four lower circles.]* You experience need, and all your struggles in earth, fire, water, and air centers of consciousness. *[He points to the corresponding circle as he names each center.]* You experience fulfillment in all of these other centers of consciousness. *[Starting with the fifth circle, the teacher points consecutively to each of the five higher circles.]* So when you have put them all together, you are freed from need, want, lack, and desire, in the sense of the formation of the divine expression.

See, the desire is the divine expression. *[He points toward the vertex of the three lines of perception.]* It is formless; it is not limited. We limit it when we descend with it. *[He again points toward that vertex and then retraces the lower line of perception.]* When we believe that we are the desire that is registering in our consciousness, that's when we limit it, and that's when we are controlled and bound by it. And that's where the forms are created. Does that help with your question? Yes, [Student B].

I have one more.

Certainly.

Then faith, it's a five. It's a certain shape. Does the shape of the five, the two straight lines and the one circle, does that have something to do with the direction of energy?

It does indeed. It does indeed. And when it's directed in a certain way, it becomes a complete circle, known as total fulfillment. It does indeed. So it depends on where you send it, you see. See, we're sending this energy all the time into the different centers of consciousness. There's an imbalance, [a lack] of equal distribution to these centers of consciousness.

See, the moment—now, for example, it's like when, at times, you'll recognize that [there is] something you would like to accomplish and you will release that from your will. Do you understand that? You'll have the desire and you will release it. You will not be plagued by it. Do you understand? Well, if you do that, and continue to do that, it shall return unto you in its fulfillment. If you permit your will to take it, from lack of spiritual exercise, breathing, and conscious awareness, it will take it down: you will believe that you are that desire [and] be bound and controlled by it, for you have denied its source. And whenever a person denies the just and rightful source of anything, they must pay interest on that denial, just like with a bank. Did that help with the question, [Student B]?

Yes. Thank you.

Now [Student S] has a question back there. Yes.

Yes, a moment ago I understood you to say the conscious, subconscious, and unconscious. You drew this—

That is correct.

I'd like to ask where the superconscious comes in.

The superconscious, which you were given many, many years ago, is a conscious awareness of all three. *[Beginning at the top left of the ninth circle, the teacher draws an arching line in an elongated C-shape on the left side of the column of circles, enclosing the entire column on one side.]* A conscious awareness of all three. That is the superconscious. Yes. A conscious awareness of all three. Someone else have a question? [Student S], yes.

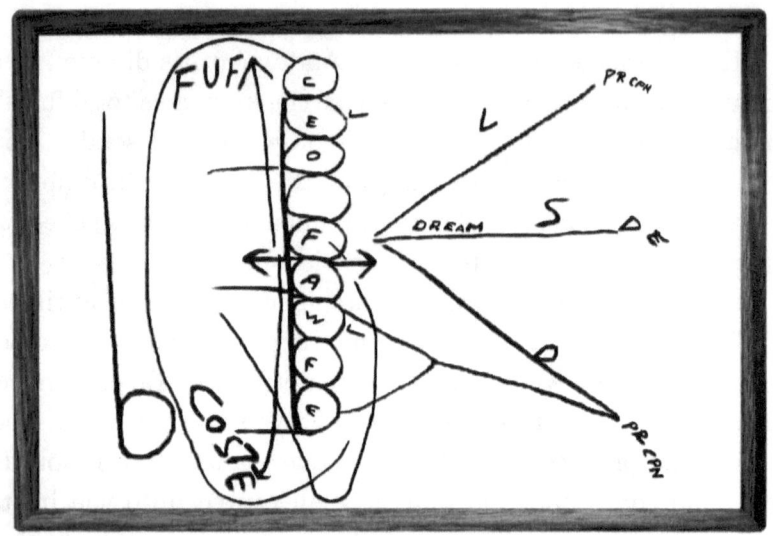

[Figure 38.5]

I'd like to ask one more, please, on the spin of the nine centers. If the pattern repeats itself on every section of three—

Correct.

—I understand, then, that there'd be six counterclockwise and—six clockwise and three counterclockwise.

Yes.

Could you, please, explain that principle that there would be so many more clockwise rotations than counterclockwise?

Well, I'll have to draw you a diagram for that. All right? So we'll have to erase for a moment. *[The teacher erases the blackboard. After he has been erasing for some time, he remarks.]*

You see how, how difficult it is to take it off? How difficult it is to get rid of something that you believe that you are; yet, so easy to put it on, isn't it? My, oh, my, it's so easy to put it on. So difficult to remove it. It is only the uneducated ego that is like a blackboard, and it is only selfishness that's like a piece of chalk. A little reason is the eraser.

All right. Now you're asking a question about the spin and the retrospin. Now we're going to have to draw for you some diagrams here. Let's draw here. *[On the clean blackboard, the teacher draws a triangle that is basically equilateral with its apex pointing upward.]* We have earth, fire, and water. And where is it located? [Student S], you've asked the question. Where is earth, fire, and water on here?

OK. Fire's on the right. Water on the lower left and earth at the point, upper.

Is that correct, [Student J]?

I didn't hear all of her answers, sir. [Student J responds.]

Oh, would you be so kind as to repeat those, [Student S]? Yes. Where is the earth center of consciousness located?

At the top. [Student S responds.]

[Student J], is that in keeping with your understanding as an older student of mine? Should tighten these a little tighter when they bring them up. *[The teacher tightens the knobs on both sides of the blackboard that, when tightened properly, prevent the blackboard from tilting.]* [Student J]?

I would say it's on the lower right. Earth.

[Student R].

Lower right. [Student R responds.]

It's on the lower right? Is that correct?

We're talking about earth? [Student R responds.]

Yes. I want earth: earth, fire, and water.

Earth is on the top. [Student R again responds.]

Earth is on the top now. Shall I go get my book? *[The teacher* may be referring to the binder that contains his teachings on Diagramology.] Now where is the earth center? You know, I have students here 17 years, 16 years, 14 years. Yes, [Student D].

We discussed that last week. Earth is the top. It's the view.

[Student R]?

Earth is the top, yes. [Student R responds.]

[Student S].

Yes, at the top.

It's at the top. [Student J], do you agree?

I concede.

Is there anyone who can—I can see, too! All right. Let's get [the] earth center. Earth. *[The teacher writes "E" near the apex of the triangle.]* Next center, fire. Who's got the fire? *[Several students laugh.]* Well, left or right? Did [Student J] want to answer that? Or one of the ladies?

I'll defer to— [Student J begins to respond.]

[Student S].

On the right.

Oh, it is on the right this week. Good! I'm happy to hear that. Earth, fire. *[The teacher writes "F" at the lower right vertex of the triangle, and then writes "W" near on the lower left vertex.]* All right. Earth, fire, and water. Now we got that principle established, haven't we? We all agree, don't we, that earth is on the top? Earth, fire, and water. All right?

Now, what is the next three? Yes, you asked, [Student S]. Yes.

Air, electric, and magnetic.

Ah! All right, now where are we going to place that? Do you know? *[After a short pause, the teacher continues.]* Well, let's put it right here, shall we? *[To the right and at a ninety-degree angle to the first triangle, the teacher draws another roughly equilateral triangle, the apex of which is quite near the apex of the first triangle.]* All right. Now where is the air? Where is it located? Which centers are the next three?

Earth, electric— [Student S begins to respond.]

I'm being a student here for these moments. Now tell me where—what the next three centers are.

Air, electric, and magnetic.

Air, electric, and magnetic! Now where is air, electric, and magnetic located? This is what you call the top of the triangle. *[He taps the vertex of the second triangle that is closest to the apex of the first triangle, which is labelled E.]* And I gave you this diagram, you older students, years ago, many years ago on your planet. Yes? You know, I want that older student. She's been here for so many years. Yes. Where, where's it located?

OK. Did you say the top? I didn't see your chalk. Did you say the top with, near the earth? That center point? [Student S responds.]

Get a little gold out here and you'll see better. *[The teacher uses a pointer to tap the vertex of the second triangle that is nearest to the apex of the first triangle.]* Right there.

That would be the air?

That's the top of the triangle. Yes. What center are you putting there?

Air.

Air. Is that correct, [Student J]?

Yes.

[Student R]? *[After a short pause, the teacher continues.]* We'll put the air center there, then. *[The teacher writes "A" near the apex of the second triangle.]* All right. Air. Next? What's on the right?

Electric. [Student S responds.]

At the base of the triangle? [Student J]?

On the right? Lower right is the electric, sir.

That's the lower right. *[He writes an "E" at the higher vertex of the second triangle. This vertex would be on the right if the apex of this triangle were pointed upwards.]* All right. Now we have that agreed upon. And the remaining center? [Student S].

Magnetic. On the left.

It's on the left this week?

Yes.

You're sure of that? All right. Fine. *[He writes "M" near the lowest vertex of the second triangle.]* The magnets have moved to the left again, isn't that lovely? There must be a new world awakening for us here. *[Some students laugh as the teacher draws a third triangle, one vertex of which is close to the apexes of the other two triangles. This triangle is at 180 degrees to the first triangle.]* There. Even drew a larger triangle there. All right, the next centers of consciousness? *[After a short pause, the teacher continues.]* This is what you call the top of the triangle. *[With his chalk, the teacher taps the vertex of the third triangle that is closest to the apexes of the other two triangles.]* The apex. Yes, [Student S].

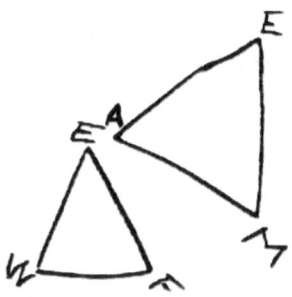

[Figure 38.6]

The odic, the ethereal, and celestial.

Is that how they're placed? [Student R]?

Yes?

Is that how they're placed?

Yes.

Where's the odic?

Odic is at the apex of the triangle.

[Student S]?

It seems that that would be the celestial.

[Student J]?

I would say the apex of the triangle would be celestial.

[Student R]?

Well, it corresponds to the electric and the air.

So what would, what would—

It corresponds to earth and air, so it, it would be the apex, the celestial. [Student R continues.]

Oh, does everyone agree now? Yes, [Student D].

The odic is the same as earth.

[The teacher laughs and then coughs.] Excuse me. I need to take a glass of water here. I have to admit that I would like a glass of water after that. Would you talk to my student, [Student S], there?

Well, the earth is the first and the fire is the second and the water is the third. [Student D explains.]

Correct.

In that tri—three at the top, the odic is the first and the ethereal is the second and the celestial is the third. So the odic . . .

[Student S]?

That's how I would've originally said it. It's just I recall that the highest center, I felt like I wanted to put at the apex.

That's the difficulty with two dimension.

Right.

It makes it most difficult in presentation. But we have two dimension; so we must work with it in a two-dimensional, flat mental world. So where are we going to place this? We start off with one, two, three: earth, fire, and water. All right? Now have we followed that same principle with the second triangle, [Student S]?

Yes, we did.

Then what do we have left to follow the principle with the third triangle? Because we're in a two-dimension, flat blackboard here.

If we do that, then it'd be the odic, ethereal, celestial.

Odic would have to be at the apex.

The apex.

From a flat perspective. Do you understand that, [Student D]?

Yes.

Yes. Well, I hope we understand it because it can become very confusing, when it is so simple. All right. Now, [Student S], we're going to place the odic here? *[With his chalk, the teacher points to the lowest vertex of the third triangle, which is the apex.]*

Yes.

Odic. *[The teacher writes "O" at the apex of the third triangle.]*

Uh-huh.

And what are we going to put down—this is the right of the triangle. *[The teacher points to the vertex of the third triangle that is on the left, which, if the apex were pointed upward would be on the right of the triangle.]* See, we have to turn this around, you see.

Ethereal.

Ethereal. *[He writes "E" at the vertex on the left of the triangle, which would be on the right if the apex was pointed upward.]* And what is the left of the triangle?

Celestial.

Ah, all right. *[He writes "C" at the vertex on the right of the third triangle, which would be on the left of the triangle if its apex were pointed upward.]* Now your question is that we have two clockwise and one counterclockwise to each group of three of the centers of consciousness, is that correct?

Yes.

And what was the rest of your question?

The principle by which there'd be so many clockwise.

So many clockwise and so many counterclockwise. And I drew this so that you could understand, right? All right. Now, what you must do is to take this diagram and location *[With his chalk, he taps in the interior of each of the three triangles.]* and you must take—where's your earth center? Is this your earth center here? *[The teacher taps the E at the apex of the first triangle.]* It is, isn't it?

Yes.

So we find this going clockwise, correct? *[He writes "c" just below and to the right of the E at the apex of the first triangle.]*

Yes.

And we find the fire center going counterclockwise, correct? *[Continuing with the first triangle, he writes "cc" near the F on the right vertex.]*

Right.

And we find the water center going clockwise, correct? *[The teacher writes "c" near the W at the left vertex.]*

Yes.

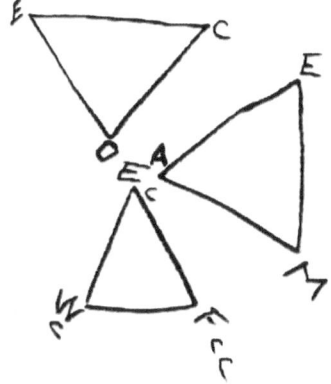

[Figure 38.7]

All right. So now pause for a few moments and think. Here are three centers of consciousness *[With this right hand, the teacher indicates the first triangle.]* that are affecting indirectly the remaining two groups of three centers of consciousness.

[With his chalk, he taps the center of the third and second triangles.] So at what point, here *[The teacher points to the E of the first triangle.]* in a clockwise spin, does this indirectly affect these other two groups *[He points to the apexes of the other two triangles.]* of three of the center[s] of consciousness? Now you write that down and do your homework. Then you will understand the question that you have asked: Why are there so many clockwise spins and so few counterclockwise spins? For they affect each other indirectly, not directly. Does that help with your question?

Yes. Thank you.

All right. Don't forget this diagram. It is very, very important. Yes, [Student B].

Is there another side?

Yes, there—

To balance it?

This here?

Yes.

Yes, there is a side over here. *[He points to the blank area just to the left of the three triangles.]* This is, this is what you are. Right over here. *[He continues to point to the area to the left of the triangles.]* All right? See here?

Yes.

This is what you are right here. *[The teacher draws a long, horizontal line with a circle that rests upon the top of its right endpoint. The circle just touches the apexes of all three triangles.]* That help you, [Student B]?

Uh-huh.

Pardon?

Yes.

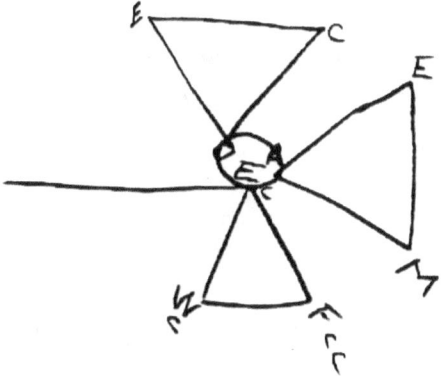

[Figure 38.8]

All right. I'll give you a moment there to write that down. You know, time passes so quickly. Time passes so quickly. Yes, [Student D].

So—

In your world.

—the bottom triangle is the lower three and that's like, in the other diagrams, the creation. And then the top one is the perception and the center one is the dream state?

Center one, yes, is the dream state. That is correct. That is correct. So, you see, I would like to be able to superimpose one upon the other so that you could see how they all come together. But you will have to do that with your notes and the little diagrams that you're making. You can see that, can't you, [Student D]?

Yes.

And [Student B] and everyone.

Yes.

See, if you had them superimposed, you would get a clearer picture for your mind. Yes, [Student S].

I hadn't formulated it yet, but I was wondering, a student just asked was there another side of that.

That's it right there. *[The teacher points to the area with the horizontal line.]*

I'm sorry, I didn't . . .

Oh, you didn't hear me when I, when I explained to [Student B]?

I heard it. I didn't . . .

[Student B] asked if there was another side to this diagram that we have just drawn here. *[With his pointer, the teacher indicates the three triangles.]* Now, you know, long ago some of you older students, I told you it was a bow tie, you know. Oh, many, many years ago. I've given you this diagram here many, many years ago. *[He again points toward the three triangles.]* A few of you students. And I told you it was a bow tie. And I didn't tell you that as a joke; it really does affect your will, you know.

But anyway, *[The teacher laughs joyously.]* this is the other side of it. *[With his pointer, he points to the right end of the horizontal line and then retraces the line.]* This is what you are, right here. *[He again points to the horizontal line.]* And don't you see how that all comes into this right here? *[He traces the circle, which touches the apexes of all three triangles.]* Do you see that? But you've got to superimpose these diagrams, then you'll find out what a bow tie you really are, sometimes. *[The teacher places both hands near his neck and then extends them as though he were pulling on a string that had been wrapped around his neck. As he does, he makes a sound that is difficult to transcribe.]* Yes, [Student L], please.

If a straight line is really a circle and the half-circle plus the straight lines in the number five of faith—

Correct.

—become an eight or infinity, is that correct?

Well, that's what you are. That is correct. Why, certainly it is correct. Absolutely. Definitely. Yes, [Student U], please.

The degrees of perception are 45 degrees.

Forty-five. Correct.

But it appears—

Between the fourth and fifth.

Ahh.

Go ahead with your question.

But it appears—

We already discussed it.

—on this diagram that there are channels at 60 degrees.

Oh, it does appear that, doesn't it?

Yes.

Does it appear that way to anyone else? *[The teacher pauses for a moment and then continues.]* I've stated clearly they're 45-degree angles. Hmm? Don't you know that all angles for a person who identifies with limit, all angles are 45? Now tell me why are all angles 45 degrees only for anyone who identifies with limit or form. All angles are 45 degree for anyone at any time. Do you know, [Student R]? *[After a short pause, the teacher continues.]* Why are all angles 45 degrees for anyone who identifies with limit or form? Yes, [Student S], there has a . . .

Because their dream of life hasn't yet become what they really are and gained the other 45 degree to make it 90 degree.

You can only experience—let me put it this way—you can only experience need at a 45-degree perceptive [perception]. *[The teacher writes "45º" above the horizontal line and to the left of the third triangle.]* Perhaps that would best answer your question. You can only experience need at a 45-degree perception. Yes, [Student R].

You'd shown in your earlier diagram that the point of perception or perspective . . .

Yes?

... the lower perspective, in relationship to the dream, is 45 degrees.

Correct.

And so that would guarantee that it would be 45 degrees.

It absolutely does guarantee it. All need is an experience of 45-degree perception. In other words, you only see half the picture. Do we understand it that way? Ninety is the nine of totality that returns unto oneself. That's 90 degrees. Don't worry about a hundred degrees. Ninety degrees is all you ever need to think about. Forget a hundred degrees. Yes, [Student Y].

Is gravity formed by the force between the counterspin and the retrospin?

Yes, it is. It is the adhesion. So now perhaps you will understand whenever you permit this dream of life that we had here a moment ago *[The teacher points to the area of the blackboard where the vertex of the three lines of perception had been.]* to descend, then you—try to understand that's how you're grounded. You are controlled by the pull of gravity.

See, once you make the step from the lack of effort with your spiritual exercises, you're on the way down. You don't have to worry about making any effort to get down there. The reason it's so easy go down and difficult to come up is because you step into the Law of Gravity. That's why you go pshhht! *[The sound the teacher makes to describe, but he gestures with both hands in a sharp downward motion.]* You see, you just get sucked up like a sponge. That's why it's so easy. This is why the human mind believes it's easy to make no effort, you see; it doesn't make any effort. Because, you see, it's under the Law of Gravity; you don't have to worry about making any effort because you're on a slide. The moment you step under the Law of Gravity, you guarantee to be grounded. You see. Yes. But, of course, indeed, it is a thrill while you're sliding. That is true. Most people register that as a thrill. That is correct. Yes.

OK. So in this galaxy, this configuration of planets with the, and the sun, and the planets rotating around the sun, is that same retrospin and counterspin that's within us?

If you will look at it, perhaps, in a different way: if you will understand that you are a universe, that is what you are—you actually—you are a universe. You are the microcosm of the macrocosm. And so the laws governing the macrocosm and the microcosm are the same laws. They are identically the same laws. Yes. [Student H] had a question, please.

Would a microcosm of all nine centers of consciousness be in every organ of the body?

Yes, they are. In every organ of the body. In every cell. Oh, indeed, indeed. Absolutely. Definitely.

And—excuse me. And that, therefore, would account for disease of organs: an imbalance.

There's an imbalance in energy distribution. That is correct. That is correct. Yes, [Student B] has a question, please.

I keep wanting to pull all those triangles together. It would be a pyramid, if...

That is correct.

...it were more—there'll be were another side to it.

Well, the other side is the one that you can't see in two dimension.

Oh.

You see, we're dealing with two dimension here. Would you not agree, [Student B]?

Yes.

How am I going to present the side that you can't see in two dimension? You have to present that. That has to deal with perception, doesn't it? Pardon?

Yes.

Yes. Of course, it is a pyramid. That's what it is. That's where the power's contained. You see, it's not limited to just this one. *[With his pointer, the teacher points to the uppermost triangle.]* Just take and put all three of those together. *[With his hands he forms a sort of pyramid.]* What does it give to you? *[After a short pause, he continues.]* You see, all you've got to do is to visualize that this is a piece of cardboard, all right? *[With the pointer, one after the other, he points to each of the three triangles.]* And these are all cut out. And so if you bring that together what do you have?

A pyramid missing a side.

No, you're not missing a side at all! *[The teacher laughs joyfully.]* Because that's what you are right over here, see? *[Using the pointer, he points to the horizontal line.]* No, no, no, no. It is true to the mind there's a side missing. Correct?

Yes.

Well, that missing side has no, no—is not subject to the mental world. It's not subject to the mental world; therefore, the mental world does not see it. But that's the side that the mental world doesn't see. You see, the mental world—and I gave it to you right here, infinity and the circle of eternity. *[He first points to the left end of the horizontal line and then retraces the circle.]* This is what you are. *[He points again to the horizontal line.]* We don't see what we are. We see what we believe we are because we have identified with limit. Did that help you, [Student B]?

Yes.

So, you see, this side that you don't see is the side that you are. This is what you really are: the missing side of the pyramid. *[The teacher points to line near to where it meets the circle.]* You see? See, the mental world doesn't see that because you are more than mental; you are that which sustains mental. So the mental world, which is limit and formation, creation, doesn't see that side, [Student B]. Does that help with your question? It is not possible because it is not within the domain where it can be seen by the mental world. Not what you truly are. Yes, [Student L].

Is that the base of the triangle?

No, that's not the base.

No?

You wouldn't say it's the base, would you?

No, it's not. [Student B responds.]

I wouldn't want it the base for me. Not in that respect. No. It's the side. You see? Just close that up there and you have one open side. Hmm? The mind cannot see that and never will be able to see it; it's contrary to the Law of Mental Substance.

And then [Student O]'s been waiting with a question. Because, you see, time—I don't have a watch on, physically—but time is passing quickly. Go right ahead.

Yes, sir. You answered it in, in your conversation, I think. [Student O responds.]

Thank you. All right, now [Student D], or was it [Student L]? Excuse me. I'll get to [Student L] and back to [Student D]. You had your hand up, [Student L]?

Yes.

Ask your question.

Because that concentration is the key to all power—and I'm thinking in terms of releasing oneself from the Law of Gravity—is that how you slow down the rate of spin, from counterclockwise and clockwise, by concentrating?

Yes. And bring balance into your life. Certainly. Because, you see, we can only experience need, as I have said several times this morning, as an effect of denial. And when we deny, we descend. Whoever denies, descends; whoever accepts, ascends. Be sure and put that in your notes. And so if you find pleasure in descent, then continue to deny and you will have plenty of it. Yes, [Student D].

Well, would you say the invisible side of the pyramid is the totality of the other sides?

It is what you are. All right. Now we'll put it another way. These three parts of the pyramid, these three triangles are what you express through. This *[He points to the horizontal line.]* is what you are. So you may see what you express through, but you cannot see with mental eyes what you are. Did that help with your question?

Yes.

But you certainly can see what you express through. And you can take it very personal and say, "I'm expressing through this flesh and bone, this hand here. I'm expressing through it, but it's not me." *[As he speaks, he touches his left hand with his right hand.]* Therefore, the question is always asked, "Then what am I?" Correct?

Yes.

All right.

Thank you.

Yes. Yes, [Student S].

Last week you made reference to moving through the Law of Gravity. You use the power of understanding?

Correct.

And I'd like to know how do you move from the eight of infinity to the nine, the power of understanding.

Well, if you want to move through the infinity and the power of understanding, then there is one thing that will move you there: is the acceptance thereof, for you cannot experience what you do not accept. You see, when a person accepts that they are the limit, when a person accepts that they are form, when they accept that, they do so at the cost of establishing the Law of Denial of what they are. So whenever you permit yourself to accept denial, to accept limit, when you permit yourself to accept that you are a form of limit, when you permit yourself to accept "This is my original thought," therefore you establish the Law of Denial and guarantee the experience of need. Do you understand?

Yes.

And so if you want to move from the question you asked, from the infinity to the understanding, then you must establish that law of full acceptance. Yes.

Also, could you please discuss how this relates to the law to divide and conquer?

To divide and conquer is the law and the reign of the mental world. One conquers parts. No one ever conquers wholes.

Thank you.

One can only conquer parts. You can only conquer the part, a part of something. You can never conquer what is, and you cannot conquer the whole. You can temporarily conquer the part.

Thank you.

A person conquers a part of their habit patterns. Would you not agree? But they do not conquer the whole of them. No. You only conquer in parts. Yes, [Student B] has a question, for our time, I see, has passed. Yes, [Student B].

So many of the numbers have the same shapes, just like a nine looked at one direction is a nine and another direction it's a six.

Correct.

And a five and a two have the same shape, just depends on how you look at it.

That is correct. Absolutely.

How does that fit in to our studies?

Well, in reference to—the question, therefore, you must ask yourself [is]: How many numbers are [there] originally? Hmm? Now, given our teachings here on nine numbers to which you can relate to.

Yes.

Correct?

Yes.

One through nine, unless you want to consider aught a number. Well, it is from the aught that all numbers were given birth. It is in their separation of the aught that you have the numbers from one to nine. You see, for example, as I said to you last week, and then, as I say, our time is up on this class, as I said to you last week, *[The teacher draws a straight, horizontal line to the right of the second triangle.]* a straight line is a circle. It's only straight because of your perception. Is that correct?

Yes.

All right. It's only a straight line because of your perception because in truth a straight line is a circle. *[He draws a circle above the midpoint of the horizontal line he has just drawn.]* Is that not what I said? All right. Your perception, taking a portion of the whole, *[He draws five, seemingly random lines just outside of the new circle.]* has given you the numbers that you have. And this is why some of them are similar: because they're in the same area of perception. Did that help you?

Yes.

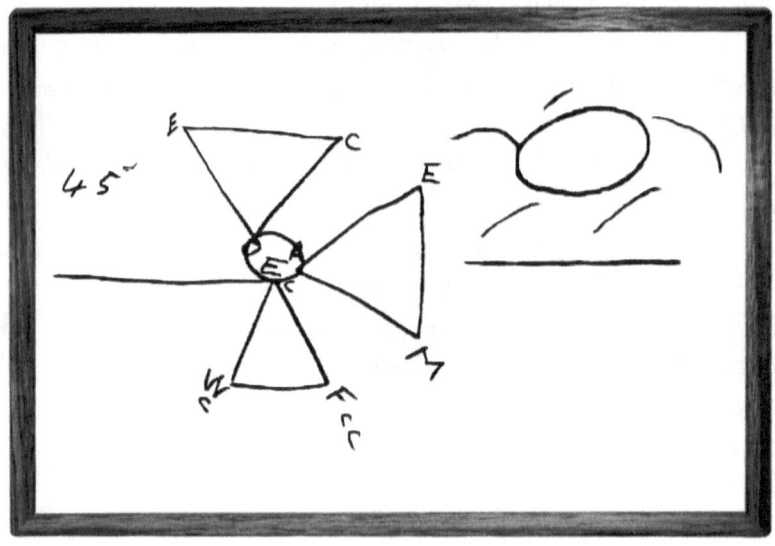

[Figure 38.9]

Yes. That's what it is. Now, I best erase this blackboard [*The teacher begins erasing the blackboard.*] and say—oh, excuse me. I promised not to talk when I was doing this, didn't I? [*After a pause and as he erases the blackboard, he continues.*]

You know, if someone would bat my erasers, they might work better next class. Perhaps I will merit that.

Thank you very much. And I see our time has passed. I will say good day. And have a nice week. Thank you.

MARCH 9, 1986

A/V Class Private 39

Now this morning I would like you to take your pen and notebook and draw the basic, simple triangle: [an] equilateral triangle. As soon as you have accomplished that, I would like you to put at the lower right point of the triangle "Denial;" the lower left, "Need;" and at the apex of the triangle "Temptation." I would also like an answer from you and I want you to speak up so that we can all hear you clearly, Where will you place Earth? Yes, [Student M].

At the apex of the triangle.

No. [Student L].

I was going to say that.

No. *[After a short pause, the teacher continues.]* Waiting for the hands. Yes, [Student P].

I would say in the middle.

No. It goes on one of the three points of the triangle. [Student R].

Denial.

Correct. Earth. When you deny what you are, you experience what you are not; therefore, you experience Earth at the expense of what you are. Where will you place Fire? [Student Y].

At the top.

No. Yes, [Student P].

By need.

Correct. Now where will you place the water center?

At the apex. [Student R responds.]

At the apex. So now what do we find from the location of denial, need, and temptation? What centers do we find, [Student S]?

The lower three.

Name them.

Earth, fire, and water.

Correct. So through what center of consciousness are we tempted? [Student L].

Through the water.

Through the water center. Mark it down in your notes. *[After a short pause, the teacher continues.]* You cannot be tempted unless you identify with your emotions. You identify with your emotions by believing that you are them.

[Student H], through what center do you experience need?

Through the fire center.

Through the fire center. Is there anyone who does not understand that you experience need through the fire center? Hmm? Are all my students qualified now this morning? *[After a short pause, he continues.]* Fine. Are there any questions about experiencing need through what [Student H] has said, through the fire center?

Through what center do you experience denial?

The earth. [Student R responds.]

And explain to us how you experience denial through the earth center of consciousness.

Identification with form.

Identification with limit guarantees denial of what you are.

Now we have spoken for a long time on the importance of your daily, spiritual exercises, for if you do not make that effort, then your identification of your *prana*, your identification locks it into those centers of consciousness and your experiences are in keeping with those centers.

Now, [Student R], what center of consciousness would you say, from your observation of fifty-some years on Earth, that most people remain in?

I guess the most predominant would be the earth center or the denial.

Yes. Which one do they express most fully on your planet?

The fire center.

The fire center. Everyone agree with that? [Student L] does not agree with it: [that] most people express in the fire center of consciousness. Yes, [Student L].

The water center.

[Student L] says it's in the water center. Any other questions or any other remarks of where you think that most people on your planet are expressing through, which of the three centers? [Student U].

I was inclined to think it was the water, the more emotion.

[Student O].

Yes. I think it's the water center because we spend a lot of the time creating.

[Student J].

My—I would say it's denial, because without denial there is no need.

Correct. And the other does not exist. So the identification is in the earth center, in limit, and expresses through those centers of consciousness.

We are only tempted by what we first judge we do not have. You cannot be tempted by what you accept. You can only be tempted by what you deny. Now do not permit your mind to deceive you that this is outside. You have to establish the Law of Denial inside.

Now everyone is fully aware of what they think they need. So when you are aware of what you think you need, pause, for it is telling you what you have denied inside yourself. Denial is in direct proportion to overidentification with limit, form, creation. The more you identify with creation, the more need you will experience, for the more denial you have established.

Now remember, you cannot fill a cup that is filled. Your cup is full. Therefore, when you permit yourself to deny the fullness that you are, your cup overfloweth. And this is why you experience no end to what you understand as need.

Some time ago I shared with you that affirmation: "I am whole, complete, and perfect." That which you are is whole, complete, and perfect. When you accept that, then you've accepted what you are and free yourself from what you are not. For whoever accepts that truth cannot experience need, for they have not denied, and not having denied, need does not exist, let alone temptation. A person who has accepted what they are cannot attach and cannot be adverse. It is not possible. For how can one attach to what they truly are, let alone be adverse to it? When you accept you're whole, complete, and perfect, there's nothing to attach to outside and there's nothing to be adverse to outside, for you are in truth everything and everywhere. You do not experience need, for you do not experience denial; and you cannot experience temptation.

Let's not forget, students, you cannot be tempted by what you are. How can you be tempted to drink the glass of water if you already are the water? It's not possible.

There's only one thing that you've got to give up: it's the limit that you believe you are. So start with your thumb and accept that truth: "I am not the thumb"— *[Reddy, the church's dog, begins barking loudly.]* You may take care of your student Mr. Red. *[The teacher addresses a director.]*—"for if I were the thumb, then there is little I could do." So start with these parts that you believe that you are.

Now, as soon as you've finished there with your notes, we're going to get to your questions. And you speak right up because you're the ones that get these lovely classes on audio and videotape. And if you don't speak up, I'm sure some of my students are going to speak to you. Yes, [Student N].

You said you can't be tempted by a glass of water if you are the glass of water.

Yes. How could you be tempted by that which you are? How can you be tempted by that which you already are? Do you know of some way to be tempted by that which you already are?

No.

You see, you must believe that you are not in order to be tempted by it. You must first establish that Law of Denial. If you are whole, complete, and perfect—that is what you are—then there is nothing that you are not. And where there is nothing that you are not, you cannot be tempted by anything, for you already are; you already are that. We are working to help you to grow in understanding, acceptance, the will of the divine Principle of Good. Yes, [Student Y].

If one was in a relationship where both beings were in this acceptance and faith, going in an upward direction, would they, then, experience true fulfillment?

Well, first of all, if they were applying this philosophy, this Law of Life, a relationship wouldn't exist, you see? You see, relationship is a birth from denial of what one is. You see, relationship does not exist without denial, which is followed by need, which is followed by temptation. A relationship is an effect of one's temptation, which is born from their own denials. That doesn't mean that two people couldn't be together. Two people can easily be together; but, you see, in being together, they are still whole and complete, together or separate. But that's not what I find in your world. Is that what any of my students are finding? *[After a short pause, the teacher continues.]* For that would be something new that I would like to learn, yes. Does that help with your question?

Thank you.

Yes. Relationship, as you know relationship, does not exist when you no longer deny the truth. Relationship can only exist as an effect of denying what you are.

Well, you take a look at the animals. There are times of procreation and when it's finished, they go their way. Would you not agree that that is what your eyes observe?

Yes.

Well, the human being is an animal, an advanced, so-called advanced animal on your planet. But that is not what we find. They do not observe and practice the principle of procreation: a season for all things. [It] has nothing to do with relationship. The dog is not interested, nor the dove, whether or not this person's going to be around next month. Does that help with your question?

Thank you.

Yes. So, you see, if they had the thinking in their consciousness and had risen to deny what they are, oh, well, then, of course, there would be many kind[s] of relationships and certainly a great many fights. Hmm? Yes. And disturbance. And discord. Yes. Yes, [Student B].

Why is the water center at the top, here, rather than on the left, the magnetic side?

Because, you see, when you deny—for example, you have, first of all, you have a denial. Now what center is denial in? It's in the earth center, correct?

Right.

So, you see, when you enter earth, when you enter limit, you deny what you are. For example, you have that experience, all students, all people have that experience when they think more of their limit, they have less of the good that they are. Would you not agree? In other words, they overidentify with creation, with forms and limit, and they separate themselves from what they are. That is the earth center.

Then you have need. Now when you experience need, that experience is not complete within your consciousness. It's ever driving you to something else. Would you not agree? And it drives you to what you understand as the fulfillment of that need. That's the fire center that drives you. Now from that, you enter into the realm of temptation. That's where one weakens what they are. Now temptation is there in the water center. All right.

Fire, an electric expression, contains within it the magnetic. The electric and magnetic are one in the same; their proportion in expression is what [makes the] difference. You see, a person is electric in their expression; that does not mean that they do not and are not magnetic. For example, you take a look, you see a person that will be extremely electric in what is known as aggression, in doing what they decide they're going to do. And yet, in other experiences in their life, they're extremely magnetic. So in order to create a judgment or form, you must use the electric and the magnetic: you must send out and attract back. You send out an electric vibration. In the electric is contained magnetic, in all electric. And in all magnetic, there is electric. So that goes out into the universe. You send it forth from yourself electrically. And, as it goes out into the universe, it attracts magnetically like-kind. So electric and magnetic are one in the same thing, but they vary in their expression of their, of their composition. Does that help with your question, [Student B]?

Yes.

So, you see—because, you see, all forms are created in the water center. They are created by temptation, born from need, the expression of denial. Hmm? So if you understand that, then you will understand why the water center is located here, you see. *[The teacher points to the diagram written in a student's notebook.]* You see, you have earth, fire, and water. Now this is a neutral point. This is a point of perfect balance, all right? That's what the apex is. That's the balancing point of the other: electric and magnetic. Hmm?

And I see what your question is. You're looking here at the earth center. *[He again points to the diagram in a student's notebook.]* You see, you're looking at the manifestation, the completion of these two, is what you're looking at. It's the perspective of how you're looking at your triangle, you see? You see, the earth center here— *[He again points to the student's notebook.]* that's where the form is completed or manifested. And it is manifested from the electric and the magnetic—Hmm?—from the fire and the water.

Right.

So if you will just turn this here, like this, *[The teacher picks up a student's notebook and turns it slightly.]* then you will get a different perspective. Can you see that, [Student R]?

[It is difficult to accurately transcribe the response of Student R.]

Yes, you just turn that. Now, you see, if you try to—try to think of it this way. I gave you the line of infinity and I gave you the circle of eternity. Eternity is your perspective of the infinity which you are. All right. So what you want to do, or start making the effort to do, is to see dimensional. You see, you're in a flat dimension. And so you have to look at these things ever in keeping with the spin of your consciousness. Now as the spin of your consciousness increases, you will awaken. And as that happens, your perspective changes and you see in three or fourth dimension. I'm trying to bring you fourth-dimension understanding into a two-dimensional creation. You turn your paper and take a look at that. Your diagrams *[The teacher again points toward the student's notebook.]* are your perspective in a two dimension. [If] you increase the spin of your consciousness, you will change from a two-dimensional to a three-dimensional to a four dimension. Hmm? Yes.

Thank you.

[Student H].

No. I'm sorry. I was just—

Do you have a question on dimension?

I don't.

[Student Y].

If you looked at the straight line in a perpendicular, if one was able to view it at a perpendicular plane, would you—

One is.

—then see the other side of—

Yes. You see, when you look at a triangle or any other diagram, through an increase, through an increase in acceleration in your consciousness, you will see all sides. Do you understand that?

Yes.

You see, you just won't see two dimension. You'll see four dimension. You'll see all sides. You'll see all of the pyramid, the triangle—because it's actually a pyramid, you see. And you will see all sides and you will see inside and that's very important. Yes. Yes, [Student L].

I made a pyramid. And each third of the pyramid is 90 degrees, and therefore it contains 270.

Uh-huh.

And a full circle or the square—

It's 360.

—would be 360. So that would mean what you are is 90 degrees?

I gave you that teaching many, many years ago. You have 10 percent free will. That leaves 90 percent. Now I think you do recall that, don't you, [Student J]?

Yes, sir.

And [Student R] and [Student S] and everyone? So you should encourage yourself. You're beginning to think in a way that you can perceive the dimension. Absolutely. Yes, in one of our other diagrams that I gave to you so many years ago is that triangle [that] is contained inside of a circle. Yes, [Student L].

And is the eye of eternity at the apex of the pyramid?

Well, of course, that depends on your perspective. If you want to know where it really is, then that is where it is. That is where the eye of eternity is, yes. It's at the apex. But sometimes, you know, depending on your perspective and depending on—because your perspective will dictate what dimension, the dimension that you see. You understand that. So as you—you could place your—when you place your triangle in a different angle, you see, then what you do, you see, you do not see as clearly. Because here is the eye, *[The teacher gestures toward the student's notebook.]* is where it really is. And then you turned it another way, you see a little dimmer. You turn it another way, you see even dimmer than that. So that, of course, is subject to your perception, you see, your perspective. Hmm?

Thank you.

Does that help with your question?

Yes, it does.

Yes. [Student O] has a question, please.

Yes. In the, in looking in three and four dimensional, is that, is that the same as viewing something? OK, we are here in— we're looking at things in a second dimension right now from a flat surface.

Yes, only because you choose to.

OK.

Yes.

Yes. All right. Well, I'm saying now, what I'm hearing myself say now, now I already done said it. So looking, coming from a third or fourth dimension, I mean, I said it in a third or fourth dimension—

Yes?

—moments ago, and that would be the third or fourth dimension?

Yes, you can perceive anything at this moment in a three dimension or four dimension. Now when you perceive a fifth dimension, you no longer have a limited form. Hmm?

OK.

Because the separation is such that there's nothing to sustain the limit.

Thank you.

See? That's why five or fifth dimension is where faith is. And that's why you can't control faith. It's beyond limit. Hmm?

Yes, sir.

Yes. I'm interested—and [you are] coming along nicely now—in doing your daily spiritual exercises, for in so doing you will perceive a broader perspective; you will be able to, from your proper spiritual daily exercises, begin to perceive other dimensions that affect your life. Hmm?

Yes, sir.

Yes.

Thank you.

Yes, did you have another question, [Student O]?

No.

Hmm? Yes. Yes, and [Student J], you won't be confused at all. You're one of my older students. Yes, [Student Y].

Is the missing part of the pyramid, is that within? Is that direction ...

The which part of the pyramid?

The missing part of the pyramid you showed.

Well, yes. It's only—I gave it to you on the blackboard. Well, that's what you are. Yes, it's only missing from an error of ignorance, and it's there waiting for you, because that's what you are. You're speaking of the last class, aren't you?

Yes.

The side that it looks to you is missing.

Yes.

Well, that is true. Many of my students believe that they are missing. In fact, they're convinced of it: they insist on need. Yes. Go right ahead, [Student Y].

OK.

And it's true. They are right.

Right.

Yes, at times they're missing. Not from my classes, be it in Divine order. Yes.

So is—that is—if one, if one could turn around and—I'm trying to get the direction—if you could, like, turn around, like, in front of oneself, would you be heading in the direction of that, of what you truly are?

You would have to make a complete turn in consciousness. And in that respect, yes. You would have to make a complete, complete turn in consciousness. That requires a drastic change, yes. Slow growth's the best growth. Gradually move in that direction. Hmm? Yes. [Student M] had a question. Thank you.

Yes. The line of infinity.

Yes?

Which was the dream state. Now on—

The line of infinity? Is that someone['s] new teaching? The line of infinity—just a moment, [Student M]. The line of infinity is the dream state? Did you teach that? *[The teacher addresses a different student.]* Who taught that? I'm interested in that fellow. Now I want my students to do a little more homework, because if I have taught that the line of infinity, after all these eons, is the dream state, then I want to know, and I would appreciate your kindness—did you understand that I taught you that what you are is a dream state?

No. It's what, I thought, we are. [Student B speaks very quietly.]

Pardon?

It's what we are. [Student B speaks more loudly.]

Yes, it's what we really are. Our perspective—do you have that diagram?

Yes. [Student M responds.]

Well, I think you should refer to that. And I'll give you a chance while I answer someone else's question. On the line of infinity being a dream state. You know, I know that you're not trying to change the teachings. It's just from a lack of effort there.

Thank you. [Student M responds.]

Yes. Yes, [Student U].

By looking from above—

Above. Yes.

—we view what we are and its potential. Could you speak a little on that potential of what we are?

Your potential of what you are? What is it that you think you need, for you are everything? So if you're speaking of potential, there's no need can possibly exist. There's no potential: you already are! According to your perception of what you are is your potential.

OK.

You see? You see, you already are. And if you only see a portion of what you already are, then that's known as your potential. Yes. Does anyone not understand that? If you only, you know, if you only see, "Well, let's see, I'm capable of doing this much. There's this much time in which I can get this much accomplished. And this is what I want to do; so all of that there's got to go." Well, that's your perspective of what you are. And because you see it in a very narrow perspective, then that's all that you can get accomplished, you see? And leave yourself in need of all the other. Hmm? You see? "O man, think humble, yet well of thyself."

Thank you.

The true self. Yes, now do you have that so you're not confused that the line of infinity [is] that what you truly are? *[The teacher addresses Student M.]*

Yes. Yes, I do. [Student M responds.]

Yes, a dream state is something else, having to do with your perception of what you are.

Yes.

You know, I'm so happy to have—you like these classes a little better here at the temple? *[In this class, the teacher was seated at the head of the dining room table and several students were seated at that same table. More students were seated at nearby tables. This was the format for many of the classes that were given at the temple that were not recorded. The recording equipment was set up at the foot of the table.]*

Yes. [Student M responds.]

It's very nice, because, you see, this way you can get to see the areas in which one needs to work. You get to take a look and see, "Now why did my mind tell me what I am is a dream state?" Hmm? What does that tell us all? See, this is what's important, you see? Don't you think that's important?

I do. I think that's very important.

Yes, yes, now go right ahead with that question.

Well, I was—

Instead of that support of something else. Hmm?

Yes. Thank you. In the triangle that we just drew—

Yes.

—of the three lower centers—

Yes.

—I was looking at the diagram of last week with all the centers running up the spine.

That's right.

And of our perspective. You know?

Yes.

And the middle runs into desire and the electric. I was wondering how those two diagrams compare.

No problem whatsoever. Did I not speak here last Sunday that you should make some effort to superimpose these diagrams? Yes, did you do that?

I tried. I had a difficult time superimposing.

You had a difficult time at superimposing one diagram over the other? What was the difficulty? This is very important, because I happen to know some of my students had such a difficult time that they didn't even try! Yes.

I was trying to do it with the spins, with, you know, with the spins.

While you were spinning?

No.

You spun too slow. What's the next question? Yes, [Student O].

Yes.

Perhaps your husband can help you there. *[Student M and Student O were married to each other.]*

OK. Thank you. [Student M responds.]

Yes, I'd like to ask, Why or how an obstruction is viewed as a distortion to the original purpose of its design? [Student O asks.]

Well, an obstruction—everything is designed to serve the purpose of its original design.

Right.

When you do not make the effort to understand the purpose of the original design, it becomes an obstruction to you. For example, if you have a tack and you have a hammer and you put the tack in the chair and you want the tack to go in the chair and you don't understand the design of the hammer and you hit your head with the hammer, then you are not serving the true purpose of the design. Do you understand that?

Yes, sir.

And so the tack doesn't go into the chair, and your head feels not too well when you've finished. Hmm?

Yes.

So you must make the effort to understand the true purpose of design of all form that you are tempted to believe that you are. And if you do not make the effort to understand the true purpose of the design of all of the forms, which are limits, that you are in service to, then they become in truth an obstruction to you, just like the hammer and your head, the tack and the chair.

Yes, sir.

Does that help you with that question, [Student O]?

Yes, that, that helps. Well, right away it helps me when I'm encountering something new or, or when I've been viewing something and it's been an obstruction for a while.

You are not in service to the true purpose of its design and your belief in it that it is you.

Right. OK.

Now you think about that, as [Student J] has a question here. And I know very well, [Student J], that you're not confused at all. It's just some changes.

Yes, sir. In keeping with what you just said is to try to recognize the purpose of the design of the forms that we serve. How do we recognize those forms and then identify what they are?

Fine. That's an excellent question. Now a person has a thought in their mind. Hmm? And they believe that they are the thought. They believe that that is them. The moment that they believe the form they have created, the thought, is them, they are in service to the form that they have created. Now the form has been created by the mind to serve a purpose. So one pauses when they have a thought and one makes the effort to understand its purpose for which they have designed it.

Now you have a thought that you want to go to dinner, correct? So that's a thought; that's a form that you have created. Now you have to pause and say, "Now I want to go to dinner. I have created this form. The purpose for which I have created it is because my stomach tells me, which is another form, that I am hungry." So you understand that purpose of that which you have designed. Don't stop there. Now you must be still and say, "Let's see, well, I want to go to that particular restaurant." Correct?

Yes, sir.

Now you've got another design that you have created. Don't stop there. For now, going on in the consciousness are the shadows of the past. And you want to go to that restaurant based upon a form that tells you you're hungry. That particular restaurant, because at that particular restaurant you had created a design that you met somebody there or that it was very nice, and all of the justifications that support the design. So now you have three forms.

Don't stop there. Now we must look at the form that says, "I want to drive there." Don't stop there because there's another form that says, "Well, I'm not going to drive there alone." Because another form comes up from the past that there was somebody else there and you had a very good time. Or you must take another look, because don't stop there. And maybe another form that somebody was in your car when you went to that particular restaurant: there's a time. You went there at a certain time for all those good experiences to happen. However, you must pause and look clearly, because the person you took at one particular time, that form may be rising up into the design and it was a terrible disaster.

So we must understand the true purpose of design that we choose to service. See, when you go to dinner or you go on a job or—what is it? Yes—you, you begin to form a deal, you see? Isn't that what they call it, you know, in business there, a deal? Then you've got all of those things to consider, to look at as the true purpose of your design.

So, you know, that goes back a long time. I think I spoke to you, oh, so many years ago in your world on motive, movement, motivation. You see, when a person feels motivated, they must understand they are motivated by forms that have been created and are designed to serve a certain purpose, you see. And they come in, and we've got to take a good look at them. Because if we say, "Oh, I just want to go to dinner," then the next thought is, which is another form, created, you know, its true purpose of design is "I want to go to that particular place. Why do I want to go to that particular place? Because when I went to that particular place I went with a young lady. We had a wonderful time there. If I want to go there—Now just a minute: there's a time design. No, we wanted a certain time. Just a moment. It was on a certain day." Don't stop there, because on that particular day the weather was just so. So therefore, what month was it? What day was it? What week was it? That's the true purpose of design, you see?

So when you have a thought to do something, you must understand when you believe that that is you, you service that design. And that design contains many, many different variables. So when you understand all those variables, when you're finished with thorough investigation, the next thing you know, you may call down and order a hamburger to be delivered. *[Some students laugh.]* You know, not always, but, I mean, when you go through the whole thing. You see, by the time you get through the whole thing, you may lose the appetite. But then again, after you get through all of that, you say, "Now just a minute. I start a new design, based upon one thing: that I'm hungry. All right, I'm hungry. I'm just going to go eat." But it won't stop there. "I've got to find a restaurant." You see? That's another design. Then you've got to be honest with yourself and say, "Have I ever been there before? Have I ever heard about it before?"

You see, you must realize that "I'm only a witness of time passing on. A witness of things that have come and gone. Never the jury or judge will I be, for I am the witness, the life and the tree." Now when you're not that, you're all those jurors—you understand?—in the courtroom of creation. So whenever you do anything and you don't pause to think—and this, in your world, is the year of the lion, the wisdom to pause—you are in service to all of those forms you have designed and created.

You know that we are tempted ever in keeping with the law. Tempted by that which we believe that we were in past days and years of creating a design, you see? The design, the creation, the form, the limit. Now this is what takes place every time you believe you are a thought. Now if that tires you and wearies you, which it would anyone, I would think, then when you have a thought, you say, "Thank you. This is a thought passing through my mind. A form created. It is not me. I recognize it. I am responsible for it. It got into my house. It is not, however, me." For the moment you permit yourself to believe that it is you, you are in service to it. That's separating truth from creation.

Now your spiritual exercises and your meditations are working to move this Life, intelligent Light, what you call the life force or *prana*. It's far more than that. That's what you truly are. And you are working to move this up through these centers of consciousness, which are all these experiences in [creation]. So it would exhaust a person to pause at every thought [and] say, "Just a minute. This is a design I created." A thought is a form; the form is the effect of what you have originally designed. However, it contains all those other designs. And when you believe that you are it, think of the laws that you are controlled by.

So you go to a restaurant and the girl has, perhaps, brown hair and brown eyes, long hair, perhaps, and looks very feminine, nice and delicate and everything. And then something goes wrong. For in the design, which is the instrument of causing the motivation to do all of that, is contained so many variables that she stops while you're driving there and she says, "Stop the car a minute. I want to put on my face or my lipstick or whatever else." And then another form that you had created, designed and created, comes in, and there's another woman at another time in your life [who] did that and you had a terrible accident as an experience. So all of that rises up—you understand?—here into the water center; and the next thing you know, you're fortunate if you even make it to dinner. So that's what goes on the moment that you believe you are the thought that is in your mind at any time. Did that help your questions?

Yes. Thank you.

You see, it's terribly exhausting, but you don't have to have that exhaustion if you just make a little effort and declare the truth. "Oh, yes, this is something I designed. I created it to serve a purpose. And who knows what's contained in all the other designs inside of it. I will have to take this time to take a look at it. Hmm? No, no, no. I am not that thought. I shall use that thought, if I pause, to intelligently examine it so that it may serve the purpose, the true purpose, for which it is designed."

You see, we're trying to make forms that we have created, designed and created, to serve certain purposes in our life without making the effort to see what the true design is. By not investigating the true design of anything, we deceive ourselves. Hmm? Now so many times you know that is true. So many times, a person designs something and says, "Oh, she's just lovely. Beautiful relationship. Perhaps the rest of my life. Perhaps even off into eternity." Hmm? Well, I don't see those things in eternity myself, but then again there was, a long time ago, when I did, you know, deceive myself, you see, by not thoroughly investigating the true purpose of my design, you see? And when I looked deeper into that and saw that somehow or other, in my ignorance, I had decided that she wouldn't boss me around, but she would do what I told her to do. It turned around the other way, you see. And I had to be honest with myself and see that I had made that error in evolution by denying what I truly am. And when I stopped denying what I truly am, I did not have those experiences anymore. Hmm? Yes.

So I'm trying to share with you to help you, for I don't see any of my students there on Earth that have the untold thousands of hours necessary for just one thought form they have created to thoroughly investigate to see what's underneath of it, you see. They are deceived by the cover. Hmm? Do you understand that, [Student J]? Yes.

Would we then get down to motive, of the original motive—
Oh, certainly.
—our motive, to save this whole examination process?

Well, the best, the best process and the fastest acceleration is to declare the truth: "This is a form in my mind. It is not me. And I am not going to allow it to deceive me that it is me." And how you do that is you make that declaration and then whether or not it's fulfilled or not fulfilled, it doesn't make any difference. You see?

Yes, sir.

There's always something else. And I assure you there always is. So the best practical way, the most practical way in the present state of evolution is to declare that truth. And every time it rises up to try to convince you that it is you [or] that you are it, oh, be very strong.

And it does it in such cunning ways. First, it'll declare it blatantly in your consciousness: "This is, this is me. This thought," instead of saying, "This is a thought form I have created." Who knows the true purpose of its design because it's been there so long ago and it's up for a feeding, you see? And declare the truth: "This is a form I have created to serve a certain purpose. I really don't know all of the ingredients. I haven't thoroughly investigated. So I'm going to take the best, most practical way and remind myself, 'Thank you. It is not me. I am in service to it. And I alone shall decide how long I shall serve it. And if it doesn't do what I think it's going to do, I will immediately discard it.'" Hmm? And remind yourself constantly of that, and then you won't be trapped in a love affair with your designs, don't you see? See, you see, we fall in love with that which we design. We believe that it is, and in so doing we service it. And it takes us who knows where because the cover's very deceiving. Did that help with your question, [Student J]?

Yes, sir. Of course.

You see. So, you know, it's just like a practical business. So you go to work there. That works out. Maybe, maybe it doesn't. It doesn't matter because you've got 20 more over here. So what does it matter if that does or doesn't work out, you see? You learn the lesson, "Well, that didn't work out. So that form, when it rises up and motivates me—I've had enough lessons with that one. It's deceived me many times from a lack of thorough investigation." You know, just like going to the restaurant, you see, for dinner. And so you could try those other ones, you see. Ever reminding yourself, "This isn't me." Now you put the effort in and you see what the results are. And if the results are not too good, you got 10 or 20 others over here that you're working at the same time, you see. A bird in the hand's worth 22 in the bush. You need 22 up there. Get them out of the bush. Does that help you in a practical way?

Because, otherwise, you see, students, you'll spend all of that time, say, "Now let me see, What is my motive?" like just going to dinner. I mean, think. You just asked the question of what's my motive to go to dinner and it's going to take several hours to research it all because there's so much in there. *[A few students laugh.]* I mean, do we all understand that, students? So that's not too practical in your world. It's much better to declare the truth, which is the truth, "I created it. It's not me. I shall do my part. And if it doesn't do its part, then from my lack of thorough investigation, it deceived me; I deceived myself by not making that effort." And have several others going at the same time, you see. Good business practice. Yes, [Student L].

Thank you. [Student J responds.]

Back to the diagram you drew last week with the centers up the spinal column. [Student L begins.]

Yes? Where are you going to place this?

I beg your pardon.

Where are you going to place this present one? *[The teacher points to the triangle diagram from this class in a student's notebook.]*

Oh, the present one?

It's a very simple one. It's a triangle. Where do you place that on there?

At the lower regions.

Yes.

Yes.

All right. Yes. And what center does it touch, [Student S]? What center would the apex touch? Earth, fire, water. What comes after water?

Air.

Air. So, you see, all of this here that I just gave unto you enters your air center. And we're talking about true purpose of design. You see? Now what is your air center? Is it affecting your toenails or your mind?

Mind.

[It] affects your mind. So your mind is being affected from all of that. Yes.

The question I had dealt with, this is along the river of life, and I believe you mentioned that the river of life flows over the top of the head. [Student L continues.]

Indeed, it does.

And back down again. And I was wondering if the celestial center is on the top of the head or at the atlas.

Do you still have a soft spot on the top of your head, [Student L]?

I think we all do.

You've answered your question then.

Thank you.

Very soft. It's always been there. It always will be there. It never gets hard, you know.

That's what I've—

Did you know that? Never ever gets hard. That's a soft spot. Remains soft.

Thank you.

You're welcome. Yes, [Student D].

Is the original design of the earth center to be the view? And is the distortion of that—is denial a distortion of that view?

Overidentification with limit is distortion of the view, which of course is denial. That is correct. That is correct, [Student D].

Thank you.

Overidentification with limit, of course, offers the bondage of belief. Yes. Now [Student S], here, has a question.

Yes. I'd like to ask since the celestial consciousness is the highest consciousness—

Uh-huh.

—I would like to ask, Why is the magnetic charge, when it would seem, being the highest, it would have a perfect balance neutral charge?

Please restate your question.

In the previous class we were placing the groups of the three centers—

That's correct.

—on the triangle with the charges.

That's correct. And what is a perfect balance?

The neutral point.

And when you have neutrality, could you possibly experience either denial or need or temptation?

No.

It's not possible. Go ahead with your question.

Well, when we were placing the final three centers—

Yes?

—the odic, the ethereal, and the celestial.

Celestial. Yes.

I understood that the celestial would end up on the magnetic point of the triangle.

You did?

And, well, I'd like to stand corrected if that was wrong.

Well, why don't you just draw it right out for all of us here. Did you already do that?

Uh-huh.

Then let us take a look at it.

OK. We had the odic at the apex.

Uh-huh. That is correct.

Ethereal at the electric. And the celestial at the magnetic.

In the higher centers of consciousness.

First of all, I'd like to ask, Is that correct?

Well, why don't we ask all of our students and see if they got it the same way that you did?

OK.

[Student R]? Diagrams, please.

I didn't have a diagram for that.

[Student J] and [Student M] and [Student B].

That's what I had. That's what I had. [Many students speak at once.]

Uh-huh. Uh-huh. So what you're asking in reference to that is, Why the celestial is magnetic?

Because it's the highest—

It is the highest.

—consciousness. [Student S responds.]

Yes. Well now, tell me something, Whenever, through identification with limit, that you think of celestial or heaven what [does] your perception of it reveal to you?

That it would get me out of the limit.

Yes. And free you from the magnetic.

Right.

Correct?

That would be nice, yes.

But didn't you understand, as we look towards heaven, we see heaven, that's our perception, we can only see heaven in the two dimension from a mental world and we can only see it as the fulfillment of our needs. Why do you think it's magnetic?

Thank you.

I was in hopes that some of these things my students would perceive. Surely, you understand that.

Now I do. Thank you.

Yes. Well, homework, you see, what you call homework would have revealed that to you.

How could you be in a heavenly state of consciousness and not be fulfilled? So in keeping with the perception, of course, it has to be magnetic. Yes.

So my next question is—

For you have to attract what you need.

Is it really magnetic in truth or is this just our perception of it?

I am giving you teachings in a two-dimensional perspective, for that is what you identify with. I am working to help you into a third dimension and a fourth. [When you perceive] the fifth one, you'll be over here with me.

Thank you. Thank you.

You see, of what benefit can a class be, if you can't relate?

Uh-huh.

And as long as you insist on believing that you are limit, then you must be nursed through a two-dimension into a third dimension and a fourth dimension. So as you view heaven, you view heaven as a fulfillment of your needs. But if you were in a third and a fourth dimension, needs wouldn't exist, and you would not view heaven that way. Does everyone understand that?

Yes. [Several students respond.]

Can I relate to you if I tell you that here is heaven? It's not fulfillment and it's not lack. I mean, you see, you can't relate that way. You can't relate in a two-dimension that way. Now, but you can relate, as long as you believe you are limit, that there is a man, another half of you, or there is a woman, another half of you, or there is someone, another half of you, that you can control and have that heavenly state of consciousness. Well, of course it *has* to be magnetic from your perspective. Is it or isn't it magnetic? It's neither.

OK. Thank you.

What is, is. It doesn't become. It just is. Our perception of what is, is the becoming stages. And we believe we are the becoming from a two-dimensional perspective.

Thank you.

When you believe you are in need, then you look out into the world and you say, "Here's my fulfillment," for a time. Wouldn't you say?

Right.

And to the two-dimensional world, of the overidentification with limit, that's heaven. And this is why people in the two dimension say, "Well, I don't—I haven't found my soul mate yet. Could this be my soul mate? In other words, is this the other half of me that [will] make me feel fulfilled and I have full control [of]?" You see, a person who believes they're only half filled—you understand?—cannot possibly be happy because they only have half control, you see? It's only half control. You got to have the other half.

I didn't make it that way. One's perception makes it that way, you see. One does so at the sacrifice of self-esteem and the goodness of life. Yes. I don't know of anyone in keeping with two-dimensional thinking believing that there's someone out there somewhere and as soon as they get ahold of them, they'll be fulfilled, I don't know of anyone who doesn't consider that heaven itself. Hmm? Yes, go right ahead. Any more questions?

Ah ...

Yes, go right ahead.

I'd like to ask another one on the nine centers of consciousness.
Yes.
We see it in relation to the river of life on the spinal cord and the prana.
Uh-huh.
I'd like to ask about the invertebrate animals or something like an amoeba. Do they have—how would their—
They have the centers of consciousness. Yes, they do. And what's the question?
And do they have a soul?
There is what you would understand as an Allsoul. You see, the human being, as you know the human being, is what is understood as an individualized soul, separate and special. You see, the dogs and cats, and the cockroaches and the little bugs, and the little mice, you know, and the guinea pigs and all of those creatures, the bluebirds and the sparrows, they don't have the glory of separation. That that is individualized is divided within. Mark that down. That which is individualized is divided within. When you accept what you truly are, you'll no longer be individualized; you'll no longer be divided within. You, of course, will be fulfilled. You are what you are. Not having denial, not having divided within, you won't experience need and, therefore, cannot be tempted.

Soul mates wait in the astral realms of consciousness. How blessed are the humble creatures who are not divided in soul consciousness.

Yes. You know, I would like to pause for one moment. In your evolution on the dividing, the individualization, when you brought up the question, in the individualization of the soul, you have a split of that which is. And it ever goes out into creation and as long as there's identification with limit, then there's ever the need, for you to always feel half there. I hope that's helped with your questions.

Thank you.

That's not what you are, but that is what you've identified with. Division, individualization, which is division within, is not limited to the Earth planet of substance. It is wherever there is form. Wherever there is form, there is limit. Yes.

And does that mean in the other realms of consciousness (astral, spiritual, celestial, etc.), since they are clothed in a form of that particular—

Yes.

—plane, therefore they are individualized? [Student J asks.]

That is correct. Whenever the Light enters, in order to express in what you understand as creation—oh, certainly, the realms—there are realms of light where there are individuals. Whenever I enter form, I enter the form; I take a suit out, whichever one will fulfill the purpose of the Light. I put it on for a time; however, I do not believe that I am that limit, for to do so, I would experience need, for I would have denied that which I am. You see, that's the division. That's the split. And you only experience that, of course, as long as you identify with what you've put on for a time.

And so I find untold millions searching around in all realms for their soul mate. All kinds of soul mates running loose. Too bad they can't get together and move on and enter the formless, that which they truly are. *[A few students laugh.]* See?

We offer to heaven what we offer to ourselves. So we've already judged what heaven is: it's magnetic, you see. It's ever in keeping with our needs. Yes. Yes, [Student Y].

Does the part of the pyramid that we can't perceive with the mind, is that—which is what we truly are. Is that correct?

That is what you are.

OK. Does that—

Everything else, from division, you have created. Divide and conquer is the Law of Creation. The Law of Limit is divide and conquer. So when you divide, creation conquers. All right? Now mark that down in your notebooks. The moment you divide, creation conquers. That is what divide and conquer is. Yes, [Student Y].

So is that what connects us to the oneness of which we all are?

The division?

No.

That is what separates us.

OK.

Then unity, of course, unites us.

OK. So my question is, we're in form with . . .

No. You are *using* form. If you believe you're in it, then, then it's got you. It has divided and conquered you. You are *using* form. Be with a thing; be with limit, not a part of limit. Yes, be with it, not a part of it.

So these, like the bow tie—I'm trying to understand—

Yes, yes. Go right ahead.

The bow tie, that is more—is that like an abstraction, more of an abstraction than an actual point within us?

It is a point within limit. Because, you see, you are limit in keeping with your belief in the suit that you're wearing at any moment. Are you aware that you're wearing several at this moment?

No.

You see, this is what I'm trying to help you with. You see, you have a thought; you believe you are the thought. You have a physical form, and in the belief you are the judgment in your mind, you have another form. And so there's one form over another form, superimposed upon another form. And a person gets very confused this way, don't they? You see?

Uh-huh.

In fact, didn't [Student M] just say to us this morning she had great difficulty in superimposing one over the other? You always have difficulty in superimposing these forms when you overidentify with one of them. Hmm? Did that help with your question, [Student Y]? It doesn't satisfy that, that other suit. I see that clearly, yes.

I—

You see, an abstraction is an abstraction in keeping with overidentification.

Where are my artists here on Earth? [Student H]?

Yes.

Answer that question I've just stated. An abstraction is an abstraction in keeping with one's overidentification.

That's right. Because if I were to go to an art gallery—

Yes.

—and look at a painting known as an abstraction, then the meaning of that, of that painting is ever subject to the meaning that I give it, which is subject to where I am, what I see in it, where I'm coming from. It may be entirely off base from where the artist was coming from. But—although it's the artist's duty to communicate his thoughts and feelings through that—

So what does that tell you? It is our perception of it.

That's right.

Doesn't it? That's what all of life in your form in two dimension is entirely dependent upon: your perception, you see. You see, it's like [Student S] asked a question, well, she wanted to understand that heaven was magnetic. Well, heaven is magnetic in keeping with your perception. Do you understand that?

Now if we ask some of the men students here, they'll say, "Oh, no, it's not magnetic. It's electric!" You see. Well, is God a woman or a man? *[Some students laugh.]* You see, that's the dimension from which you are perceiving, you see. I'm trying to help you to gain a little different perception, you see, a different perspective, so that you may broaden your horizon and then you won't see it's an abstract if it doesn't fit in with a two-dimension limit that we overidentify with at any moment. For, you see, it is abstract to one who is viewing it from an overidentification to a particular level of consciousness. To them it is abstract. To them it has to be: "Heaven must be magnetic. No! Heaven must be electric. No, no, no. Heaven neutral? No, it can't possibly be neutral because I don't identify with neutrality." Do you understand?

You see, how many of my students, who believe they are limit and the form, and the suit that they have chosen in keeping with the law at this time, say, "Heaven is neutral. I feel good in that neutrality." No, no, no, no. [For them] heaven is either magnetic or electric. It has to be one or the other, you see, because it has to fit our perception of it, our own perspective. Because without fitting our perspective, we don't relate. And when we don't relate to that which we perceive, it's abstract, I think you call it. Yes. Yes.

So if you were, if your perception was more of a feeling of heaven, let's say, if you, if you perceived it through feeling, then would that be . . . [Student Y speaks.]

One perceives that which is through a broadening of one's horizon through an acceptance of what they truly are, which is the will of Good. And so, as long as a person denies what they are, their perception is ever in keeping with what a narrow view they will allow of what they are. That's like one of my students saying that what they are is a dream of life. Wasn't that the statement, [Student M]?

Yes, it was.

From a lack of homework, you see. My, time is passing quickly, you know. Very quickly. There, [Student N] had a question there. Very quickly. Yes.

Yes. I was wondering faith is in, in the center in the subconscious on the diagram we put the three together and the middle three was the subconscious and the shadow and that's where faith is also. I was wondering—

Faith's in the shadow?! Is that what you're—

Well, it's in the same middle—

Well, now I want my students to start studying a little bit here because, you know, I want to know that if I have made an error, I want to be corrected. I don't recall having taught that faith is a shadow.

Fire is in the shadow. [Student O offers his perspective.]

Pardon?

Fire. Earth, fire, and water— [Student O continues.]

That's darkness. [Student N offers her perspective.]

It's light, shadow, and darkness. [Student O responds.]

Yes? And do you have faith down there?

No, sir. Not in, not in— [Student O responds.]

I found a lot of belief down there. But I'd like to know if there is some faith down there.

No, sir. [Student O responds.]

Hmm?

No, sir. [Student O repeats.]

Now, [Student N], don't you think you should study a little more on that particular area?

Yes.

Pardon?

Yes.

Faith is something that you do not control with mental substance. Hmm?

Right.

I know we are often tempted to do so, but the only result we get is belief and bondage. Hmm?

Right.

Extra-long class today. My channel already gave you two classes. Now this is your third one. Yes. Yes, [Student U] has a question.

Can we increase the rate of spin of the centers without increasing gravity?

Well, if you understand that gravity, what gravity is, as I've already given to you, and you want to increase the rate of spin while you still believe you are the center of consciousness that you've overidentified with, no. *[The teacher laughs.]* That's very clear. Does that help with your question?

Yes, sir.

No, there's no shortcut around thataway. No, no, no. The law is very specific and very detailed. Now you study there and you'll see that. Yes, [Student M] has a question here.

OK.

And move right along with these questions. It's very important.

In regards to the spin, it was said that clockwise was the earth, counterclockwise—

That was all given. Yes.

Right. OK. Now, why is it going clockwise, counterclockwise, clockwise again? Is there a balancing between the two—there's three centers—

Fine. I understand your question, and I answered it for my student, [Student S], just last Sunday. So she can answer it for you.

OK. [Student M responds.]

Because I've already answered it last Sunday.

That's where he drew the bow tie diagram with the four triangles. [Student S explains.]

Yes. [Student M responds.]

And when you draw it out, he said that they were interrelated within each group of three. [Student S continues.]

Right. [Student M responds.]

OK. So you have to draw that out and then that's what was left. Did you do that? [Student S continues.]

I did that. Yes, thank you. [Student M responds.]

And she has a question that I answered for you last Sunday. So go ahead.

That's the way it was left with me. [Student S responds.]

Then what's the problem? What's the question? *[After a short pause, the teacher continues.]* Did I not clearly state to you, [in] the class last Sunday, that it spins in a clockwise and counterclockwise? Hmm?

Yes. [Student M responds.]

What was the question, [Student J]?

What was her question? [Student J responds.]

[The teacher laughs joyously.] I'm so happy. Well, I did answer the question. So do you understand the question? *[The teacher addresses Student S.]*

I understand the question. I'm not sure I completely understand the answer. May I— [Student S responds.]

Oh, you don't understand my answer?

Well—

Yes. You should speak right up there. It's very important.

Last week he gave the diagram and he said now you study it and perceive it. He didn't answer—he didn't take it all the way out. [Student S continues.]

Uh-huh. [Student M responds.]

But— [Student S continues.]

Well, how much study and how much perception have you gained? This is seven days later, I think. Yes.

When I drew it out and looked at it, all the center points— [Student S continues.]

Yes?

—coming together were all in the clockwise spin.

Uh-huh.

The very center where they all came together—

Uh-huh.

They were all going clockwise.

Uh-huh.

OK.

Yes, what does that tell you?

That tells me that it's coming in.

Uh-huh.

OK. And then all the, the charges on the outside were alternating.

Uh-huh.

Clockwise.

You made the effort.

Right.

Uh-huh. Uh-huh.

So then I was—see, I haven't gotten the full way yet. But I was trying to look at this inner center, spinning clockwise. And then the outer center is kind of a balanced spinning.

Well, now let me say this much: if you've done your homework, you've got that far—

Uh-huh. That's as far as I've got.

I'll give you just a little bit more. And you do your homework, because I'm not going to do your homework for you. You understand? Now let's stop for a moment. Are you attracted and pulled into anything that does not accelerate in a clockwise motion? [Student R].

Are you attracted and pulled into anything that does not accelerate in a clockwise [motion]? [Student R repeats the question.]

Yes. *[After a short pause, the teacher continues.]* Now visualize in front of you, perhaps, what we would call—you're an artist, [Student H]. Now if you want something—someone pulled into something, would you have it accelerated in a clockwise or counterclockwise?

Clockwise. [Student H responds.]

And now you explain to all my students why, because they should have all have perceived this on last Sunday through a little bit of homework.

Well—

What, what happens to your mind, which you believe you are, when you look at anything that's spinning in a clockwise motion?

Oh, I'm, I'm falling. I'm entering in. It's—

That's how you enter.

Right.

All right. Now you should have perceived that. Now how do you get out?

Counterclockwise.

Uh-huh. The way out of a thing is the way you got into a thing. So counterclockwise is clockwise, depending on the dimension [and] your perceptive [perception] of the dimension. Do you understand that? So you get into all of these confused states and all of these needs and everything. How do you get into them, [Student H]?

Through the clockwise connection.

Now you should have made the effort and took a look at the centers that go clockwise. And you should also have taken a look at the ones that go counterclockwise. Yes. [Student S].

When this was originally given with the nine—

Yes.

On its side—

Uh-huh.

With the circle of eternity.

That's right.

We were told there was another circle of eternity on the other end.

That is correct. That is correct.

I'd like to ask if this one is this way.

Yes.

Does the one at the other end of the line of infinity spin the other way?

Yes.

Good.

Depends if you turn around.

Good. Thanks.

Keep an eye on what's behind you.

OK.

You see? Because, you see, the spinning—you see, that that is on the right is spinning clockwise, and that that is on the left is spinning clockwise, becomes counterclockwise according to your perspective.

OK.

And the dimension in which you're looking at it. You know, I might have to ask some of my assistants to come down here and give a few basic art classes. Do you understand that [Student H]?

I would agree. [Student H quietly responds.]

Pardon? *[After a short pause, the teacher continues.]* You enter that which moves in a clockwise position.

Right. [Student H responds more loudly.]

You are repelled by that which moves in a counterclockwise position. Is that not correct?

Correct.

Well, then try to apply that simple principle right there in the diagrams that you have received. Hmm? You see?

Now when you look at anything—and I'll say this before we finish the class because we've gone way over time here. I'll say this: When you look at anything—and you've got this basic diagram today—[and] you believe you are tempted, try to understand that you are moving in a clockwise, accelerated increase of spin of your consciousness. Now you have that because that's how you, that's how you moved into temptation, you see. You move yourself into it. You enter it. It's like—what would you call those things in your world? A pinwheel?

Vortex? [Student R responds.]

A vortex, you see. You see, it's the—it pulls you right into it, you see. That's clockwise. Now if you want to—when you think you're tempted and you do not want to be tempted, you see, you must change the spin in your consciousness; by changing your perception, you will change the spin. If you tempt to change the spin and do not make the effort to change your perception, which would change the spin, then that resistance will adhere you to it. Now do you understand? See, you must make the effort to move to the center of consciousness which is spinning in the opposite direction, for that changes your perception of what you've allowed yourself to be tempted by. And in so doing, you see, you will be pushed out of it, instead of pulled into it. Yes.

In order to make that change, in a prior class you made mention of it takes the will of the electric going—

Correct.

—into the water.

Correct.

And to prepare ourselves so that we won't have the shock.

Correct.

And I'd like to ask how to do that.

Well, one is often shocked by what they believe that they are tempted into. Usually they're shocked after they get in there. *[Some students laugh.]* Rarely are they shocked in another way. It's usually while they're in.

Thank you.

You know. You see, what happened, you entered the hole, the vortex, you enter the hole, and while you're in the hole, you see, you're just pulled like a magnet. And then you—something happens inside and a change of consciousness starts to take place, and you are now identified with a counterspin at a high accelerated speed, equal, ever in keeping of the spin you got in clockwise, and it's a terrible shock. It's a terrible shock.

You know, it's a great shock, to form, to be born. That's how you got to Earth. You got to Earth in the spin and into the vortex. Now you know how to get out of it.

Oh, I must say good day. Keep your questions for next class. Time passes quickly, as I said; time in your world, such a deception. But, you know, as long as you're going to believe you are limit and form, then we must all, in limit and form, pay the price of that deception, you know, created by our ignorance of investigation of true design.

Thank you and good day.

MARCH 16, 1986

A/V Class Private 40

Please be seated. Good afternoon, students.

Now we'll spend a few moments here in this class on a review. [Student S], you can read some of your review notes here for the class.

That was given?

Last week.

Last week.

Yes.

Thank you. First of all, we started with the equilateral triangle with denial and earth at the lower right; need and the fire center at the lower left; and at the apex, temptation and the water center. And it was stated that when you deny what you are, you experience what you are and identify with the limit, which guarantees the denial of what you are. And that's, like, you come into the earth.

Uh-huh.

Should I [carry on]?

All right. No, that's fine. Any questions here today on last week's class? Yes, [Student O], you have a question on last week's class.

Yes, sir. [He speaks quietly.]

Speak right up, won't you?

Yes, sir. I would like to know what is the relationship or the correlation in reference to perspective and dimension.

Yes, well, for example, we don't have our blackboard up today, but that's all right. You have a pyramid there in front of you, or what you call an equilateral triangle. Now according to your perception of it, it looks like a triangle and you see it in two dimension. Now if you stand with a perspective looking down at it, then you're going to see a different dimension. If you look at it straight, as you're looking at it on your little notepaper there, then you only see one side of it. Actually, of course, there are four sides to it. Hmm?

Yes, sir.

Now we all understand that this pyramid we've drawn here, this triangle, is four-sided. Do we all understand that? *[After a short pause, the teacher continues.]* All right. Now, I'm glad you've brought that up, because in reference to these diagrams, you have four sides of an equilateral triangle: you have the northern side; the southern side; you have the eastern side and you have the west side. Now you have a choice of entering the apex of the triangle by your ascending on either one of the four, so-called, sides of the pyramid. Now which one, which side does a wise man choose in his efforts in ascendance? [Student R].

The left side.

Now you have—let's call it north, south, east, and west. Which side would you travel up? Would you travel the north side? The south side? The west side? Or the east side? Yes, let [Student R]—

My first inclination is north, but then [my] second thought says east.

Yes. Well, ofttimes it's best to wait for your second thought because the eastern side of the triangle is the best one on the pyramid to travel up. Because, you see, when you turn to the east and you ascend on the steps, the eastern steps, then you always have the Light before you. What happens when light is in front of you and what happens when light is behind you?

There are no shadows when the light is in front, and when the light is behind, you have all the shadows that are there.

Does everyone understand that? This is why, in your thoughts, you see, as you ascend, you always ascend on the eastern side. If you do not ascend, if you do not turn to the east, then you are distracted and controlled by shadows. And what are shadows, [Student R]?

Shadows are—

What is a shadow? We have given that before.

A shadow is the image—I was trying to remember what the definition was, but my own definition is the image of forms created—the judgments, solidified judgments.

That are?

Reflection of solidified judgments?

That are in the way of the Light.

Yeah.

Is not a shadow an obstruction to the Light?

Yes.

A shadow is an obstruction to what you are. *[After a pause, the teacher repeats.]* A shadow is an obstruction to what you are. Now as soon as you have that [in your notebooks], let's move in our consciousness. Of the four choices you have, you've already stated the choice that shadows do not exist. Is that correct?

Uh-huh.

And what was that?

The eastern side, facing the Light.

When you face the Light, no shadow exists. When you face the Light, no form controls you. In the moment you face the Light, there is no shadow, there is no obstruction. Now, therefore, in order to continue, for you here on Earth to have these classes, you must face the Light daily, frequently. How do you face the Light, [Student R]?

By going within.

By separating truth from creation, you face the Light.

Uh-huh.

When you declare the truth, your consciousness turns to the Light. You declare the truth when you do your spiritual exercises and when you state your affirmations, your consciousness turns to the Light, where there are no shadows. And where there are no shadows, there are no obstructions. That reveals to you that shadows only exist in the north, south, and western poles of consciousness, correct?

Uh-huh.

All right. Now write that down in your notes. Shadows exist north, south, and west.

Now there are three centers of consciousness beginning with earth, fire, and water. You cannot experience obstructions, you cannot experience shadows—you have that on your notes. You have it on tape, anyway. You cannot experience shadows, you cannot experience obstructions, if you are not identified; the river is not blocked in one of those three centers: earth, fire, water. Now remember, the obstructions are judgments, which are created in the water center. That has already been given to you. They express through earth, fire, and water. When you believe that you are earth, fire, and water, you are obstructed by your own creations. Yes, [Student R].

I'd like to ask which of those three functions correspond to which points of the compass.

That's a very good question and that is forthcoming. Make a triangle. Place north, south, and west on your triangle. Have you done that? *[The teacher looks at Student R and then continues.]* Oh, no, you place it first and then I will correct it for you, if any correction is necessary. Some of my students are very illumined; therefore, they don't need to be corrected. A triangle. What happened to your sense of humor this morning? Oh, it's afternoon in your world, yes, of course. North, south, and west. Do you have north, south, and west? *[The teacher addresses Student R.]*

Uh-huh. Uh-huh.

Now tell the class where you have north.

Well, I put north on the left side.

Well, you should put north at the apex.

OK.

And where do you have south?

On the right.

That's correct. And west?

On the left.

It's the only place left. Now where do you have the centers on that triangle? Earth, fire, and water. You already have that in your notes.

Uh-huh.

Now let's superimpose them on the north, south, and west.

Well, fire and earth are on the left and right.

Yes? You have earth, fire, and water.

And water's on top.

Yes. Well, now tell me something, even in your physical world, don't you understand that the North Pole affects the water? Or haven't you had that in your education? Pardon?

Uh-huh.

You haven't had that?! Who has had it? Well, there are some of us who know. Of course, it does. Is the northern pole a magnetic pole or not?

It is.

Well! You see the correlation, as my student [Student O], says between water and magnetism? Pardon?

Uh-huh. [Student R responds.]

Fine! Then you have no problem [with] north, south, and west, do you? And you have no problem making some effort to stay out of all three places. Hmm? You know, let your head face the pole; make sure your being is someplace else.

Now changing the molecular structure of an obstruction. [Student H], my channel shared that with you the other day, you and a few other students. How do you change the molecular structure of limit or form?

Through the friction-adhesion principle.

Uh-huh.

The clockwise spin and the counterclockwise spin, raising it to a heated temperature.

Uh-huh.

For a liquid form—taking it from a solid into a liquid form.

Correct. All form, all form is first liquid. Do you have that down in your notes? Now in your world, I'm sure in your studies in your Earth world, you would understand that forms, before they are liquid, they are gases, correct?

Yes, sir. [Several students respond.]

Well, now tell me something, What is a gas compared to a liquid? Yes, [Student U].

Chemically, they're identical.

Correct. They are identical. Now what is the difference in their expression?

The intermolecular adhesion forces—

Yes?

—are less in a gas.

Than they are in a liquid.

Correct.

And on so through a solid, correct? So now we start moving into an understanding of changing the molecular structure of an obstruction or a form or a solid. Now when you have a solid object, in order to change its molecular structure, it must move, be moved in consciousness from the earth center of consciousness to what, [Student R]? *[After a short pause, the teacher continues.]* Say that you—

To the fire?

Correct. And when you have a solid, what is the next stage that it is evolved to?

To the water.

To a liquid.

Uh-huh.

Correct?

Uh-huh.

All right. Now make that—put that in your notes.

Now this object here, known to you as a glass, *[The teacher adjusts a glass of water that is on the table at which he is seated.]*

is and exists only because you create it in your consciousness. That's its only existence. Now you can say to your fellow student, "Does that glass exist?" And your fellow student will say to you, "Why, of course it exists." It exists because they have created it in their consciousness as you have created it in your consciousness.

How did you create these solid objects? You created it through the very process of entering your planet Earth. When you accepted division from what you are, what you call in your world individuals, when you accepted that law, you guaranteed what that law had to offer. And what does that Law of Division have to offer? It has to offer to you what you know as forms or limit. Therefore, if you ask your fellow student, "Does that glass exist?" your fellow student says, "Of course it does," for they have accepted division of what they are, the same as you have. Therefore, it exists. And because you have created it, for you it exists; therefore, you are bound by what you create because you believe you are your creation. You see?

You see, you believe you are form. Because you believe you are form, you are controlled by form. Therefore, to those who believe they are limit, they are, by the law, controlled by limit. So when you have an obstruction, although you have created it, for you it exists. In truth it does not exist at all.

Now if I seem to be going too fast for any of you, well, you speak up. But you be rest assured you have homework to do. You have homework to do, yes.

All right. Now you know how to change form through its various stages until it returns unto a gaseous form. What controls the realm of gases? [Student R]. Which center—

Fire.

—controls it?

Fire.

Which center—in which center, rather, do the gaseous forms exist? Earth, fire, water, or what?

Air.

Air center! Put it down in your notes. And also put down: earth—solid; fire—transformation; water—liquid; air—gaseous.

Now [if] you want to change the molecular structure of a solid—and please do not misunderstand me. My interest in revealing these laws to you is [to] change the greatest solid you'll ever experience: it's known as your judgments. They are very solid. For whoever does not change their solidified judgments can never expect to change or transform an object outside of them.

Now you have a judgment that is an obstruction in your path. Do you understand that, students? *[After a short pause, the teacher continues.]* And you want to transform it; you want to change it. Hmm? All right. What do you do? Where do you move that judgment? Yes.

[Are you] asking that question? [Student O asks.]

Well, I am. I'm asking my students, yes.

The first thing, we—I think the Friends told us is to accept its right of existence. [Student O continues.]

Correct. Accept—what does that do to your consciousness when you accept the right of its existence? Yes, [Student O].

It separates the truth from creation.

Yes, when you accept its right of existence, you respect the purpose of its design. Remember that the obstruction was first designed in your consciousness before it became solidified and known as a judgment. You must respect its purpose of design. It has a purpose to serve. All right? Does everyone follow me on that to this point? All right. Yes, [Student O].

Yes, sir. After, after we accept the purpose of its existence . . .

You accept its right of existence. Right. When you accept the right of existence of limit, you respect its purpose of design. Yes.

And, and then, generally—I don't know. I have to think about it.

Fine. [Student B], do you have some expression on that?

I think then you'd have to go to the fire center.

Correct. The fire center. And what do you do in the fire center? What happens in the fire center?

Well, you would heat it or give it energy. [Student R speaks.]

You would heat it or give it energy. What happens to the objects you've placed there? If you take your judgment and you send it into your fire center, what happens to it? Hmm? Yes, [Student U].

It gets transformed into a liquid.

It gets transformed into a liquid. Correct. Now what center of consciousness is liquid?

The water center. [Student R responds.]

Speaking on the lower centers of consciousness.

Water center.

It enters the water center, doesn't it?

Yes.

Yes. Hmm? Now after it has entered the water center—now remember, it's earth, fire, and water. You now have it in the water center, correct? It's now in liquid form. What's going to happen to it? Yes, [Student U].

Well, if it, if you continue to add energy to it, it will rise to another, higher level. It will become a gas. And enter the air center.

But where're you going to get energy from?

From the fire. [Student R responds.]

Uh-huh. Yes, [Student B].

Fire and water are steam.

Correct. That's what sends it into a gaseous state.

So it's the balance of fire and water. [Student R observes.]

Correct. Correct. Now you've heard in your world that thoughts, they fly. Is that not correct? All right. Now I'm trying to show you what happens with your thoughts and your judgments and how they go out into the universe. They go out in a gaseous state. They go out in what you understand as the air center. Now how do they return, [Student R]?

Ah—

You've sent a form out in a gaseous state. Solidified in your consciousness (earth center).

Uh-huh.

Born as a form in your water center. Transformed and sent out from your universe in the air center or a gaseous state of form.

The way out is the way in. So it would come back as a gas.

Now you're beginning to perceive something. *[After a pause, the teacher continues.]* Through what motion do you send it forth? Well, let's put it clearly: through which spin that you have received would you send it forth?

Clockwise.

Clockwise?

Clockwise to send it forth.

Clockwise? Everyone—

Counterclockwise! I'm sorry. It's the retrospin that sends it out.

Yes, that's counterclockwise.

Yeah.

Definitely. So when you send out something, it goes out by the Law of Retrospin. It goes out into the universe.

Now tell me: how are you receptive? What state of consciousness must you be in to be receptive to a retrospin of form in the universe and in the atmosphere? What state of consciousness must you be in? Now don't forget the various laws you have received on friction and adhesion and don't—and study your notes and then tell me. Yes, [Student O].

Magnetic.

Yes, magnets attract. What is, what spin is a magnet, [Student R]?

A magnet is, is clockwise spin.

So you cannot be receptive to the gaseous forms, which you understand as thoughts and judgments in the universes, unless you are in a magnetic state of consciousness. Do you understand that? So you receive, therefore, through which center, [Student R]?

The air center.

Which is being controlled by what center?

Fire and water.

Remember, the magnet is in the water center. Hmm? All right? Tell me: what is belief? Is it electric or magnetic?

Magnetic. [Student R continues to respond.]

Indeed, it is. That's how it controls you. Yes, [Student L].

Did he say you received through the air center?

It went out through the air center. It is received through the air center and enters the magnet, the magnetic or the water center.

Now what do you do with that form now that it has entered your universe through the air center and is a liquid in the water center? What do you do with it? What do you do with it? Well, look at it this way, what do you do with a thought form that enters your consciousness?

Pass judgment on it. [Student R responds.]

Believe that it is you. If you take a thought and you move it into the fire center, a thought that you receive, you move it into the fire center, then you are working with it intelligently, for it to enter the faculty of reason, which is located where?

In the air center.

Uh-huh. Now we're moving. Therefore, it is not in anyone's best interest for their own good to accept a thought form that has not gone through the purification from the water-air— the water-fire center balance on into the air center, where the faculty of reason expresses. Otherwise, we're known as very credulous beings, which means, of course, as I've stated so long ago, easily imposed upon.

All right, are there any questions on that, students? Yes, [Student D] has a question this morning. Excuse me, this afternoon in your world.

You send out and you receive the gas form through the air center.

Correct.

And move it down into the fire center and work with it there. And then move it back up into the air center?

Yes, because it reenters your universe in the air center as a gaseous form. It immediately descends into the water center. It very rarely is balanced in the fire center. Does that help you, [Student D]?

It goes into the water center from the air. OK, I think I—

Yes, now look at it this way: that which enters our universe descends.

Right.

Can we understand that?

Yes.

Look, all points inside point down. All points outside point up. *[After a pause, the teacher continues.]* Oh, I wonder if I've made that clearer for you all. Is that clear for you, [Student R], this morning?

Well, I have to kind of dig that—

[The teacher laughs.] Yes, [Student N].

The way I understood it was you said it's not wise to consider a thought form until it's been purified by the lower, by the fire center and then moved up into the air.

Well, you can't even consider it, 'til it enters the faculty of reason, which, which exists in the air center, [Student N].

But the, but the pure—let it go through the process down there first?

Well, it won't do it on its own; you have to make the effort—
OK.
—to balance it out with your fire center. It has plenty of water because when it enters your universe, it enters from the air center and descends immediately into the water center. So you have to make the effort through your own will to move the form from the water center into the fire center, where it will be balanced and, through that balance, will enter the faculty of reason in the air center.

OK. Thank you.

Yes, you see, you must first descend to ascend.

OK.

Yes.

Is that why confusion happens a lot of time? Because the effort isn't made to, to take a look at things a little closer without—

That's very correct. You see, the forms remain in the water center.

Oh.

The thoughts, which are forms in the consciousness, the effort is not intelligently made to move the form, or thought, or judgment, from the water center, where it is fully expressing itself, into the fire center for balance, which would in turn, as it is balanced in the fire center, move it on to the faculty of reason in the air center. Yes.

So then is it necessary to go to the earth center? It's not after that . . .

No. One sends it to the earth center from the air center through the process, if they choose to solidify it into physical, what you call, physical matter.

That's what—OK.

Does that help you in the endeavors you've been working on?

Yes!

They've been stuck in the air and water centers there.
Yes.
Yes. Certainly.
Thank you.
Yes. Yes. *[The teacher calls upon Student S.]*
It seems that as we move it up, from a solid to a liquid and then to the gaseous state—
Uh-huh.
—that the molecular structure is accelerated.
It is. That's the only way to change it.
And therefore, takes on energy. Is that correct?
When, in the spin, when it is accelerated, of course, it does absorb energy, yes.
And then when it comes down the other way, it seems that as it's slowed . . .
It releases it. Yes, that's correct.
And I'd like to ask, Where is it absorbed from and where does it go to in that process?
Well, it is absorbed from your being and is returned to your being. So you're either exhausted or filled with vitality ever in keeping of what you're doing with the forms that you are creating and receptive to.
Thank you.
And this is why sometimes, you see, a person says, "Oh, I'm totally exhausted just from looking at that person, let alone talking to them." You know, sometimes, you see, don't you—you know that, don't you, [Student J]?
Yes, sir.
"Oh, I'm totally exhausted!" just by being in their presence. Well, you see, you're not intelligently working with the forms that are in the atmosphere that are registering into your consciousness. And consequently, you're totally exhausted from those forms as they [are] absorbing the energy. Yes.
Thank you.

You're welcome. Yes, [Student B].

You said that it was not in our best interest to accept thoughts that had not gone through the purification process.

No, it's not.

Well, if we don't accept them, then are we denying them?

No. You see, when I said it is not in our best interest to accept them until they have gone through—we have put them through the process to enter our faculty of reason, what I mean to say is that you do not permit—you accept their right of existence; you do not permit them to use your being, unless they're willing to go through that process. You see? So it doesn't mean that you deny their right of existence, but you do have certain regulations that govern them. And that's your responsibility to see that they abide by those regulations before they can enter your house. You see, if you open your door and—perhaps you don't like people carousing in your little home; then you tell them, "These are my rules and regulations. If you wish to abide by them, you're welcome. And if you don't, you're not going to enter." Yes. Does that help with that question?

Yes.

Yes, [Student B].

Thank you.

Certainly. [Student N], please.

What, what would it be like to move from the water to the fire?

Well, many people say that they become very angry when that happens. Yes.

OK. And then when you want, and then that gives you the energy to bring it, whatever it is, if you want to bring it into form.

Why, certainly. Certainly. You bring it into balance so that you can send it up to the faculty of reason in your consciousness. You see, try to understand that a form, a judgment does not want to leave the water center.

Right.

Once it gets home, it is not about to leave. And it takes the conscious effort of your will to balance it with the fire center. It's like anything that is born. You see, you take a little child and the moment it comes out of the little sack of water, you hear quite a little sound of joy, wouldn't you say? To some, it's a joyous sound; to others, it's most irritating. It depends, of course, on who believes who it belongs to.

Uh-huh.

Yes. Now if you believe it belongs to you, then they're sounds of spiritual harmony to your ears. If you don't believe that, you have a problem, usually.

If you don't believe it belongs to you?

That's right. Well, do you like to hear a little child screaming that doesn't belong to you? Pardon?

No.

But if it belonged to you, it may not bother you so much, would it?

True. [Student N speaks softly.]

Pardon?

Yes.

Yes, well, you would try to do whatever is necessary, so it could have what it wanted. Well, now you're dealing with the same thing with a judgment and a thought form in your consciousness. Born in the water center, it doesn't want to leave.

Right.

And so you must make conscious effort to send it to the fire center for balance in order to move it up to the light in the faculty of reason, up there in the air center. Hmm?

Thank you.

Yes. Yes, [Student B].

Where does it come in to just ignore?

Where it comes in just to ignore, the principle to ignore, is when you have recognized its right of existence and in that

recognition, in your recognition of its right of existence, you awaken to its refusal to follow your rules [and] regulations governing the home it has entered. Do you understand that?
Oh.
You see? And so you don't battle with it. You see, if you—you know, to battle with a form created, understand this, is an effort on your part to suppress it. Hmm? And it is no effort on your part to educate it. So, you see, when you refuse and battle its right of existence, you become its victim. Do you understand that?
Yes.
You do not demonstrate the law which is the principle of ignore. You see, you've recognized its right of existence. You've accepted its right of existence. You have awakened that it refuses to follow the rules and regulations, which you are responsible for [in] your own little home, you understand? And when it makes that refusal, you ignore it. If you fight it, it will bother and disturb you. And whatever bothers or disturbs you in truth is controlling you. You don't want it to control you; so don't fight it. All right?
Thank you.
Certainly. Now just because you don't fight it, doesn't mean you're going to do what it wants to do. Of course not. Yes, [Student H].
I was just following that. [Student H speaks softly.]
Pardon?
I was just following that statement.
Yes. Now, [Student J], what are these questions here that you have.
I have a couple of questions written down, but I don't have my glasses and I can't read them.
Well now, you know something? I will just excuse you to get your glasses.

I don't have—I don't have them with me, sir.

You didn't bring them with you! Well, perhaps I could see what those questions— *[The teacher tries to look at the student's notebook and then laughs joyously.]* Well, how do you like these informal classes?

I love them.

Well, I don't think my channel's glasses are going to serve you too well.

No, sir.

Hmm, can the secretary see for you? Or she can't read your writing?

Probably.

[The teacher laughs again.] It's all right. That's all right. That's fine. Now are there any other questions here today? I keep calling it morning and I know it's afternoon in your world and things are more peaceful here. Yes, [Student M].

Yes. I was wondering about the principle that everything first must descend in order to ascend.

Well, certainly. Now, think. You're speaking about form and limit, correct?

Correct.

Well, now ask yourself the question: you have a solid; you have a liquid, and what do you have beyond that? Do you remember? Gaseous.

Gaseous. [Student R responds.]

Correct?

Correct. [Student M responds.]

So if the gaseous does not descend, it doesn't become a liquid, does it, [Student U]?

No, it does not. [Student U responds.]

And if the liquid doesn't descend, it doesn't become a solid, does it? Now as long as I have students on Earth who believe they are solid, then they must descend graciously before they can ascend. Now, [Student M], try to understand: you surely would not blame me or my channel because I don't believe that I'm solid flesh and bone? But I grant your right to believe that you are. Therefore, I grant your right to insist on descending, as long as you don't deny my right to ascend. All right?

Yes.

Yes.

Thank you.

Yes, [Student L] has a question on descending there.

No, I think I have a question—

On ascending? Oh, wonderful!

—on the northern—

Yes?

—the southern—

I'll have to call you by number then, if you're ascending.

No. [Both the student and teacher laugh.] *Forget I said—*

Yes, yes, yes. Number 6, go ahead, please.

[Student L laughs again.] *You gave us the north, south, east, and west on the, on the triangle. How does that—*

I gave you north, south, *east,* and west on a triangle?

North, south, and west . . .

I gave you north, south, east, and west?

North, south, and east. [Student R remarks.]

North, south, and west. [Student O remarks.]

North, south, and west. I'm sorry. East— [Student R corrects himself.]

North, west, and south. [Student L remarks.]

Now let's pause for a few moments and look at that pyramid, north, south and west, and let's see what that means that I have students that insist I put the east there. Hmm? Now let's take another look at that, shall we, please?

Yes. [Student L responds.]

Yes. Now, now, [Student R], let's take another look at that in here. And what does that represent? [*The teacher points to the diagram in Student R's notebook.*] What did I tell you that means?

These are the levels of consciousness within us.

Yes. Yes. Now you want to descend? Is this what Number 6 is telling me? She wants to descend?

I— [Student L begins to respond and a few students laugh.]

Well, east does—east doesn't exist there.

Right. [Student L responds.]

You see, earth, fire, and water, there is no east. It's north, south, and west. Yes. You go right ahead, Number 6.

Now I'm wondering how it applies on the pyramid. Does that apply to each plane on the pyramid? Does— [Student L asks.]

Are you referring to an equilateral pyramid?

Yes.

Did I say that that one was equilateral? It's missing one side. I gave you north, south, and west, didn't I?

Uh-huh. Yes. [Many students respond.]

And the east was— [Student R remarks.]

Well, now, let's, let's rise above it. And let's look down at that. North side, south side, and west side. Is that a four-sided or a three-sided pyramid?

Three sides. [Student O speaks quietly.]

[Student B].

Three. [Student B responds.]

I never did say that that was an equilateral, four-sided [pyramid], did I?

No. [Student B responds.]

Not on that one. On the one before [that] I gave you, I made it very clear that it was four-sided, didn't I, [Student J]?

Yes, sir. [Student J responds.]

Yes. Yes. Now students, you're coming along, but let's listen to the classes. Hmm? Yes. Yes.

I was seeing it as a triangle instead of a pyramid. That's what my mistake was. [Student L remarks.]

Yes, but didn't we discuss at last class, here, that we must move from the flat, what we call, you call flat-heads, two-dimensional, into the three-dimensional and four-dimensional? And then we can all rejoice when we enter the fifth dimension. Yes. But let's first move out of the flat-head vibration, you know, into the three dimensions, all right?

Yes. [Student L responds.]

Yes, [Student B].

You've said that the three centers are 45 degrees.

They're 45 degrees.

And then the next three are 45. And then 45—so, and then, 45 degrees, say, for what we are. That's only half a circle.

That's correct.

What's, what's the other half?

All of us. No, I'm not, I'm not just being humorous. I understand, of course, that is what you perceive is half a circle. Hmm?

Yes.

Now let's look at this half a circle in the atmosphere, all right? Well, it's half a circle we're looking at.

Right.

Is it a half a circle as we look up at it? Hmm? [Student U]?

No, it's a circle.

It's a circle.

If it's a half a sphere, it's a circle. [Student U continues.]

Correct. So we look up and we say, "That's all of me." Now that's one perspective, isn't it? Now let's go and look at it sideways and tell us what does it look like?

Half a circle. [Student U continues.]

A half a circle. So looking at it from that side, it's a half a circle. Right? Now let's rise above it all and let's perceive it from above. What does it look like?

A circle. [Student U continues.]

A circle. So we have to move from a two-dimension at least into a three-dimension and a four-dimension to see that the answer to your question is totally dependent on the perception of the observer. Hmm?

In other words, you're saying that the circle fills up. I mean . . . [Student B responds.]

The circle doesn't fill up, but you fill up.

I see it's filled up on one half and the other half's just vacant. [Student B continues.]

No, you see, you see, it does not exist as half, for half is dependent upon the Law of Relativity. What do you have to compare it to? You see, a half is a whole to one who is not the illusion which they have created by the panorama of passing limit. Do you understand that, [Student U]? *[After a short pause, the teacher continues.]*

For example, now you say you see, from that position, you see a half a circle. Now we move to another position: we see the half a circle as a full circle. Well, the question, therefore, is, Are we a whole circle or a half a circle? As long as there is that question, it is dependent upon our perception, for we are now, once again, in the *maya* of illusion. Perhaps I'm not, no, I'm not—yes, [Student Y]. We'll, we'll get it cleared up for you, [Student B] and everyone else. Yes.

Would it help one, then, let's say you look out the window and you see a tree. And you actually are viewing the tree as two-dimensional, but if you start picturing things in their completeness of actually viewing, would that help? To, like, to train oneself to start looking at, at . . .

Well, for example, we have created a half a circle. Would you agree to that? *[The teacher addresses Student U.]*

Yes. [Student U responds.]

We have created what we know as half a circle by our perception. Would you understand that?

Yes. [Student U again responds.]

May I borrow your pen and pad here, please. *[In this class, as in the previous one, the teacher was seated at the head of the dining room table. Some students were also seated at that table, while other students were seated at other tables in the dining* room. *Student R was seated to the teacher's immediate right and it was his notebook that the teacher asked to borrow.]* Really, for this I should have set up the blackboard, but we didn't. That's all right. Now you are looking here—this is what is. This is a complete circle. *[The teacher draws a circle in Student R's notebook.]* All right? Now you're looking here *[The teacher seems to make a mark below the circle.]* and you see, perhaps, you will see a portion of that circle, correct? *[The teacher gestures toward the lower arc of the circle and then draws several lines between the mark below the circle and the circle.]*

Correct.

Well, if you understand that you are—your reality is what you created by the panorama of limits, the movement of limit, if you will understand that, then you will understand that this here, *[The teacher appears to again gesture toward the lower arc of the circle.]* and this perception thereof, is what you have created. Now if you move yourself over here, *[The teacher marks a point to the right of the circle.]* and you're perceiving it this way— *[He draws several lines radiating from that point on the right toward the circle.]* See here? And perceiving it that way, you still see half! Correct?

Correct.

All right. Now if you move yourself over here, over here somewhere, *[The teacher makes a mark to the left of the circle and draws lines between the mark and the circle.]* forty-five, you still are seeing half. Correct? Do you understand that?

Yes. [Student R responds.]

You understand you're seeing half?

Yes.

You're perceiving half. Now put yourself up here, you see. *[The teacher makes a mark above the circle and draws three lines between that mark and the circle.]* And it's still half, isn't it? You've got to accept the Law of Personal Responsibility and put yourself right in there. *[The teacher makes a point in the very center of the circle.]* Now it's whole. Because, you see, that's what you are. You see, you are not what you are perceiving. You are not what you are creating. You are the creator. You see here? *[The teacher turns his notebook around and places it in front of Student B, so the student could clearly see the diagram.]* See, that's what you are. So you can only see from outside half of what you are. You must go inside to have the awakening of what you are, the fullness of what you are. You cannot, it is not possible to perceive the fullness of what you are, for what you perceive is ever in keeping with the illusion that you have created.

But it's still 135 degrees. [The teacher laughs.] *Even if I'm in there, it's still 135 degrees, isn't it?* [Student B questions.]

No. No.

That's full?

No.

No?

No. No. No, there's no way possible. There are no degrees. Degrees is what we have created. It's an illusion. It doesn't exist. I give you angles and perspectives of what you have created. *[With his pen, the teacher points to the marks outside of the circle.]* That is an illusion. What you are is right there. *[He points to the point at the center of the circle.]* That's what you are. *[The teacher may be pointing to the center of the circle.]* You are the circle. You are—on the inside, you are aware that you are it. When you move outside of it, you look at it and believe you're it and can only see a portion thereof. Do you understand that, [Student Y]?

Yes.

You see? You see, you cannot awaken to what you are, what you truly are, as long as you permit your identification to be in illusion. *[Student R reclaims his notebook and adjusts it so that it is now directly in front of him.]* Oh, I gave this to you, I think, long ago. This, these triangles right here. *[The teacher retraces some of the lines going toward the circle.]* I think I gave those to you long ago.

Uh-huh. [Student R responds.]

You must enter—you know, so many of you—talk to the mind about entering the void and the first thing, the first reaction you get is a terrible fear because the void is not something that there is reference to in the world of illusion. Do you understand that? So, you see, unless you have reference, you have a relative experience, you see. What happens is you leave the realm of gravity. And when you do that, you no longer have this division in consciousness; you are no longer individual. Yes. Yes, [Student Y].

So, so you're, you're actually completing the circle by moving within. The circle—

Why, yes, because, you see, how you see yourself is ever dependent upon the illusion that you create. And that illusion that you create is ever dependent on your belief of your experiences, which in truth are the movement of limit. Yes. Does that help with your questions?

Yes.

Yes, [Student O].

Would you give us, if there is a correlation or relation between the dimensions and liquid, solid, and gas state?

The correlation? Didn't I—

The dimensions. I mean, like if . . .

In what respect?

Is a gaseous—OK. We perceive in dimensions. All right. Is a gaseous a third or fourth dimension?

Oh, I see, I see what you're asking. Third.

Third. The gaseous. And the liquid?

Second.

And the solid?

First.

OK.

You are counting from the bottom, aren't you? Hmm?

I don't . . . [The teacher laughs.] *OK.*

Yes, but now I don't want to move too, too quickly for you. And I don't want you to waste energy in the obstruction. *[The teacher reaches for Student R's notebook, which is handed to him along with a pen.]* So let's put a circle around here. *[The teacher draws a circle in the notebook that seems to encompass his first circle as well as the various points of perception.]* It's not such a nice circle, but it is a circle. It's a circle to your eyes. All right. Where are we going to move here? How do you get inside of something that you believe that you are by the limits of the experiences you have created? *[Starting at the lowest point outside of the first circle, he seems to redraw the different lines of perception. He then redraws the lines to the right of the first circle. And then moves on to the point above the first circle and redraws those lines.]* How do you get inside? Hmm?

[Reddy, the church's dog, who is off-camera, seems to step on the teacher's microphone cable, which gets the attention of the teacher.]

Hello? *[The teacher seems to address Reddy. The teacher readjusts his microphone cable.]* Yes.

Now that's what we, that's what we have to work with here. *[The teacher redraws the lines from the left of the first circle. And has now redrawn the lines from all four directions.]* See, you have north, south, east, and west. And you know that you have to travel along the eastern path in order to have the obstructions removed. They do not exist as you face the Light.

Now when you do your meditations daily, which you all—from this day on it's absolute: it has to be done. And so we won't go into that. We'll just put someone in your world to monitor it, and check every single student when they enter the door. So we won't waste any time on that. Hmm?

Now the question is, How do you enter what you are when what you believe that you are, so much of it you fear? Hmm? Yes, [Student O].

OK. We, what we believe we are, we're, we're solids. I mean, we're pretty solidified in it.

Yes, that's a solid. What you believe you are is very solid. Yes, yes.

So—

That's correct.

So—

Yes, you're on the right, you're on the right path there.

Well, you've been telling us we have to break it down.

Yes. You must change the molecular structure of that which you have created. Yes. And I have shown you how to change that molecular structure. And I have given you the different breathing exercises, which are in truth changing those molecular structures, when it's properly done and it's done consistently, daily.

Yes, sir. OK.

Yes?

OK.

I've shown you how to move it from a solid to a liquid into a gas. Yes.

Yes, sir. And that's, that's far as I done got. I mean, I, in my under—in my knowledge and understanding of the teachings.

Well, you see, we cannot awaken to what we truly are until we make the effort to go through that process of changing the molecular structure of the limits that we have already created and that we believe that we are, you see. Yes, [Student N]. [Student N] has a question back there.

Oh, I was going to say through—you asked us how do we enter what you are when we, when what we believe we are we fear. And my answer to that was through faith.

Correct. That is correct. That is correct, [Student N]. Through faith. It's available to us there.

When—some of my students have had the experience—when you begin to enter the void, how do you feel? Hmm?

Insecure. [Student R responds.]

Insecure. Insecure. Now why does a person, when they begin to enter what they truly are, experience insecurity? Yes, [Student Y].

It's unfamiliar to what we've been in.

And that which is unfamiliar?

Is something we can't control. [Student Y continues.]

Correct. So this reveals to us that our water center, and that which is created in it, is dependent upon what the mind judges it can control. And we judge we can control whatever we make effort to become familiar with. Why do we judge we can control that which we make effort to become familiar with, [Student Y]?

Why do—would you please repeat the question?

Yes. Why do we judge that we can control whatever we make effort to become familiar with? How does that work? It's very important that you should know. Pardon?

I, I don't know.

Thank you. [Student L].

I think you become, you become it. And when you become it, you understand it and know what to do with it.

Well, that's so nice and sweet, and I wish I could say that's true. Thank you. Yes, [Student O].

Because, I guess, we have the knowledge that we know we're creating it there and we judge that it's ours.

I wish that [were] true, too. However, let's say this: we make effort to become familiar with something or anything or anyone that we first judge has a weakness that we must study so we can control it. That's how our minds work. That's how the mental world works. So we become familiar in the sense of studying and ever watchful of the slightest weakness. And, of course, the

weakness is ever in keeping with how superior we feel that we are. Do you understand that, [Student Y]?
Yes.
Now we understand why familiarity breeds contempt. Hmm? *[The teacher laughs.]* Oh, I have your notebook! No wonder you're almost asleep. *[The teacher addresses Student R and returns his notebook.]* Pardon me.

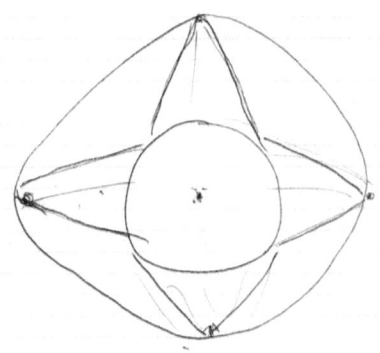

[Figure 40.1]
[The image above is a copy of the actual drawing.]

All right. Now are there any other questions here today? In your world this so-called illusion of time goes so quickly. Hmm? Yes.
I'd like to know what center the east corresponds to.
What center would you place it in?
The air.
Far beyond that.
Oh, then way at the top with the Light? The celestial.
Uh-huh.
OK. Thank you.
Forms created in the water center, known as judgments, are ever on guard and ever watchful of what's going on in the air center. So as the Light in its decent into form enters the water

center, the forms from the water center, that we believe at times we are, immediately, *immediately* remove as quickly as possible what is not in keeping with what they judge is in their best interest. Hmm? Yes, [Student J].

Since the breathing exercise changes the molecular structure of a thought—

It does.

When we're, during the course of our day, encountered with an important thought, important to us, should we then immediately, prior to forming some kind of a judgment about that situation, do that breathing exercise nine times? And then consider the situation.

Correct. Because you will at least experience what you understand as a double thought or a contrary thought, for you will have two forms: one from the water center and one being created within the consciousness through the faculty of reason. So then you must make an intelligent decision.

What would be the time factor? Say you're in a group of people or [with] another strange person and we can't just immediately go ahead and do that breathing exercise. What time-frame factor would be beneficial for something like that?

Most important would be a stillness of the mind, of course, and of the body, because when, with the—the mind is not still if the body is moving. You understand that. So an absolute stillness of the mind and body, and an honesty with one's inner being to awaken in consciousness to the forms that are appealing to their forms. Now, how does that experience take place? Well, you can always do a breathing, without anyone—[when] you're exposed to other people, uninitiates, you can always do a slow breathing so that you can gain a little awareness of the forms that are appealing to your water center. Yes. And then you won't be easily sold. Hmm?

Thank you.

Yes. But you must be perfectly still. You can smile or you can look out the window, but you must be perfectly still in consciousness. Uh-huh.

Thank you very much.

And then you'll be aware of what's in the atmosphere that is affecting you.

When we do this still breathing, should it be through the left nostril?

No. You—

No?

No, it should not when you're—no, no, no. It should not. When you're doing that particular breathing, I'm giving you now, as you say, you're exposed to uninitiated people, then you breathe very slowly through the mouth. Just open it a teeny, little bit and exhale through the right nostril.

The right nostril.

Yes. Now you control that by your mind, you know. You see, so many people make little or no effort to control their breathing, and their breathing is then controlled by the magnetic influences on creation, and the North Pole. And as the tides flux and flow, so does their breathing. So they are then the victims of creation, for they believe they are creation. They become the victims of the whole creation. So most people do not and cannot—they think they cannot; of course, they can—adjust their breathing. Because [when] you get yourself emotionally upset, you'll see what happens to your breathing. Yes.

When one does their affirmations in a crowded place—

Uh-huh

—and say one has the ability to switch back and forth in the nostrils, is it not in one's best interest to use the left nostril?

It's not in the best interest—

In a crowded room?

No, it's not in the best interest.

Should—then should one breathe through the right nostril? And when doing one's affirmations in a case like that?

Uh-huh. When you're exposed to that much in the atmosphere. Yes.

Taking it one step further then, is it not beneficial to breathe through the left nostril consciously in a crowed group?

There are times when it could be beneficial; those are rare. You have to sense the basic feeling or vibration of what you have exposed yourself to. Yes.

Then I take it—am I to assume, then, that breathing through the left nostril consciously should be very carefully done in select places?

Oh, yes, it should be—one should use great discretion with it and discernment. One should definitely use discernment with their spiritual exercises.

Particularly the left nostril.

Particularly. Certainly.

Thank you.

That's how the forms enter. Yes.

Thank you.

Air. Yes.

In a spiritual class, when we're in our class here, is it advisable, then, to breathe through the left nostril? [Student S asks.]

Well, I'm not afraid of you, so I, *[The teacher laughs.]* so I don't have any problem that way. And my channel doesn't have any problem that way. You see, when one is in a spiritual class, such as you are here today, the forms that are extremely detrimental, effort is made to remove them from the class before they have an opportunity to totally pollute and contaminate you as students. That consideration has always been shown to you, as students. And as recent as just an hour or two ago, I left and Isa and the workers tell me they did great work here for your sake. Is that correct? *[Isa Goodwin is Mr. Goodwin's mother. She was a member of the Spirit Council that governed Serenity and through Mr. Goodwin's mediumship, she would guide, correct, and expose the students.]*

Yes.

Not that I doubt my assistants, but great work was done. The entire decontamination squad came in for your protection. So, you see, the question of whether or not a breathing [exercise] at these particular classes is truly begging—considering the evidence reveals that phenomenal effort is always made to bring in the decontamination squads and remove those forms from the atmosphere so that you would not be exposed to them. Yes.

I think what I was really asking and wanted to know is if breathing through the left nostril would make us any more receptive to the teachings.

Of course, it does. It makes you more receptive to the forms in the atmosphere, and this is why such great effort is made in your private classes to see that those forms are removed so that—there is a responsibility, not only of myself, of my channel, and all our assistants, to see that those forms are removed before a class goes into session. Don't you feel that there was great effort made in the years that you have been here to see that those forms are removed? Now, if you have those forms prior to class, it's more difficult. If you have them after class is over, then it, of course, is more difficult. But you may be rest assured here at this table and working with you in these private classes those forms are removed. Did you not have some of that experience this morning?

Oh, we certainly did.

Uh-huh. Well, you see, you were being considered as students, what was fair and equitable for your efforts in being students, that those forms be removed and not be here with these spiritual teachings in class. Do you understand? Yes. Yes. So, yes, you are more receptive, of course, when you are breathing through the left nostril. *[The teacher drinks from his glass of water.]* Might want a little water on that. Yes.

Yes. OK. I've been breathing; I've been taking in air through my mouth.

Yes. Your cleansing breath.

In my cleansing breath.

Yes?

And should I be, should I be, would it be more beneficial if I do it through my nose?

No, the cleansing breath is the cleansing breath, and it serves a wonderful purpose. And one should do their cleansing breath every day, many, many times a day. Because the more you do your cleansing breath, the better off you're going to be. It's the ones not doing their cleansing breath that get trapped and can't get themselves out.

Yes, sir.

Yes.

When, I was, I was—what is it in reference to us breathing through our nostrils then?

Well, we're talking about another exercise, [Student O]. Hmm? Yes. And I have given you, I think, if you will please check your notes—you do have a lot of notes on the breathing. Hmm? That you should consider that. You were given that.

Through my, for my nostrils.

You were given that.

I'll check.

You weren't given that?

No, sir.

No. [Other students also respond.]

Hmm?

Some students were, sir. [Student J comments.]

Some students were, yes.

I think the question dealt with the exhale, though, on the cleansing [breath]. Not the inhale. [Student S remarks.]

Oh, I see. Yes, you were given the exhale. Is that correct?

Yes, sir. [Student O responds.]

I see. All right. Well, now as we gain more control of these forms, so they don't get polluted anywheres near our classes, then we'll move on to—I think, perhaps, you're speaking of the power breath, some of you, are you? Yes, all right. Coming along. Now be grateful for that. Seems to be rather a low-energy vibration here. I mean, the forms have been removed, but now we have this, ugh, *[The teacher makes a sound that is difficult to transcribe.]* terrible form. I think we ought to work on that. Hmm?

Now let's have questions in what little time here is left in your world, so we can move right on. Yes, [Student B].

Then you drew a big circle around that.

I did indeed.

And is that the big sphere that we talked about in one of the real early classes?

Yes. That is the larger.

It's—OK.

It is.

OK.

Yes, it is only, perhaps, difficult—the only difficulty in the perceiving and the understanding is—you try to understand the years that you have looked at a flat, two-dimensional world. And as you make effort to perceive a three-dimension or a fourth-dimension, then you will have a greater understanding, because you will have a different perspective. Yes. Do you have a question, [Student R]?

No, sir.

Yes. Well, I'm not finished with class, yet, so this sleepiness [will] have to go away. Yes.

I have one question here that I haven't asked, but I, I don't know if you answered it or not, but you—

Well, I don't know if I can either, [Student O]. I'll have to check with the, with the Light that I serve. Yes.

Right.

I'm sure that they can, if that's in order. But I will check to see if, if it's possible that I could merit learning that. Ask your question, please.

Yes, sir.

Yes.

What I was saying is I thought you, maybe, done answered it already.

Oh, I see! Might have answered it already. Ask it anyway.

Yes, sir.

We'll see—

Yes.

—if you've done your homework.

Is a center of consciousness at one position on a two-dimensional view is in a total different position on another center of consciousness?

Well, now, *[The teacher laughs.]* I understand your question. You want to know its position. Well, its position is dependent on your perception.

Right.

Do we understand that? You see, for example, when you perceive something, that's its position, right? Then you move and you perceive it differently and the position changes. Correct? So ever in keeping with your perception is the position, for *you* have created it.

Right.

Hmm?

Yes, sir. OK.

Yes.

OK. In, in, on the bow tie—

Yes?

OK. On, on the two-dimensional—OK. We have three triangles.

Correct.

OK. The, the way I understand it, the earth, OK, the earth, fire, and water—

Yes?

—is clockwise. They, they [are] moving in a clockwise—OK. And then we have the counterclock—now which one would be the counterclockwise? And then back to the clockwise?

Yes.

That's what I'm trying to figure out.

I see. And did anyone else perceive that from that class, [Student U]?

It is my understanding that the earth center went clockwise.

The earth center does go clockwise. Now I'll be right back. Pause the camera for a moment. I'll be back in a few moments. *[The video camera stops recording. When the teacher returns, it is turned on.]* Is it on there now?

Yes, sir. [Student R responds.]

All right. [Student U], you were explaining, because we want to move on with that so we can conclude our class today. It's running quite long. You were explaining to the class the earth center is moving clockwise. Did we all understand that? I like to have all my students understand from their notes. Yes. Do you understand that? *[The teacher addresses Student S.]*

Uh-huh.

You did understand that. You do. All right. Now go ahead. *[The teacher now addresses Student U.]*

The fire center is moving counterclockwise. [Student U continues.]

Yes.

And the water center is moving clockwise.

Yes.

That pattern is repeated through the other six levels of consciousness.

Yes.

There is a rotation as we move around the triangle, from, going up the levels of consciousness—

Uh-huh.

—of a clockwise movement.

Yes.

From earth, fire, water, around the triangle there's a clockwise motion.

Yes.

Now—I didn't—if that answered [Student O]'s question . . .

That answer your question, [Student O]?

Now, what I'm—OK. Are you saying that—OK, those centers stay stationary and, and we are moving through these centers? I mean, we're—

That which you truly are is moving through those centers. Correct. Yes.

OK. All right.

That which you are. Yes.

OK. OK. That which we are. So all I'm—well, OK, some is not going to stay the same, then. Something is going to change if, if somebody's—something is moving.

Uh-huh. Uh-huh.

If we're, we're moving—I thought that the triangles was rotating.

Uh-huh. That's correct. They are rotating. That is correct. So if you permit yourself to identify with the center as your river, that which you are, is moving, then you trap yourself by the force that is exerted by the movement of those centers. Do you understand that, [Student J]?

Yes, sir. [Student J responds.]

That was your problem—wasn't it?—this morning for you students. That through a lack of some of you students' spiritual, daily exercises, you believed and were bound by that very process, you see? That's what it's all about, [Student O]. Do you understand? You see, when you are moving the river, then you must accept the responsibility that goes with it. That responsibility is to do your daily, spiritual exercises daily. Without so doing, you will not be able to leave the centers that you trap yourself in. You see?

Yes, sir.

Yes.

OK. OK. I understand that some things we're supposed to be able to bring down on earth on, on the two-dimensional and, and be able to, like we draw angles, see it, so to speak.

Yes. You can see a part of it.

OK. Yes, sir. A part of it.

For two-dimension only offers a part of the whole.

OK.

A very limited part. Yes.

OK. Thank you.

You're welcome. Yes.

Could I please ask [Student U] for a clarification on what he said? Did— [Student S asks.]

Yes.

Did he say that earth, fire, and water were rotating clockwise?

Yes. See, my students have seventeen different interpretations of what has been given. Shall we spend the time to put it back and to go get our videotape to prove what was given? Go ahead. Go ahead. Because we're going to close our class here in a moment. We must close up.

I'd like to just ask him if I heard that correctly. I was trying to follow what you said. [Student S continues.]

I thought— [Student U responds.]

You have it here. *[The teacher addresses Student R and taps his notebook.]*

—that [Student O] was referring to the clockwise rotation of the centers around the triangle. With earth as the apex and fire in the lower right and water in the lower left, that movement, going up through the levels of consciousness, represents a clockwise motion. To my understanding. [Student U explains.]

Thank you. Just wanted to make sure I heard that. [Student S replies.]

Uh-huh. [Student R], did you have any question on that?

No. No question.

Yes, [Student B].

So it's the same with denial, [denial] is clockwise.

Yes.

So it stays the same? . . . clockwise. [Student B speaks very quietly and it is difficult to transcribe all of her words.]

Pardon?

Whether it's denial that we're in or is that like the last week's class? That was . . .

That's the spin.

That's the spin.

That is the spin. You see, it's like when, you know, in order to bring about a change, you must retrospin, you must do the direct opposite of what you have been doing. Now when a person finds themselves trapped into a center of consciousness and having great difficulty, then the only way to get out of the center of consciousness is to do the direct opposite with their forms, with their creations, with their thinking, of what they did, you see?

Now you'll go out the same way you went in, but you'll start a retrospin. You get out of something through a retrospin, and you get into something from a clockwise spin, you see. For the magnet is controlling the clockwise spin. Do you understand that? Magnetic forces. Electrical power is controlling the retrospin or the counterclockwise. So when you find yourself in something, as my student[s] [Student H] and [Student P] did this morning, when you find yourself in those conditions, trapped in those realms, you must do the direct opposite of what you have been doing in order to get out of them. Yes.

I'd like to ask clarification, then, because denial was given at the electric point. [Student S remarks.]

That is correct.

Then it is correct that it would have the counterclockwise spin?

Denial has the counterclockwise spin? What you deny you do not accept, do you?

Right.

So if you deny it, you push it away from you or you 'tempt to. Is that not correct? Yes, of course it has that spin.

So—

But your adversity becomes your attachment. So what you deny you in truth accept.

Right. But then wouldn't that be drawn back to you in the point of need?

Of course, it is.

On the clockwise.

Why, certainly.

OK. Thank you.

It's drawn right back into you. You see, you say, oh—you know, you see, you make a judgment and say, "I would never do something like that." Time passes and you do exactly what you said you would never do. Whoever says they will never do something only establishes the law to be sure that they do it. So, you see, you're working with these clockwise and counterclockwise spins. So that which you throw out from you, that which you resist, you in truth are attracting. But surely you students in creation know that anyone who resists your efforts and temptations becomes, surely, more desirable and a greater challenge.

Would you not agree? You know, the more a person resists, the more desirable they become. How does that happen? It happens through this: what I am giving to you, you see?

So you got yourself into something; then you must start thinking the direct opposite of—you know what you thought in getting into it. So you have no problem there. Now you've got to think the direct opposite of what you [were] thinking because you now want to get out. In other words, you've got to go through a retrospin. You've spun yourself into it. Whatever you get into is a clockwise spin and pulls like a magnet. And whatever you get out of is a retrospin. Yes.

I—in a diagram I drew for myself I discovered that counterclockwise—

We're running out of time. [Student R quietly whispers to the teacher.]

—was clockwise just by turning around 180 degrees.

Yes, certainly. Now I must say good day because we are running out of time of over an hour and a half, my cameraman tells me. *[The teacher begins to remove his microphone.]* And I wish you all a very fine week. I know that you will have one. And— Oh! I'm still talking. Well, I'll say good day.

Thank you.

MARCH 23, 1986

A/V Class Private 41

Good morning, class. Please be seated.

This morning is such a very special occasion. We'll begin our class with your progress and your spiritual efforts of late. And I wish to state, first, of the many affirmations that have been given to you, the most important in helping you through your present state of evolution are "The Laws Be" and "The Spiritual Environment." *[Please see the appendix for those affirmations.]*

Now I do wish to make a correction, as my channel, yesterday, slipped into error in respect to "[The] Spiritual Environment." [It is] "You are in a controlled spiritual environment." It is not designed to state that "I am in a controlled spiritual environment." The reason for that is an affirmation to assist you in separating truth from creation, from what you are and from what you believe that you are. So when you state it, as my channel has so religiously stated it correctly for so many years, you are speaking to that, when you say "*You* are in a controlled spiritual environment," you are speaking to what you believe that you are from what you truly are. Therefore, when you are, at times, plagued with these various forms, as man is the creator, you are speaking to that which you have created, that it shall obey you in keeping with its purpose of design.

Remember now, that forms are created by mental substance and you are the true support and controller of mental substance.

Now those two affirmations dissipate from your universe and from your aura the forms that you have created. They do so by separating truth from creation by placing you, in consciousness, in a position to control what you have created.

And I'm happy that you have these magnetic tapes. *[The classes were recorded on either audiotape or videotape.]* Magnets serve their purpose. Without them, there'd be no creation. And that you have those to check your notes with because I realize for some of you it may be rather fast writing.

Now, with your spiritual exercises and especially in flooding your consciousness, a flooding of your consciousness—I did speak to you some time ago about flooding your consciousness. Now what you're going to experience will, of course, depend upon your continuity of effort. And when you permit yourself to stop casting the Light that you are upon that which you have created, then that which you have created will seize the opportunity to submerge or drown you in the water center of consciousness.

Whenever you speak forth these spiritual affirmations, whenever you make the effort to do your exercises, be sure that you are in a vertical position, your form. Now you may contemplate and rest at a maximum 45-degree angle of your form. To go beyond that degree is to place you under the control of magnetic influences where the forms have been created and where they truly exist.

Now this ancient symbol of the cross [is] symbolic of the burden that man carries through creation. If you will note, the cross is two simple lines. The vertical line is, of course, longer than the horizontal line. When you permit yourself to believe that you need, you immediately place yourself on the horizontal line of magnetic consciousness and drown in the water center.

And while speaking on that, I also wish to speak on the one number that has not been discussed in these classes. You've gone through all the numbers, on through the 9 of totality. And you've even moved ahead in to the number of power of 11, the God above and the God below. We have not discussed with you here on Earth the number 10. Now first of all, to a mental world, what does the number 10 represent to the human mind? It's composed of a 1 and what else? [Student U].

A zero. A naught.

And what does zero mean to the mind? An aught.

Nothing.

It means nothing. That is correct. And so to the mental world, the number 10 is the oneness of nothing. That's what it is. However, to the Light, what the mind conceives as the one of nothing is in truth what you are. You are the no-thing perceived as something in keeping with your own perspective.

Now in keeping with the class[es] you've already had over these past weeks, [Student R], what is the definition of eternity? *[After a short pause, the teacher continues.]* What is the definition that has been given to you as a class of eternity? What is eternity?

That's what we are.

Yes, but there's a specific definition been given to you. [Student U]?

That is, eternity is what we perceive we are.

Thank you. [Student B].

A complete circle.

A complete circle. Our perception, as I have given to you before—do you have the answer? Our perception of infinity is what, [Student R]?

Our perception of infinity . . .

Is eternity. That's what we are. We are eternal. And that eternity that we are is our perception of infinity. So as we perceive infinity, we experience eternity.

I've also spoken to you about the flatness of a two-dimension. When you place your consciousness in the horizontal position, you are two-dimensional; you only see two-dimensional. Now how does one place themselves in a horizontal consciousness? Quite simple. Usually that's where one is because one believes in keeping with one's references, which are dependent upon one's experiences; and therefore, what you are not and can never be you believe that you are.

Remember, the teachings you are receiving and [which are] expanding your consciousness are only a bit confusing to a two-dimensional consciousness. It's time, after all these many years, to move you beyond this flatness of a horizontal consciousness into the vertical perception that you may know beyond a shadow of any doubt what you are, why you are, and who you are.

Now we'll take just a few moments this morning for some of your questions. Do you have any questions this morning, [Student J]?

Yes, sir.

Oh, you have your extra eyes this morning. Good. *[In an earlier class, Student J was unable to read the questions he had written because he had forgotten his eyeglasses.]*

Yes, sir.

My channel usually has his, though ofttimes he sees better without them. Yes.

Yes, sir. How does one change the spin when entering into the vortex or into the magnetic, how does one change the spin from clockwise to counterclockwise to reverse entering, to reverse to get out?

Correct. Friction. Friction. Friction. The way out of a thing is the way into a thing. Now try to understand that we go into a clockwise spin through a friction, and we move our self into a counterclockwise spin through a friction, the direct opposite movement in consciousness. For example, a person is thinking and from that thinking the result is a disturbance in the universe that they are not happy about. And they want to move out of that, that they, like a magnet, are being pulled into.

Now remember, whenever you enter this vortex, you must realize that you are entering it through the magnetic field of consciousness. Objectivity exists as an electrical vibration; it is a positive vibration. It is electric. In other words, when you experience the entering, you are literally being magnetically pulled through the water center.

Now, for example, let's put it into experience. You have an increasing experience that you find distasteful. To what is it distasteful? It is distasteful to the created form—that is the thought that has been created—and that thought form is what is disturbed and is not happy. Because the experiences that that form is encountering and is being pulled into—remember the form is created in a magnetic field of consciousness. That's a magnet. That's why when you're pulled into these experiences, you're pulled in by the form that you have created in the water center of consciousness. Therefore, if you will realize that and pause for a moment, you will understand and you will experience that it is only your emotions that are being affected. The emotions are being affected, which reveals to anyone that that which they have created in their mind is created in the water center of consciousness.

Being created in the water center—for example, all judgments are given birth in the water center of consciousness. And what is a judgment? A judgment is a thought that has been formed and solidified by belief that it is what we are. All right? So we have a thought and we have a feeling, we believe we have a feeling, for the thought is formed in the water center of consciousness. Then we have emotional feelings rise up, revealing to us that our thought form is solidifying itself into a judgment. Now we have created that to serve a purpose in our life. Correct? Yes, people create a thought form to serve a purpose. And we must understand its true purpose of design.

Now all thought forms are created as an effect of denial of what we are. All right? Now does everyone follow me so far? *[After a short pause, the teacher continues.]* We create a thought form as an effect of denial of what we truly are. Therefore, in the creating of them, they are cemented with the belief. You see, they contain all this magnetic. They're created in a horizontal consciousness. So the form is created. It goes out in the universe. And through that magnet is being pulled right in. And *we* get pulled with it, for we believe that it is us, for we have created it.

You see, what we create we believe—say that a person—now you take—[to] carry on with this, it's going to take a little while because I want it clearly understood. A person takes and they have a thought of creating, let us say, a chair. They have the thought of the chair that they want to create. And they see it in their mind and feel that that's what they would like to create. Now that starts to move to take its full shape in our consciousness. As it does so, we begin to experience certain feelings of our accomplishment that hasn't yet taken place. All right? We do that in business, too, don't we, in the material world?

Yes.

Of course. But I'm speaking of a chair. Because chairs are so important, you see, because it's a cushion for our foundation. *[The teacher clears his throat and many students laugh.]* Excuse me just a moment. I've warned you all about looking to see what's behind you, but so few people do anyway in the earth realm. Now, so we are creating this chair and we begin to feel, "Oh, that chair's going to be so comfortable for me. I just rest in that chair. I will feel so good in that chair." So we're now talking not just about a creating of a chair, we are now talking about the benefits that we are going to experience after this chair is completed. Correct?

Yes, sir.

And now from that, you see, we got about twenty other thousand things of what we're going to do in that chair. Some of them we're consciously aware of: very, very few. So now the true purpose of the design of the chair has been added to and totally contaminated. And if we're really in denial, we'll say, "Now let's see. I must make this chair a little bit larger because this person's going to be sitting in this chair with me. They have to be just this certain size because otherwise they won't fit. And I don't want that chair too big because I don't judge it'll look too well where I'm going to place it." All right?

So now we have the chair. We have our self sitting in it in this water center, you understand, in this horizontal consciousness. And we also have a little space for a certain person to sit there. Now we've already got them described in our consciousness. A certain height. Definitely a certain weight. A certain size. They got to fit right there. That's how much room's being allotted from them, and we don't want to be squeezed our self. So all of these different things are now being created from one desire: to have a chair.

All right. Now from that we start to go to work. Either to take the money and go out to the store to buy one or we may feel a greater accomplishment if we build it our self. Well, let's say we're going to build the chair our self. So we start through the process of getting the lumber and cutting it and all of this to build this chair [in] keeping with the design that we have made. Well, while we're in the process of building this chair and we're cutting the lumber and we're getting the cloth and the cushions and all of that, it would be nice if that was the only thing that was going on. But that's not what's going on. You see, all the reference, because that's hidden in the creating of this chair, all the reference of the people in our life that we have ever seen, had any involvement with of any kind now rise up to see if they are going to be able to fit in that chair. You see, because we made a space for one other person. So while we're making the chair, all of those forms are feeding off of our energy. Hmm?

Now we, at times, in making the chair, will perhaps hit our thumb because we hit the thumb instead of the nail because at that moment in charge of our consciousness was a form from the past who got very emotionally upset because back here in our mind *[The teacher gestures toward the back of his head with his right hand.]* we told him no, that space was not for them.

Do you understand that? Now all this is going on beneath our conscious awareness.

Finally, the chair gets completed. And we have fed all of these forms through the Law of Reference. And we find that we're sitting in our chair and there's no one there but us. And we don't feel well about the chair at all. There's something wrong. There's something missing. That space is not filled. So we go to work and we go to find someone, but each one that we find doesn't quite fit. Because all of the other forms, during the building of the chair, are activated and in our consciousness, demanding that that spot's for them. Now we create all of this. Do you understand?

So we're speaking now of this vortex. Through this magnetic spin, we go into that and there we are, and we're involved and we're trapped. Business, chairs, tables, whatever. How do we get out? The way out is the way that we got in. We have to free our self through a counterspin in consciousness to move from the horizontal plane of consciousness into the vertical. To do that it takes a counterspin in the consciousness. Now that counterspin will take place, for example, through your proper breathing exercises and especially through your affirmations that I've spoken to all of you this morning. You see?

You see, try to remember that when you have these experiences, you have trapped yourself in a horizontal consciousness in the magnetic center, the water center. And to move from that you must free yourself from identifying with the forms that you have created. And to free yourself, these, especially—of all of the affirmations given to you students—these two, "The Laws Be" and especially "The Spiritual Environment" affirmation, both of them, are designed over eons of time to serve the specific purpose of freeing the soul from that which they have created.

Now one does not escape, of course, their personal responsibility, but who on Earth is to judge that, in keeping with your personal responsibility, by saying your affirmations you have not fulfilled the Law of Personal Responsibility? So, you see, the benefits of doing your spiritual exercises and especially these two affirmations, if you will flood your consciousness with them, you will begin to feel them. And as you feel that which is taking place, which you truly are, these forms, you see, will not receive your energy. Therefore, you will not be trapped by them magnetically, and you'll not find yourself out of the vortex completely.

Now everyone has within them that which they are. And that's the power. And that's what does it, when it's properly applied. It will only work for you. It can only work for each individual. You cannot, in any way, affect another with it. You can only affect that which you are, you see, because that which you are will rise.

Now, you find something terribly disturbing in your life, terribly disturbing. And you want to move yourself from that. Immediately flood your consciousness with those affirmations. Especially "The Laws Be." For that is what you truly are. *[Please see the appendix for the complete text of those affirmations.]*

When you declare what you truly are, you identify with what you are. And when you identify with what you are, you are freed from what you believe that you are. You see? You see, you will not even experience, once fully flooding your consciousness, you will not even experience what those created forms are doing or not doing because you will not have any interest. Do you understand that?

Yes, sir.

And by not having any interest, you will move on in consciousness, and you will continue to evolve. For they have been created to serve their purpose and when they no longer serve their purpose, you understand, you no longer want them in your universe. Now when you no longer want them in the universe, because they won't behave anymore and they're doing what—you have designed them to do one thing and from a lack of discipline they're doing their own thing, you see. They, out in the atmosphere, they will find like kind, and they'll find another house. And they will find someone who doesn't care about what they truly are. And they'll go in and take up space in their house, you see.

You see, that should not be a concern of yours. That is an interest of mine here in these classes because, you see, I have a responsibility, and so does my channel, that those little wild ones running around loose because, while the students are in the temple, we have a responsibility that they don't come and be totally polluted. Of course, the law is the law. But we have a responsibility to depollute the atmosphere constantly and to correct that, you see, for they will rise up. And if the effort isn't made, they'll take control. And then those in the atmosphere, that someone else has driven out, they're out looking for a place to live. And there's plenty of houses that have their doors wide open and no one on duty, let alone on guard.

So that's what will do it. That will do it. You continue on with your cleansing breath. But, you see, you'll find yourself at times, it's just plagued and bombarded and you can't seem to get rid of it.

Now remember, the brighter the Light, the darker the night. So the more you do your exercises, the more you do your affirmations—and I'm talking about hundreds of times a day. I'm talking about being on guard right around the clock. I'm talking about the last thing you [do as you] lose consciousness you're saying your affirmations, especially those two: "The Laws Be" and "The Spiritual Environment." I'm speaking of saying it the moment that you awaken, the moment you awaken. I'm speaking of saying it all during the course of an evening. I'm speaking about, even when you're watching a movie, keep flooding your conscious—because you can watch and hear a movie and you can enjoy it. You'll find out how much you can enjoy it because you won't have all those forms in the way of it. Does that help you, [Student J]?

Yes, it does.

You see, because the more—you must realize, and I know you do, that in the universe of creation and form, there's a payment for all attainment. The payment that each student has to make is not paper. Not on a spiritual path. No, no, no, no. The payment that each student has to make is the effort from the wisdom of experience. You see, we've got all these experiences, and we finally rise up to the realm of consciousness of wisdom, you know. Because knowledge, you see, knows much, but after it's known all it's going to know it boosts us to the next step, which is called wisdom. And finally, we awaken in order to have harmony of any kind and enjoy life, that effort must be made.

You see, you have two choices as students in creation. You have the choice to remove yourself from the Light of the temple or to make constant effort. That is not something imposed upon you. That is something, in order to maintain your sanity, that is absolutely required. If that effort isn't made, then there is great, great question over the mental stability of any student. Any student. You see, the more that you receive of the Light, the greater effort must be made to control the darkness, you see. So you receive—and this is something that is being constantly monitored by the Light that I serve: that how much can be given to a group of students without any one student suffering irreparable damage from a lack of effort of the absolute, *absolute* necessity of their affirmations and their spiritual work. If that is not done and if the consciousness is not flooded, then mental stability of the student is in great question, of any student. Did that help with your question?

Certainly, sir.

You see, you see, it doesn't mean that you have to remove yourself from creation in order to remain on a spiritual path.

What it simply means is this is the first time in your world that this much Light has been given to students who have any time in creation. And therefore, this school is a much more difficult school in the sense of the mental world, for you spend time in creation, but you have the golden opportunity to separate what you are from what you create. You have that constant experience, you see? You see, you come into the Light, and if you come into the Light identifying with what you believe that you are and [are] not making the spiritual effort that is absolutely required for all students' sanity in this type of a Light, then there's no way possible to maintain what your world calls mental stability. It's not possible. Did that help with your question, [Student J]?

Yes, sir. Thank you.

So, you see, the uniqueness, in that respect, the true benefit is that teachings and the Light that have always been reserved for temples where the students are freed from any exposure to creation [are made available to you]. This is the first time it's *ever* been brought in your world in the midst of creation. Therefore, that which controls creation is certainly more challenged. I know my channel feels that "Why did it have to be right in the midst of the battlefield?" but that's really not the point. The point is that each student, their soul, all of you, through the eons of evolution, are strong enough to maintain mental balance, if you follow the rules. And that *is* the rules. If the rules are not followed, there is no way possible that we can blame or put our responsibility on to someone else. I've made it very clear, I think, to all of you: without those exercises, there will not be the continuity of what you understand as mental balance. Because, it will not.

The Light is a great challenge, especially when it's in the midst of the forest of creation. A greater challenge, indeed it is! Hmm? But who is it a challenge for? It's a challenge for each and every one of us for the Light that we truly are or for that which we insist on believing that we are. So the challenge in truth is really inside of our self. Each and every one of us. Does that help with your questions on that?

But you will find, if you do that religiously, when they rise up to plague and take control of you and you seem to become totally helpless, [and] you cannot shut them off in your mind—remember, they only exist in your mind and emotions; they're mental substance; they're not soul—and you cannot shut them off, it is because the affirmation, the flooding of the consciousness is not being done consistently and frequently. Hmm?

Now it's no big chore. What is the big chore to declare that which you are? "The Laws Be" that's what—that's what you are. "Spiritual Environment" that's what you are. Of truth and freedom. That is what you are. However, when you state that, you must realize that you are casting that which you are, the eternal Light, upon the shadows, that which has been created. And they're going to scream. And if you don't stay on guard, you see, then they'll come flooding in. And not only that, they'll bring all of the, all of the stragglers from old creation. From the streets and gutters of creation, they'll bring them all in with them. *[The teacher laughs joyfully.]* Yes, yes, indeed. They will. Because that's how they work. All right. Is there any other question on that?

Now if anyone feels that you have not received sufficient information in reference to maintaining your mental stability, I assure you, neither I or my channel will stand in the way if you choose not to continue with such an important step in your evolution. I wouldn't want you to feel that in any way you have been deceived. I have always stated that the Light is greater than a nuclear explosion. It is something you can't play with. There's no way that you can manipulate it. And if you will follow the rules, you will not lose your mental balance. If you do not follow the rules, it is guaranteed. The rules are quite simple: flood your consciousness. You even have the exact words in which to do it. And be on guard [of] changing any of them.

Hmm? Yes. [Did] that help with—all right. Someone else have a question while were working on this here?

Because, you see, you are receiving what is a direct threat to illusion. And because you are receiving that, that makes you an enemy of illusion. And whether you like it or don't like it, you made your choice to be in class. You are receiving what your soul has come for. And that which is created is not only threatened by it, it is determined to destroy it inside of you. You see? Inside of each one—determined to destroy that Light that is rising inside of you. So first it goes through all its temptations, and it knows all of our weaknesses. And it works on that. Try to understand, children, that I spent eons on the desert. That's why I'm grateful for a little ant. I see no difference between the angels and the ants. No, none whatsoever. Yes, [Student Y], please.

In the affirmation "The Laws Be"—

Yes.

—what does "Holy be the identity" . . .

"Holy be the identity." Now what does the word "Holy be" [mean]? Now let's say this affirmation.

> Our being is the consciousness truth
> Holy be the identity—

[As the teacher speaks the beginning of the affirmation, many students join him.]

The identity, now, is the indentation of the being into creation. Now do we want it holy or do we want it something else? Now when you declare it—now try to understand this: we all identify in order to maintain limit. This is limit. *[The teacher gestures with both hands toward the physical form of his channel.]* All right? Our mental form is limit. Our astral form is limit. Now in order to maintain a vehicle through which to express in worlds of limit in creation, in order to maintain that, we must identify. Do you understand? That is the law. There's no other way to maintain form without identification. All right? Without—creating a limit is the only way to maintain form. All right? Fine.

Now remember, in the creating of limit, in the creating of a form, it isn't just you [who] have created a form; you have called upon the nature spirits and all of those other entities that are responsible for the manufacturing process to create it. Now you are the superintendent of all of that and all those workers in the factory. And you'll really realize it when you go to leave your physical form, when the Isle of Hist separates, that's when you will realize it. For if you have permitted yourself to believe that you are the forms that you have created, the spirits controlling the water center, the element of water, will not leave. And you will have great difficulty in leaving the form.

So when you declare "Holy be the identity," you are accepting and recognizing that your identification is a divine principle and that you are using that which you have created. You cannot, and never shall, be that which you have created. Do you understand that? Now does that help with your "Holy be the identity"? It doesn't say my identity. It doesn't say [Student Y]'s identity. "Holy be *the* identity." Yes.

Thank you.

Any other questions? *[After a short pause, the teacher continues.]* Now let's go on with that. Yes.

Yes. You—am I correct in understanding that, that we are extract[ed] from the universe to create the form if—it latches into us, it identifies with—

Yes. You are responsible to feed it. Now, for example, look at the elements you have been given: earth, fire, water, air, and on through the varying centers. Now do you think that water just appears? There are nature spirits. That is their work. *They* are in charge. Those are the water elements. Those are the water spirits. Then you have the earth spirits and you have the fire spirits. And when you have all this upheaval on your planet, when you have these great earthquakes and volcanic eruptions, when you have [these] typhoons and hurricanes and all this great destruction, you have great wars going on between the nature spirits. Now those wars go on because—you see, the nature spirits also are the workers who keep our form together. Do you understand that?

Yes, sir.

You see, there isn't some so-called God that implants a seed and it grows automatically. That's the responsibility of the nature spirits. Now when the thoughts of man are so discordant and disturbing, they affect the vehicle that he is using—and the vehicle that he is using is manufactured, maintained, and sustained by the little nature spirits. Do you understand that?

Now when these nature spirits get all upset, representing fire, water, earth, air, etc., they start to war amongst themselves. And when a sufficient number war amongst themselves, you have this disturbance in the atmosphere; you have volcanic eruptions; you have all types of destruction. Do you understand? Now, you see, your ancient civilizations on your planet well understood the nature spirits and worked with them. They are intelligent and you are responsible for their care. So when you do not identify—"Holy be the identity"—with the vehicle that the nature spirits have created and you ignore their responsibility, you pay a dear price for that. For, when they get upset, they have no problem retaliating. They represent the elements of form. Does that help you with your question?

Yes, sir.

Hmm?

Yes, sir.

Yes. Now, you see, you want to transform something? Well then, first of all, you must first recognize and accept their existence, for they're the ones to whom you must speak in order to transmute lead into gold or anything else. You see, *they* are the servants for the fulfillment of the law. Yes.

So, you see, when you go to do something and things don't work out for you, well, you have disturbed the nature spirits, the vehicle that you are in. And you say, well, you get all frustrated and emotional. Why, certainly. You have directed more intelligent energy to feeding the element water, the water center, the nature spirits controlling water, than you have to the fire and the earth. And so certainly, you see. You've transgressed the law.

You see, the nature spirits are not the law; they are the servants of fulfilling the law. Does everyone understand that? You see?

Yes, sir.

All right. Now someone else had a question. [Student B] has a question here this morning.

Then the word holy, *is that, does that encompass the whole,* w-h-o-l-e?

Correct. That's right. It encompass—why, certainly. It recognize[s] and accepts the true purpose of all design. Therefore, it accepts "Holy be the identity." "This form is manufactured by the nature spirits. I am responsible to those who have manufactured this form. This form is not me. This is manufactured by the nature spirits. I am using this form." And when you declare that truth, "Holy be the identity," you understand—see, whole is divine, for it leaves nothing out. It's not limit. You see? Now you may spell *holy h-o-l-y* or you may spell *holy w-h-o-l-e*. Either way, that which is whole is all. That which is all is divine. Hmm?

So when you permit your mind—remember, your mind is controlled by what nature spirits?

Air.

Air! When you permit the nature spirits of air to receive more vital, life-sustaining energy by your identification with them at the sacrifice of your water element, your earth element, those other nature spirits get very upset. They're not getting their share of the meal. Do you understand that? And now you know how you are when you don't get your share and you have to sit and watch somebody eat five times as much as you get, and you got a little small portion. And you've finished and you're still hungry and they're still eating. Well, now remember, they have intelligence. They are intelligent. They are not eternal soul; they are creation and they have the element air, which is mental substance. They are not vicious. They retaliate. They experience rejection and they express retaliation ever in keeping with what they understand as survival.

So if you give less *[The teacher may have intended to say "more".]* energy to the nature spirits of the air, your mind, than you give to the water spirits, then the water spirits are going to be all upset. And if you give more to another element of the nature spirits, then you're going to start experiencing time-pressure: there's not enough time; there's not enough this; there's not enough something else. Yes, [Student S].

Do the electric and magnetic centers—are they controlled, also, by the nature spirits?

All centers are controlled by nature spirits. All centers of expression, you understand that, is the responsibility or the work of the nature spirits. Your form is only by the grace of the divine evolution and meriting the form that would offer you the most lessons, for the lessons that you have to learn in creation on Earth. And you have a responsibility to share equally with the various centers of consciousness, the elements, which are the nature spirits. And when you don't, then they retaliate. And if you believe that you are the nature spirits, if you believe you're the skin and bone, if you believe that you are that, then *you* will experience their upset. And the more you believe that you are the form, the more that you will experience, with all of its fullness, their retaliations and their rejections. Does that help with anyone's questions? Yes.

For the law is very just. It's ever in keeping with overidentification. Overidentification is selfish, a lack of total consideration, and those responsible for form in the fire center and the earth center, well, they'll just really retaliate for not getting their just share.

First of all, you must realize they are intelligent beings and they know how much you're distributing. And they know what the others are getting and what they're not getting. Now if you give those dessert and you don't give those dessert at the same time, then they're going to retaliate. Do you understand that? And if you're overidentified with the water center, when you go to leave your physical body—many, many of you, perhaps, are aware that some people, they just get filled with fluids and they can't seem to release those fluids. Well, there's an overidentification with the water center. And the water center is there having its feast, and the other centers of consciousness are starving. And there's a serious problem. This is why so many people have great difficulty in leaving their form, you see. There's an imbalance with the nature spirits. A total imbalance. Yes.

Is the dis—is the sickness pneumonia, would that be . . .

Well, you understand there's a problem with the air center, [these] air spirits. There's a problem with improper balance or energy: intelligent energy direct[ed] to that center of consciousness of which they are responsible. Hmm? In form, you see? Yes, any other questions on that? Hmm?

You see, first of all, you have the nature spirits to consider. Most of them, you see, the real gluttons of nature spirits are the water spirits. They gobble up more than anything. And if you'll look around you will find that more people get more emotional than they do pause and think. So, you see, they get a great deal of feeding, you understand, those water spirits, the nature spirits of the water. Yes.

You see, if you would make a little effort to study some of these so-called fables and stories throughout the eons of time, then you [would find] contained within them is these great truths, you see. But you must have the key of reason to unlock the door. Yes, [Student H] has a question this morning.

Yes. It's in reference—and this ties it in with what you were speaking about last week, when you were talking about the forms in water center are ever vigilant about any truth or Light that's coming into the air center.

Oh, yes! Why, certainly. You not only have the nature spirits to consider, you [have] got all of those forms that you yourself have created. Remember, they've all been created in the air center.

Yes.

You know, created in the air center of design and formed in the water center. You see? So here we have this great battle between the air center: what we think and what we believe. And so people have this battle all the time, you see. All the time they have this battle.

You know, so many years ago, you know, we weighed out, carefully, the advisability—so many students in those days, well, you know, there was always this thirst, this thirst of proof, you know, of our world, you see. And specifically of myself. And my channel, you know, he was so tired of hearing that over the many years, you know. And, of course, I had told him, "Of what import is it? Let us—if they must judge, judge the tree by the fruit that it bears." Well, we weighed out very carefully to see what would be in the best interest of bringing these laws to your world. And in all reason, the most detrimental thing that could be done is for us to bring you any sensational phenomenon to entertain the water center of consciousness, the very thing we are dedicated to free you through and bring some balance about. Yes. Does that help with your question, [Student H]?

Thank you. Yes.

Yes. Yes. Well, you haven't felt sleepy for a long time, have you? *[The teacher addresses Student R.]*

No.

Like that. That's, that's good. Yes, you haven't had flu for a long time. Don't worry. You'll, you'll recover. Yes. Yes, [Student S].

I'd like to know if friction and adhesion, if they're inversely proportional, like if you increase the friction, is the adhesion lessened?

No. Friction, if you increase the friction, you certainly increase the adhesion.

Thank you.

Yes.

I had a question—

That's how you get your attachments.

OK.

You see, you see, all you have to do, you see, is our adversities become our attachments. Well, what is an adversity? An adversity is a constant spin of irritation. You see? Until such a point [that] you become adverse to it. And the moment you become adverse to it, the next thing, you're totally attached to it. You see, instead—that's the principle of friction and adhesion. You want to adhere something, you want to be attached to something? Well, just direct a lot of energy to friction with it. You'd be amazed. Well, don't you know that, that people in—what do they call it now?—free relationships! I think it's a new thing in your world. I think it's called free relationships or free marriages. And if my understanding is correct, it implies to do your own thing, live under the same roof, and share the money. I think that's what it implies. But anyway, you see, there's a lot of, there's a lot of friction there, you see.

Uh-huh.

And would you believe that in free relationships, they call them in your world, and free marriages, they do their own thing and they're more attached than ever before? Don't you find that interesting? You see, here's all this friction and all this upset, you know, because of free marriage, you see. And there's always this suspicion, and there's always this question, and there's always this irritation and friction, and they become more attached than ever before. Yes. Go ahead with your question.

I'd like to know if it's correct that in the gaseous state that there's less adhesion than in the—

Well, it's more refined. *[The teacher laughs joyfully.]* Yes, yes, it's more refined. [In] the gaseous state you don't have the water, the water spirits to work with. Yes, yes, indeed. Yes.

Now remember, in working—I am aware, of course, over a long time, that there are those who have received some Light. There are teachers in your world, and in some of the other worlds that I visit, who have bargained with the nature spirits. Well, now let me tell you something about the nature spirits. Did you ever bargain with a three-year-old child? Hmm? *[Several students laugh.]* Now if you think you're going to get a good deal out of it, first—what do they call it in your world?—take a dry run, someone once said. *[Many more students laugh.]* Take a dry run with a little three-year-old and tell me if that's what you want to bargain with. Because you will always come out on the short end. I can assure you of that.

But, you see, now, think. So many people bargain, and they don't realize that they're bargaining until the nature spirits come in to claim what they have worked for. You see? You see, oh, yes, there is such a thing, of course, of working with the nature spirits of the earth, because that's where money [is]. And so when you permit yourself to bargain with that, you're going to pay dearly; you're going to pay a lot more than you get.

And when you permit yourself—you see, I told you there's only two functions that could take you out of the Light, your eternal being: those two functions are the earth center and the fire center. You see? That's the, that's the creation, that's the real creation. You see? That's, that's the solidified creation. Earth and fire: money and sex.

Now when you bargain with those nature spirits, you're bargaining with a three-year-old child, and you're going to come out on the short end. I guarantee you. You'll always come out on the short end because following those nature spirits, guaranteed, are the water spirits. All the emotions, you see.

See, study your senses. Understand creation. Creation is limit and form. There isn't some divine Light that just plunked you there on Earth, you understand. You have all of these mountains of workers representing—they work in the elements, you see. So when you turn to money, before you—to the earth center, to the nature spirits controlling earth, you see, when you turn to money, if you turn to it before you've turned to the Light within your being—if you do not turn to the Light first, if you don't put God in it, forget it, for you're bargaining with a three-year-old child, and you're going to come up short every single time. Whether you're bargaining with the earth spirits, the earth nature spirits, or you're bargaining with the fire nature spirits, be rest assured, you're going to come up on the short end.

See, when you put what you are first, then you can come to an agreement with the earth nature spirits; you can come to an agreement with the fire nature spirits. But you must put what you truly are *first*; then that is the Light. Those nature spirits respect the Light, for they do know, beyond a shadow of all doubt, without the Light, they would not only have no food, they'd have no sustenance, they'd have no Light. *[The teacher may have ended his statement with the word "life."]*

You see, the nature spirits governing your form, you must realize, only exist as long as you are in that form. Now when that form goes, they too go. They go to annihilation, back unto the source, the all source of old creation. So, you see, they hold on. They don't want annihilation. And if you permit yourself to overidentify with the nature spirits, then you think you're going into oblivion. That's your great difficulty in moving through this seeming void into what you truly are. Your nature spirits won't let you go through, because if you go through, they're petrified that they will lose and they will be annihilated. Do you understand? Because, after all, they're intelligent, and they've seen their buddies and their friends go to annihilation back unto the source when one of the forms passed on, you understand, one of the physical forms. You see, your only fear of death is your overidentification with the nature spirits in that water center. Yes, [Student L], please.

Then the void, the seeming void is actually the unknown to the nature spirits in your mind.

No, no, no, no. It's just the opposite, my dear. My goodness, the void, the great void is your freedom from the nature spirits, and it is the entrance through which you must pass to enter the Light which you truly are.

Oh, thank you.

Oh my, yes. It's just the reverse.

Thank you.

Yes. And so when there are changes in your life, when, you know, in your evolution, your nature spirits get upset because they get afraid. And if you overidentify with your form, then you experience their upset. Of course, you're responsible for them.

Thank you.

You see? But I realize, of course, that's not you. That's the creation. Yes, [Student D], please. Good morning.

Good morning. OK. The nature spirits are annihilated at death, but the form—

The death of the form.

Yes.

The physical form.

The physical form.

That's correct.

But the forms that we've created go on with us beyond our physical existence.

Into mental world and the mental nature spirits, the air spirits, continue on, [Student D].

I see.

But your earth spirits don't, for that's returned unto the source. You understand?

Uh-huh.

And then, when you are, when you have your so-called death to the mental world, then your air spirits, they return unto the source. You see? You see, people who, from lack of effort, over-identify with their form experience the nature spirits. Because they believe they are their form, they experience that which has truly manufactured their form and continues to sustain it as a physical limit, you see. That help with your question?

Yes. Thank you.

Yes. Time is passing quickly now. Are there any other questions this morning? Yes.

Do the nature spirits of the odic, ethereal, and celestial, then go on for a much longer period of time?

Well, yes, indeed, you see. Yes, indeed, they do. Of course. Because you stay there a lot longer. Your time on your earth realm is very short. It's actually numbered in seconds.

And do the spirits of the higher three levels ever help work on the ones of the lower, since—

Well, they do their best. They don't bargain with them. They do try to help them and to calm them in reference to their upset. The same as you would a little three-year-old child. But the angels from the realms of Light and the realms of reason, they will speak to them and be strong with them, be kind with them, and work to guide them into a little bit of reason for their own good.

And so you come unto the temple with these, of course, these many nature spirits, which you are tempted to believe that you are, and the Light works on those. And that's just the nature spirits. Now you have all the other ones that you create.

Now we have a lovely anniversary. *[The teacher may be referring to the anniversary of Modern Spiritualism.]* And I see the time is up; so you can have a very nice day. *[The teacher begins to remove his microphone.]* And I'm happy to see—oops, I always do that, don't I? *[The teacher refers to his practice of removing his microphone before he finishes speaking.]* Well, someday I will change. *[He picks up his microphone, which had been set on the table.]* You know, I'm not used to one of these things here. There. Good day. I will remind myself, perhaps, next time. There's many things—there's no justification for it.

MARCH 30, 1986

A/V Class Private 42

Good morning, class. And please be seated.

Now this morning we'll continue on with the class we had last Sunday. And we will specifically discuss what is known as the wandering soul. Whenever the vehicle, through which the soul, by right of design, is expressing itself and is denied the right of access by the vehicle, the soul is known, then, as a wandering soul.

Now fortunately, you have this all on magnetic tape, so you can always check your notes with the recorded tape.

So we find that each time we deny what we are, we establish the law through which our soul is sent to wander in the universe. And at times I have mentioned to you, some of my students, that you are not at home. Now the affirmations that have been given to you, as I stated in our last class, have been designed from eons of effort to help the soul to remain in the vehicle that, by design and the laws of evolution, it has merited for a time.

The declaration, "All things are possible," is the voice of truth and is the light of your soul, ever in keeping with that, by the right of design, you have authority to control.

Now we'll get to your questions this morning. So you may raise your hands, if you have any questions on what we are discussing. Yes, [Student U], please.

What happens to the water center nature spirits when a liquid is transformed into a gas?

Whenever a liquid is transformed into a gas, the water spirit, the little water spirits, the nature spirits, of course, they, in keeping with the laws of creation, they battle and fight for survival. And so it is that whenever you are communicating with an individual who is controlled at the time by the water center, known as the center of emotions, known, also, as the center in which all thoughts are created as judgments, and solidified, then you must realize that in the effort to bring the light of reason, you are instrumental in helping them to move from a water state to a gaseous state. Consequently, you must prepare yourself for what is known in your world as a battle. That help with your question?

Yes, sir.

Yes, certainly. Yes, [Student Y], please.

Where does the soul wander?

The soul wanders out into the universe ever seeking a residence through which it may express itself by the Law of Design and the Law of Divine Purpose. Yes, [Student L], please.

Is that how those souls that are in the, in the astral plane wander and try to get into the bodies of those on Earth? Because they're wandering souls?

Well, now you're speaking now in reference to another type of situation in which a person who no longer, from laws that have been transgressed, has a form or house through which, or vehicle through which they may express. In keeping with the Law of Evolution of the soul, it may find itself earth-bound in its effort to fulfill its true purpose in its evolution, to express through form or in a house. Consequently, that is true: some that are not as evolved remain on the earth realm ever trying to get into any house, which is contrary to the Law of Personal Responsibility and merit, rather than to make the effort to get into the house that they have merited in their evolution. Do you understand that, [Student L]? Yes. Yes, [Student J], please.

Since everything created has three parts—

Correct.

—what are the three parts?

The three parts of creation?

Yes, sir.

The positive and the negative brings about the balance of the neutral. Now for example, there are two parts to creation. There is *one* truth. There is *one* infinity. And that is known, of course, in your world as neutrality.

When you bring into balance the centers of consciousness, which compose the house of clay in which you are residing as a soul, an individualized soul, when you bring the centers into balance, then you experience what you truly are. Until the centers are brought into balance and kept in balance, then you experience what you are not. Experiencing what you are not is an effect, an effect of an imbalance between the centers of consciousness through which that which you are is expressing. For example, for each thought the mind forms, there is an idea which the faculties are ever attempting to express. And so if you will understand that for everything you create, there is a cause. So the cause and that which is created must be brought into balance.

Thank you.

You're welcome. Yes, [Student B] had a question, please.

If the mind is so in control that the soul can't express, does it go out, does it wander then?

Yes. Well, like in any law, you see, there is—you take the whole, what [is] known in your world as 100 percent, and any time you permit mental substance 51 percent control of the vehicle through which the soul is expressing, then the soul cannot reside. The soul must have 51 percent control of the vehicle through which it is expressing. If it does not have 51 percent of control of the vehicle, then it goes off into the universe to wander ever seeking a vehicle in which it may express itself. For its true purpose of design in its evolution is to express through form, to awaken form that it may, in so awakening, recognize and accept the source which sustains it. Yes. That help with your question, [Student B]? Yes. Someone else here has a question. [Student S], please.

Yes. I'd like to know what happens when there's a wandering soul and it's way out of balance, more than 51 percent of something else is in control.

You're speaking of the vehicle?

Of the vehicle.

Yes. Correct.

And what happens when that soul's spiritual bank account is zero, as far as divine grace? How do they get the help to get back in?

Well, there is where you have what is—one of the students asked a little earlier, in fact, it was [Student L], about these souls that are earth-bound and will accept any vehicle that they can get in. There is no divine grace left. Yes.

And then I'd like to know how do they work to eventually regain to the point where they should be.

That the soul may return into the vehicle through which, by the Law of Evolution, it has merited for its expression?

Yes.

Yes. Well, first of all, you have to understand that mental substance is the very instrument that has taken control over that which sustains it. Now by so doing, the soul is sent off to wander, as the forms created by the mental world take control over the vehicle. Now, you try to realize that as the soul is driven out to wander in the universes, there is still a connection between the soul and the vehicle, for the vehicle cannot live or survive without the sustenance of that which you are, which is soul, a part of the whole. Therefore, in reference to your question, How does it merit returning to the vehicle that it has merited in its evolution? it has to pay its debt for the sellout to the mental world. And I'm sure all of my students know who controls the mental world. Yes.

Thank you.

Does that help with your question?

Yes. Thank you.

Yes, it must work its way and pay off its debt. You see, for example, whenever one permits themselves to believe that they are the forms they have created, in so believing that they are the forms they have created they give control of the form through which the forms are created (they give control over the vehicle) and, in so doing, experience temporary satisfaction at the cost of building a debt which must be paid back with interest to the mental world. And that pay back is work in what is known as the salt mines of creation. Yes.

Thank you.

Yes, for without salt, there is no creation. Yes.

Is, is the soul or one of the, the term of the—is it one of the nine bodies?

The soul, that which you truly are, is that which sustains the nine bodies that the soul expresses through. Yes. The soul is not a body in the sense that a body, as you understand it, is limit or limited. That which you are is the Light. That which you believe you are is that which you have created. Yes.

So you, you stated that there—the soul is out there wandering, trying to find a residence. I mean—

Yes, for the residence that it was in. The one that it paid for, through its own merit in evolution, you understand. By denying what we are, we believe what we have created. By believing what we have created, we permit the created forms to take control over the vehicle or house that we have earned in our evolution. Now it's like a person, you see, you live in a house. You've bought it. You've paid for it. The mortgage is paid. And you're paying the taxes upon it in your earthly realm. And you're very satisfied that, whew, that debt's now over.

However, how would you feel if you left to go to the store and when you returned you found you were locked out, for a lot of aliens had come in and taken over your house, after you had paid the debt to purchase it in the first place? You wouldn't be very happy, would you?

No, sir.

All right. Now the soul is driven out by that very system. By permitting the mind, that which is created, to convince them that that is them, they are doing exactly that, as you would go to a store and return, and you can't get in your house for someone else has moved in and taken over, after you paid the debt for earning the house in the first place. Do you understand that?

Yes.

Yes. Now if you permit yourself—now this is what is so important in reference to [Student L]'s question—if you permit yourself—say, for example, here is your soul out here, and here is the vehicle through which it is able to express. *[The teacher first gestures to his left and then to his right.]* It's earned that house, that vehicle. So it has been driven out by these strangers, these aliens, that are in that house because you have permitted yourself to believe that you are the forms that your mind has created. Do you follow me so far?

Yes, sir.

All right. Now this connection here—to sustain that house, you are still connected to, but you are not there. It's like a thin cord that connects you to the house that you have earned, all right? But you are not living inside of it; you're out in the cold. Now if you permit yourself to become emotional and angry because strangers have moved in and taken over your house after you have paid for it, then your wandering soul wanders in the earth realms and will enter any house that it can get into because it's out in the cold. So you have to understand, when you leave your house and if you remain in a realm of consciousness, that cord that connects you to the house, if you remain in that connection through the water center, then you will become angry that someone has moved in and taken over your house and won't let you in. And your soul will wander in the earthbound realms. Do you understand that?

Yes, sir.

Now, however, if, in leaving your house, you have left it in that sense through the air center or fortunately and hopefully through the center of consciousness of the air center and through the light of reason, then you will come back to your house, you can't get into your house and you will go to work in consciousness, through this connection of this line, this cord that connects you to your house, you will work with the laws that you understand. And in so doing you will become an instrument through which the forms you have created can be driven back to the substance from whence they have been created, and you once again reside in your house.

Thank you.

You're welcome. Yes, [Student D], please.

How do we leave our house, if we leave it, how do we leave it through the air center?

You leave it through the air center [when] you leave it through the light of reason. For example, if you permit yourself to continually overidentify with the house that you are residing in, your mind and your body, then you cannot leave your house through the light of reason and apply the laws through which you may return. Does that help with your question, [Student D]?

Then if we identify less with our house, we go out through the air center?

Yes, if you will understand that your house, your body, is a form that you have merited in evolution, if you will ever remember that it is not you—it is something that you are using; such as your mind and your body, that it is something that you are using; it is not you, and by that declaration, you separate truth, that which you are, from creation, that which you are not—then you will leave through the light of reason, and you will return in keeping with that same law. Does that help with your question?

Yes. Thank you.

Yes. Yes, [Student Y], please.

How does one know when they're in the mist in terms of this? How—

When they're wandering?

What's the sign of whether you're—what would be the sign if your soul is wandering in the earth realms to, compared to—

Yes, yes. I understand your question. Well, the sign is very evident: it's known as the lack of reason. The denial of personal responsibility is an expression of the lack of reason. The lack of reason reveals to anyone that the soul is not at home; that it is wandering. Now the soul doesn't get pushed out by the forms and remain wandering as a set law. Some souls wander for centuries and for eons of time. Then in your experiences on your planet Earth, your soul may wander for an hour, a half hour, a day, a week, five weeks, six weeks, ten weeks, you see? But you must realize, the more that your soul is driven out of its house and left to wander, then it weakens the possibility of regaining control over the house that it has merited. Yes.

So . . .

Need drives the soul out of its house it has earned, for need is an effect of denial. And that is the destiny—the destiny of denial is the wandering of the soul. Yes. The destiny of denial is the wandering of the soul, that which you are. Yes.

I understand that. I also have one more question.

Certainly, [Student Y].

What is the first step, if one perceives that one's soul is in this process, what—and it's serious.

Yes, it is very serious.

Yes.

Yes.

What is the first step one can take if—the affirmations? Would that be—

Yes, the first step that one can take—you see, the affirmations that have been given to you is to declare the truth of what you are and to awaken to the truth of what you are not. So through the affirmations and an acceptance of personal responsibility—now try to understand that there is no light of reason when there is denial of personal responsibility. So when a person denies personal responsibility for all their thoughts, acts, and deeds, they are experiencing the lack of the light of reason. They are experiencing that which—they are not experiencing what they truly are, you see. What they truly are *is* the Light. The Light is reasonable. Therefore, when a person is not expressing the light of reason—and we know inside of our self—then try to understand: the soul is not at home. It is wandering. Forms created by the mind have taken over the house that the soul has earned in its evolution.

Now you may liken the takeover of your house to you[r] experiences on Earth. You leave the house [and] you leave the doors open. And people come in and they go to work—and how are you feeling today, [Student R]?

Good.

Thank you. The people come in and they take over your house.

Now there's one thing about what you understand as freeloaders: they like to share. They love to share. I think you call it sharing. What it truly is, is converting. Now try to understand people who take over someone's house pay nothing for it, take it over, and then they have all their buddies and friends—and the word passes very quickly that there's a free pad down the street, so to speak. Now if you will realize that what they are really doing, they're passing the word there's a free pad. They got there first. So by entering that so-called free pad, you are in debt to the ones who took it over. Do you understand that? So there's really nothing free at all about it. You see, it's not the air center at all. It's some other center of consciousness. There's nothing free.

And so therefore, the ones who heard about the free pad, so to speak, now move in. They're in debt to the ones who took it over in the first place, and so the ones who took it over in the first place, they feel better for they've now converted someone else and they have someone else to work for them when they want to call the debt due.

Now the purpose of the fall of the archangel known as Lucifer, his very existence is dependent upon conversion. Without converts, he cannot maintain and sustain his throne. He must have subjects, which he works diligently to convert. It's like a pyramid system, and he's up at the top of the realm below. He can only remain at the top and his throne can only get higher, as long as he can convert others; he increases his kingdom. Do you understand? All right.

Now that very same principle goes to work when we permit our mind to deny what we are and we experience need. We say that we need this or we need that. We will get this or we will get that, but it is not enough, you see? For the conversion process has just begun by the denial and the experience of need. So in that respect, the mental substance never ever gets enough, for it is, by its very nature, by its very nature, a pyramid system on which he who sits on the top of the pyramid must ever convert to make his throne even higher. Do you understand? Yes. Does that help with your question? Yes. Yes, [Student O], please.

Yes. So are we, we are, are we destined to return to this house and clean it up before we move on or—

Well, yes. Oh, yes, you must return to the house you've merited in evolution. Now if the physical house is long gone, then you have to work even harder because you've got to get in one of the other bodies that are left, still in keeping with the law. So, you see, just because the physical body leaves, you've still got the mental body. And you've got to get back into that house, for when they take over the physical body, it's because they've first taken over the mental body. Hmm?

Yes.

Yes. Yes, [Student H], please.

Yes. Back to what you were just talking about, the pyramid system—

Yes.

—Lucifer, and need. How does applied appreciation work on this pyramid system?

Well, applied appreciation is the Law of Gratitude, which recognizes and accepts personal responsibility, which, in turn, permits your soul, that which you are, to express its light and that's known as the transfiguration through the Law of Reason. Yes. You see? Be ye transformed through the light of reason. Yes, [Student N], please. Yes.

I was wondering when we're experience of—we're learning something new and we have—we're fighting ourselves. Is that judgments and forms being—somebody else being in the house at the same time when we're trying to learn something?

Correct. And it is contrary to what they desire, for they are interested in their own survival. So as long as you permit yourself to believe that that is you, you will have difficulty in making any change. The difficulty in making change—you see, the intensity of density, as [Student J] knows, is measured by acceptance. So if you find yourself in a density and a battle of these thoughts and forms that you have created, it simply reveals you are having difficulty in accepting, accepting the possibility.

Of change?

Correct. You see, a part of a person's mind says, "Oh, I want to change so much," while the other part of their mind fears and says, "I don't want no [any] change at all. I am secure emotionally in what I am familiar with." A person having difficulty with change soon realizes that they are overidentified with the water center, through which emotion and fear and judgment are expressing themselves. Hmm?

Thank you.

Yes. One does not make change easily, as long as they are in those centers of consciousness. Yes, [Student J], please.

In relation to the water center, what is the relationship between sugar and the forms created in the water center?

Well, yes, there's a direct relationship. And that's a— *[The teacher coughs.]* Excuse me. There is a direct relationship. Now, security to the mind is ever dependent upon the sweetness of experience. Now perhaps you could take note of that. I do hope you are. Security to the mind is ever dependent upon the sweetness of experience. And the sweetness of experience is as sweet as its service to our judgments. Now, for example, [say] you meet a young lady. [If] she services your judgments well, then she's sweet to the security of your emotions. Would you not say?

Yes, sir.

All right. Well, would not anyone say?! And so in speaking on sugar and candies and these other things, the human mind is designed, by its very purpose of design, to be an expert substitute. It can and does substitute anything to service the judgments that it creates. Do we all understand that?

You are not the human mind. You cannot be the human mind. The human mind is a copy. It is a substitute. In other words, if the human mind and the forms known as judgments it has created, if it cannot get it one way, it'll get it another. That includes a candy bar. Now do you understand the answer to your question of sugar? Pardon?

I don't—

[The teacher laughs joyfully.] Well, when a person permits overidentification with the need created in the water center and a person permits themselves to overidentify with that center of consciousness, then there are forms there who tell the being there's a need. A need for security. Now remember, it's speaking from the water center. Now to the water center, the security is the sweetness of experience. Would you not agree?

Yes, sir.

Well, now there in the emotional water center, there's a sweetness of experience with sugar. Isn't there?

Yes, sir.

A person feels, "Well, now let's see. I don't feel too good." So they get a candy bar. Would you not agree?

Yes, sir.

And for a short time, they feel better. All right. Now let's look at the chemical process that's taking place. Let's analyze that for a moment. When you permit yourself to believe that you are a need that you have created by a judgment, you change the blood sugar and the physical chemistry of your body. Now the chemistry of your body must be kept at a certain balance, and if it is not, you find yourself imbalanced, physically, created by the mental world, and you must bring about a balance. And there are many ways to bring about that balance. One of which, of course, is security to the mind, to the water center, by the sweetness of experience. Try to understand that the physical body reacts upon the mental body, and the mental body reacts upon the physical body. And there is a chemical change that takes place ever in keeping with our thoughts, our judgments, our identification to what they offer, which is our need. Hmm?

Now if you find that, at any time in your experiences, that the forms created in your water center that they can feel secure by sweetening your experiences in life in a certain way, then that's what you do. Hmm? And you feel secure for a time. Only for a time. When you permit your mind, in the water center of consciousness, when you permit identification with the forms and other people are not doing what your created forms say they should be doing and you've permitted yourself exposure and identification with that, then you must sweeten the experience in order for the chemical balance to be maintained and sustained in your physical body.

Am I speaking too quickly on this or is it beginning to relate?

It's beginning to relate.

You see, you see, because, you see, the mental body affects the physical body and its chemistry. The physical body and its chemistry affects the mental body and its chemistry. You see, there's a chemistry to the mental body. I know that it is not usually discussed in your world, but as sure as there is a chemistry to your physical body, there's a chemistry to all the other bodies. Well, without chemistry, bodies or limits do not exist. There is no such thing as limit or form or creation without chemistry, you see? You see, even your astral body has a chemistry. All bodies have chemistry. All forms have chemistry. Without chemistry, form does not exist. Yes.

Now the question is, What are the chemicals of the chemistry of a particular body and how to adjust it? Well, there's a part of you that knows beyond a shadow of any doubt that certain chemicals are—there are very little of them in your body. They're being drained and depleted. And so that part of you, that inner part of you, that knowing part, it will get those chemicals in the way that it can get those chemicals based upon its own experiences in life. Well, it's kind of like some men, they get very thin when they get married. Some women, they get very fat when they get married. There's a chemical change taking place ever in service to the judgments that they identify with. Hmm? That help with your question?

Yes, sir.

Yes. Someone else have a question? [Student B].

When the soul wanders, does it take these other bodies with it, like—

No. No. There is a—when the soul is out here wandering, it's like a thin thread. It's like a golden thread that's connected to the body. The soul out here is not in control. It views what's going on with its, with its vehicle that it's supposed to be in. You see, it gets to view it. It takes a look at it, you see, and it knows that it must get back in there. But, you see, that's going to take great effort on the part of the soul to drive out the forms that it has permitted to enter. Yes.

Is, is the soul a spiritual body?

Of course, the soul is a spiritual body. The soul is the covering of the divine, eternal Spirit.

So the chemistry is changed in this body.

Corr—

... form body, physical body— [It is difficult to transcribe a few of the student's words.]

That is correct. To such an imbalance that the soul can no longer reside in it. It only has a thin cord of connection. Absolutely. Absolutely.

And the astral body stays with the physical body?

The other bodies stay with the physical body. Correct. And that which affects the physical body affects the astral body, which is inside of the physical body, [and] also affects the mental body and the other bodies. That is absolutely correct. Yes. There's been such a chemical change that the soul is actually, literally driven out. In other words, the chemistry is not harmonious anymore with the soul. There's 51 percent chemical change. You understand?

Yes.

Yes. That's what happens. Yes, [Student B], you have another question.

It was on the chemistry of the soul. [The student speaks quietly.]

Pardon?

It was on the chemistry of the soul. Can—does the chemistry of the soul change—

No.

—when it's out there wandering?

No, the chemistry of the soul does not change. You see, you see, what happens is the vehicle—now try to understand this. The chemistry of the soul is ever in keeping of [with] an individualized soul and its evolution. Now the chemistry of the soul enters the chemistry of a mental, physical, and astral body in keeping with the laws that have been established in evolution.

Therefore, each person's chemistry is a little bit different—do you understand that?—as each soul, in that respect, chemistry-wise, is a little bit different. All right?

Now, so here's a form, a body; that [soul] enters at the moment of conception; the soul enters. Its chemistry is harmonious with that particular body. All right? For that chemistry is an effect of laws established. That is the suit that the soul may wear during its journey on Earth. Now if that chemistry is changed drastically by a person allowing the created mental thoughts, those forms, from taking over the house, then the chemical harmony between the soul, which has earned the body at the time, is so different, so drastically different, that the soul is literally driven right out. You see?

Now for the soul to enter again, the chemistry of that body must be changed. So as you create a thought and believe that you are the thought, you solidify the thought form into a judgment and the chemistry of the body changes. Did that help with your questions?

Yes. Thank you.

Yes, that's what happens. Now [Student H] was waiting for a question, please.

That explained my question.

All right, fine. It's very mathematical. It's very, very simple. When you look at it in the way that it truly is. Yes, [Student O].

You said that, stated, rather, that the mind is a copy or substitute of—but you didn't say of what.

[The teacher laughs.] It is a substitute. It is not what you are. It is a very poor substitute. And the mind, because it is a substitute, it will substitute anything in order to service that which it has created. Yes. It'll substitute anything and everything. Blind, crippled, crazy, or retarded, from nine to ninety, it will substitute anything in service to its own creation. Yes.

In service to its own—well, well, the mind must have some idea of—

Minds don't have ideas, but they do have thoughts and judgments. Thank you, [Student O].

Well, it must have some thought or, or judgment as to what it's trying to obtain or this feeling or this so-called feeling of the Allsoul. I mean—

Well, the mind is constantly, by its very nature, trying to absorb—it's a great sponge—and [tries to] control everything that it can absorb. Its true purpose is to convert. Yes. Just have someone disagree with you and see what happens to your mind. Especially if your mind has created a judgment that you're right. Hmm? And because you believe that which you create is you, then you have quite a time in the water center, wouldn't you agree?

Yes, sir.

Have you, have you never had your wife tell you that you're wrong?

Oh, yes.

Well, it didn't make you happy.

No, it didn't.

Yes. You didn't make you happy, because it didn't service the judgment that you had that you were right. Correct?

[If the student responded, it is difficult to transcribe his response.]

Well now, there you are, you see? It's a great substitute. Go ahead.

OK. Well, what's in control at the time is the most solidified judgment, right? What's in control of the mind at—I mean, something, something is, it's running and controlling and manipulating.

Why, yes. It's the servant of old creation. The thing that you aren't. And you know who controls creation.

OK.

You see, the king of creation, he's a wonderful loan shark. Now he'll loan you all these things you think you need. Hmm?

Right.

Once he's got you hooked, he'll call in the debt with phenomenal interest. Hmm? Yes, he's known as the greatest of all loan sharks. Oh, he'll loan it to you, and for a long time. Because the longer he loans it to you, the greater interest that you got to pay on the debt that you owe. Do you understand that?

Yes.

Yes. Well, now that's known as temptation. Yes. All loan sharks work through the principle of temptation. They appeal to your weakness, never to your light of reason and your strengths. They only appeal to your weakness. Something for nothing, you see.

Yes.

But the debt has to be paid someday. And when he comes to collect, he collects. And what is the one thing the king of creation wants from you? What do you think it is?

Service?

Absolute service. And absolute service can only be obtained from you by the king below when you are totally convinced that that is you. That's when you start paying your debt, with all its interest. So if you convince yourself you are denial, you experience the need, and you are tempted to serve the loan shark.

Now [Student M] has been waiting with a question.

Yes.

Yes.

The soul and the form are in harmony when the soul enters at the time of conception.

That's the only way the soul can enter, is through a chemical, harmonious vibration, yes.

Now as time goes on, our minds change and begin to believe what we are not. More denial, at times, occurs. There's—

Become overidentified with creation, yes.

Yes.

The indentation into creation. That's correct, yes.

As that process happens, our chemistry changes.
Correct. Your chemistry changes. Correct.
And when our—and when our chemistry changes to such a degree our soul leaves, through either the light of reason, the air center, the gaseous form—
Uh-huh.
—or one of the lower centers, be it water, earth, fire.
Uh-huh. Correct.
Now when the soul leaves through one of the lower centers, other than the air center—
Correct.
—to get back in—there's that fine line—to get back in, the affirmations are the way back in. Like, the way out is the way back in. But if the way out is through one of those centers, does the soul return back in through one of those centers?
I see your point. Now, say that your soul leaves through the fire center, all right?
Yes.
The way out of a thing is, is—the way into a thing is the way you got out of the thing. And the way out of a thing is the way you got into the thing. Vice versa. Now, that's the principle of it, not the personality or form of it.

Say, for example, your soul has been driven out through the fire center. There's been a chemical imbalance that has been created by your mind; the soul can no longer reside, and it leaves, at a time, through the fire center. All right. Your soul is out into the universes wandering, looking at its house [that] it's been driven out of. Through the affirmations you have been given, that is instrumental for you to rise in consciousness, through this thin line that is connected to the house, to rise in consciousness up into the air center and into the light of reason. You can do that through the Law of Objectivity; that's from the separation of truth from creation. Then your soul will reenter into the form through the light of reason, through the higher centers of consciousness, and you will see the transformation of the house. And you will say, "My, that person's entirely different now." Because that process has taken place.

Now for a person who, in their evolution, has not yet awakened to the process of how to exorcise the demons that have controlled their house, then they can be exorcised by someone who has merited, through the law in evolution—a driving of the demons out is known as an exorcism. However, the demons will only stay out as long as the exorcism process continues, for that's the change in the chemistry of the house. Do you understand that?

Thank you. Yes.

Yes.

Thank you.

Yes, [Student N], please.

Does the chemistry continue to change as you move up?

Why, yes—the chemistry of the house or the body?

Yeah.

Oh, yes, certainly it changes. It becomes more compatible with that which you are. The higher you rise in identification in the centers of consciousness, the more compatible your form is to that which you are, your eternal soul. Yes.

And then I had a question about the statement that was made, the higher the, the higher the rise, the—no. The greater, the greater the fall—wait a minute. [Student N pauses for a moment.]

It's all right. You have it.

The fall is never greater than the rise. [The teacher laughs joyfully.] *The climb. The climb.*

It's all right. We under—I know we all understand. "The climb is never higher than the fall." Is that the one you're referring to?

The climb is never higher than the fall.

Yes. That's one. All right. Yes.

The climb is never higher than the fall.

Well, if you climb with your mind in conviction that that which you create, your thought forms, are you, then you fall in that which you are, your eternal soul. Yes. Because you change the chemistry into more of the mental substance.

But if you rise in, in soul—

Then—

—and you sustain it—

That's correct. Then you find yourself less identified with limit and with form, and you experience, certainly, a more harmonious life.

Thank you.

That's what your affirmations are designed to assist you in accomplishing what you have just said. Yes.

Thank you.

You're welcome. Yes, [Student L], please.

In The Living Light *book on page 110 [in Discourse 39]—*

Yes?

—you speak of the lessons being dissected so that we can learn, then, because the mind is so filled with confusion and all.

Do you have the book—you have it before you there?

I'll read it now. "The pattern—"

This is the page 110?

One hundred and eight.

It's page 108. Yes. I don't see the book there, but I will accept your word.

I've written it from the book.

Yes, yes. Yes, I know. We must always be alert to the falsifying hands of the copyists, mustn't we, [Student L]? *[Many students laugh.]* Please read it off.

A portion of a sentence says, "The pattern—"

A portion?

"—will be complete—" Yes, it is not the whole sentence.

I see. All right.

"The pattern—"

It's out of context then.

"The pattern—"

All right.

"—will be complete before you leave your earthly shell, as complete as possible to your understanding." [The student misquoted the text. The complete sentence is, "The pattern will be complete before you leave your earthly shell, as complete as is possible to your present understanding."]

Yes, now the pattern you're referring to is which? This is out of text, but—yes.

Well—

What is the question?

That's what I was asking.

On page 108, what is the question?

The question is, Is it the pattern of the teachings that they're speaking of—

The teachings?

—or the pattern of the—

But you've read it out of text. I think, I think you should bring your question next class.

All right.

And read the full text from the book. All right?

Yes.

Because, you see, whenever we take something out of text, we are filled with implications, you see. And when we're filled with implications, we keep wandering farther from the Light of truth.

Oh, thank you.

Yes. Don't you think that's important, [Student L]?

It certainly is.

Bring your textbook. Yes. Hmm?

Yes, I will.

Yes. Because, you see, you're referring to a certain discourse that is discussing a certain realm of consciousness, and to take a part of that out of text and to apply it to this, when it could be very well applied and mean, very clearly, something entirely different. You want to read the discourse. And then, I think—for the benefit of my own students. That's why I asked you, "Is that the book there?"

No.

It's a new kind of book. I hadn't seen that one before. Yes, someone else have a question? Yes, [Student S] here, please.

Earlier you said that the physical body—

Uh-huh.

—was dependent upon the soul there for its . . .

Sustenance.

Sustenance.

Correct. That is correct.

So I'd like to ask, When the wandering soul is out—

Yes?

—then is there a great decline in the physical balance?

Well, there is, as I stated earlier, there is a connection of a thread between the soul and the body. Otherwise, the body, as you know it, as a being, a live being on Earth, does not exist. And, for example, as far as the chemicals are concerned, the chemicals are passed through the cord. You know, it's like a child, you know, in the embryo stage. And you have this little cord, and you snip that cord.

Uh-huh.

You see? Well, you see, prior to that it was feeding completely off of the mother. The mother's soul was sustaining that, you see?

Uh-huh.

And because, as the negative and positive poles come together, that's when the soul enters. The little soul, you see, enters the form. Now when that form comes out into your world as a physical form, it reveals to you that there is a cord between the source and the baby that's connected to the source. That physically reveals that. Well, you see, as above, so below; as below, so above in reference to the principle of the law. You have a cord also that connects from the source, that is, your soul, an individualized soul, into the form. And through that, the chemicals are passing. Does that help with your question?

It does. Thank you.

Yes. Now [Student D] has been waiting with a question.

Now this, it goes back to the water. You were talking about water and sweetness. And I've thought about the fact, well, on Earth there's, like, sweet or bitter waters. And salt waters and—

Water? Yes, may I, may I make one statement here in reference to water? It is my understanding we were discussing the sweetness of experiences in reference to feeding the forms and the judgments, which are created in the water center. Is that correct?

Right.

Is that my recall?

Yes.

Yes. I don't, I don't think that we discussed sweet and sour water, did we? Yes. Or sweet and bitter water?

Well, I, I was thinking about the fact that there are those kind of waters on the Earth.

Yes, there are. And so that would be a new question for discussion, wouldn't it?

Yes.

Yes. Yes, I like to kind of keep everything nice and clear so we don't get confused, as [Student L] was reading out of text, which was bringing in an entirely different perspective. So now the question is in reference to sweet and bitter waters of the planet Earth? Is that the question?

In salt and fresh with the—

Yes, there are salt—that's true. There is salt water on your Earth. There is fresh water. There is bitter water, and there's sweet water. What was the question on the waters of the planet Earth, [Student D]?

Well, I wondered what connections, since everything is interconnected, what connections there were between these waters and I was having a feeling about the centers.

Yes, they are, because the nature spirits are the ones responsible for the water center. But then again, I'm sure you realize that we have sweet personalities and sour personalities; and it's not restricted to so-called human beings. It also applies to nature spirits. They have the sweet little ones and they have the sour ones. A lot of sour ones and some bitter ones. Does that help with your question?

Yes.

Pardon?

Yes.

Yes. You see, it's very important that we maintain and sustain a perspective in our discussion so we do not become confused. You understand, [Student D]. Now someone else has a question that's been waiting. It was [Student U]. [Student U]'s been waiting and then it's—yes. Oh, time passes so quickly, you know. My!

Is there a direct relationship—

In your world. Yes.

—between the chemistry that's out of balance and the soul being forced to leave the body? I mean, the question—

Oh, yes, yes. When the chemistry of the body is changed to such a point that it is no longer harmonious with the chemistry of the soul, then the soul is driven out of the body. Yes. Now try to understand, as [Student D] has just asked, the form of the physical and mental body is composed and maintained and sustained by the nature spirits. All right?

Right. [Student U responds.]

See, man is the creator. These nature spirits create earth and fire and the water and all—now, now their responsibility is that chemistry. Do you understand that? That's their responsibility. They mix the chemicals and make sure that that maintains and sustains the body as the body should be sustained in keeping with the soul's chemistry at the time of entrance. Now if you take and permit your attention, through which this energy from your soul [is directed, to be sent excessively] into the water center, then you have a chemical change and an imbalance—do you understand that?—

Yes.

—in the chemistry in the water center of your body at the sacrifice of one of the other centers. That chemical imbalance—do you understand that?—is no longer harmonious to your soul, and your soul is driven out. So you have to understand that your thoughts and your judgments, formed and created, are feeding energy from the soul directly into that center of consciousness. Those centers of consciousness, their maintenance is dependent upon those particular elements of the water spirits or the nature spirits for the fire center, the earth center, and etc. Do you understand that?

Yes.

All right. So we must realize that as we create forms in our mind and we solidify those things with what we know as judgments in the water center of consciousness, we are upsetting the chemical balance of the mental and physical body. And then it becomes no longer harmonious with the soul that is feeding them. And the soul is driven out. Hmm? Yes.

Now can the soul leave the physical body in circumstances of harmonious chemicals—

Does it many times. Many, many times. However, an awakened, a person awakened to their soul does not leave their physical body without certain, what you would call in your world, protection. After all, my channel had a terrible time even letting me in, let alone—because his soul had to go when mine came in, you see. And that was a most difficult thing because his water spirits didn't want that happening at all. Yes, go ahead.

Then there would be some sort of chemical test, would there— in the body when the soul had been driven out there would be a chemical change—

Oh, there's definitely a chemical change. Absolutely and positively. Definitely. That, that can actually be measured in your physical world, the chemical changes. Certainly. You see, the weight change of a soul leaving a physical body is simply the effect of the nature spirits who control the water center of the consciousness of the physical body. That's why there's a weight difference.

Are they leaving the body then?

Well, they're leaving the body because the soul has left completely; and the Isle of Hist has separated and so there's, there's a weight loss. There's a measurable weight loss to the physical body when the soul permanently leaves. Why, certainly. It's not only a weight loss, there's a loss of several chemicals. Yes.

This is one of the great difficulties in the soul passing on harmoniously. Usually it is the water spirits who do not want to let go because they've been overfed. That's why it's the water spirits. And this is why you will notice in hospitals or institutions, when a person is 'tempting to pass on, there [are] these problems with the water center, the chemicals dealing with the liquids and the fluids. That's always the problem. They've over-identified with that center of consciousness. And now they're not going to get fed; and they get all upset [and] cause all kinds of chemical problems in the body.

Yes, our time is moving right along. Yes, [Student O], please.

Yes. There's a chemical harmoni—they, they stated a moment ago that a chemical harmonious vibration is present during conception.

Yes, in order for the soul to enter, that is true. It has to be harmonious to the soul's entrance. Correct.

OK. That doesn't necessarily mean a, a neutral state.

Oh, no, most certainly doesn't because we've got to see the little soul there—no, no, no, no. No, no, no, no. That's an entirely different subject, the moment of conception. Lord forbid. An entirely different subject. Couldn't possibly go into that today. Not conception, no. Not that type of conception.

Yes. Thank you.

My! [Student S], please.

When a wandering soul attempts and gets into another body, a foreign, physical body—

Yes, that is true. That happens many times. It's a very common thing in your world. Yes.

—is there an awareness of that, the wandering soul, the person of the wandering soul?

Oh, the soul that is out there wandering and has to look and see somebody else taking their house over, yes, there is an awareness.

No, I meant when, when they go into another body themselves when they take over . . .

Yes, it's like moving into another house. Yes.

Then do you take on a different identity or how do—

Well, sometimes they do, and sometimes they have a problem letting go of the past one. And then I think in your world they call that—you have terms for that—multiple personality or something. Yes, yes.

OK. Thank you.

But we usually don't discuss these things. Only in these private classes because there's too many factors, too many doors that open up and cause problems for people.

Thank you.

Yes. Yes, it looks like time has passed. Yes, [Student N] here.

So when we create, you were speaking of the, the . . . in creation and creating judgments after you have the creation. When we, when we have a desire, and we bring it into form— [It is difficult to transcribe a few words of the student's question.]

Yes.

—is it best just to accept it then and to evolve it? Instead we, instead we seem to—I seem to make judgments about what I've created, instead of—

Yes. Well, the only reason you make judgments about what you've created is because you believe that you are your judgments. When you no longer believe [you are] your judgments, you won't have problems in accepting what you've created. You see, we only have problems accepting in what we've created when we believe our judgments and it didn't turn out the way that it should have. And, of course, therefore it was somebody else's fault. I think you call those things circumstances or something. It's always a vehicle through which you may deny personal responsibility. Yes.

Right. OK.

Yes. Yes. And the denial of personal responsibility absolutely guarantees the lack of reason. Hmm?

Thank you.

Yes. Yes, [Student B], please.

Does it matter whether the soul's awakened or unawakened as far as wandering?

No—well, it matters in this sense: an unawakened soul hovers over the earth realms and will get into any house it can get into while another soul is out. You see, it's extremely serious, of course, for a person, for their soul to leave and not to be aware and be able to bring it back in, because they don't know who's going to take over their house, you see. And the ones who move in on them, the freeloaders, may not let them back in again. And if they don't let them back in, then they're out there wandering.

And because it is their purpose of design, of the soul's entrance into creation, to have a vehicle and a house to express itself, then, of course, you have that drive to enter a house because that's your purpose of being. You see.

So it certainly does matter whether or not the soul is awakened before it gets driven out, because if it's not awakened, then it's destined to hover in the lower realms of consciousness just to get into a house. Any house will do. It doesn't matter what house, you see. You see, that's what happens during the process of a person, you know, they think they get attached. And they're attached to the forms and then the forms, you understand, they always—you must realize about attachment, it's always something that is beyond your control, what one attaches to. That's the delusion: the denial of personal responsibility. And so if a person becomes overidentified with a person, the possibility of the other person, in their efforts to control, and the other person in their efforts of dependence that their soul may just leave and another one enter, you see. Then someday they wake up—it's usually called the morning-after sickness—and say, "Where was I last night?" I think that's what it's all about.

And I think—I see that our time is up. Now I won't take this off until I say good day. *[The teacher refers to his microphone.]* Have a very good day, please. And thank you. We'll see you next Sunday. I did it anyway, didn't I.

APRIL 6, 1986

A/V Class Private 43

Good morning, class. Please be seated.

Now that everyone is seated here, we'll begin our class.

Today we'll discuss, for a time here, vital life force. It's very important that you understand that vital life force is essential to the form in creation of a thought. Now when you create a thought in what you understand as your mind, this vital life force is used for the purpose of the creating. As the form that you have created goes to serve the purpose for your creating it, the resistance or friction to its movement is known to your mind as experience.

Now as you continue on with your efforts in these classes or in any class of a spiritual nature, by the nature of your effort you become more receptive to Light, which is energy, which is vital life force.

Without conscious effort to bring about changes in thoughts created by your mind, you experience an increase in the intensity of forms you have already created. And so the so-called struggle of awakening spiritually is ever in keeping with the constant efforts that you make to bring about changes in the direction that you are sending the ever-increasing vital life force that you become more receptive to. Now as you flood your consciousness, you will find that you will gain, once again, conscious control of directing this ever-increasing energy that you experience as you turn to the light of reason.

Now we'll take a few moments for your questions on the classes here. Yes, [Student B], please.

Why is vital life force? Why isn't it vital life power?

It's force the moment it becomes formed or limited. You see, force is power that has been restricted. Do you understand that, [Student B]?

By the mind?

Oh, yes. By the vehicles. There are nine vehicles, of which the mind is one. And so it is that functions are undeveloped faculties, as force is restricted power. Whatever you limit, by your vehicles—in this sense we're speaking of the vehicle known as your mind—whatever you limit, you restrict; whatever you restrict, you build a resistance to; whatever you build a resistance to, you create a friction. That friction becomes an adhesion. And that is the difficulty between a person gaining control and moving from belief that they are what they have created and acceptance that they are the creator of it. Yes. Yes, [Student M].

Yes, here, what you were just speaking of, this resistance or this friction to the movement, what is the resistance to the movement?

The resistance to movement is that which surrounds limit. You see, for example, if you take—you create a thought: well, the thought is a limit of this power. The creating of it is vital force. So when you create or form that, you separate it from the whole. When you separate it from the whole, it has a resistance to the whole. I think, perhaps, you can best relate to that when you say, "Now this is my thought. This is what I want to do. This is what I'm going to do." You see? So you have separated that from its source, from that which it is. You see, first of all, you are all and everything. When you take and create, and separate, you tempt to separate what you are and you believe what you have created, you believe what you have separated—you understand?

Yes.

Then when you create that limit, that which surrounds it, which is the whole, resists its movement. Do you understand? You see? Perhaps in another way. If you take and study nature and you see, for example, a little family of birds or insects of any type or animals, and one of the animals is born different than the other animals, then the parent that is responsible for the birth will 'tempt to destroy it rather than have it contaminate the whole family. Hmm?

Yes.

Yes. You see, those are the laws of nature, based upon what is known as the instinct of survival.

Thank you.

That which is different must struggle to survive. Hmm? For it has separated itself from the whole. Yes, [Student Y], please.

Is there a location of the vital life force within us?

Oh, yes, I've given that to you *so* many times. The river of life, which is the vital life force, which is also known as the *prana*, flows from the base of the spine, flows up through the earth center on through the celestial center and returns. Yes, it is a continuous flow. And when it is obstructed in any of the centers of consciousness, in those centers of consciousness the vital life force is therefore being directed to the forms that have been created on those centers of consciousness. Yes.

Thank you.

Yes. And [Student J] has a question this morning here.

Ah, no, I don't, sir.

Well, it's coming. *[The teacher laughs.]* Thank you. [Student N] has a question.

Does—

You just had a meditative thought, I see. All right. *[The teacher addresses Student J.]* Yes, [Student N].

Does self-esteem come from belief or is it a, is it a faculty?

Oh, no. The esteem of self, the gratitude for the vehicle that one has earned to express that which they are, is in the realm of the faculty of reason, which that center has been given to you. Do any of you students recall the location or the center of the faculty of reason that's been given to you?

Nose. [Student B responds, but speaks very quietly.]

Pardon?

Right between— [Student M responds.]

Yes, [Student B].

The nose?

Yes, I didn't mean the part of the anatomy. The center of consciousness. Through which centers of consciousness does it flow?

The fourth and the fifth. [Student B continues.]

The fourth and the fifth. Which are?

The air center and the electric center.

Correct. Yes. So does that help with your question, [Student N]?

Thank you very much.

Yes. Yes. Now [Student M] has a question.

No, I was just answering—

I see.

Thank you.

All right. You see, your breathing and your affirmations have been designed, as I've stated before, over eons of time, for they have proven to be the most effective in order to help you to move from a center of consciousness in which, through overidentification, you have created, temporarily, an attachment. So the forms created by the vital life force, through those centers of consciousness that you find yourself overidentified with, you cannot remain in those centers at the time of declaring the affirmations and the breathing exercises you have been given. So the forms created before your view disappear. They disappear from your consciousness in the sense that you, your identification, moves from that center of consciousness into another center of consciousness. Yes. Yes, [Student J].

Why is it, then, while we're doing our breathing exercise, particularly watching the film for that eighteen-minute period of time, is it so difficult to concentrate?

It is difficult to concentrate because the forms on the center through which you have overidentified don't want to let you go. You see, try to understand whatever you create with your mind is sustained by the vital life force through an identification or direction of the vital life force for them to move and be active and to live. They only live as long as you, through identification, direct vital life force to them, for, as I've stated so many times, they are soulless creatures. Yes. Yes.

But if we're making a conscious effort to keep our mind on what we're doing, namely in this case the, the exercise—

Yes.

—and watching the film and listening—

Correct.

—and we're, we're receiving audibly and visually—

Correct.

—and trying to concentrate, and yet it is so difficult.

Why, yes, because there are other centers of consciousness that it is not affecting. Hmm?

How can we make them affect these weak centers of consciousness?

Well, they're not weak. They're really quite strong. The sense of touch and the sense of feeling, those are quite strong centers, you see. There are five of the so-called senses that are affected for the forms have been created in those centers of consciousness and have, through the creation process, been created by more than one or two or three of the senses. So how we do that is by accepting—for example, visualization has an effect upon all of the centers of consciousness. Now anyone who, in their life, has fantasized and fascinated is well aware that all centers of, all of their senses of consciousness, all their senses, their physical senses, they are affected by that which they create, you see.

So you want to know how to— *[The teacher laughs and then coughs.]* Excuse me—how to create a stronger—you see, what you're doing when you're saying your affirmations and when you're doing your spiritual work, you are creating a form. You do understand that? Of course. And, for example, all forms created serve their purpose of design until we believe that we are that which we have created, then they no longer serve their purpose of design and they are then in service to creation. For we believe, then, we are creation, and then they become what is known as demons. You see? So that reveals that forms created on the center of consciousness that you are trying to move through were created with more than the sense of sight and the sense of hearing. You do understand that, don't you, [Student J]?

I think so.

Well, you see, now you can—you must learn to activate the other senses of consciousness. You see, the centers of—the senses activate. For example, you think of something; and you see it and you hear it and you can feel it and you can smell it, if you believe, truly, in your creation at the moment. The danger is that a person continues to believe what they create. And when they do that, that which they have created takes control of them.

You see, as I spoke to you so many years ago about visualization, visualize a cloud. People say, "Well, I have difficulty creating anything in that cloud." Correct?

Yes, sir.

You see? Well—or the fountain exercise. Well, the only difficulty in creating is because that is something new to their mind. If they were given something that they had already created and believed that they are, they'd have no problem whatsoever. But then that would be fascinating, fantasizing, and going into deeper bondage, you see? You see, it's like a person—if you concentrate on something that you desire, with all of your senses, you see—if it is something that you truly desire, then all your senses become activated, if you have something already created to help you in your mind. Would you not agree?

Yes, sir.

You know, if you see something and you have in your mind, "Now I really like that. I like that very, very much." Well, you have a form that is telling you they would like to have a little assistance. So go ahead and create another one. And another one. And another one. You see? So when you go to do your spiritual exercises, you don't have all of those assistants created. They're, they're—you have assistants, but you must realize they're not as strong as those other ones that have been created. Hmm?

Yes, sir.

You see? So that's the seeming difficulty to the mind: is that in relating it doesn't have something that—now say, for example, if you wanted to create a form that, oh, you would like to lay down like a lounge lizard and take a little nap now, I don't think you would have any problem at all. I think you'd go to sleep very soon.

Yes, sir.

You see? In a matter of seconds, a person can do that very well. Or you want to create now, "Oh, it's so nice here at the beach." And the tropical winds are blowing, you see. I can see them myself, you see. And what happens is you create that with your mind, then you can feel the cool breeze and everything that goes with it. You see, because you are a creator. God is not a creator. Man is the creator, you see. So you can, and you do, create anything that you want to do. You create it with this vehicle known as your mind.

So when you have difficulty creating something, you must realize that you've got to make the conscious effort, the conscious effort to *feel* that. You don't have something relating to that [that] appeals to the senses, for the senses have become controlled by all the forms they have created in the past. You see?

Yes, sir.

But it's not impossible. It's not impossible. And after all, you're able to concentrate better than you used to, that is, on spiritual things.

Yes, sir.

Hmm?

Yes, sir.

I mean, you know you never had any problem before in life creating on, ah, concentrating on certain other things.

Yes, sir.

There's no problem at all. You see, some people have no problem at all on sleeping. But they go to sleep just like that. *[The teacher snaps his fingers.]* They don't have to think about it. Not even for ten short seconds. And they go right off just like that. Because they already have a form, you see, that is totally solidified, has many, many helpers, you see, over the years. And so you say the word *sleep* and they go— *[The teacher makes a sound that is difficult to transcribe.]* They're gone. Something else is there, you see. The form's immobile, you see.

Yes, sir.

Except, perhaps, for snoring and a few of those things. *[Many students laugh.]* And, of course, that's all in keeping with the forms created. That help with your question?

Yes. Thank you.

Yes. Certainly. Now [Student Y] has a question.

We—you're saying that we, we're creating these forms and then they manifest as experiences in our life?

The movement of the forms created, the effect of the movement is a resistance or a friction; that's what you understand as experience. You see, a resistance to a movement is a friction. You understand that, don't you? *[The teacher addresses a different student, who does not verbally respond.]* So, you see, a person— in the movement of the forms, the activating of the forms, which is the movement, there is a resistance to that movement. It is known as an action and a reaction. A movement and a resistance; a friction, an adhesion. And so you fall in love with many things. Hmm? Is that not true?

That's correct.

Well, what is that falling in love? What that is, is the experience that's taking place within your mind that you fall in love with. Yes.

So—

Because it appeals to your senses. It appeals to that which you have already created, you see.

So that comes first. You're going along through the day and you're creating . . .

Oh, yes, yes. People create things constantly. This is why I work to encourage them: in your creations, create something that will serve you well—you see?—and help to, once again, permit you to become the captain of your ship, which is in truth, your purpose in life: to be the master of your own destiny and the captain, of course, of your own ship. And so these forms that are created, which you would consider, in your world, angelic or forms of Light—for they're created in the light of reason to serve the purpose of their creation, you see?

Yes. You make a conscious effort to declare the truth. That creates a form for you. You see, truth is individually perceived. It is individually perceived for it is only perceived by the vehicle and what the vehicle will allow in. That makes it individually perceived. Truth is not individual. Truth is individually perceived. Hmm? Yes.

So if you're having a repeating thought in your mind—

Yes.

—then you know that you, that's a sign that you're caught in one of the centers, probably in the functions, you're—

Well, it does reveal that your vital life force is being used by a form you have created, yes. And definitely the forms are created on the different centers of consciousness. Yes. And if you will look at that, when you have a repetitive thought, you will see a form that has been created that is very insistent, very demanding, [and] extremely selfish. Yes. It considers only what it was originally designed for and nothing else. Hmm?

Thank you.

Does that help with your question?

Yes, it does.

Yes. Yes, [Student B].

So when we're saying our affirmations, if we're creating forms when we say them—

Oh, yes. You create forms in creation. Yes.

—then they'll work the same way as the ones—

Absolutely. As above, so below. You create them for the purpose of awakening your consciousness to remain identified with the faculty of reason. And that transformation takes place, for those forms, those angelic forms, are the ones that go to battle in the realms, you see. You see, you have the soldiers of Light and the soldiers of darkness. Well, they are created, you understand that, in those realms. So when *you* need help, you know, when the soldiers of darkness have practically, completely annihilated you, as far as [your] peace and harmony and balance and reason, then, you see, you need the armies of Light. Those that you have earned through your own efforts, yes. They go to battle when you activate them.

So then when we have thoughts that we put feeling [or] soul, our soul into—

Yes?

—do those have a different, I mean, does something—what's different about them?

What's different—oh, my, yes. On the battlefields they survive.

Uh-huh.

They survive, for they're the strongest soldiers. You see, they receive in their creation much more vital life force. That makes them much stronger. You see, you have the five senses of what you understand as the physical world. When you put all of the senses into the creation of a form, you have a very strong soldier, either for Light or for dark. Yes.

Thank you.

Yes, [Student L], please.

Are the angelic forms, do they have soul?

The ones you have created? Only in the sense that you have directed vital life force to them. Now this is an important thing to understand: there are angelic forms; of course, there are what you call angels. Of course, they are souls in form, certainly. We're speaking now about the forms that [you] have created.

Exactly.

They're either Light or dark. Well, they no more have an eternal soul than that which you have—you continue to supply the vital force, the energy for their continuity. Do you understand that?

Yes.

You see, you see, try to understand it's like the difference between the created forms of the mental worlds and the astral worlds, soulless creatures. And try to understand the nature spirits—something entirely different—that are responsible for the various elements of your physical body and your chemistry of your mental body, you see. So it's like when a person—the moment you believe you are the vehicle through which you are expressing, then the vehicle through which you are expressing has a direct reaction upon what you are. You see?

Yes.

You see? It's not designed that way. So you take a person who believes they are physical substance, for them physical substance has a definite action upon them. And their resistance to that action from physical substance is a resistance or a friction, which in truth is an adhesion, which increases the attachment to the form that they first believed that they are, you see. And so you will find people who are easily and quickly affected by physical substance, and you will find people who are not so easily affected by physical substance. Or you will find people who are affected by physical substance in certain areas of their consciousness and not affected at all in other areas of their consciousness. That, of course, is ever dependent upon the forms that they have created and the belief that they are those forms, who, in turn, are in service to the realm of physical substance or mental substance or astral substance. That help with your question?

Yes. Thank you.

Yes. You're welcome. Yes, [Student D], please.

The created forms of the shadows fear annihilation. How do the Light forms, who have no soul, react to annihilation?

Yes. Thank you very much for your wonderful question. Well, of course, reason has no fear. Therefore, the action or reaction is self-evident. Do you understand? You cannot experience fear, when you're expressing the light of reason. And angelic forms are created in the light in the realm of reason. That's why I have stated, "Keep faith with reason, for she will transfigure thee."

And, of course, why is reason referred to as "she" or magnetic? Because "she" is a servant of your creation. And that which serves, as you have created it, of course, it is magnetic. Of course, it is in that respect a "she." Yes, go ahead.

Do they have an awareness that they will return to—return to the Allsoul? Is that correct?

The forms you have created are created—they realize that you are their parent. Now if you're talking about the Allsoul and you're talking about the nature spirits or you're talking about other forms, that's something different, [Student D]. We are talking about that which you have created and you are the parent of.

Yes.

Yes. So they return unto the substance from which they have been created. You see? For they do not, they do not have soul. Remember that if you'll study your Living Light textbook, you will see where it is clearly stated, "The soul can and does all things create." *[This quote is from Discourse 17 in* The Living

Light, *the textbook for the students, and was republished in* The Living Light Dialogue, *Volume 1.]* If you will study your textbook there. God is not the creator. Man is the creator, you see. Yes. Does that help with your question there, [Student D]?

Ah, then one more.

Certainly.

So these Light forms, when they are, when we cease to exist, they cease to exist.

Well, when you—now just a moment. Now when you cease to exist, do you mean in the physical world?

Yes. In the physical world.

Well, no, they're not physical substance; so they would not cease to exist because you left a physical vehicle. No. They go with you, of course. Light, dark, and indifferent. Yes. And mostly indifferent. Thank you. Go ahead, please. *[Many students laugh.]* Because they are very selfish, you know. They don't care what you want. They're going to do what they were designed to do. Like it or not. Yes. That's the way they are, because, you see, they have—especially the ones of the mist of the darkness because, you see, they have one slogan, [and] that's the only banner that they fly: "My way or no way" is their banner, you see. It doesn't matter what you do once you've created them in the darkness.

Now the ones created in the realms of Light, they take a look [and say] "You want me to change that? Yes, all right. I change that." You see, and they step aside. Yes, and another one comes in, and he does that job that you now want done. That's the angels of Light. Those are the created forms of Light, you see. The other ones say, "My way or no way," once they've been created. Therefore, you see, they easily tempt you, you see. They're tempters. Oh, yes, indeed. Certainly. Because they know once they [have] got you, they'll do whatever they want to do. They know that, you see. And there's nobody going to stop them. Yes, [Student D].

I, I will consider that.

Except the soldiers of Light. Yes. You should see the battlefield someday. Yes, [Student N], please.

Soldiers of the Light, the forms of the Light, we express the same as, as—can take control of us the same as the forms of darkness?

No, because they're created in the light of reason. They know better. You see, they know better. The forms of darkness don't know better. They don't know any better. You see, as I said, their banner is "My way or no way." Once they're created, it's always their way. Oh, yes, yes. You can ask them to stop trying to do this and that, that means nothing. No, they'll laugh at you. Yes.

And reason is designed to serve creation?

Reason is not designed to serve creation. Its very purpose is to cast the Light upon creation, for, you see, people who believe they are creation are not identified with the realm of Light. Now people who understand that they are using creation, that they have created these different things, you see, then they know the purpose of their design, and there is no problem. Reason is not something that is created. Reason is a servant of the Light. It's an expression of the Light. Yes. Does that help there, [Student N]?

Thank you.

Oh, my, yes, yes, there's quite a difference there. Therefore, these created forms that you have created in the Light through the faculty of reason, they do not fly the banner "My way or no way." They know beyond a shadow of any doubt that forms created are vehicles. And that they are a vehicle. And that they are designed to serve a purpose. And they do not tell you how long that purpose is to be. Hmm? No, no, no, no. Only the forms from below, they tell you. They tell you, "Oh, no, no, no. I'm going to do what I'm going to do no matter what happens to you." Oh, yes. They'll tell your mind that, you know. Yes. And they will convince you—because you believe you are that which you have created—they will convince you if you're not on guard that that's you. Yes, [Student Y].

This is in a little different direction, but I wanted to know—

Well, [a] different direction is ofttimes the best direction, but not necessarily so. So let us carry on and test this new direction.

OK. Last class you talked about the wandering soul and I wanted to know—

Oh, I—may I say one thing?

Yes.

I think, if you will check that class, I referred to the wandering souls because there's more than one. Yes. Certainly.

The wandering souls. And I wanted to know is it possible to draw the soul back in through a particular center in one's being, conscious—

Well, I think you will find we discussed that. And if you will keep faith with reason, you will not have any problem being concerned about where your soul is. Because your soul will know where it is and so will you, the vehicle. Oh, yes, indeed. Yes, yes. Yes, and another thing, as has been spoken by, oh, so many different teachers over these many centuries, the eyes are the reflector, you see, of the soul. And so you look in the eyes because they show everything. The eyes show everything to an awakened person, yes.

Thank you.

What do they show? They show all that the vehicles have created. Oh, yes, indeed. And they also show who's in control at the moment. It's very important, the eyes. Of the vehicle, the most important are the eyes. Hmm? But, then, what do the eyes represent in the Living Light Philosophy? Yes, [Student L].

Awareness.

Awareness. Of what benefit is life if there's no awareness of it? Hmm? Yes, the eyes are so very important. Are there any other questions this morning? Yes, [Student N].

The soul creates all things.

All things. That's correct. For it.

For it, for its design—

Well, the soul creates—let us, let's stop a moment. The soul creates all things. The soul creates the vehicles through which it expresses. Do we understand that?

Yes.

Then if we believe we are the vehicles that the soul has created, then the vehicles turn around and create everything you could possibly imagine. Now do we have some understanding and Light there?

So the vehicles can have, can create as well as the soul?

Why, certainly. All you have to do is believe you are the vehicle, and the moment you do, it creates anything it wants to. And you think you're it. Now, [Student J] here this morning has brought this up very clear. He has had no problem in creating whatsoever various forms from life's experiences. Correct? But a little difficulty, just a little, temporary difficulty in creating these forms so that he can be left alone and experience concentration. Correct?

Yes, sir. [Student J responds.]

So, you see, [Student J] has already spoken on it this morning, if you were following on that.

Yes.

Yeah.

Thank you.

Did that help with your question?

Yes, it does.

Oh, yes, yes, yes. Let us not get confused. See, of course, there's good in all things. Well, there has to be good in all things because when you go back to the source, you find out who created all things. But you have some very unruly children when you believe you are the vehicles that your soul has created, and the vehicles are turning around creating all those things. Then you have difficulty in seeing good in all things. But if you trace it back, you find that it all comes from the Principle of Good, you see.

Everything wanders from Good, or God, and is destined to return to that from whence it has wandered. So we're all destined to return to the Source from whence we have wandered. How we get back there, of course, there are many slow boats to China in your world . . . *[The teacher speaks very quietly and a few words are difficult to transcribe. Several students laugh.]* Some sleep most of the voyage, of course, and miss, miss the lovely, lovely experience.

But I've always tried to think that quality is what pays. And it's better to go first class than down in the hold, especially if you're sailing. Well, what is the benefit of sailing if you're going to be down in the hold? You can't even see the water, let alone the sails or the sky. Yes. So if you must sail, let's go first class. Hmm? *[Many students laugh.]*

Thank you.

Otherwise, try flying. Yes, now [Student P] has a little question this morning.

Oh.

Oh, yes, you do.

I was—in one of the recent classes you were speaking of speeding up the spin when you—

Yes. Yes, yes, yes. The spin and retrospin?

Right.

Oh, yes.

And I have a difficult time in meditation because . . .

You spin off?

Not in the right way, I don't think.

Well, no, I didn't say you spun off in the wrong way. I just said, "You spin off."

Yes, I definitely—

Yes, yes.

I was—

That's a wonderful talent that you have. Some people do have that talent. And it's nice, as they broaden that, then they can spin off in the right things, something that, you know, will be a benefit to them.

[Student P's response is difficult to transcribe.]

Hmm?

I was wondering if there's any—if there was some greater understanding that I could have in, in . . .

Well, now you have no problem in the spin off.

No.

The only thing that you would like changed is the form that you're spinning into, isn't that correct?

Exactly.

Yes. Yes. Well, you see, of course there's a phenomenal magnetic pull there from experiences. And, of course, they're always hungry and thirsty, and they want to feed all of their buddies so they can put on the dog, I think they call it in your world, at your expense. Well, tell them they're not going to put the dog on at your expense anymore. Yes. So, you see, what—you know, it's almost like a type, what in your world you would call, self-hypnosis. You find yourself going shhhhhhhh. Hmm? But the form that you're going into, you don't appreciate. Isn't that correct, [Student P]?

That's true.

Yes. Well. Well, now, you apply these classes that you've been given. You spend a little more time listening to your tapes. Spend a little more time in viewing your tapes. You hear? And if you will do that, you will find that you'll be able to bring about a balance between that spin, and you'll start to get a little bit of retrospin.

You see, you have no problem moving off into that realm. Now in that sense you and my student here, [Student R], have a lot in common there. You both seem to, what your mind says, just drift off. Is that correct? Well, a person who drifts off without a conscious choice of drifting, they're not sailing, you know. They're drowning, you see. Because they haven't made a conscious choice. Now you make a conscious choice and say, "Let's see, oh, I think I'll go to Samoa this moment." And here you see the beautiful, lush high green mountains there. And then you see this beautiful little cove there. And there are sailboats and all. The temperature's about ninety-seven right now, you see. And everyone there—there's just a wonderful warm breeze. And the next thing you know you're just relaxed. And, of course, you wouldn't stand up and experience all that. You have to lay down. It makes you sleepy, you know. *[A few students laugh.]* And you just—the next thing you know, you're just right off and you're right there. Correct?

Right.

Well, you see, you have a wonderful, creative imagination, you see. Well, you make a conscious choice of what you're going to create before you pass out. Because what you are creating is what you're servicing. Your vital life force is creating that and animating that, you see? You see, you're doing that all of the time. That is what creation is. You see, you have these experiences and you create all of this. And your mind can create going to the islands, perhaps, [and] can create a little grass shack there and a little music there. And just you and the ocean and the beach, you know, and everything. You have no problem creating that, do you?

No.

Might even have a little bicycle there, if you feel you can get up off of the cot long enough to pedal it, for about five minutes. *[Many students laugh.]* So, you see, you have no problem creating that.

No.

But you have created all of your experiences the same way.

Right.

You see, the same way, everybody is creating their life. We create that. And so the thing is that we have forgotten that we have created what we are experiencing. We have forgotten that because we believe we are that. And so we say, "Well, now I am creating here in the islands. I'm lying in front of this little grass shack. The sun's just right. And the breeze is so wonderful. And I have some good music. I don't know where it's coming from because I don't [have] telephones or anything. And maybe one bicycle around the back; of course, that's kind of modern for that little island there. And a little canoe, perhaps." And you see, you say, "Oh, well that's just a fantasy." Well, all of your experiences are created by fantasies. Do you understand?

So you say, "Well, I've had a good week—no, I had a bad week." Well, that's something you've created in your mind. And you believe that; you believe your creation, and you're convinced, and then you're there with all of your senses.

You see, I can go to the islands or anyplace else I choose to go in the universe in a moment. Now I don't permit myself to say, well, that's just a fantasy, because I know the whole thing is an illusion each moment and each day that's formed. You see? You see, but you have this delusion that this is real (reality). *[The teacher grasps the glass of water on his left.]* And this is a dream I'm creating, *[He seems to grasp an imagined glass of water on his right.]* when the whole thing is a dream. And the only difference between reality and fantasy is that you believe you are the fantasy you have created and the other fantasies you're yet to believe that you have created them. Do you understand? You're yet to believe that you are them. So here's reality: your belief in the fantasies you created—you understand? *[The teacher gestures toward the glass of water on this left.]*

Correct.

And here's fantasy: something you've created, but is not yet reality because you don't believe it's you yet. *[He gestures toward his right, to his imagined glass of water.]* That's the difference. Known as the dream of life. Dreamer, dream a life of beauty before it turns into a nightmare. Before the dream starts dreaming you is the truth of the matter, which, of course, becomes the nightmare indeed. Hmm. Yes, [Student Y].

So are you saying that we actually have dreamed this?

You are dreaming it.

How about before we came into form, did we dream it?

When you're out of form, you're not dreaming. You only dream when you're in limit. That ought to tell you something, shouldn't it? The reason that—you see, you dream when you're in limit for you believe you are limit. That's known as experience. All of that. The movement of the limit into the all is a friction, a resistance from the all and that which is separated from it. And you believe you are that. It is a dream, you see. You dream it each moment. Because you believe what you have created is you, and, of course, that's experience. Yes, [Student Y].

So how is it different?

How is it different? You have dreamed many dreams. Some of them you no longer dream as just a passing page in your book of life, correct?

Right.

So it's no longer a reality to you, is it? The only reason it is no longer a reality is because you no longer dream it. It's only a reality when you dream it and believe you are that which you are dreaming. That's the *maya*. That's the illusion. I do hope that—you will follow. You will all follow, because you're all moving along nicely. Yes, [Student O].

Yes.

It's a dream. The table is a dream. You have dreamed it. Yes.

Yes, would you speak on the word hallucination?

Hallucination? That's something that dreams you.

That's something . . .

Uh-huh. "Dreamer, dream a life of beauty before your dream starts dreaming you." You see, that's something that you have dreamed and you believe you are the dream. And in keeping with the society you are exposed to, they're not dreaming the same dream, and therefore you're hallucinating. Do you understand that? Well, think about it for a few moments so that you can absorb it.

Now, let's, for example, take our little picture box over to parts of South Africa where they've never heard of a radio, let alone a television set. And the chieftain says to you, "That's a hallucination. That's a—you're hallucinating! Don't tell me all that. That's a hallucination." He'll tell you that. Do you understand that, [Student O]? Because, you see, they have not had the experiences; therefore, they have not created the forms; therefore, they do not believe that which they have not created. Do you understand that?

Yes.

Listen to this tape several times when it's over today, and I know you will understand. Certainly. You see, that exists for us that we have created and convinced our self that we are the creation by believing it. Otherwise, it does not exist. Well, to many people, you know, I do not exist. They will take a look at my channel and say, "Well, yes, that's him. But no, no, no. He's a hallucination." Because, you see, they don't have those created forms. Do you understand that?

Yes.

But then I can sit here, you see, and look at all of you and say, "Oh, my, what a hallucination. Where am I? *[Many students laugh.]* I'm supposed to be in a class somewhere giving a class." So I could, I could convince myself the same way, you see. Hmm? I have no problem. I have plenty of experience with that. I spent a long, long time as a magistrate, you know. I have no problem at all with making, creating forms and solidify[ing] them. I was a professional at it. I had no problem at all. It came to me very natural, one might say. I'd rather say very easy. But anyway, there's nothing natural about creating forms, even though many do it. Oh, yes. It's popular in creation. Definitely. But one doesn't necessarily have to say that it's natural. Hmm.

Thank you.

Did that help you?

Quite a bit.

Yes. Yes. The form isn't happy, but I know that your soul is quite, quite awake in that respect. Yes. You see, you see, if you go and tell someone your experiences, and they have not created what you have created—in other words, they have not dreamed a similar dream as you have dreamed—they'll tell you you're hallucinating. You see? A wise man knows to keep his mouth shut. And when he chooses to discuss anything, he first pauses to see if they're having similar hallucinations. And then he has a rapport, and then there's no problems. *[Many students laugh.]* Yes. Oh, yes. Yes, [Student D].

When you're drifting off and you have this fantasy of the south sea island—

Well, there's a difference between drifting off, which means that someone is calling you, that you don't have control of, and consciously making a choice to, perhaps, sail on to the North Pole. Yes. With the polar bears or something, you see. You make a conscious choice, [Student D]. It isn't something that—I mean, if you want to take control of that which you create, you make a conscious choice of what you're going to create, how long you're going to service it, that is, how long you're going to hallucinate yourself. You understand that, as [Student O] just got through speaking. How long are you going to dream the dream? Do you understand that? Now if you believe you are your creations and if you have that talent, then you say, "Oh, I drifted off here and I drifted off there. And I drifted off someplace else." Because that which you have created you believe that you are; so when it comes to call, you're onboard, and that's all [there is] to it.

It's known as being shanghaied. Yes. Thank you. Go ahead with your question. Quite popular in your world. I see a lot of people shanghaied.

But you answered part of it.

Yes.

I, I was thinking about the fact that you're aware that when you're creating that Samoa fantasy, the island fantasy, but this moment of creation which we're in right now, like, I couldn't say that I'm aware that I'm creating this moment, where I would be aware that I was—

Why, certainly. Because you believe you are this moment that you have created from other moments that you have created that are similar. And so you total—they totally convince you. Of course. There's been more than one class, you understand.

Oh, I see.

Does that help you?

Yes. Thank you.

Well, you see, some people will go and look at a picture box and they will absolutely convince themselves that they are the participants that are playing on the stage. Do you understand? Now, are they hallucinating? What are they doing? To one who does not create that for themselves, they say, "That person's a weirdo. How could they possibly cry when that's only a picture over there?" Hmm? You see? Yes.

What is reality? I've said to you before: a conscious realization of passing events. And what is a conscious realization of passing events? A belief that you are that which you have created: the passing events. My goodness, yes. Yes, [Student H], please.

Would someone, for example, a scientist who is trying to, to prove something, for example, Christopher Columbus, trying to prove the world was round, did he have to no longer believe in the moment that he was in and believe in a different moment?

Yes. He had to create in his mind that which was contrary to popular thought at the time. He had no problem doing that; he was very independent with a very large ego. I don't know how much of your history reveals it, but he had a lot at stake. And he absolutely was the type of person that had no problem in convincing himself of whatever he created. Now he created something different than popular acceptance had created, though there were a few who had no problem with creating an Earth that was round instead of flat, you see, for he had an insatiable need to control. And so he created an Earth for him in his mind that was round, and he had difficulty convincing others. Hmm? However, through some personal interest in him from people who were in the position of finance, he managed to fulfill and satisfy himself—and her—that the Earth was round. And you've all benefited ever since. Yes. Is there anything else to your question?

No. Thank you.

Yes. Yes, [Student J].

Why is it important for us to be aware of what's behind us at all times?

For what is behind us is what is coming forward to bring to you experiences that you usually do not care for. They are behind you because from their experiences they know that you don't want them in front of you; you don't want to go through it again. So they come in the back door, you see, in order to get in your house. You see, a person that you kick out of your front door, if it insists that the house belongs to them, will find a way to the back door. Hmm? Yes.

How can we practice that and put it in to action on a daily, moment-to-moment basis?

Through an absolute, absolute conviction of creating that which you, in the light of reason, choose to create. Now through a conscious effort on your part to declare the truth, to, to be more [in] acceptance and encouraging of your possibilities, you understand, you will create encouraging-possibility forms in the light of reason. You see, in the light of reason to you, the great creator, all things in your domain are possible. Hmm? Your domain is not subject to someone else's domain. The first thing you want to refrain from doing is depending on what someone else does with what you have created. That's the first step. You see, you must care less—and even more not at all—what they think, what they do, how they will react to it. By your being concerned of how anyone will react to what you are creating, you create reaction forms. Do you understand that? Now they all take place within our own mind.

It's like a person that goes for employment. And they have created certain forms: they would like to have money and etc., and they would like to have better experiences than they've been having. And so they create these forms of what they want. And at the same time, by their belief in what someone beyond their control will or won't do, they create these reaction forms. Do you understand that?

Yes, sir.

So the person goes for the employment. Depending on the employer, the employer will sense either these forms that one has created to get the job and etc., or they will sense the reaction forms that the person has created. Now if they sense the reaction forms, they'll get an inner sensing that this person is not qualified. They will justify it out because this person is not convincing them because they cannot convince them because the employer is receptive to the reaction forms that they have created. Did that help with your question, [Student J]?

Yes, sir.

Yes. And so you say that some people have no problem selling themselves or their product—which is really themselves. You see, a person selling a product has first sold themselves by convincing themselves that he is the goodness of the product that he has judged. All right? So a person first sells a product to themselves by believing they are the product, that is, the goodness that it is. So what the person is then doing, the person is then selling themselves. I mean, they're handing out a book, but they're selling themselves. Do you understand? Now if they have created at that time of creating that process, you see, if they have created reaction forms, that is, concern of what someone else will do with their effort, oh, then they [have] got a real problem. They're very poor salesmen. Would you not agree?

Yes, indeed, sir.

That, that's what it's about, [Student J]. Yes. Yes. First, convince yourself, you see, and refrain—you know, I told you long ago that common sense is the lack of self-concern. You see, the lack of concern. Now do you understand? It is the concern—it's poor business sense—it is the concern that creates what is known as reaction forms. The concern is creating forms that say to the mind, "What will this person say? What will they do? Will the deal go through? Won't it go through?" They're this; they're that. And it goes through all those processes of justification, but the person must realize they have created all of those. [You] don't want to do that. That's not good, that's not good business, you see. You see, the practice of good business is the lack of concern. You see?

Yes, sir.

Not responsibility. Concern. Oh, my, there's all the difference in the world. Yes, [Student L].

Thank you. [Student J responds.]

And those forms travel with a resume as well as any other—

Why, of course they do. Why, certainly. They travel with anything that you touch with any of your senses. You have created them.

Thank you.

And they travel along with it. Yes, yes, [Student U].

On occasion when I'm in that situation, I will go through possible responses that other people may say. Now is that in essence creating reaction—

That's concern; that's concern of what you cannot control. Whoever is concerned over what they cannot control is a person who is not freed in the Light and in the truth and is a person who is not demonstrating personal responsibility. In other words, their life is dependent on what the someone else does or doesn't do, for they have created that as they deny the truth of personal responsibility. It's an error of ignorance, you see? You see.

So I've tried to teach you over these many years to give what you have to give and to care less what the world does with it. For if you care what the world does with it, it is a created form you have created, and you call that upon you for the thing you fear the most befalls you. And you've created forms of concern which are filled with fear of what someone else will do with it. Do you understand that? And that befalls upon you, you see. You see, faith in the mind is fear, of course. You see, you can't say that there's fear in reason because reason is a soul faculty. It's not the mind. It's a faculty of the soul. Yes.

Yes, how are you doing on your sixty minutes today? *[The teacher addresses the technician recording the class.]*

I haven't even been keeping track.

Oh, why don't you keep track today? How many minutes do you have left?

Oh, we still have—it's about sixty minutes now.

Oh, isn't that nice? Just about sixty minutes. And you didn't even keep track. Well, see how quickly time passes. Well, there's no guarantee it'll fit on one of your C-60s. *[A C-60 is an audio cassette tape that has a sixty-minute capacity.]* So my students and their soul [have] much more value to me than sixty minutes.

Now I'll take this off before I finish speaking. *[The teacher refers to his microphone.]* Thank you very much. And have a very good day.

[After a short pause, he continues.] You thought I couldn't keep time. *[All the students laugh.]*

APRIL 13, 1986

A/V Class Private 44

Good morning, class. Please be seated.

This morning we shall take a couple of notes here. The question is, In what center of consciousness does the human ego reside? Second question: Upon what is judgment dependent? Third question: What is the defense of judgment? Next question: List the ways in which we are controlled and the centers of consciousness that are represented by that control. List the ways in which we are controlled and the centers of consciousness represented by that control. *[The teacher spoke slowly and repeated himself in order that the students could take more accurate notes.]*

Now we'll pause for a moment so you can write down all your answers. And I will try to get to those before class ends this morning. [I'm] sure that'll only take you a moment. Considering my students have been doing so well with their homework. Of course, I didn't say which students. Or which class.

[After a short pause, the teacher continues.] All right, that's plenty of time for your answers. Now we'll go to this discussion of spin and retrospin. Now you have been given over this long time now, how you enter the spin and how you free yourself from the spin, how you move in consciousness in retrospin or spin. And so we'll be a little bit more, perhaps, specific today in respect to that. You have many teachings. You have, "Broaden your horizons." You have, "Accept the possibility." You have, "All things are possible." Now stop and think. Whenever you declare the truth "I accept the possibility," you move from the spin that you are being controlled by, that is a form you have created, into a retrospin. Whenever you move into retrospin, you free yourself from what you have created.

Now there are many, many ways in which you have been given that teaching. Such as, think of something different than what you're thinking of. Of course, thinking of something different just moves you into a temporary retrospin and back off into another spin, for there's another form waiting immediately for you to service. So to broaden your horizon moves you from the spin created by your overidentification with anything that your mind has created, and in so doing you literally move back into the Allness that you are. Now in the Allness that you truly are, all things are possible. So by the declaration, "I accept the possibility," you move from that which is controlling you to that which you are.

Now I want you to write down here today, here on your notes, which you have, many times, been given to you, [but is now given] a little bit differently. You know, if it doesn't get in one way, it's destined to get in another because you're more than one center of consciousness, as everyone is. I want you to put down one, two, three, earth, fire, water. Then I want you to put the numbers four, five, air, electric. That's separate from the one, two, and three. Now I want you put down six, seven, and eight. And now, [Student R], what do you think that is?

Magnetic . . .

And?

Odic and ethereal.

That's correct. Put that down. And what is the ninth?

Celestial.

You just gave me magnetic, odic, and what else?

Ethereal.

Ethereal.

And then celestial.

That is correct. All right. Through what center—question—[It will] take you a moment to answer, I know. Through what centers of consciousness are all functions expressed? [Student R].

Celestial.

Well, I think you should recon—

Oh! All functions. I'm sorry. Through what center are all functions—

No. Through what centers are all functions expressed? What functions—through what centers?

Magnetic.

Through what centers of consciousness—now you have nine centers there, right?

Yeah.

Now, of those nine centers, which centers are designed for the purpose of the expression of the functions?

Oh, which group? OK. It's the earth, fire, water, air, electric, and magnetic.

Well, now this is where we have to do a little more study. We have the earth, the fire, and the water centers, correct?

Uh-huh.

Now we have the air and the electric. That's number four and five, isn't it?

Uh-huh.

Now through which of the centers does the faculty of reason flow?

Air.

[Student B].

Through—between the fourth and the fifth. Between the air and the electric.

Fine. Does everyone understand that? All right. Now reason is a faculty. Do you understand that, [Student R]?

Uh-huh.

It's not a function.

That's correct.

It's a faculty. And it is between the fourth and fifth centers of consciousness. So it is between the air and the electric, correct?

Uh-huh.

Now take your little groups here. You have a group of three: earth, fire, and water. *[The teacher gestures to indicate a group to his immediate left.]* Would you say those are faculty expressions or functions?

Functions.

Those are functions. Now let's take four and five and separate it up here, like you've done. *[The teacher gestures to indicate that group is directly in front of him, but somewhat distant from him.]* Now over here, let's take six, seven, and eight. *[He now indicates a spot to his immediate right.]* And what do you have in six, seven, and eight?

Magnetic, odic, and ethereal.

Magnetic, odic, and ethereal. Now take your magnetic, odic, and ethereal and superimpose them over your earth, fire, and water. You know I spoke to you several classes ago about: I understand the difficulty about the flat or two-dimensional thinking or viewing. If you will superimpose that over your functions, what do you have, [Student S]? How do they correspond?

You have the magnetic over the earth.

Yes.

The odic over the fire. And the ethereal over the water.

Yes. All right. Now does that help anyone with some inspiration here of what we're discussing on these things? [Student R]?

I'm not sure what you're getting at, yet.

Yes, [Student S].

It seems that the magnetic, odic, and the ethereal would be the expression of the faculties balanced over the functions of the earth, fire, and water.

Uh-huh.

And the reason, expressed between the air and electric, as the, I guess you'd call it the conversion—

Uh-huh.

—where you can transpose one to the other.

Correct. That is correct. The transfiguration—yes. Because you literally are transformed between the fourth and fifth centers of consciousness. All right?

All right. Now let's—why don't you draw what you—perhaps a scale... *[The teacher says a few words that are difficult to transcribe.]* Put over here a triangle. Perhaps we'll need to bring our blackboard back. Put over here a triangle and put over here another triangle. *[The teacher first gestures to an area of the table on his left with his left hand and then to an area of the table on his right with his right hand.]* All right? Now between the two, connect it with a straight line. Hmm? *[With a finger of his right hand, he traces an imaginary line on the surface of the table connecting the two triangles.]* Do that. Put over here your earth, fire, and water. *[The teacher gestures with his left hand on his left.]* And put a, and put a straight line across. All right? *[He again traces a straight line on the table.]* Put a straight line right across there. *[The teacher indicates where the line should go on the diagram drawn in the notebook of Student R.]*

Perhaps this will help you a bit more in understanding. From the apex. That's correct. Connect the two apexes with a line. All right. Now try to see this in something besides a flat dimension. You can do that with your imaging and your imagination. All right?

[During this class the teacher and the students were seated at the dining room table at the Serenity temple. From his position at the head of the table, he could easily see the notebooks of the students on his immediate right and left. Student R was on his right and Student S was on his left. As he spoke, he monitored what they wrote in their notebooks.]

Now let's put the proper centers where I have given them. One, two, and three. Six, seven, and eight. Does everyone have that? Yes. Is this a line on the bottom? *[The teacher addresses Student S.]*

Yes, I erased that. [Student S responds.]

Oh. Perhaps you—I give you a moment to redo it.

OK. Thank you.

Remember, whenever you make an error, it is in your best interest to lay it aside and start again, for you come under another law, and you come under the control of other forms that you have created.

Thank you.

Don't try to patch up what you have done, whether it's something on a piece of paper or anything else. Do not try to patch up. It is much more difficult. It is—wisdom reveals begin again. Begin anew. In any endeavor. Hmm? Especially a spiritual one. But in any endeavor. You start all new. Do you have that, those centers, [Student R]?

[Student R does not respond verbally, but the teacher scrutinizes his notebook.]

Earth, fire, water.

Uh-huh.

Magnetic, odic, ethereal. Do we all have that? *[The teacher examines the notebook of a different student.]* Yes.

Well, I'm encouraged because soon, be it in Divine order, all of these diagrams and things, you will be able to see on your picture box there. And it will be done so that you have a little bit, perhaps, better idea of what we're trying to express here. So that you will have your little magnetic tapes and can study them.

Now does everyone have that down there? You see, our purpose is for you to think and think more deeply so that you can arrive in consciousness and not just have it fed to you; you've got to use some initiative thinking. Hmm?

All right. Now we have three centers here and we have three centers here and we have what you call a straight line here. *[The teacher gestures to the diagram drawn by Student R.]* All right now, we're missing what numbers from here? We're missing numbers four and five. Is that not correct? All right, so we have a straight line that represents, now think, four and five. Hmm? All right. Put a four up here over this line. *[The teacher points to the line near the apex of the triangle on the left of Student R's diagram.]* And put a five over here. *[He now points to the line near the apex of the triangle on the right.]* Now that controlling the functions is the number four, representing security to the water center. And that that is the faculty's expression is number five, known as faith. So let's get that cleared up there in our minds, all right?

Now, what do we believe? That's a question. Think about that. Yes.

What we deny. [Student U responds.]

And what we deny, what feeling, what experience do we have in consciousness? *[After a short pause, the teacher continues.]* That which we deny we are adverse to. That which we are adverse to, we fear. So remember that our security is based upon our fear, when we are in the functions or those centers of consciousness.

For example, when you make effort to broaden your horizon to go into a retrospin, you experience fear. What is it that you fear? You say you fear the unknown. You fear that which you do not relate to. You fear that which you've had no experience with. We always fear what we've had no experience with, which reveals that we are controlled by our fear. And so our judgments, as an expression, of course, which they are, of what we have created—that's how they work in our mind. We believe what we fear. And we believe what we fear is what we are. That is not what we are, but we believe that. Any questions on that this morning? *[After a short pause, the teacher continues.]*

For example, a person fears not having enough money. They believe their fear. They certainly don't believe something else. They believe what they fear. And when you believe what you fear, you are controlled, of course. Now if you declare the truth,

"All things are possible. I accept the possibility," if that passes through the centers of consciousness where these forms, created, are controlling you, then you will have *that* experience: you will be freed from that fear. Yes, we only believe what we fear. That's known as the false gods with clay feet. We believe them because we fear them. Does that help you, [Student J]?

Yes, indeed, sir.

Do you have a question on that?

Not this very second.

Yes. Yes. Now there's much here. Let's have questions, any questions here at this time. Time passes so quickly in your world. Yes? Yes, [Student Y].

Is water at the apex of this tri—is it water or is it fire with water—

All right. Now what is your answer to the question, In what center of consciousness does judgment reside?

Ah . . .

[Student Y]?

Yes, sir. I said the odic, not the—

Odic? *[It is difficult to transcribe a short comment made by the teacher.]*

No, I'm sorry.

Ah, we must have a lot of questions. I have a lot of questions here, considering the answers I'm receiving. I've many, many questions.

That was the ego. Excuse me. I—

What center, in what center of consciousness does the ego reside?

I said the odic.

The odic? The ego is a function of the senses [and] could not possibly exist in the odic, which is an expression of the faculties. Now the ego resides, and I—anyone have an answer to that? Yes, [Student U]. In what center does the ego reside?

I put down water.

Why, of course it does! I mean, where are judgments created? [Student B]?

In the water center.

Correct! So if you want to be controlled by what has been, all you have to do is to express what you understand as emotion, which is an identification with the water center of consciousness. So you spin yourself into the water center and, of course, that's what you're going to experience. The water center is the residence for what is known as the human ego. Yes. Yes, [Student Y].

So I'm—

Far from the odic center of consciousness.

OK.

Yes.

Excuse me.

However, you see, if you will superimpose these two triangles that I just gave you, you will have much more understanding. Go ahead with your question, [Student Y].

I'm still uncertain about where the water—if the water's at the apex.

[The teacher laughs joyously.] Tell me something about the apex of anything, would you consider it the most valuable and most important?

Correct.

Well then, let's first get the judgments in their proper center of consciousness, and especially the human ego, which is the house of all judgments, you see. Let's get it in its proper place in the water center. And let's get it far off from the odic center. Now what do you have when you superimpose the faculties over the functions as just given to you? [Student S], do you have an answer for [Student Y]? *[After a short pause, the teacher continues.]* [Student R]—

I— [Student S begins to respond.]

Do you have an answer? *[The teacher addresses Student S.]*

I had an answer, but I—there's some question about it. [Student S responds.]

Well, earth, fire, and water is how I gave it, wasn't it?

Yes.

So, what do we have in that respect, [Student R]? I gave it in that order.

Well, I have earth on the lower right corner.

Yes.

Fire on the left lower corner.

Yes.

And water at the apex.

Yes. Well, I can tell you in answer to your question water is at the apex.

Thank you. [Student Y responds.]

However, you had, you had earth at the right?

Uh-huh. [Student R responds.]

Now you're going to have to look around from a different dimension and put it where it belongs on the left.

You see, try to visualize: here you have a little triangle, which in truth is a pyramid. And can't you turn that in your consciousness so you can see it from a different perspective? Because you must see it from a different perspective. Yes.

[Student B], can't you? Or [Student U]? Or [Student P] do that? You see, if you have an equilateral, three-sided triangle and this is what you've drawn only flat here, and in your perspective, if you look at it, you will see that, as is given here, here the earth center, you understand, is magnetic. We understand Mother Nature, it doesn't change, you see. So you've got to look at it in the atmosphere of your consciousness, you see. You see. You've got to, once again, declare your right to creating the forms, instead of the forms that you have created, creating you. Yes.

Yes, someone else have a question there. [Student D] has a question this morning.

In an earlier class—

Yes.

—we were told that the earth is the view. Why is it at the bottom on this triangle?

The earth is the view?

Yes.

Yes. Read the note, please, that you have there. Because taking things out of contents [context]—I think I spoke last, last Sunday—didn't I?—to [Student L]. Did you bring your book this morning, your study book? *[The teacher addresses Student L.]*

It was the Sunday before and I brought it last week, but it didn't come up. So I didn't bring it this week. [Student L responds.]

Oh, so it's not here today?

No.

Oh, did I guarantee to speak to the question last Sunday or a coming Sunday?

Last Sunday. [Student B responds.]

I declared that I would speak to it last Sunday?

I think you did. [Student B responds again.]

Do we have the record here? *[After a very short pause, the teacher continues.]* I'll check the records. Thank you very much, [Student B]. That which is important to us we're willing to carry two weeks or two centuries.

I'm sorry. [Student L apologizes.]

It's quite all right. I know many of us carry many things and down the road of life, so-called, we consider them, finally, to be burdens and set them aside; they're too heavy. Yes, [Student D], read your notes, please.

Yes, on the note diagram that I have, that I was referring to, is what you call the bow tie diagram.

Oh, yes. The bow tie. All right. Fine.

Earth was at the top.

That's correct.

It was considered the view. And my question is, Why is it at the bottom on—

On this here?

Yes.

Because your perspective is changing. And when your perspective change[s], you see earth on the bottom. You no longer see it on the top in the view. Now I have many students in many classes who—it is true—still see, from their perspective, earth on the bott—on the top. And then there are others who see, as you evolve and broaden your horizons, you will see earth is not the top; it's the bottom. And it's totally dependent upon your own perspective. And your perspective is ever dependent upon your evolution or broadening of your horizons, which places you into a retrospin. Did that help with your question, [Student D]?

So the original, where earth was at the top as the view, that was when we were in spin? And that—

That is correct. That is correct. I mean, you just tell a person who declares that they absolutely are in the greatest love they've ever known in the universe, and you just try to convince them that that's a perspective from below and I don't know how long you will exist in that realm. Pardon? I'm sure you've had that experience, haven't you?

Yes.

Yes, yes. It's perspective, you see. It's perspective. You see, when you're trying, working to do your homework—and more homework is definitely required from some of the answers I'm getting here—you can't look at this as though you're going into a school and studying geography or algebra, because you're studying them from a very flat perspective. You've got to get into a different dimension in consciousness, which I see, at times, some of my students here have no problem whatsoever.

The form is so detailed; it's in three-dimension[s] and pops right out in front of everyone. Yes. Now are there any other questions here? *[After a very short pause, the teacher continues.]*

All right. Now let's go to the answers you've had so much time now already—look at that—to study the questions here. Let's have your answer to question number one, [Student R].

Water center.

Read the question.

In what center does the ego reside? [It] was in the water center.

Yes. Now, how did you come to that conclusion.

Because I overheard the answer given to somebody else. [Many students laugh.]

That's how you got to your conclusion.

That's how I got to that particular answer, yes.

Oh well, you get E for effort this morning and H for honesty. *[More students laugh.]* Yes. All right, [Student S], question number two.

Question number two: Upon what is judg—judgment dependent?

Yes. Upon what is judg—judgment dependent? Yes.

I put comparison.

Well, that's not the answer. Yes. [Student P] has an answer.

I put down fear.

It's not the answer. [Student H].

Denial.

No. You had one question; *[The teacher addresses a student who has just answered.]* so I'll go to [Student B] now.

Need.

No. [Student D].

Belief.

No. Oh, it's something we're so familiar with. [Student R]?

Experience?

Experience! *[All the students laugh.]* Now show me a student who doesn't have experience. *[Students continue laughing.]* Do I have any virgins this morning? *[Students again laugh.]* In the respect of no experiences. If I do, would you raise your hand, please? I don't think so, no. No hands? We all have experience.

Judgment is dependent, of course, upon experience. We form a judgment of compare; we compare from experience. Do we not see that? If you don't have experience, you have nothing to compare to. So when you want to go to the root cause, you see; [people] like to say, go right to the horse's mouth. You know, everyone's interested in riding. So go right to the horse's mouth. Yes. Did you have another answer, [Student P]?

Ah ...

Beyond experience?

No, I was thinking about the next question. It's just—

Oh, the next question. Oh, wonderful! Read it off, please. And your answer.

OK. What is the defense of judgment? And I put down justification, but I also put down pride. Because it's the handrail of ...

Well, of course, it's the handrail of ... certainly. *[The teacher says a word that is difficult to transcribe, but it may have been "temptation".]* You know, it's like a brass knob, you see.

Uh-huh.

It requires a lot of polish. Constant polishing. Now stop and think. Of course, it's justification.

Right.

You know, that's what defends all judgments. You see, when you create a judgment, which is based upon experience, at the forming and the creating of the judgment, surely you realize it's not one thing, because in its creation, it has all of its little soldiers of defense to defend and protect it. Hmm? Yes.

All right, now, the next question. Who has the next question here? [Student O] has the next question and answer.

They say, list the ways in which we are controlled and the centers of consciousness represented by their control.

Is that how you have it written down, [Student B]? Now because we—

The centers of conscious represented by that control. [Student B responds.]

Yes, it's, [Student O], the centers of consciousness represented by that control.

That's what I have, but I somehow read what I read.

I know. I'm glad that you have that, but it isn't what you read.

OK.

Unless I have got wax or something in my ears this morning. I do hope I haven't.

I have, "List the ways with which we are controlled and the centers of consciousness represented by that control."

Correct. Yes, you have all those centers now.

Well, the centers that I have are, it's earth—

Good.

—water—

Very good.

—and fire.

Good.

And the ways which they control us are through money, ego, and sex.

Well, just—that's quite simplified, yes. Yes, but that's, that's correct. That is correct, yes. Very, very good. Now do we have any more questions there, [Student R]?

Questions?

Yes, you have some questions there.

Oh, there were some more questions there, I think. Through what centers do the functions flow?

Yes.

And that was given. It was the earth, fire, and water.

Oh, my, you're brilliant this morning. *[Many students laugh, including Student R.]* Very illumined. Class is so illumined this morning we won't have to stay too long today. Yes. You know, there are others, really, [who] are seeking a little, a little more Light. I have such [an] illumined class this morning. Yes, [Student U], did you have an answer for me this morning?

Ah . . .

Hmm? Perhaps it's the weather. Something has sprung forth.

No—

I don't think it's a tulip because tulips [are] long passed. I think they passed in your world may be, what, [in] February perhaps, or March. This is April? Sure, this is April in your world, isn't it?

April.

No more tulips. No. The wind took them away. Yes.

That was the last question that I had recorded here. [Student U responds.]

Good. Now are there any questions on class? *[After a short pause, the teacher continues.]* No questions? Isn't that nice. [Student J]!

I'd like to get the answer to that last question. What centers—

Question number four. [Student R interjects.]

—do the functions exist? [Student J continues.]

Through what centers—Is that what you have, [Student R]? Through what centers of consciousness do the functions express themselves? Hmm? What question do you have there? *[The teacher addresses Student R.]*

Well, through what centers do the functions flow? [Student R responds.]

Yes. All right. Now that's the question you have, [Student J].

Was it, was it functions flow or exist? [Student J asks.]

They flow.

They flow. [Student J repeats.]

Oh, they do flow. Yes, they're just like a river; they keep right on a' flowing. Now, you know, it's most encouraging—be right with you, [Student Y]—it's most encouraging. This is where your study is required: to understand how it works. When you understand how it works, you start making the step intelligently not to be controlled by it because you understand how it works. You must understand how it works, you see. So that then you can use this creative process for something that's beneficial, never forgetting that which you desire to control which is beyond your dominion of divine right shall, by the law of your own desire, control you. Hmm? Let us not forget that.

So whatever you desire to control that is beyond your right of control—for example, you try to control an individualized soul, you try to control something out there that is not in your domain in keeping with your own evolution. For that which is individualized, as an individualized soul, means exactly what it says: it is divided; it is individualized. Divided from the whole. Forget about soul mates so that you can control another soul because you'll only do yourself in. All right? That's very important, yes. Very, very important. What is in your domain in evolution for you to control—you understand?—then that is your responsibility to do so. But when you tempt yourself and desire to control that which is beyond your limit of right in that respect, it shall, by that very law, by that law of transgression, you see, it shall control you.

Remember that all thoughts build a bridge. Where is the bridge going to? Do not forget that. All thoughts are little bridge builders. They build a bridge. Make sure that you know where the bridge is going to, because wherever it's going to, you shall find your destiny; that's where you shall be. Hmm?

Yes, [Student Y], you have a question, please.

Yes, sir. Thank you.

You're welcome.

Is—I want to understand magnetic is superimposed over the earth?

[Student R], have you done your work here this morning?

Yes, that's what I have. [Student R responds.]

Is magnetic— [Student Y asks.]

Earth is magnetic.

Earth is magnetic. And it has nothing to do with water? Water—is water magnetic? [Student Y continues.]

Class, what is your understanding from all these classes? Is water magnetic? [Student L] has an answer.

Water is both magnetic and electric.

[Student H]?

That's correct.

[Student P]?

I thought it was . . . I'm confused right now.

[Student B]?

I thought it was magnetic.

[Student U]?

In the cleansing of hands after healing—

Exactly. It's neutral. [Student P interjects.]

—it cleansed everything. [Student U continues.]

That's correct. That's correct. [Student R], tell me something: what happens when you put two magnets together?

Depending upon the polarity—

That's what we're talking about.

If it's negative to negative or if it's south to south, then they repel. If it's posi—if it's north to south, they attract.

Uh-huh.

So opposites attract and likes repel.

That's right. Now you're talking about healing. *[The teacher addresses Student U.]* Now do you understand the purpose of the water for healing? [Student B]?

Uh-huh.

All right. Do you have any questions there, [Student Y]? Yes, she does. Why don't you share that with her? *[The teacher addresses Student B.]*

I do have some understand[ing], but I'm still a little lost. [Student Y remarks.]

No, that's all right. You won't be lost long because we don't remain in the water center forever, you know. None of us do. Go ahead, [Student B]. I want you to speak to my student [Student Y].

About water? [Student B inquires.]

She's lost in the magnet.

My understanding is that water, then, is both electric and magnetic depending upon its use. [Student B shares her perspective.]

Correct.

Its direction. [Student B adds.]

Correct. That's the same thing as earth is below or earth is above. Do you understand that, [Student D]?

You see, didn't you have a whole class—why, certainly you did. Hasn't been that long ago—on perspective? On your perception? Hmm? Perception. Form changes ever in keeping with our perception. Write that down. Form changes ever in keeping with our perception. Is there anyone who would like to disagree with that? [Student U]?

No, sir.

Do you understand that, [Student B] and [Student P]?

Yes. [Student B responds.]

Yes. So, you see, if you will go and do your homework, a little more homework on that that was given to you on the blackboard, and you'll say, "Now just a moment. What is my perspective? My perception?" You see? "Because what I am looking at is ever dependent upon my angle to it. Why is it dependent upon my angle to it?" How does that work? Do you know, [Student R]?

Because the horizons—as your perspective rises—

Now we're getting there. Go ahead.

—*as your perspective rises, your—*

And how does your perspective rise in this teaching?

By . . .

By what?

. . . balancing the flow of energy.

By a broadening of the horizons, which frees you from the mist of the created forms. Go ahead.

So—

You're on the right path.

—*as your perspective rises—*

As you broaden your horizon, your perspective, your perception changes. Go ahead.

You see more clearly—

Correct.

—*the truth and you see less of the forms that stand in the way of it.*

That's correct. And so therefore, the form changes ever in keeping with your perception of it. Now, you've had that experience your whole life. You meet a, you meet a boy, for example, [Student Y], and he's just beautiful. He's absolutely handsome. Well, that's the perspective you have at that time in your evolution. Your horizon—you're in a spin cycle. Do you understand that? And when you move, in time, through experiences, you understand, to a retrospin, you broaden your horizon, you raise your perspective of the form you're looking at, and you have an entirely different view.

Now the question is, Did the form change? Pardon? The form does not change. It is your view of it. And your view of it is dependent on how narrow or how broad your mind is that you identify with. You see? Does that help with it? Yes, [Student Y].

So would that have a correlation with, with your horizons, broadening your horizons, would you go from a perce—a perspective of, from a function perspective to a faculty?

That is the whole purpose of evolution. You move from the peashooter to the all. Absolutely. And then, you see, you don't have to be so worried and fret and frustrated about this attachment or that attachment, about this frustration or that frustration, for you have finally permitted yourself the allness that you are in consciousness. So you move from these functions into these faculties and you bring about a balance with it. Yes. Yes, [Student O].

I have a question. I'd like to ask, How is that [one of] one's hallucination is more prevalent or dominant than another?

Well, what is hallucination?

That's when, you told me, when we, when we believe what we dream.

Yes. Yes. Yes. And I don't think we have any problem believing what we're dreaming, do we? I don't think so. Yes, [Student O].

I don't think so.

Do you believe that you're sitting here at a table?

I accept that I am, hopefully.

[The teacher laughs.] Well, I don't see any problem with that at all. "Dreamer, dream a life of beauty before your life starts dreaming you." That's very important that you understand how simple in truth that really is.

Yes, sir.

You have an experience. Why do you have an experience?

I, well, I—

An effect of what you've dreamed.

Right.

Right?

Right.

And were you doing the dreaming or were the judgments that you had created that you believe that you are for a moment dreaming it for you?

Ah . . .

You see, there's the question.

OK.

Who is doing the dreaming?

OK.

You see? "Dreamer, dream a life of beauty before your dream starts dreaming you." You see, you believe you are the experience. *[After a short pause, the teacher continues.]* Do you believe you are the experience or don't you?

I think I believe it because I know I'm responsible, regardless if even if the judgment did create it.

Yes, you have that responsibility. Because if you decided to make no effort and let the judgment create a nightmare for you, that doesn't change your responsibility for allowing the judgment to create a nightmare for you. Hmm? Does it? That's correct in that respect. Yes.

Thank you. That helps.

Hmm? So you must ask yourself the question, "Now just a moment. This is a dream. Am I dreaming it? Or is it a judgment that I have created and serviced? Is that, is that thing dreaming it? Who's doing this dreaming? I'm experiencing it, but who's in charge?" Who is in charge? That's the question we ask our self. Now just who is in charge here? If you find you have no control in the water center, then you know very well who's in control. You know very well. There's no question about it at all. That which you have created you are now believing that you are, and the water center is drowning you. Hmm? For a time. Yes.

Thank you.

You're welcome. Any other questions this morning? You know how quickly time passes in your world. I see the clock. Would you like to watch it a little more diligently so you—

No, thank you. It's quite all right. [Student R, who is responsible for recording the classes, responds.]

—can fit it on to a C-60? *[The teacher refers to an audio cassette tape that had a sixty-minute capacity. If class was longer than an hour, it went on to a C-90 audio cassette tape.]* Yes. Yes, [Student O].

Would, would you speak on reactionary forms?

Reactionary for—Oh, I see. You mean on those, those things that retaliate in your mind when you're dreaming that way. Yes. Well, you see, there's ofttimes, of course, you know, a person has an experience whereas a form has taken control, some judgment they made; they believe that they are the judgment. And then the judgment goes to use them to express itself. And it doesn't have its way. In other words, the purpose of the design of the judgment becomes thwarted. It doesn't get what it is after, and it's designed to get a certain thing in life, you see.

We design them for that. We create it. We create a judgment form to do a certain job for us, all right? And now when we create that judgment, along with the creating of the judgment, it has all its defense mechanisms. It has all those other soldiers, known as justification, you see. And so we have experiences. We come up against someone else's judgments, you see. And they're expressing and they don't agree with each other. And so we don't get our own way because you have all these other considerations in the mind at the same time. And that's all being weighed out by these forms.

So you go home and you find out that you went and retaliated against someone. You retaliated against them because your judgment didn't have its way. Do you understand that?

Yes, sir.

Well, you see, this is why you have that affirmation. You take control of your mind. Because it's your mind. It's in the purpose of design, being your mind, to take control of it, you see? It's when we tempt to control something that's beyond the rights of our mind that we find we get controlled by it. You take control of your mind, [which] means to take control of everything you've put in there.

Yes, sir.

Do you understand that, [Student O]?

Yes, sir.

Hmm? You see? You see, try not to forget that it's your mind. It's purpose of design is to serve *you*.

All right.

It's purpose of design is not for you to serve it.

Right.

You see? So there is more than one way of looking at anything. There's definitely two ways in a world of creation. You look at it from below, with the functions. You look at it [from] above, with the faculties. *[The teacher points first to the triangle on left in Student R's notebook and then to the triangle on the right.]* Now when you balance these faculties with these functions, when you balance these centers with these other centers, then you will be in consciousness between the four and the five, where this light of reason flows; it will transfigure you. Yes, [Student L], please.

Does that line between four and five, between the two apexes, represent the light of reason?

That is where the light of reason flows. It is a line: the line of infinity.

Oh, the line of infinity.

Yes, [Student R]. I'll be right with you, [Student Y].

It was stated earlier that the water center is the residence of the ego.

That is correct.

What is it—

It's the house of judgments.

—that resides in the etheric center?

Now that's a question I want all of you to write down. And we'll see how you're going to do with your homework. The water center is the house of the ego. Why is it the house of the ego, [Student B]? How is it the house of the ego?

Because that's where we create forms.

Correct. And believe that we are them.

Our egos are just created forms.

That's all they are. You see, a person says, well, this person has a large ego; this one has a small ego or this one has practically no ego. That's total foolishness and absolutely inaccurate. Everyone has a, what you might consider, a titanic ego. It depends on what they do with the forms they create. You see, you have to have a large house of ego in order to accommodate so many tenants. *[Some students laugh.]* So there's no such thing as a little, small cottage of an ego. They're all mansions. Castles, perhaps. They're huge-istic. Because they have to have so many rooms to accommodate all those tenants. Do you understand? Plus all their buddies that sneak in, you see. In the back door. Yes. So that's ridiculous. Ridiculous. Yes.

What was, what was the other question here? Do you have another question? *[The teacher addresses different students, and after a short pause he continues.]* We talked about the water center and you want to know about which other center of consciousness?

I was asking about what resides in the etheric center. [Student R responds.]

Yes, which—oh, in the ethereal center. Ah! Now tell me something. You received way back in the 60s, 70s, 80s—my, so long ago in your world—you received what was the faculty for the balance of what you understand as the ego. *[After a short pause, the teacher continues.]* Money, ego, and sex. What, what goes with money, ego, and sex? What's the faculty?

Faith, poise . . .

Faith, poise, and humility. So put it down. You've got your answer early. You should have known it anyway because I've given you this many times. Poise. What is poise?

The sense to pause.

Yes! Inaction. It's not reaction. It is not action. It's inaction. Do you understand that? Well, now when you have this problem here with this great castle, known as the human ego, with so many tenants, well, that's when you move in consciousness inside to the corresponding center for balance. Poise. Yes, [Student P].

Then also we have duty, gratitude, and tolerance.

Well, yes, you have faith, poise, and humility.

Right.

And you have duty, gratitude, and tolerance.

OK. So—

The faculties that were given to you.

OK. So it's the tolerance is—that's when you have to, when you, when you stop and because you realize the form that you've created and you don't want to battle with it, but you want to be— is it tolerant of yourself—

Yes.

—if you've created it—

Yes. Anyone who is not tolerant of the forms they have created cannot express tolerance to another.

So that's, that's actually poising the ego in that moment? Not to judge the form that you've created.

Well, for example, the ego is the water center and poise is in what center? I just gave it to you.

It's fire. [Student D responds.]

Poise is in the fire center?! Oh, my, oh my, my, my! *[All the students laugh.]* My, class is almost over. My, my, my! Now I want more homework done here. More homework done here. [Student R]?

Ethereal. [Several students volunteer their response.]

It's in the ethereal. [Student R responds.]

[Some students continue to laugh.] No, no, no, no, [Student D], be patient there. We'll get to it all. My, oh, my. More homework [must be] done here. More homework. Here, we're speaking of the ethereal center of consciousness, the step before the celestial! My goodness sake's alive, what is the fire center doing

up there?! *[Many students laugh.]* How did that get up there? I cannot change my perspective that much. I can turn around, but not that much. No. No, no, no, no, no. Oh, my. All right now, time's almost gone for us now. Yes, [Student D], you have a question. And [then Student Y] has a question.

OK. I said fire, but I was thinking of the, the faculties and the functions and the overlay of the—is that located, what we we're talking about, is it located in the odic, which is the overlay of the fire?

[Student S]? *[The teacher looks at Student S, and then looks to Student R and taps Student R's notebook.]* You did the overlay. Both of you. What does it show to you? Does it show you the odic?

The odic overlays the fire, but— [Student S responds.]

Well, yes.

—what was the question?

Yes. But, you see, she got that confused with the ethereal, which is the step before the celestial. I never found anything truly heavenly about the fire center at the expense of all the other lovely centers of consciousness. Thank you. [Student Y], please.

I was wanting to know where would nine be, the number nine in the, in the . . .

Very, very important question. It's the one number that you don't see there. Well, that's not only the one number you don't see, you don't even see a number eleven there, do you? Do you know where number nine goes, [Student R]? You've received plenty of teachings.

No.

We're talking about this diagram now.

The line of infinity.

That's what nine is, isn't it?

Uh-huh.

The line of infinity. And what is its circle?

Reason.

No, no, no.

Ah, ah ... in ... ah ... I'll get it. [Student R laughs.]

You don't have to believe you're eternal, you know.

No. Eternity.

Yes, [Student P].

Circle of eternity. [Student R continues.]

No, I was scratching my head. I was thinking. [Student P responds.]

Oh, that's good. That's good. Perhaps you'll scratch a little lower and think deeper.

OK. [Student P responds.]

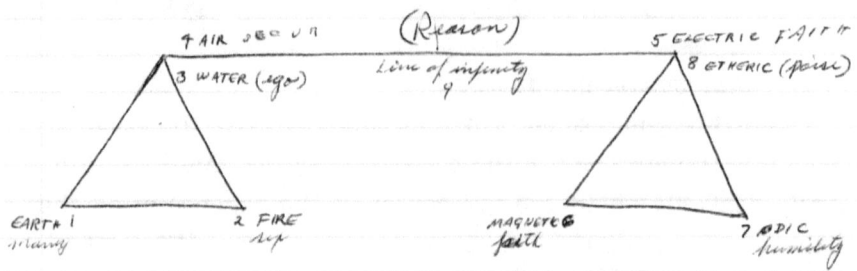

[Figure 44.1]

[This is the figure that was drawn in the notebook of Student R, who sat to the right of the teacher.]

All right. Now let's get our study's here, a little more on our homework. A little bit more on our homework, so we don't place the fire center next to the celestial and so we don't get the other centers confused here. Because what is truly important is that you understand the centers are inside of you, first of all; that you are identifying with these various centers at different times through the course of a day or a night; and that is not what you are, but it is what you have created.

Just because you are responsible for what you are creating does not establish a law that you must remain there. And you can change just like that. You change through the affirmations that are given to you. And always accept the possibility, as long as you do not use that Light of truth to transgress the divine, immutable law and take control of something that is not within your divine right. So that which is in your divine right—and we all know what's in our divine right, and we also all know what is not in our divine right, like controlling someone else. Because we first must learn to control our self. And even when we do, we are not, by divine law, able to control someone else. Do you understand that? So we all know what is our divine right.

So whenever you enter one of these things you have created, such as an obstruction to what it is you truly wish to do and are working to do, declare the truth. Flood your consciousness: "I accept the possibility." Now when you accept the possibility of something, you do not permit the form to be created by your mental substance that it shall or shall not be. That's the one trap that most students fall into. Do not allow yourself that temptation and that luxury. It's very, very detrimental. You accept the possibility while refraining from the creating of a form that you're going to get it or not get it. All right? Because when you accept the possibility, you go into a retrospin and you will have different experiences. And I can assure you they will certainly be better, for the experiences in life that are numerous, rather than the ones that are limited to a rote and a constant repetition, are surely the best. So accept the possibility.

Say, for example, you're trying to get something worked out in your business. Well, you see what you have created; you say, "I accept the possibility. I accept the possibility." But you must be on guard that in that declaration of truth a form is not created that that's going to work or that's going to work or that's going to work. Don't do that because you'll put yourself right back into the trap. All right?

Time has passed. Thank you very much. I think, perhaps, we fitted this onto a 60, did we? *[The teacher again refers to a C-60 audio cassette tape.]*

We just might have, yes. [Student R responds.]

Oh, isn't that nice. Lovely day. Must be your birthday. *[Some students laugh.]* Thank you very much. Good day.

APRIL 20, 1986

A/V Class Private 45

Good morning, class. Please be seated.

Good morning on this beautiful morning. I expect that you have been working on your homework this past week. And today we will continue on with our discussion on these centers, which are in truth the bodies of consciousness.

Now you've already had your nine centers which represent the nine bodies of consciousness. It's important that you realize leaving your physical body is not something that you learn; it's something that all beings are indeed most proficient in. And we'll have that discussion this morning.

Now I know that you realize that at times you seem to think you feel one way or you feel another way, or you believe this way or you believe that way. That, of course, is ever in keeping with the center of consciousness through which you are overidentified with, and that is the body that is in your physical body at that time.

Now are there any questions on that? [Student J], do you have any questions on that this morning?

If we know better, and yet we find our self in a lower level . . .

Yes, one of the other bodies are in—

[In] one of the other bodies.

Yes.

And yet we're—and we're aware of it.

Yes.

Why don't we, or how can we make more effort to get back to where we should be?

Yes. Now it is true that it is difficult to overcome a magnetic force field. For you must realize that in order for that which you are to leave your body, that which you are not, which is one of the centers of consciousness through which your true being is expressing, is held there by a magnetic force, a force of gravity. Now overcoming gravity, as you will study your notes, is dependent upon your proficiency, through understanding, of the retrospin. Now a person, for example, they hear the word *retrospin* and they say, "Fine. Well, now how do I spin out of what I have magnetically permitted myself to be pulled into?" Because it's literally a force field. It's actually what it is.

So a person finds themselves, for example, in a certain thought pattern, which is in truth the thought patterns which are the responsibility of a particular body or a center of consciousness. For example, let's take one of the centers or one of the bodies that most people in their evolution become extremely, extremely familiar with. Let's take the fire center or the fire body. Now, of course, we all realize that that is the second body or the second center of consciousness: earth, then fire. Whenever a person permits themselves to overidentify with physical substance, they, at the exclusion of their other bodies of consciousness, permit a building of a force field of the earth body. For example, if a person believes that they are the physical hand which they are using, then through that belief they become bound, and that earth body is the body that is usually at home in the house of clay.

Now the affirmations that have been given, as I've explained before, have been designed over eons of time to, what you would say, the bodies would say to you is most irritating. You will find that the spiritual exercises that you have been given are irritating to certain bodies of consciousness. Have you not had that experience?

Yes, sir.

For example, when, you know, you have the awareness that you are experiencing a terrible upset. Perhaps, the water body is in charge at the time or in control of the vehicle. And you have a slight awareness that that is not you, but it is controlling you for a time. Well, that slight awareness is the early stages of freeing oneself from the magnetic fields.

Now the water center is where the so-called force of the field truly is. That is the force of the field. For example, you cannot remain, that is, your earth body and your fire body cannot control your vehicle without the use of the magnetic force field of the water center or the water body. So a person remains out of their body and one of the other bodies, such as [the] earth body or fire body, one of the other bodies take[s] use of their vehicle. And therefore, working on the water body, which is the true magnetic force field, is where one should work.

You will note that when you are believing that you are the fire center, when you believe that and the light of reason is cast upon that, the irritation is an effect, of course, upon the water body. One becomes emotionally upset, you see. See now, some time ago we discussed irritation awakes the soul. It awakes the conscious[ness and] permits the true body, the soul body to return. Do you understand?

So when you find yourself controlled by any of these various bodies or centers of consciousness—which is, of course, the effect of directing intelligent energy to that center. You see, when you direct intelligent energy to a center of consciousness, you send a call out into the universe for that body to come in and take control over you. Do you understand? So, for example, the more you think about something, the greater is the force field that is built up to permit that body to take control of you.

So you'll find that there are times when you're going to do your affirmation and it becomes like a rote; it has no beneficial effect; you don't seem to be able to get out of that center of consciousness, for that particular body you've overidentified with doesn't want to leave and is not about to leave, but you still know inside of you that that is not you. It is because you will find that the water center has had more use of your vehicle than all the other centers of consciousness. But, of course, it is most encouraging—and it is the early stages of freedom—to have the slight awareness when those other bodies are in control of your vehicle.

So when you declare your affirmations, you will find, at times, you can't remember certain words, you get extremely irritated, you don't have the energy to say the next line, for example, or you just say the heck with it and go on about and service the body that's in control. Yet, if you would just pause for a moment and continue with the repetition, you understand, of the affirmations, you would find an experience of what you understand as anger begin to take control of your being, of your vehicle. And that is when—that anger is coming from the fire center. And it is coming in to balance out your overidentification. The water body and its forms have taken control, and so you experience that in your mind, and you call that anger inside of yourself, you see. I know you've had that experience a few times. *[The teacher laughs.]* Does that help with your question, [Student J]?

Thank you, sir.

Yes. It's very, very important to separate truth from creation, to declare daily what you are as you view what you are not. You see, you take a look and say, "All right. I am that which moves these fingers. But I am not the fingers. And because I am not the fingers, I can do with the fingers or without the fingers." For, you see, if you are overidentified with the physical body, if the physical body is in control, then the emotional body, where the magnetic force field truly exists, you see, that will upset you to no end at the very thought that you would be without fingers. But you realize you would only be without fingers in a physical world. And you would only be without them because you have overidentified with a physical world, and the earth body is the body that is in control, you see. You see, your fingers that you view in a physical world from the physical body exist in all the other bodies of consciousness. Hmm? They exist all the way through the celestial, you see. The same fingers. The very same fingers. Now any blemishes upon the fingers are ever in keeping with overidentification to the particular body that you've allowed to reside in your little house at the expense of the other bodies of consciousness, you see.

You see, if you overidentify with anything, you must realize that that is the body that is using your vehicle at the expense of the other bodies. Hmm? See? In other words, it's overstayed its lease in your little house. Way overstayed it. And time for it to get out for a while.

Yes now, you have a question there, [Student U]?

Well, then, as, as the blemishes physically diminish over time, does that demonstrate a redirection toward a different—

Well, certainly it demonstrates and it reveals less overidentification with that particular body. Now, for example, you take a person that has a freckle. And they have one freckle. The next thing you know, they see 2. The next thing there's 3. Then there's 5. And then there's 50 and then there's 5,000. You understand? All right. Now that is a person who is overidentified [with] the physical, the physical body, the earth center of consciousness, they have so overidentified with, they actually believe that they are that body. And through that belief—do you understand that?

Yes, sir.

They look at the physical world and they compare what they judge their body looks like compared to someone else's body. And the more they identify with that, the more energy they feed to that, that which was once one freckle becomes ten million freckles. You see?

Yes, sir.

In fact, I worked with one of my students years ago and explained to her very clearly that freckles were the angels' kisses, you see. Those were God's kisses, in order to help bring about a balance with the increasing freckles upon the physical body of the person. So once it was accepted, you see—remember, humor is the salvation of the soul. You see, that is received as humorous by the intellect, by the mind. You understand that?

Yes.

That is rather humorous. It isn't such a bad thing because it's actually God's kisses, you see? So when you do that, you change, you introduce into the consciousness another judgment. That judgment serves the vehicle known as humor, which in turn, the balancing of the soul may have a chance, in that respect, to bring about some degree of balance. Otherwise, the person becomes so freckled they wouldn't know what to do with themselves, you see, having judged that freckles are not beneficial to them. You see? You see, a person who has a problem with freckles, even though they are God's kisses in that respect, a person who has a problem with freckles is a person who is self-conscious and aware that people are looking at them because of their freckles and has already judged that they have something, an asset, that is much more pleasing to look at and that the asset that is pleasing to their mind to look at is not being looked at because the freckles are in the way. Do you understand that? You see?

Yes, sir.

Yes. Yes, you have a question this morning, [Student M].

No, not yet. Thank you.

Oh, you don't? Well, no is a question, too, you know. Most people think that no is a statement. No is a question. Do you know why no is a question, [Student B]?

No. [Student B responds and many students laugh.]

Do you know why—that's another question. Do you know why no is a question? It's not a statement. What does—when you say no, though it is God's direction, it's a question to the mind. God's direction is always a question to the mind. Now why is no—yes, [Student U].

Why not? That's the question that popped, that—No. Well, why not?

Yes. [Student B].

Well, when I said no it also meant that I wanted it explained. I was asking.

Correct. No is a question to the mental world and to the human mind. And that is why no is ofttimes God's direction. Hmm? For it is a question to the human mind. Do you understand why, how no is a question to the human mind, [Student J]?

No, I don't understand.

No. *[The teacher laughs joyfully.]* That will be a question. When a person says no, they always experience, well, like you dare say, down the road, "Now why didn't I say yes to that?!" Because, you see, what says no is never secure. In other words, when a person says no, they leave themselves in doubt. Now why does a person, when they say no, leave themselves in doubt? Now remember that no is ofttimes God's direction. But to the human mind, it is always a question. [Student B]?

Because you've denied that you do know.

You have denied that you do know. You say no. Someone says to you, "Well, I would like to go on this nice journey." And you say, "No!" After you have said no, there are mountains of questions and doubts that rise in your mind. Do you understand that, [Student Y]? *[After a short pause, the teacher continues.]*

Now they may not come immediately, but they always come. "Had I done this, this may not be that way for me now." "Oh, if only I had done that." But you must remember that at those times you had said no. See? So no is always a question to the mental world. Hmm? What is the one thing that no introduces into the mind that causes it a state of confusion and doubt? [Student R]? What does no introduce into the human mind? Yes, I'll be with you in a moment, students. *[The teacher addresses other students.]*

Temptation. [Student R responds.]

Well, if you can call fear "temptation," it certainly introduces that. No introduces fear to the human mind. How does it introduce fear? Because it leaves the human mind in doubt that it made the right decision. The human mind is always in doubt. It's always in doubt. Hmm? In fact, if it wasn't for doubt, the human mind would not exist. It would not exist.

You see, first of all, you understand that no is denial in consciousness. No, in that respect, is a denial. And whatever the mind denies, it always remains in question of the possibility. Hmm? Now you put that down, you see, to any experiences in your life and you will see the shadow always comes up. Perhaps a year later. Ten years later. Twenty years later. Fifty years later. "Why didn't I take that deal?" Hmm? Right, [Student J]?

Yes, sir.

You know, there are times when [you say], "Oh, I should have taken that deal." Correct?

Yes, sir.

"But I said no."

Yes, sir.

So, you see—remember that total acceptance is the will of the Principle of Goodness. It's a total acceptance within the consciousness. Always the possibility. Hmm? The possibility. Now that's a lot to think about. A lot to consider.

[Student H], you had something to say.

Only when you were asking a question. What I had in my mind was that it was introducing possibility. The possibility that that—

You made a mistake.

—you made a mistake.

It always does. Whenever you say no, when the human mind registers someone saying no, there's always the suffering of the possibility, you see, "I should not have done that." Correct?

Yes, sir. [Student J responds.]

"I should not have done that. I could have done it a different way." Hmm? Well, you see, you have all of these different bodies coming in and out. And then you have those who are insistent that the house belongs to them, and they don't want to leave at all. Hmm? Yes, [Student L].

You taught us years ago that, through the Law of Duality, every no has a yes.

Of course, it does. Well, you just say yes and no to your mind with any question, and you will find yourself in a total state of confusion. You don't know what kind of a trap you got yourself into. Say yes one second and no the next. On the same request, you see. Just say, "I'd like this. No! Yes! No! Yes!" People say yes and no. *[Many students laugh.]*

Now try to understand that this is going on in your mind anyway. You see, you've lost conscious awareness of it. You see, you go out, perhaps, to water the tree. And you know what your mind does, that you've lost conscious awareness of? It says, "Yes! No! No! Yes! Yes! No! Yes! No! Yes! No!" And you feel all this frustration and upset, you see. But it has happened so many times, you see, it has become a pattern in the consciousness.

You see, someone says, "Well, would you please do that?" You say yes. And the minute you say yes, you also say no. You see? And as you do that, you take a look at what you're going to do and say, "I'd better do this. No, I don't want to do this. Yes! No!" *[Many students laugh.]* And then all these things go on in the mind of, "What'll happen if I don't do it." You see? And then these other forms come in and say, "Well, if you don't do it, you're not going to get that. Now you know that you want that." And you see, all of this takes place in the human mind constantly, you see. Constantly.

And this is why in the human mind, there is no peace there. Peace is beyond the mental world. Because you have this yes-no business going on constantly, you see. And the human mind and those forms are always weighing out, "Now if I tell that person no, when I want such and such, they may tell me no. I better say yes." And so you're constantly going against—you see, what it is, now when you say yes and no and that mind's going on that way—all human minds do that—what do you create with this yes and no? What is the principle we're discussing?

Confusion. [Student U comments.]

You have friction, don't you?

Uh-huh. [A student different responds.]

You see? You see, you create a friction in the consciousness. Now what is the result of friction? What comes from friction?

Adhesion. [Student U responds.]

That's right! And so there's your bondage: your belief that you are your mind. That's constant. See?

Now I'm not saying the human mind doesn't serve its purpose. It certainly does, when you're aware of how it works. But we want to—we're here to be aware of how the human mind works. And through that awareness, we can make the gradual, slow steps to say, "All right. Fine. This is how it works. I'm aware of how it works. Therefore, I'm going to make greater effort, through my daily exercises, to go beyond that, where there's something reliable. I'm tired of this yes and no business." Hmm?

Well, it's like a girl—if you ask her for a date, she says yes and then you tell her what time she is to call you, because that, I think, is the system nowadays in your world down there, and you say, "Well, you call me in an hour." And she calls you in an hour, because you told her yes, and some other, something else is happening in your mind, you say, "No!" And then you go through all of this rat race of this yes and no. Usually, you have some kind of a justification to support the no, don't you see? Isn't that true how that works?

Yes, sir. [Student J responds.]

You see? This happens all the time. It happens all the time. Yes. And then, if, of course, if the caller, if the girl says, well, they're going to do this and that, then she appeals to your other forms; and if you're weak, you'll get into those other ones. And those other ones will say yes. And the next thing you know, you've gone from no back to yes again. But how long you can stay in yes, when no is waiting to take control, that remains to be seen. And someone else had a question here.

Yes. I wrote, as you were speaking, if there is, if there was no doubt, the human mind would cease to exist or—

That is correct. The human mind cannot exist without doubt. How could it possibly exist? It has established the very principle of the Law of Doubt: it has denied what it is, you see.

Oh.

You see, that which denies what it is lives the luxurious life of doubt, you see? Yes. You see, you know—oh, why do you experience doubt? You experience doubt about events in your life and what's going to happen and what has happened and what is happening and etc. Well, the only reason you experience doubt is because you've denied what you are. You see, when you no longer deny what you are, you no longer experience doubt. What is, is. There's nothing to doubt, you see? You can only doubt because you have denied. This is why, as you practice and you make the effort at total acceptance within the consciousness, you free yourself. From what? You free yourself from denial. And when you free yourself from denial, you no longer experience doubt. You cannot experience doubt until you have established the Law of Denial. Yes.

There's a lot to think about, [Student J].

Yes, sir.

You should smile when you have a lot to think about. Better for you to do the thinking than something else that has been doing it. Wouldn't you agree?

Yes, sir.

And besides, you're better this week. You're better this week. Yes. The good doctor spent a few days there with you. Yes.

Yes. Thank you.

But you are better. Yes. Oh yes, yes, yes. Those forces are long gone. *[The teacher laughs joyfully.]* Take care of your health.

Yes. Thank you.

Yes. Yes, does someone else have a question this morning? [Student H].

Yes. Thank you. When a person winds up totally confused that he doubts his own capabilities, he doubts that he's even done anything or forgets and so on, how, how does this work with what you're speaking about, this friction-adhesion?

Well, you see, first of all, you see, from the friction you're absolutely, you adhere to it; and therefore, you're totally attached and believe that you're that. You see, it comes only from denial, you see. You see, early in life a person like that would deny what they are, you see. They would dream of the many things they want to be because they have denied what they are.

A person dreams of being great as an effect of denying that which they truly are, you see? You see, you say a lot of people, they dream of being great. Well, great is ever dependent on the forms they have created that tell their mind, "Now this is greatness." You see? You see, when you deny you are great, that which you truly are—for that which you truly are is the Light, you see? Now when you deny that you are great, you ever experience a life of dreaming to be great, and you ever experience an unfulfilled life, for you've denied the fullness that you are. You see?

You don't have to keep denying that which you are. And you will know when you have stopped denying that which you are because deep inside of you, you will feel great, and you will be aware of that. And a person who feels great doesn't have to go around the world telling everyone how great they are. People who go around the world telling everyone how great they are,

are people who are just crying, like voices in the wilderness, for the greatness that they have denied. You see?

Greatness is not something that you can go and create. You see, you cannot create what you are. You can only create an illusion, you see. You can only create an illusion of what you are. You cannot create what you are, for you are greater than creation. So how can you create what you are? Show me someone who can create God. No. That comes from denial, [Student H]. That's an effect of denial, you see.

You know, a person who has denied what they are is also a person that is ever in need of being told how good they are or how great they're doing. You see, they can only survive, they can only live with themselves as long as someone is puffivating them. Otherwise, they cannot live with themselves. They are miserable for they've denied what they are. And they have tried to create what they are. You cannot create what you already are. The cup overfloweth. You can't get any more in it.

You are whole, complete, and perfect as the Light. That is what you are. Now all attempts to copy what you are, you must realize, fall without constant puffivation and support. You see? For you believe you are the counterfeit. You understand? So you believe you are the counterfeit, which is your payment for denying what you are.

So when you separate what you are from what you think you are, then you won't have any problem about anyone telling you how great you are. You won't even hear the word. Because you know what you are. When you know what you are, you don't have to have someone tell you what you are. It's people who don't know what they are, who have denied what they are, who need people to tell them what they are, you see? You don't need anyone to tell you what you are. You know what you are. You take a few moments to accept what you are. Hmm?

And woe to those who think for a moment that what they are is physical substance, because they have all those parts to cause them all those problems. You know, if a person uses their hand to satisfy people, then in time they believe that they are their hand. No eyes. No ears. No mouth. No teeth. No nose. No toes. Just a hand. So you see? That's what it offers. Show me someone that is happy or even fulfilled or satisfied just being a hand. Can you image a hand flying around the universe? Can't walk or anything. It's just a floating hand. No.

[After a short pause, the teacher continues.]

Well, how is [Student D] this morning, with all of her questions? As I say, the illusion of time in your world of identification passes very quickly. I assure you. And I'm on time this morning, you know.

Yes, you are. [Student D responds.]

I'm on time each morning. Ofttimes I'm waiting on someone else, but I'm on time. Yes.

I accept that.

Well, thank you. That's kind of you. *[The teacher laughs.]* Yes, [Student D], you're so kind today. Thank you. Yes.

Well, I'm not aware of my questions at this time.

Oh, don't feel bad. I would not mistake your kindness for weakness. Thank you. Yes. Does someone else have a question? Yes, [Student B] has a question this morning.

Going back to the water center—

Yes.

—is self-pity and belligerence and those kinds of expressions, are those from the water center?

Yes, they are defense mechanisms to protect the body. You see? You must realize that everything that is created, everything that is limited, is under the control of the king, the great king-judge. And we all, I think, know who king-judge is. He [is] down there. *[The teacher, sitting at the head of the dining room table at the Serenity temple, turns to his left and looks down directly at the floor.]* Oh, long way down. Can't see him this morning. But anyway, be rest assured he's there. *[The teacher laughs joyfully.]* So, you see, those are defense mechanisms, you see. They defend that body. Yes.

And when a person believes they are that body, then you have, as a defense mechanism, you have the pity of self, you have the belligerence, you have all of that foolishness, you know. Like you're, perhaps, used to experiencing with a little child who doesn't get his own way. You see, when a person becomes upset and they say they're upset and they reveal that they're upset because they don't have their own way, what they are telling you [is], "The body that has me in control right now is going to have its own way at any cost or any expense." You see?

So try to understand that these centers of consciousness, which are in truth the nine bodies of being, their very purpose of design is to defend themselves. You see, they're not truth. You see, I spoke to you long ago: truth needs no defense. Truth doesn't have need. Truth does not contain need. Truth just is. Falsehood needs and requires defense. So when you are communicating with anyone, especially when you're communicating with your bodies, you will see very clearly they require defense. They justify because that's a part of their defense mechanism for they're creation. They are not truth, you see? You see? Truth needs, nor requires, no defense. It just is. And crushed to earth, to the old physical body, it shall rise again. It shall always rise again, for that is the law. Without that rising again and again and again, there would be no creation for it sustains the limits, you see. The limitless sustains the limit. And the only thing a person defends is the falsehood of their own belief, is one of their bodies, you see.

Now a person may stand and communicate their position in life and what they're responsible for, and state it clearly. But that's not defense. No, no, no. Because a person who defends is constantly justifying and—and first of all, the body has judged that the threat is from without.

Now my channel went through quite a bit here just yesterday explaining to, I think, some of you students in very vivid detail that that is a person known as an emotionally gay person. You see, an emotionally gay person is a person constantly defending themselves and justifying and experiences self-pity and etc. Yes, in fact, it caused quite an upset here in the temple, my assistants inform me. Just yesterday. Yes. But, you see, he was instructed to inform you of the truth as you would relate to it. And, you know, it does wonders for what you believe you are to face the possibility that you may be emotionally gay. Both men and women. Hmm? I think that he did a fine job. Did a fine job.

Any questions on that, you know? The thing that you fear the most befalls you. So if you're afraid of being emotionally gay, well, continue on, you only guarantee it. I mean, after all, you will prove to yourself that you're not the form. *[The teacher laughs.]* Isn't that lovely? You see, so there's benefit to all of these things, you see. You'll prove to yourself beyond a shadow of any doubt, "Oh, you're not that earth body. Why, you're not even that mental body. Why, you're not even that water body." Oh, yes, yes. Our adversities, indeed, become attachments. Isn't that lovely? Yes, it's just wonderful. If that's what is necessary to inspire you out of the limit and experience what you truly are, then, if that's what you want, that's fine, you know. [Isn't there] a saying in your world, different strokes for different folks? Many paths to the same Light. Yes. Any other questions?

So please don't blame my channel if you find that you are emotionally gay. I assure you he's done nothing to help you on your way in that respect. Yes, [Student L], please.

Yes. In last week's class, you spoke of the two equilateral triangles.

Yes.

And the line of infinity that goes between the two apexes, which is four and five.

Correct. Correct.

Now—

That's very important that you understand. Yes. Yes.

—it was mentioned that controlling the functions is the number four, representing security to the water center.

Yes?

And that that is the faculty's expression is the number five, known as faith.

That is correct.

I'm wondering how, how it controls, how four would, would represent security to the water center.

Look at your world of creation. Now tell me how many poles are there? Hmm?

Poles? Two.

Two poles and two what else, [Student R]? Or don't you know?

I'm not sure. [Student R responds.]

Well, you know there're two poles. It's called the north and south.

Oh. [Student L responds.]

And what's the other? *[After a short pause, the teacher continues.]* What do you call those?

Direction. [A different student speaks.]

Oh, you call those "direction"?

No, I didn't say that. [Student L reacts.]

Yes, [Student N].

Spins, the, the, counter—

All right. Now let's, you know, I should really bring a little pad, now that our blackboard's not there. But maybe someday it'll be again. *[The teacher borrows the notebook of Student R, who is seated to the teacher's immediate right at the dining room table.]* Let me borrow your pencil here. You don't mind if I borrow the back page here, I don't think. You have plenty of paper. *[The teacher turns to the back page of the notebook.]* Oh, something on there. *[The teacher laughs.]* Something on the back page. Now— *[Many students laugh.]* It's interesting. I won't bother to look at it. I don't need to. Now you were discussing this little diagram here, isn't that correct?

Yes.

Don't expect me to be an artist, you know. *[The teacher draws two equilateral triangles and a straight, horizontal line that connects the apex of both triangles.]* All right. Now you were discussing here the four, *[The teacher writes "4" above horizontal line near the apex of the left triangle.]* which represents the security to the water center. And you were discussing the five. *[The teacher writes "5" above the horizontal line near the apex of the right triangle.]* Now you got your faculties *[He writes "F" just to the right of the apex of the right triangle.]* over here and you have your functions over here. *[He writes "F" just to the left of the apex of the triangle on the left.]* Note they both begin with F, won't you? Yes. Well, they do!

Yes.

Or didn't you note that? All right. Now don't get— *[The teacher laughs joyfully.]* All right. Now you've asked the question why does four represent security to the emotions and to the water center. And I stated to you there are four poles in your world of creation. I told you, and you agree, that there is the North Pole and there is the South Pole. *[As he speaks the name of each pole, he writes an "N" a bit above the apex of the triangle on the left and an "S" a bit above the apex of the triangle on the right.]* Correct? *[After a short pause, the teacher continues.]*

All right. Now what does the North Pole and the South Pole represent to you? What weather, what weather conditions, [Student R]?

Cold.

They both represent cold. Let's put cold here. *[The teacher writes "COLD" slightly above the N.]*

Is north and south at the two apexes? [Student L askes.]

Well now, are we going to answer all these questions at once? *[The teacher writes "COLD" slightly above the S.]* Or are we going to continue on here? We could go on to a different discussion if you would like, yes.

I apologize. [Student L responds.]

All right. North and south here are both cold. Now in your world of creation, you know it is not possible for creation, as you know it, without two hot areas. *[The teacher places the notebook in front of Student R and places the pen on the notebook.]* So what is hot?

The equator. [Student R responds.]

Well, I better do the line for you. *[The teacher turns the notebook slightly toward himself and picks up the pen.]* This is what you call hot, right? *[He draws a straight, horizontal line beneath the N and the S.]* We'll make a straight line for the equator. Now where's east and west? Where do you put east and west? Or don't you know? I put north there on the left and I put south on the right. Where do you put it? *[The teacher addresses Student R.]*

I would put west on the left and east on the right.

[The teacher writes "W" below the straight line representing the equator so that it is also directly below the N, which is above the line.] All right, you would put west on the left?

Yes.

Is that what you said?

Yes.

And you would put east . . . *[The teacher writes "E" below the straight line representing the equator so that it is also directly below the S, which is above the line.]*

Underneath the . . .

Under the South Pole.

Yeah.

Now why would you do that?

Well, it seems to me that the east belongs over the, over the faculties rather than the functions.

Well, it does! Well, I'm happy someone is doing some homework around here. So the east here is over the faculties, all right? Let's make that *F-A-C* here, the faculties. *[The teacher writes "FAC" even with the straight, horizontal line near its right endpoint.]* And where is the west?

Over the functions.

And the west we'll put that *F-U-N*. *[The teacher writes "FUN" even with the straight, horizontal line near its left endpoint.]* Because most people think functions are fun anyway. So let's just abbreviate that. *[Some students laugh.]* You know. *[The teacher coughs.]* Excuse me. So we have fun and fac over here, don't we?

Uh-huh.

Oh, yes, it's quite fun. All right. Now we find over here, according to what you have said, and I want you all to speak up here, we find over here we have the faculties south-east. *[The teacher points to the right endpoint of the line.]*

Uh-huh.

Is that correct?

Yes.

All right. Now if we have the faculties south-east and we have the functions north-west and we have the equator, this equator— *[The teacher retraces the straight, horizontal line.]*

Uh-huh.

—going straight through. *[The teacher indicates the upper horizontal line.]* And this equator, which you have your four and five on, that is your equator. *[He now indicates the lower horizontal line.]*

Now [Student L], tell me where north and west is for the functions and where the south and east is for the faculties.

I don't see clearly from here what you've drawn so— [Student L responds.]

Do you mind if I tear this out of your notebook? *[The teacher addresses Student R.]*

No. [Student R responds and the teacher tears the sheet of paper from the notebook, but only a portion of the page is torn free. A part of the page remains in the notebook.]

Oh, that's interesting. What part did we tear off?

The cold part. [Student R tears the remaining part of the page free from his notebook and hands it to the teacher.]

Oh, how unfortunate. That's where you preserve things, you know. Here, would you pass that to my student, [Student L]? Did you ever know of anything being preserved in a warm climate?

No. [Student L responds.]

Did anyone know of anything ever being preserved in a warm climate?

No. [Another student remarks.]

[Figure 45.1]

[This is the actual image drawn by the teacher and a close examination will reveal the tear.]

Now, you have south-east, correct?

[A few students respond, but it is difficult to transcribe their responses.]

For faculties. Do you preserve anything when you enter the Light?

When you enter the Light—

Yes. [Student S], do you preserve anything? Can you take limit into the Light?

No.

Of course not. Because the Light sustains limit. You cannot take limit into the Light. So whatever you preserve, north-west, in those—there's the area of your functions—cannot be taken into the Light. So why does four represent security to the emotional body? It represents security for that's where everything is preserved.

Oh.

Yes, now someone else had a question. You cannot, you see, it's like your human memory. Your human memory is totally dependent upon the north-west in that respect. Why do you face north, your head? North? If your head faces north, where's your face, [Student J]?

Your face would be south. [Student J responds.]

Hmm. That's right. That's right. Now you—I told that to you, I think, some time ago. You and a few students of mine. Yes, someone had a question down there.

Yes. [Student D responds.]

Yes, [Student D].

In the physical world, we can preserve things by drying them in heat. And I just wondered what—

What happens when you dry something?

It loses all its water.

That's right! Now my students are beginning to do a little homework here. It loses all fluid.

Yes, yes.

And what is the emotional body? What center of consciousness is it?

It's the water center.

It's a fluid center, isn't it? Well, now we're getting somewhere because class is almost over here now. Now do you understand?

Yes.

Put your head to the north and let your face go south. Yes. I'm happy to see that we're doing some thinking. A little deeper. Uh-huh. Yes, [Student O].

Would that hold true also for the, the hemispheres of the brain?

It certainly does. It certainly does. They have their own location.

Now, where—[Student D] was interested in that and I know you all are—in what part of the human brain [are] the controls of the fire center, [Student D]?

Isn't that back in the back down low, the thalamus—I'm not sure what the name of it is.

It is. It's down low. That's correct. It's correct. Now where's the location of the water center in the human brain? What controls—where's the center that controls what you call the emotions?

That's above the, right above the whatever the first one is.

That's right.

The hypothalamus?

That's right. It is.

[After a short pause, the teacher continues.] You see, as far as preservation, like you have stated, things are preserved by drying them. But not as they are. They lose all the water center. And they lose a large portion of the other centers of consciousness, [Student D]. You see, have I not taught you that functions are undeveloped faculties? Pardon?

Right. You have.

Well now, perhaps, you understand what, how they become developed. Hmm?

They dry out.

Have you not had in studies of all these various religions and philosophies that you are purified through the fire center?

Yes.

Is that not correct?

Yes, it is.

Why, certainly, because what happens when you give something fire, does it not lose all its fluids?

Yes.

Well, my children, my. So let's take our thoughts and forms that sometimes we believe we are and let's move them through the center of consciousness where they can be purified. Hmm?

Now remember, I'm not speaking of the fire center that's below the water center. We're talking of the next center, the light center, you see. The higher center, for those are the fires of the Light. Try to understand [there] is the fire of the Light and the fire of the flesh. Hmm? Don't mistake the fire of the flesh for the fire of the Light. My, oh my. You know how to tell the difference between the fire in your consciousness of the fire of the flesh and the fire of the Light? Would anyone like to know how you tell the difference in your consciousness? Yes, [Student P].

I would like to know.

Oh, you would like to—certainly. Certainly. I think we should all know. The fires of flesh cast a shadow and the fire of the Light does not. And why does the fire of the Light not cast a shadow? [Student R].

Because there are no forms in between.

That's right. There is no obstruction to it, you see. We depend upon our obstructions and relish in the conquest thereof. We do. In those realms, we depend on our obstructions. Yes.

Could you, please, explain that a little further, how we depend on our obstructions?

We always want what is not in our divine realm of control. And we find what we always want to be an obstruction.

Thank you.

For we transgress the law. We first judge it is desirable. And that which we judge is desirable, we first judge we have a need of. You see? First, we deny. And from that denial, we experience the need. And we judge that there it is: "To fulfill what I need." See, we've already denied that we have it. We first must deny that we have it. We first must deny that we are it, you see? You see, you cannot want, need, or desire anything that you have accepted you are. For example, say that, "Oh, I would like to have that lovely rose out there." The instant you accept that you are that, you no longer experience the need of it, for you have no longer denied the truth. You see? Accept that you *are* it, and you won't have to experience the need for it because you can't experience need without denial, you see.

So, don't you understand, the human mind depends on its obstructions and relish[es] and thrills in the conquest thereof.

Rather silly in a way, but it's how that realm works. For each denial, you must experience its equal need. Deny your goodness and you'll search to find it. You will not find it. Oh, you will be often deluded from the temptation of the search, but you will not find it, for it cannot last. It is an illusion. Illusions cannot last. You create illusions, but they cannot endure. You must constantly think of them, which is directing energy to them, for them to continue.

So each need you experience, which is an effect of your denial, which establishes the Law of Illusion, you delude yourself. And you can only sustain that for a time. It constantly must be fed energy. That which is created by energy must constantly be fed energy. So when you accept what you are, you won't have to be fed energy, for you are energy. So how can you be fed what you already are? You can't. Yes, [Student L]. Yes.

Yes. Thank you. I have a question regarding something you said last week. It was regarding the law of starting over when you make an error, instead of trying to fix the error. Would you expand on that?

Well, certainly. When you are in any project or constructing anything or forming anything in your mind and it is not what you consider quality or correct, then you must accept the demonstrable truth: that your efforts in creating it were partially or wholly controlled by forms you have created that you are not. So it is by far a wiser, wiser policy to take that which has been created by what you temporarily believed you were but you are not and to set that aside to return [to] the source from whence it has cometh, you understand, and to start anew. You start over, you see? And you make the effort to be freed from the forms you have created in order that you may express your true being. And because your true being is quality, your manifestation of your effort is quality. So, you see, you can tell, clearly, whether a person, you understand, is at home when they do anything or they're not at home. And if they're not at home, someone, something else is, you see.

So this is why quality is so critically important in anything. Quality in your thinking. Quality in your efforts, no matter what it is you do. Because, you see, the quality, which is the fruit of your act, you understand, that which you have created, reveals clearly to you who was in control of your body and your mind when it was brought into being, you see? You see—and this is another thing I have to reserve for another class—a child is born and comes from the fruit of the womb of the women of your world. The child is ever in keeping, its quality, the quality of the child—the form we're speaking of, you understand; you've got to understand that the soul has earned in evolution that particular form—the quality of the form of the child is in keeping with what forms were at home from the moment of conception on through.

And I see that, my, oh, my, our time has passed. Thank you. Now have a very good day. And I look forward to seeing you next Sunday.

APRIL 27, 1986

A/V Class Private 46

Good afternoon, students.

A little encouragement for your soul: today's recording shall not be erased. So I know to some of you who believe you are the mind, that is certainly encouraging. *[Although the students met at the temple on the previous Sunday, May 4, 1986, there is no recording of a formal class with that date.]*

Today we're going to realize, I think, that the teachings you receive are demonstrated in our lives, in our thoughts, and in our activities, for you have come to that state in consciousness where you must make the effort, for survival in the Light, to consciously choose what you are or what you believe you are. And no one, no one makes a choice until they've had sufficient experience in what they believe they are is no longer desirable. And when what you believe you are is no longer desirable, you search, you seek, and you begin to make the effort to find what you are. And perhaps from these experiences, you will understand desire, the divine expression.

When the direction of desire reveals to one, repeatedly, that a direction of that divinity must be changed by the will which is guiding it, then we begin to experience something beyond what our beliefs have offered to us.

Attachment to our fruits of action exists in magnetic centers of consciousness.

Now we'll come to your questions this afternoon. You are free now to raise your hand with any question you have. Yes, [Student U].

Why is it that we cannot control what we believe we are?

The reason that we say we cannot control what we believe we are, the reason that is done is because we have yet [to have] sufficient pain in that to be inspired to make the change. For example, you say, Why is it we cannot control what we believe we are? We control what we believe we are, for we have created that belief. Once having created that belief and experiencing what you understand as the glory of its effect—it isn't that you cannot control what you believe you are, for you fully controlled that creation in order to create it. So if you understand that what you believe that you are is what you have created, and from that creation that attachment does not allow you to control it. It is your attachment; it is your magnetic center of consciousness. As long as you insist on identifying with your magnetic center of consciousness, then you must pay the price of what it offers you. "I cannot control what I believe that I am." That is the magnetic center of consciousness and the forms which you identify with, which offer to you that is what you are.

Thank you.

So you've already demonstrated in order to create that, you've already demonstrated your control over it. Yes. Yes, [Student M].

Yes. You were saying attachment to our fruits of action exists in the magnetic centers—

Correct.

—of consciousness.

Correct.

Now the water center being . . .

One of them.

One of them. And the others being the nine bodies of the water center of . . .

Well, first of all, I have a question for your question.

Yes.

Does form exist in the nine centers of consciousness?

Yes, but I think on a diff—on a different sphere.

Correct. Correct. So now what is your question? *[After a short pause, the teacher continues.]* Now that you have considered more of the question, what is your question?

OK. I have felt, I guess, the attachment to the fruits of action is a function.

Functions are undeveloped faculties.

Yes. And the functions—

The soul can and does all forms create.

Yes.

So if you identify with the undeveloped faculties, then, of course, one has a lot of payment and grief.

Yes.

There are functions which are undeveloped faculties. Then there are faculties which are grown up.

Yes.

For example, I'll, perhaps, put it another way. A person gives birth to a child. She convinces herself in the water center that that is the fruit of her efforts and, in so doing, establishes the law to be controlled by it. A person gives birth in the sense they are an instrument through which the birth is made possible in developed faculties, and they are aware that they are an instrument through which that was made possible. They realize that they in truth are only an instrument of the creation. They are not the creator themselves of it. And that way they are not controlled by it.

You have a child. You believe that the child is the fruit of your own creation. The child grows up. You go through many experiences. It offers to you the same delusion that you are under at the time of your conviction: that that's yours. Denying the truth. The child grows up. You grow up. And in time you have no problem with the attachment to the fruits of your action. Would you not agree, [Student B]?

There is a transformation that takes place as you grow up and educate your uneducated ego. That's the difference between a function and a faculty. When you pass into the higher centers of consciousness, and we start into the faculty of reason, you realize that you have a personal responsibility and you accept your personal responsibility; and you grant that in your growing up to yourself. However, you have already granted the direct opposite to what you believed at that time was your creation. Does any mother not understand that? Pardon? Do you understand that, [Student B]?

Yes. [Student B responds.]

All people? You see?

Yes. [Student M responds.]

So as the teachings have been revealed to you, the soul can and does all things create. It does. When you identify with the creation in what is known as faculties, developed, you see, developed functions, and then you do not have the problem with the attachment to that because you no longer believe that you are the creator. And in refraining from that belief, you're freed from that bondage, and you are not filled with denial and need for glory of what you have accomplished. Yes.

Yes. Thank you.

Yes, [Student J], you had a question there.

Why does it take pain before one wants to effect a change in their life?

Well, the lord of the universe, that is, the lord of our universe responds to that which is painful and that which is pleasurable. You see, form offers duality. It offers pain and pleasure. It offers joy and sadness. So the awakening, that faculty of reason to shine over the lord of the universe—you see, the lord of the universe is your will. You direct intelligent energy; your will alone directs that. When experiences repeatedly reveal to you that the direction of your will, the effect of that direction of your will brings unto you pain, there is the natural instinct of survival that is instrumental in redirecting your lord of the universe, your will, that law, to something different than what you've already experienced. So that awakening does not happen until survival of what you desire is at stake.

Now to some people it takes a great deal of pain for—and suffering—for them to awaken and redirect their will into a different direction, you see. And then there are some people who say, "Well, I've never suffered." And they continue right on creating the same forms that cause them so much suffering. That's why it takes pain. In form, which is duality, there's always the choice: pain or pleasure. When the pain is sufficient, one redirects the energy flowing through them by their will. When the light of reason shines over the lord of the universe, they start on a new direction or a new path.

Thank you.

Did that help with your question?

Can I ask one more?

Certainly.

Why can't, why can't one, why can't a child learn this right up in front without going through that?

Yes, a child does, if they're properly guided. Now, you see, to form governed by the Law of Duality or two, you offer to a child, "If you do that, this is your experience. If you do this, that is your experience." So with a child, you offer them the law. The law is duality. "Insist on doing that and then this is your payment." You see, payment and attainment is a dual law that governs all limit. You can call it cause and effect, which reveals to all of us payment and attainment, doesn't it? You see?

You see, we seek the attainment without considering the payment. So a child must be guided to learn. "The attainment is ever waiting for you. This, this desire that you have created in your mind can be fulfilled. Here it waits for you in keeping with the law you have established. However, this is what you must pay for that attainment." Then the mind takes a look at how much it costs to get that. That is when you establish the law, which a child will learn from experience that he go[es] inside, you see? "Oh, no. No, that's too expensive. And so therefore, I no longer desire that attainment. I desire this one over here, for that one, my experiences reveal to me, all of my experiences, is it's much too expensive for that." Hmm? You see, creation is a playpen. Choose wisely, choose wisely.

So, you see, creation is like going to the department store. And you take a look at many different items. And you have a desire for that over there, you see. And you look at that and you want that very badly. And then you say, "Oh, I had best take a look and see how much that costs." You see, the payment, you see. And so you take a look at the payment and say, "Well, this over here is just as good." Because, you see, you're bas[ing your choice] upon the experiences that you've had: to take that that you really desire has cost you so dearly that you're willing to settle for second best because to your mind, at that moment, that's too much cost, you see. So payment and attainment is the law that is governing form. Does that help with your question?

Thank you, sir.

You know, a person says, "Well, let's see, I would like to have an automobile. Now I'd like to have an automobile so that I can move around and not have to be dependent on what you call other transportation." Dependent on someone else's will, you know. Perhaps they come early; perhaps they come late; perhaps they don't even come at all. And so you have the desire to have wheels of your own. And so you go out and you look at all kinds of wheels. But you can be rest assured that your mind's got: "Now how much will that cost me? How much is the whole thing going to cost me?" Then you begin to make decisions based upon your desires and your fears and all of your forms of experience. Does that help with your question?

Yes, sir.

Now that is how all minds work. They always work that way, you see. Therefore, "O suffer senses not in vain for freedom of your soul is gain." This is why the experiences that you encounter here in the school, you make them necessary. And there's good in that, of course, because in time it will inspire the students to make different choices. Because they have paid sufficiently for the choices they have made. And survival, survival of what they value is now registering in the consciousness, you see. And so the mind will say, "Oh, no, I've been through that enough." And it will make changes, you see. Therefore, the teachings without the application are worthless.

Now I don't want to say that the teachings aren't being applied. I certainly know better than that. They are being applied. I would like to see them applied in a more beneficial way to the soul. They are certainly being applied in benefit to the functions, you see, the undeveloped faculties, in far too many ways. However, that is absolutely necessary in order for the student to be inspired so they don't have to experience so much pain and suffering. Hmm?

So, you see, pain and suffering serves a very good purpose. It helps to free us from the attachments of the forms we have created and make an intelligent choice to create something different. You see, as long as we insist on identifying with the mental realm, then we must use the laws that will control that realm in our consciousness and make intelligent choices, you see? You see, try to understand, if you have children who have established patterns that they believe that they are, well, those forms, known as patterns, well, they're not going to give way easily. And to some it takes a great deal, and to others, not so much. And then, they're in and they're out of them, you see. And hopefully out more than they're in. Hmm? Of the patterns, of course. Does that help with your question?

Thank you, sir.

Yes, yes. Because, you see, creation is a price tag. All creation is a price tag. Whatever thought you think is creating a form. There's a debt you pay with that form, you see? And a wise man pauses and says, "Now just a moment. There is a price tag on this. I wish to see that price tag. Help me within—the Light within—to see how much that's really going to cost. How long will it take me to pay that price tag?" So you always want to look at the price tag. You see? "How much will this form that I am tempted by cost me? How long will I be in debt? Will it be

10 years? Will it be 20 years? Will it be 2,000 years?" And then you'll reach a time you don't want to pay that debt anymore. You see? You don't want to pay that debt anymore at all. Well, you see, the reason you don't want to pay that debt is because you did not make the effort when you were tempted to have that, that form, you did not make the effort honestly inside of yourself to the Light within you [to perceive] exactly what is that price tag. How much does that cost? Cost, not in dollars and cents. Cost in years and ofttimes centuries.

You see, had I asked, when I was on your planet, "How much does that cost? I want to see that price tag,"—I did not have that awareness. Had I had that awareness, I wouldn't have spent so much time in the desert. Do you understand? See, I did not have that awareness at that time. And so I know, and I'm trying to help all of you to know, that all forms have a price tag. Creation is a price tag. So choose wisely what you buy, because the debt, you'll keep on paying. You must take a look and see how much it's going to cost you in order to make an intelligent decision. Yes. For it can cost you for untold centuries. It certainly has cost me for centuries. Though it's long ago, it seems like just yesterday for me. Very expensive. Very expensive. A luxury I am no longer tempted by. Thank you very much. Any other question on that, [Student J]?

Not at this moment, sir. Thank you.

Yes. And so this is what we [are] here [for], in this lovely little school, this day, is to awaken to that, you see.

Or did I not speak to you, why, just here, last Sunday was it? *[Again, no recording exists of that class.]* Did I not speak to you on the great deceivers and the great actors and actresses? Well, my assistants tell me—because I went off and took care of my other schools, you know. I wouldn't be tempted to wait on how long it's going to take some of my students to come to some light of reason. And so when my other classes were finished, I came here to meet this class. Didn't I speak to you just last week about Mata Haris and actresses and deceivers? Well, they're in all of us, you know. They exist in our mental world. Hmm? Did you not have that experience today, a little bit, with Mata Hari? Did you not have that experience? You had that experience, just a little bit, with all of these different things, you see. And Sarah Bernhardts. Now you must realize that whenever we work to defend a form we have created in our mind, that defense requires wonderful acting because, you see, it's the illusion, you see. And so it requires that in order to perpetuate it, you see. Yes. Does that help with your question?

Thank you.

Yes. Did you have a question, [Student O]? [Student S] has a question; so I'll come to her and get to your question next. All right. Let's let the ladies come first today. It is Mother's Day, you know.

Thank you. [Student O responds.]

And that's something that one in your world usually considers ladies first.

Yes, sir. [Student O responds again.]

Hmm? Yes, like going through a door or something. Unless we consider our self ladies. I don't consider myself a lady. I don't need anyone [to] open a door for me. Yes, [Student S], please.

I'd like to ask, How do you check the price tag on creation?

Oh, my, so expensive. Yes, yes, yes. And if one is not used to checking the price tag, then, of course, for one's mind it could be a little difficult. One pauses and sometimes, you know, one goes into what they consider is a meditation—you see?—and they ask what they believe is the Light within them. You understand that? And if the desire for the form they have created is greater than their acceptance of the Light and God and Truth at the moment, then the desire will take the form of the Light, you see. And of course it won't show the price tag. You see? And it will convince the mind, "It doesn't matter how much it costs. I'm going to have that anyway."

So, you see, that's how the angels of darkness wear the garments of the angels of Light. Because they only wear the garments, you see. And so when a person has a desire, a desire for any form they have created—because remember, what we may desire outside is actually what we desire inside, and what is outside is reflecting that which we have created inside, you see. I'm sure all my students understand that. And so with desire, we must pause and make the effort daily to go to the Light within our self.

Now there's one thing about any form that we have created: it cannot sustain itself without continued energy directed to it. This is why it's so critically important—I've always taught my students to spend seventy-two hours with anything that they desire or decision that they make. Spend seventy-two hours to give them the opportunity to come to the light of reason within them. All right. Now, I've also taught them that the way out of a thing is the way into a thing. I have also taught you students that depending, ever in keeping with how much energy is directed to the creation of form, it will take equal energy to free oneself from the form they have created. I've also granted that to you.

So a person takes a look at a desire they've created with their mind. And they go inside. They make that effort. And they do not go by the letter of the law. They go a little deeper to the spirit of the law, for you have seventy-two hours with the desire you have created. Well, the question has to therefore be, "Have I only spent seventy-two hours of directing energy to this form I have created?" Now if we spent three years directing energy to this form we have created, then it's going to take equal amounts of energy—you understand that?—and direction of that intelligent energy, you see, before we can even get to the seventy-two hours. Because, you see, we've got all this debt back here. Do you understand that?

Uh-huh.

Instead, a person has a desire, say, oh, well, 9, 11, [or] 10 years ago. All right? And they've spent, oh, say, 9, 10, [or] 11 years directing intelligent energy to the desire form they have created in their mind. And then the day comes and the possibility, "Ah! Now I can get it fulfilled. However, I will take 72 hours in keeping with the letter of the law of the spiritual teachings that I am studying, I will take 72 hours to see if that is in my best interest by the Light within me." Well, the Light within you doesn't even get close to showing you what the cost is because, you see, there's a 10-year debt going on. Does everybody understand that?

So, you see, the letter—that's how the letter of the law killeth. And the spirit of the law giveth life. So after a person finds out, [that is,] they awaken from experience how heavy the burden is, how great the debt is, and they ask God, "Well, how long must I pay for this?" Then one must be honest with themselves and say, "Oh, God, how many years did I work directing energy to this form I've created? And how much of my energy did I give to creating that?" And then, if they're honest with themselves, they say, "Let me see. Well, it was only 10 years. Wasn't 11 at all. It was only 10 years. So I have now 10 years."

"Does that mean I've got to pay for 10 long years?" No, it's just like a debt you incur at the department store. You have a ten-year contract, and you can pay that off, if you like. Sometimes you have to pay a penalty clause payoff, I think you call it, but, you see, there's always the possibility in a contract.

You see, what you want to understand: you make a contract with a realm of consciousness that is the divine right of the angel Lucifer. Now if you will understand that's who you've made your contract with, then you'll be very specific about his cost, you see.

So when you desire from creation, you are asking Lucifer, the fallen angel, the king of those realms, for that fulfillment, you see. You see? So when you're working expecting your fulfillment of your desire to be fulfilled in a mental world [you are] not declaring the truth, "O God, free me from this desire that I have stolen from you. Free me from that." [If you release it to the Divine,] then, you see, it returns unto the source. It may or may not come to pass. It shall always come to pass in principle. It is not guaranteed to come to pass in form.

So when you have a desire and you specify the personality of the desire, and you are not grateful for the principle of the fulfillment of the desire, then your contract is with the fallen angel. And the fallen angel does not reveal the price. And what he will do, he will simply leave you, if you insist on the cost from the fallen angel. If you insist on your desires in life being fulfilled by creation, you see, then you must expect to pay Lucifer's price, no matter who expects from creation. You see, I've taught you that in so many different ways. I've taught you accept from God, and you will not expect from man. "Man" in that sense, of that particular part of the teachings, being creation. Do you understand that? But if you insist on expecting from creation, you must be willing to pay the debt that he extracts.

Now I can assure you that the fallen angel's debt goes far beyond your physical life experience. It goes through many, many realms of consciousness. He does not let go until he's extracted every ounce. A contract that—no intelligent person would knowingly, consciously make a contract with creation. Yes. Yes.

In the Rotunda...

Yes?

... on those teachings, we were told—and I'd like to ask for clarification—that at that time we make a contract with the Light and the darkness—

Correct.

—before coming.

That's correct.

How would one come without having to make a contract with the darkness? Is that possible?

Why, certainly. There are many souls that enter what you call creation that are not convinced that they are creation.

Uh-huh.

You see, you have to understand you're fulfilling, anyone is fulfilling a contract with the fallen angel and, therefore, is dependent on creation for their goodness in life. Does that help with your question?

Uh-huh. [Student S speaks very softly.]

Pardon?

Uh-huh.

Yes. Now, you see, as you move—as in all contracts, all contracts are negotiable. They're all negotiated. Do you understand? They're negotiated between two parties.

Uh-huh.

All right? So in the contract and in the negotiation, you are never, no one is ever left without turning to the Light for their fulfillment in life. Even when the contract is made in the Rotunda, contained within the contact is always the opportunity. That always exists, moment by moment. To grant the service and—you grant service to the Light by accepting from the Light. You grant service to the fallen angel by expecting from creation. Hmm? Yes.

May I ask one more? If we do incur the debt to Lucifer ...

Oh, it must be paid.

Now you said something about we can renegotiate the contract—

No. No, no, no, no. We can't renegotiate the contract. No, we don't renegotiate. The contract is negotiable at the time that it is made at the Rotunda. And, you see, for example, a person, you see, here the little soul waits in the Rotunda. Here's all the experiences of their evolution. The contract is made between the Light and the darkness. Because without the Light, there is no darkness. It doesn't exist. There is no creation. Therefore, the fallen angel and his henchmen must make their contract with the Light—all right?—before your soul can enter into creation. You understand that? And into those realms.

And so in that contract, which is negotiated, you have, or anyone has, a debt they must pay to the fallen angel's realm in keeping with their evolution. In that contract is ever the opportunity: "I do not expect from creation." When that declaration is demonstrated, you understand, by anyone, they accept what comes from the Light in principle. So a person, moment by moment, in keeping with the negotiated contract that's already been established, they have always, always the opportunity: it's ever at hand. "I no longer choose. I do not choose to expect from creation. I choose to accept from the Light within. And I have no problem." Yes.

Well, then what about paying off that debt though?

Show me one soul in creation that is not tempted to expect from creation. The debt gets paid off. The debt gets paid off. Yes.

You said that, like—

I know what you're saying. Yes.

You can pay it off in ten years and then you can, with a penalty, pay it off, maybe, sooner.

Well, you're talking about creation. Show me a contract in creation [that] doesn't have a penalty clause, if they don't get their interest. Would you agree, [Student B]?

Yes.

So, you see, you see, the fallen angel has put all these penalty clauses in. Do you understand that, [Student O]?

Yes, sir. [Student O responds rather sleepily.]

Good for you! Would you like a glass of water?

No, sir. [Student O responds much more awake.]

All right, then, you tell that thing it's a lovely day. Yes. *[The teacher addresses Student S.]*

Well, my question is, If we are considering paying it off, how do we know that we can afford the penalty payment and not hang ourselves again by overextending our self to pay it off sooner than would be reasonable for us?

That's the light of reason. You see, you live in a little house in creation?

Uh-huh.

You make an intelligent choice whether to pay it all off with a penalty clause and will you survive after that in the way you desire to survive? Is that not, is that not a question—

Right.

—that you intelligently answer?

Uh-huh.

Well, same thing. You're talking about creation.

OK.

You know, whether it's a house, a glass of water, or your physical form, you're talking about creation. You see, any time you expect from creation, then you must accept the demonstrable truth that you are paying the fallen angel. Therefore, before you expect from creation, say, "Just a moment. Just a moment now, Lucifer. You show me"—you see, if you demand of Lucifer, the fallen angel, for him to show you the price tag, if you demand that, he must show it to you or leave you; and therefore, the desire will go. You see, you see, if you demand that inside of yourself and say, "I desire this. Oh, I really want that." And you demand of Lucifer, he must respond to the Light. And he will show you the price tag. It is rare he will show it to you. He will leave you and you'll have the desire no longer. Oh, no, it's very, very rare. Only if he judges that by showing you the price tag for that item that you desire that he has trapped you for even a greater debt will he ever show you the price tag. No. No.

Because he can't get his workers that way. If he shows his price tags, you see, he can't get his workers. And he will show his price tag if he judges that by showing you the price tag for the satisfaction of the desire that you have, that the one he's got hidden behind him, after you're trapped, is much more expensive and a much greater debt. Because he has to first judge you that you're that weak, you see. Now his judgments are based upon the contracts that [have] been made in the Rotunda.

Uh-huh.

You are never left without the Light. But you alone must choose the Light. Yes.

Thank you.

Does that help there with your question?

Yes. Very much. Thank you.

Yes. And [Student L] has a question this, this afternoon.

I recall something about 51 percent. If we have accomplished 51 percent—

That is correct. What is that 51 percent?

Soul accomplishment, I imagine.

Fifty-one percent. What number is that, [Student L]?

Six. [Fifty-one is a 6 because 5 + 1 = 6.]

That's right. And what does the number six represent?

I think it represents oneness, but I can recall double manifestation.

It certainly does. What does it represent, [Student U]?

Divine love.

Divine love!

Divine love. [Student L remarks.]

When your love is divine, you're 51 percent in the Light; you don't have to worry about expecting from creation.

Thank you.

And you best not let Lucifer tempt you what divine love is. "Oh, love divine a servant be / 'Til selfishness imprisons me / And warps the reason of my mind / Into the madness of the blind." *[Please see the appendix for the complete affirmation, which was first given in Discourse 25.]* I would suggest you students repeat that until it really reaches your heart. Yes, [Student Y].

So you're saying that expectations bind us.

Expectations bind us for they tempt the functions to serve creation. You see, what is a temptation? Is it not an expectation? [Student J]?

Yes, sir.

I mean, are we tempted by anything we don't expect to get?

That's true. Yes, sir. [Student J responds again.]

So, you see, temptation-expectation belong to the fallen angel. You see, that's part of his, what you would call, his con game. But he doesn't show you the price tag. Yes.

And so acceptance— [Student Y continues.]

Is the will of God.

It frees us.

Acceptance frees us. You see, a titanic ego is an atom of rejection. Would you not agree, [Student R]?

Yes.

Did I not personally give that to you some time ago?

Yes, you did.

A titanic ego is an atom of rejection. You see? So all you have to do is to reject the divine right of the Light to express and you have total dedication to the fallen angel, you see.

So that's what it's all about, you see. This is what we're talking about. This is what you're experiencing. You see? Accept from God. Accept. You have a desire? Give it to God. Return it to the source. It is a divine expression. And don't tell God when you're to experience it. Forget the personality of the desire, for the moment it's got personality it belongs to Lucifer. Accept the principle of the desire, then you have the divine expression, but that takes divine love within your own being; that takes the expression of the love divine within you. Yes.

So I know this is a very mental question.

Well, that's what we're here [for]: to discern the difference between our faculties and our undeveloped faculties, known as functions. Certainly.

So when you accept something from God, is it a sense or a feeling that you know it's from God? We've—it's so easy to be led astray.

When you accept from God—you see, first of all, when you steal the divine desire, the desire, the divine expression, when you steal it from its realm of consciousness, you put a limit on it. Then your desire takes on personality. It takes on form. You understand that? Now when that happens, your mind begins to expect its fulfillment of it. It expects it. That establishes the law for the forms to come and tempt you. And they don't show you the price tag. So you're getting exactly what you wanted. You don't like it when the price tag comes due. You see?

You see, there's no way possible the fallen angel could operate and show you up front the price tag because you would never be tempted. There's no possible way. If someone told you, you have a six-year service of 10 hours a day, 6 days a week, for 10 years to pay for an ice-cream cone, would you accept it? Pardon?

No.

Well, that's what he does. That's what he does. For a few moments of pleasure. How long does it take you to eat an ice-cream cone that you must pay 10 years, 6 days a week at 10 hours a day? Well, take a look. I think it's a very, very poor contract myself, for anyone to make. Hmm? It's certainly not worth it for such a momentary satisfaction of a desire.

Accept from the Light. Because, you see, when you accept from the Light, it is guaranteed without a price tag. Only creation has a price tag. Now, the mind, if you believe you are creation, then as the Light rises within you, you will say, "Oh, this is a terrible price tag, walking on this path of Light. It's just a terrible price tag." Why, certainly, to your mind, who is controlled by the fallen angel, of course it's a terrible price tag. No price to your soul at all because you are awakening to that's what you are. That help with your question?

Yes. Thank you.

Now [Student O] had a question that's been waiting there for us. I'm happy to see that you're feeling better, [Student O]. Your little soul got back in there.

Yes.

Yes, oh my, what [an] irritating thing. Worse than irritating. Irritation wakes the soul. Your soul couldn't be woke. It was way over there. *[The teacher points off to his left, as he looks directly at the student.]*

Yes, sir.

I'm happy to see that you're back. Hmm. Yes. Now go right ahead with your question.

My question, yes.

I [would] have lots of questions [if] that thing got in temporarily and used my body. Hmm.

Yes.

Yes.

Well . . . [Student O paused for a moment.]

Well, perhaps I could help you with a question.

Yes.

Make a little effort there to help you with that question.

Thank you.

It is difficult for the mind to understand why students don't have more value. Would you not agree?

It's difficult—it is difficult for the mind.

Yes. That's what the mind says, isn't it? Doesn't the mind say, "This is something else. They have no gratitude. Look at the hour that classes have started. What's the matter with them [that] they can't see the Light?" Doesn't the mind say that?

That's something the mind would say.

Yes. I'm happy that you know you're not the mind, [Student O].

Yes.

I'm very happy considering that thing down below coming in and trying to say that while I'm here working with my students, including you. You see, just because I'm talking to [Student S] doesn't mean I can't see and hear what, what's going on down there. Hmm? Tolerance. There is no success, there's no spirituality without tolerance, [Student O]. Hmm?

Yes.

Surely you understand that, don't you? Well, you tell that thing to stay behind you. Far behind because you're looking at it. Hmm? You do that. And then, don't you see, you won't feel so badly. You see? Try to think. If something makes us feel badly, could that be from God? Could that possibly be goodness? Goodness can't make a person feel badly.

No.

If you feel badly and you have experiences that are not good, then we have to say, "Now just a moment. How could, how could I possibly call that God? God is good. Why do I feel bad? Well, God's not here. Let me get God in here." Wouldn't you agree?

Yes.

You see? And so even though the fallen angel is so clever and even though the fallen angel, because he controls the mental world, he controls limit, even though he knows all of the words of the Light, you understand, he's still a counterfeit. And he shall always be proven to be a counterfeit. You understand that?

Yes.

You see? He will always prove himself to be a counterfeit. Every beast shall show its face, and its day shall be known. You see?

Yes.

See? There's the difference. You know, my channel allows himself to be tempted [with] "It's just not worth it"—well, [if he overidentified with that thing] I wouldn't be here speaking with you through his form this moment. You see?

Right.

So he has to work on that because he knows that's not good, doesn't make him feel good, that can't be from God.

Yes.

Do you understand?

Yes.

You see? And besides, if you have to depend upon something outside of you for goodness, that can't be from God either. Because that has a debt. You see?

Yes.

God is not a debt. No, no, no, no, no. God is not a payment and attainment. God is. Truth is. You don't pay for truth. You can't buy it and you can't sell it. You see? It's what you are. That help with your question?

Yes, sir.

You do look better. Yes, your children look better.

Thank you.

Yes. Yes. You see, it was a very important question. I was looking to just see how long he was going to stay in there, you know, as I'm working with my other students. You see? So you made a little effort there. Not a good feeling, is it, [Student O]?

No, sir.

To have that thing come inside and take over your mind like that, you know. Sneak right in behind you, like a thief in the night, you know, and steal your form like that. Not a good thing. No, I wouldn't appreciate that at all. I have had too many experiences eons ago. Leave me out in the desert. Not even an ant to communicate with. And, you know, I like to communicate. I always did like to communicate. Oh, yes. Yes, yes. Yes. I never considered myself, like some of my students think my channel is, a motormouth. I think you call them motormouths. I've never considered myself that. You see.

Yes, sir.

Because I can stop when I want to stop. Yes. Anyone else have a question here? I didn't say that my students called my channel motormouth. Some of them believe that, and I'm trying to help them with their conviction and their bondage. Because no matter how much they believe that my channel is a motormouth, I'll just stay longer and see how much of a motormouth [I can be] to help them with their convictions. Hmm?

Thank you.

Well, isn't that what they call them? Motormouths. *[The teacher addresses Student R.]*

I've heard the expression, yes. [Student R responds.]

Well, indeed you have. *[Student R laughs.]* Yes. *[The teacher laughs.]* Now [Student H] has a question here this afternoon. And I have to work to not to say "morning" because I've already taken care of morning classes. I had to make a change there, but that's no problem.

Well, this is in reference to a couple of classes ago.

It's always pertinent to the Light, if it comes from the Light. Yes. Thank you.

Thank you. When you were speaking about how the student could get locked into the water center and it's difficult to say the affirmations—

True.

—and then you get through that by just a constant repetition of those affirmations.

That is correct.

And then, it was my understanding, that you said that there followed an experience or feeling of anger—

Yes.

—at that point.

Yes.

That's what I'd like to ask about. How does that, how does that happen? You said that the anger balances that water center.

Yes?

But how does that work, that that anger comes in? I'm unclear on that.

Oh, you're unclear on that? You're unclear that when you're in the water center—

Yes.

—and you use a repetition, through which the Law of Change is made possible, that you become angry? Your belief that you *are* the water center and the judgments you have created in there and your experience from that creates a condition that you know as anger, doesn't it? Would you not agree, [Student B]?

Sure. [Student B responds.]

You know, when you're in the water center and you're playing with the forms you have created and you're constantly repeating a demonstrable truth, the Light, then the energy is going to that which you are now moving towards, the Light, at the sacrifice of the forms that you believe you are. So in that transition process you become very upset and very angry, would you not agree?

Yes. [Student H speaks very quietly.]

Pardon?

Yes.

You see? You see, it's just like, you know, and I'm sure you've all had experiences right here, you see, that when my channel and his workers work and do what they can to help you to help yourself to free yourself from service to that realm, to Lucifer's realm there, you become very upset and very angry; then you experience a wonderful relief, you see? One experiences a relief when they finally stop all of that labor done there in the salt mine. And they say, "Oh, just a break." I mean, that's what your experience is. That's what anyone experiences. So you kind of sit back and you kind of rest and you smile and you feel real good. And then time passes, sometimes an hour, sometimes even almost a day passes, and you start thinking about self; and the forms come in and they tell you different things. And you believe that you are them because you're overidentified with self. And then they look at one person: whoever helped you to wake up gets all the rash. Would you not—do you not understand that?

Now in your world you like to say you always hurt the one you love. How many times has my channel said to us "Don't, don't—I don't want love any more. I don't want any love. Because it's absolutely guaranteed I get all this other. So please stop loving me. Everyone."? That's what he said. He says he wants the—he wanted the angels and—he didn't ask me personally because he knows he'd have a problem: he'd got it from me—but he asked a few of his other assistants: Please instruct them all that, that he doesn't want your love anymore. He'd rather have your hate because love costs too much. That's what his mind [acts] like. Do you understand that? All right. Fine.

You know, when you have spent your short life, this short time on Earth—you know, he spent his time on Earth [in the] experience [of] the love of the Light within him; then his mind cannot choose to have the love of form when he sees it's so terribly costly. This is why he's asked us to inspire the students; and his mother told me, "You call that inspiration, Richard?" Well, then he got what he wanted. He didn't get love, but he did get instruction. You see. No, this is so, so, so childish and so ridiculous. And life is so beautiful.

You feel better now that those, most of those judgments are gone, lying down there? *[The teacher addresses Student O.]*

Yes, sir. [Student O responds.]

You see, they're tickling around your wife's toes. *[Student O was married to another student who was also in class.]* I see them, but don't worry. They're only this big and they were that big. *[The teacher first gestures with his fingers of his right hand indicating a few inches, and then gestures with both hands indicating a couple of feet.]* So that's fine. Yes. You see, one should make effort to be tolerant with oneself. And if one is tolerant with oneself, they'll have no problem granting it to others, you see. A little bit more tolerance with [Student O]. The more tolerance with [Student O] will grant a lot more tolerance with all our co-students. Wouldn't you agree, [Student O]?

Yes.

Yes. You see, it's difficult to understand, "Well, why does [Student H] do this? And why does [Student S] do that? And why does this one do this? And why does that one do that?" Well, there's a reason for treason for all of us in form, isn't there?

Yes.

Hmm? You see? And to think, "Well, they should know better." Well, then we have to say if we had their evolution, if we were walking in their moccasins, would we really know better? Well, we don't know 'til we walk in their moccasins for at least a mile or two, you see. Hmm? Yes. Because then, you see, they turn around and they look and say, "That [Student O]. [Student O], why does he do all those things? Well, that's so stupid. He's an intelligent person. Why did you do those childish little things?" You see, because they think the same way. Sometimes.

Yes, sir. [Student O responds.]

You see? And, you see—and like we sit here and we say, "Well, how possibly could that [Student R] sit there and doze off to sleep in these classes?" Well, you think I'm not aware? I have a very good foot. I can let him have it. You know where, you know. *[Many students laugh.]* But I think in your world you usually use the knee. But I'd rather try it [with] my foot. Same place, you see.

Yes. [Student O responds.]

If he dozes off again. [Of] course he'll have to stand for me to accomplish that. With my foot. Hmm. Feel better? Good!

Yes. Thank you. [Student O continues.]

Any other questions there? Yes, [Student S] has a question here this morning.

I under—

Ah, this afternoon! I wouldn't want to mislead anyone. This afternoon. Yes. In your world, it is afternoon. Yes.

I understood you to say in a prior class that—

Yes.

—at the equator one is more receptive, at times, to the Light.

Correct.

That these poles, north and south, that's more the neutral point. Then the other week, we had in class where we place the north [and] west I understood—

Correct.

—over the functions.

That's correct.

And the south [and] east over the faculties. [The student may be referring to Figure 45.1 in this volume.]

That's correct.

And I'd like to ask you, Why are schools, you mentioned, were in the east, but in the very cold parts—

Why?

—rather than in the warmth?

Cold to Lucifer, warm to the Light.

I see.

Hmm.

OK.

Do you understand that? Because I know you've always had great pride in the letter of the law. I know that you seek—No, no, no, no, no. I know that you seek the spirit of the law.

I do.

But that does not in any way stop the desire for the letter of the law.

Uh-huh.

You see? And it's important that you be detailed, you see. But what is much more important than being so detailed to the letter of the law, what is so much more important is that you use it to serve the spirit of the law. Hmm? You see, it's like a person, you know, they learn many things, [Student S]. They learn many things, the spiritual laws and things, and the angel that has fallen always waits to take the credit and feel the sensation, which in your world you know as glory, you see. Yes, there's a reason for treason. There is a reason for everything. What is cold to your mind is dependent on the forms you believe that you are. And always has been. You see?

Uh-huh.

And so I stated clearly that changes shall come about within the school. The alternative to not making those changes in this little school is for the Light, which has already guided us to do so, to take our channel, so our work can continue on Earth, to another location, where it's very, very cold. It's very dry and very windy. All of the things that he doesn't like. No trees. There are a few scrubby bushes. And it's very high. And the atmosphere is very thin. And it's far, far away from all that other. Hmm?

Yes.

And so, you see, when one desires something, one must take a look at how much it costs. For him, [the teacher's channel, Mr. Goodwin], it would cost his fondness for warm climate and [being] nice and comfortable, and beautiful trees and flowers and etc. That's the price he would have to pay. Oh, he would pay it. He wouldn't like it. But he would pay it. But, don't you see, I also know that you students wouldn't like it. For I also know what your desires are, and knowing your desires, I know your adversities. Hmm? Yes.

Any other questions? Yes, [Student L].

We we're told, not specifically in a class, but here in the temple—

Yes?

—that if we followed, if we keep our eye on the Light during the transition and don't look from left or right—

Yes. Could I clarify something? First of all, I have a question. Who told you?

Mr. Goodwin.

Well, that's fine. Always, you want to know who's telling who. And what are they telling. Now, go ahead with what you were telling me, because, you see, you tell me you were told here in the temple. Well, [Student R] could have told you. [Student J] could have told you. [Student M] could have told you. [Student B] could have told you. [Student H], your boy, could have told you. [Student D] could have told you. [Student N] could have told you. [Student Y] could have told you. [Student U] could have told. [Student S] could have told you. Have I left anyone out? *[After a short pause, the teacher continues.]* [Student O] could have told you. Thank you, [Student O].

Now, you were told here in the temple.

Yes.

By my channel.

Yes.

Yes, go right ahead now.

I'm looking for clarification also.

Well, so was I. And that's why I spent that time before we continued with your question. Clarification, you know.

Yes.

Clear communication is clarification. Clear communication's clarification. Go ahead. Yes.

During transition, if we don't look to the right or left—

Now may I ask a question of you? Looking to the left or right, is that a deviation from what you're on?

From what?

Well, would you call it deviating?

Instead of looking at the Light and follow—

Correct. Would you call that deviating from the guidance?

Yes.

Fine. Now go ahead. So that we can all understand what happens to deviates. Yes. *[The teacher laughs joyfully.]*
That's what I'm asking is, if we keep our eye on the Light—
Yes. And do not deviate.
That's right.
Yes.
And arrive at the, at the, I think he said the Halls of . . .
Of Repose. Yes.
Yes.
Yes. Yes. He should say that. He certainly knows that much.
Yes.
Yes. Well, of course, he knows. My, I wouldn't want to call him back, you see. Yes.
If that takes place . . .
If it takes place?
I mean, if you've done that—
Oh, I see. I see, yes.
—and it takes place, do we still have to go back and serve Lucifer anyway?
Well, you're only talking about one incarnation! You're only talking about one page of a contract. You're talking—yes. Yes, you see, just because you went to the Halls of Repose, you return to the Light—you see, where do you think the Rotunda is? The Rotunda's there in the Light. It negotiates for your next incarnation, you see? And oh, yes, absolutely. Definitely. You certainly don't think that's the end of it, do you?
No, but I didn't think about all the rest.
We've already been through it many times. Experiences have been, I would think, sufficient. But then, well, they're obviously not. You see, as long as—the Light is not known unless there is something through which it is known. And that knowingness is limit. We've discussed this many times, haven't we? You see?

Here—there's Light. Light is everywhere. It's never absent or away. Here's the obstruction to the Light. A dense obstruction. A very light obstruction. And so if you have—if you make yourself a very dense obstruction to the Light, then you see many shadows that you believe that you are.

How do you make yourself dense to the Light that you are? By overidentifying with what has been created. So you overidentify with your form, you understand?—which you are responsible for its creation. Oh, you certainly are responsible. You have brown eyes or blue eyes or green eyes for a reason, you see. We have all of this, the temple—the temple is what you're inside of right now. And this is a temple. *[The teacher gestures with both hands toward the physical form of his channel.]* It's not what you are. It's only the temple through which what you are is expressing itself.

So if you permit yourself to overidentify with the vehicle that what you are is using, then you become a very dense obstruction to the Light that you are and are easily tempted by the shadows that your obstruction to the Light which you are creates. Does anyone not understand that? A person easily tempted is one who is totally overidentified with the vehicle they are using and are tempted by the shadows that are created by their obstruction to the Light.

So a person can easily tell at any time whether they are a great obstruction to what they are or they are just a small obstruction to what they are, because we all know how easily we are tempted. Do you understand?

Yes. Thank you.

Yes. Yes, [Student Y].

In the process of the payment, which you, you spoke of paying the price, so I—so you're in the process of paying back what you have incurred, through your actions. Is that correct?

Well, you're paying the price—you have a desire. You expect the fulfillment of the desire from creation or what you're able to do with your mind. It has a price tag on it. You rarely get to see the price tag. And as I stated earlier, you only get to see the price tag if the fallen angel makes the judgment that by allowing you to see this little price tag, he will have no problem when the big price tag comes. You see?

OK. So is it—so if you're, if you have incurred, you know, you know by your, by your experiences in life—

Yes.

—that you, that you have a debt, that you are in the process of paying for what you have desired or . . .

Yes.

So my question is—

Be encouraged. Go with your question.

OK. That—OK. That helps. So you just be encouraged. Because you don't know how long it's going to take you to . . .

That is correct. And if you concern yourself with how long it will take to pay off the debt that you have incurred in an error of ignorance by not demanding to see the price tag, then you are only serving the darkness below by incurring another created form, which will offer to you discouragement, until your mind will tell you it isn't worth it, and you'll go down in total service into his salt mines.

OK. So encouragement—

Self-concern will do that because self-concern is an over-identification with Lucifer. You see, self-pity, as I have taught you, is the most destructive force you will ever experience. Well, self-concern, concern of the self, is a child of the pity of the self. So anyone who permits themselves the luxury—and indeed is it an expensive luxury—to express intelligent energy, that which they are, through the function of the pity of self is a worker who is not working 10 hours in service in the salt mines, [but] is a person who is working 22 hours out of 24 in the salt mines and is so used to being down there, mining the salt with his or her tongue, that they're no longer aware that there is any other world and, therefore, cannot accept the possibility that there is something beyond the mental world because they've spent so much time in the salt mines. And, of course, that which we place our attention upon we have a tendency to become. Yes.

Soon. *[The teacher directs this comment to Student R, who is responsible for recording this class.]*

Oh— [Student Y continues.]

Did you check the time? Soon. *[The teacher again addresses Student R.]*

Soon. [Student R responds.]

Well, I have a clock, too, you know. I'm a little familiar with illusion. Yes, [Student N], because we do have—well, here, do you want to look at my watch? *[The teacher shows his wristwatch to Student R, and then addresses Student N.]* Yes. Yes. Yes.

Here, if you have made a contract in the world and you, and you've got a certain job that you've said you're going to do, how do you know when it's, when it's time to go or you can leave it?

Don't concern yourself, because in so concerning yourself you incur another debt to creation. That's overidentification with self and offers the pity of self, which is the most destructive force in the universe. You give it to the Divine.

So if you feel like you don't want to be there anymore you just go or . . .

No. You will know deep inside of yourself. There's an inner awakening when it's time to go. Yes, [Student D]. We have time for just this last question and you know your illusion here passes very quickly. Yes.

This is a question about the question that [Student L] asked about the Light, keeping our eye on the Light.

Yes.

I've been trying to visualize doing that when I meditate. Is that a good practice?

Oh, indeed, indeed, indeed. It certainly is. Now remember that the Light must not be allowed to—do not desire the Light too bright.

Yes. Well, it isn't too bright.

Do not *desire* it too bright. Yes, [Student J].

I was under the impression that we're supposed to concentrate on peace and not think of anything during—

You should concentrate on peace, but you understand that [Student D] has already gone through that and hasn't had satisfactory results. So now she merits another experience.

What should we do?

Well, I would do what I was told to do. And you're a seventeen-year student of mine. Peace is the power. Light is its expression.

Thank you.

I've spent my time trying to encourage my students to go directly to what you call the horse's mouth. However, if you'd rather go to the tail . . . *[The teacher removes his microphone and it falls to the floor, which makes it difficult to transcribe a few words.]* Oh, my! Would you take care of that? *[The teacher asks Student R to attend to the microphone.]* Thank you. And, of course, therefore one must pay accordingly. Oh, thank you. *[The teacher again addresses Student R.]*

Good day.

MAY 11, 1986

A/V Class Private 47

[This class was recorded outdoors in the garden of the Serenity temple, near the east pond with the waterfall on. The sound of the waterfall often masked the questions asked by the students.]

Good morning, students. It's so nice to be out here in the fresh air. Can you hear me this morning? Fine.

So we'll continue on with our classes and this morning, due to the fact that we have some new equipment, I'll expect our cameraman to keep his eye on this timing and do his part there and to let me know, because its battery, what you call a battery-controlled piece of equipment and depending on the energies, it will depend on how long it lasts. Maybe you don't know that about what you call batteries, you see, until you understand your own battery. Now I think we'll speak of batteries this morning, considering we have a battery class. Yes. It's not a batter class, but a battery class. There is a difference. All right.

Now I know you've heard about human dynamos—you hear me back there all right, [Student D] and [Student N] and everyone? You've heard about human dynamos. Well, they're battery powered. So you find yourself exhausted. And when you find yourself exhausted, you find yourself irritable. In other words, you don't seem to have the energy to cope with things as you do when you feel charged. And so in your world everyone, of course, runs around looking for a charge. Now people get charged like batteries get charged. They all get charged in different ways, you see, and depending on what, in your experience, you judge made you feel good, well, that's the charge you get. And so you get irritable and upset and not very harmonious because you're in need: your battery's in need of having a charge.

Why is it in need of having a charge? Because you've depleted the energy that is in the battery, and your battery charge lasts as long as you identify with the realm of consciousness and the center of consciousness that the battery is charged on. Now of all my students here, who has the answer to which center of consciousness charges their battery? Good question for today. Yes, [Student M] has an answer to which center of her consciousness charges her battery.

The electric?

The electric center?

Yes.

The electric center charges your battery. Is that it?

Light of reason?

Well, that's what charges your battery? Well, it would be so nice, [Student M], if that was true. Yes. Thank you. Yes, [Student N]. Now what center of consciousness charges your battery?

The emotional . . .

The emotional center of consciousness—

Water center.

The water center charges your battery. I see. And anyone else? Oh, [Student R] has a battery charge there. Which—

Fire.

The fire center charges his. [Student D]?

Mine also is fire.

The fire center charges yours. Anyone else? [Student S] has a—Yes?

I think the celestial does because God does it.

Yes, and do we feel the charge? Are we able to identify with the celestial and feel the charge? You see, I was asking a question for each student. Which center charges their battery? Not the teachings, you understand. We know those, but which one do you feel, that you identify with, charges your battery. Each student, you see. Now one has the water center. Now [Student M] has the electric center. [Student R] has the fire center. [Student D] agrees with that center. What center charges your battery? *[After a short pause, the teacher continues.]* Well, there's earth. And there's fire, and there's water, and there's air, and there's electric—

I guess it's between the air and electric.

Air and electric. I see. Perhaps I got the questions not quite clearly presented to you. Which center of your consciousness do you identify with and believe thrills you? Yes, [Student O] has an answer for that.

The water.

Perhaps I used the wrong word. I think perhaps *charge* would be better explained to you as thrill. Yes. Which center thrills you?

The water center of consciousness. [Student O responds.]

Your water center thrills you. All right. Which one thrills you? Which is truly a charge. Yes.

The water center for me, the house of the ego. The water center. [Student U responds.]

Your water center thrills you, charges you. Yes. I see. Which one charges you?

It seems like I'd say the water, but I know it drains me the most. So I don't know what the answer is. [Student S responds.]

Well, that's interesting. Now there's one thing about a battery: Does it charge and does it discharge? So if you identify with the discharge of the battery, then you feel drained. Would you agree to that? And if you identify with the charge, then you feel thrilled. Is that correct?

Right.

Well, you see, now I think we're getting there. This is very important to understand the charge and the discharge of your battery, because we got a battery here that we're working with. Oh, how fortunate, though, it comes in a little case. You slip it in. You take it out. You put another one in. All it needs is a boost of electricity.

Anyone else have an answer to the center that charges them? *[After a short pause, the teacher continues.]* Well, now, let's, as I spoke here, just a moment [ago] here, to [Student S] and she answered you that she thinks it has to be the celestial center that charges her because her water center totally drains or discharges her. Well, now we must understand the center of consciousness with which you identify that gives you the charge also gives you the discharge.

So when you go to be charged, remember that unless you make the effort and you're capable of controlling your identification with the centers of consciousness, you must experience the discharge just as much as you experience the charge. Do all my students understand that? So when you go to say, "Oh, I need a charge. How long will I be discharged from this charge? Is this a fast charge? A slow charge? A two-day charge? A one-day charge? Or a 20-minute charge?" This one here's about a 60-minute charge. More likely a 45. The camera, that is, you see. The little thing. Do we understand that?

All right. Now where are we then? We stop and we think. Need is a charge or a discharge? [Student S].

Discharge.

Need is a discharge of what?

Energy and all that we are.

Well, all discharges are a release of energy. All discharges are a release of energy. What I'm asking you this morning is—what was your question? What was the question I asked you?

About the discharge. [Student S replies.]

Pardon? [Student J], you have the—do you know what question I asked?

[There was no audible response from Student J.]

[Student O].

You asked was need a charge or a discharge.

Good. Good. You took the cotton out of your ears this morning. I'm happy to hear that. Is need a charge or a discharge, [Student S]?

Discharge.

Is a discharge that—do we all agree, students, that need is a discharge? [Student D].

Well, the fulfillment of need— [Student D speaks rather softly.]

I'm sorry, no one can hear you. Shall we turn off the water[fall]? Pardon?

The fulfillment of need, seems to me, would be a discharge.

All right. Now, [Student L]. Thank you. [Student L]—

I think—

—is need a discharge of energy or is need a charge of energy?

It's a charge.

Pardon?

I think it's a charge. It charges the forms.

Thank you. [Student N].

Isn't it both? Because after—if you have the need, then that's, you're going to get a charge from it, but then after you get the need fulfilled, I mean, it's a discharge first and then after the need is fulfilled, it's a charge.

All right. Now let me move on here with the class, and tell you that discharge—need is a charge of the forms created by one of the centers of consciousness and simultaneously a discharge of the center of consciousness known as the celestial. Now it is a discharge of energy; it is a charge of energy. So when you identify with a center of consciousness and experience the forms you have created, they are created by energy. They are activated by energy. So that is a charge of energy. You are releasing energy from your being, which is a discharge. Now from what center of consciousness—now all energy enters you through the celestial and all through the centers of consciousness. Now which center of consciousness is being discharged when you permit your mind to state and declare need? Which center is being charged and which center is being discharged? Yes, [Student O].

OK. The center that's being discharged would be the celestial and the—

Not the celestial. The celestial sustains and charges all centers.

All centers.

Yes. We want—you see, for example, take nine centers of consciousness. You are charging what center of consciousness when you tell yourself that you have need? [Student P].

The water center.

Yes. You are charging the water center at the expense of the discharge of what other center of consciousness? Yes.

Celestial. [Student P responds.]

No. The celestial center of consciousness [is the center] through which all energies flow into all centers of consciousness. [Student B].

Magnetic.

No. In what center of consciousness does the faculty of reason flow? Pardon?

Air. [Several students reply.]

Pardon? [Student B], speak up.

Between the fourth and the fifth.

And that is what centers?

From air and the electric.

All right. Does everyone agree to that as students? So whenever you charge—and you charge from declaring in your mind need or denial—you charge the water center at the discharge of the—which center, [Student B]?

Air.

And?

And electric.

Air and electric. All right? Now does everyone understand that? So if you identify with the water center of consciousness that you are charging with this energy, then you have the thrill of the charge of the forms that you believe you are, and therefore you experience that as a charge or a thrill from your identification with that which you have created. And then you move in consciousness to other centers of consciousness, between the fourth and fifth, the air and the electric, and you feel this phenomenal discharge. Do you understand that? So, you see, there is a quick charge, a slow charge, a one-day charge, a weekly charge, and so you try to understand that. It's so nice we have this battery here this morning to have a battery class.

Now I've spoken to you about these things in other ways. But you always charge a center of consciousness at the discharge of another center of consciousness. And that's what's been happening with all of these experiences around here: the personal experiences that you have been having are in keeping with your charging and your discharging. Now one moment you're all charged up, and those forms use your mouth and go do their things and use your mind. You believe that you are them because you are now identified with the center of consciousness that is being charged. Then you're taken on through, through guidance, through discipline, to the center of consciousness of the faculty of reason, and you are totally exhausted and appear to be, temporarily, a little angel with sprouting wings. Hmm?

Now you can witness clearly with a child the charge and discharge system. It's much easier to witness it in another, because, you see, you don't have their particular forms created, unless you have established that law known as attachment. And if you've established that, you pay the price. But if you look objectively, that means freed from attachment, then you will see a child moving into this water center of consciousness, experiencing this great charge, and then you [will] see the child, if he doesn't have its own way and you are a disciplinarian and guiding them properly and very firm with them, then you'll see them melt like butter and appear to become a little angel. That's only temporary until there is an awakening within the consciousness. Yes, [Student O].

Is there a pattern to, say, like the air and the electric, do they govern the lower, the lower three centers of consciousness? In other words, any form created in the lower centers, three centers of consciousness, is automatically discharged through the air and the electric?

That which is above is ever above that which is below. Now, for example, the lower centers of conscious[ness] are always subject to the higher centers of consciousness. And if you want to experience a beautiful life, then all you have to do is make the effort, through the guidelines that have been given to you, to maintain yourself, that is the separation of truth from creation, into the higher centers of consciousness where the faculty of reason flows. You must reach at least the fourth and fifth center of consciousness in order to experience the abundant good of life. You must reach that, you see. Everything else is a system, whereby, you look at something to purchase. You are deceived by its cost. You take it. It's gone. And you keep on paying for it. You see? So you must rise up to the fourth and fifth center of consciousness or go through that experience in the lower centers of consciousness.

Thank you.

Yes, [Student D].

Do all—do we need to charge ourselves?

You don't need anything. That's where the problem is. Because you believe you need, you experience this constant charging and discharging. Every charge is a discharge.

So if we get beyond need, then we don't need, then there's no charge or discharge?

That is correct. Because when you move beyond need, you have moved in identification in the centers of consciousness between the fourth and fifth and higher centers.

And you're—

It doesn't exist.

And you're still in form?

Oh, yes. You are still in form. You have separated truth from creation. You have then identified with what you are, and you no longer are experiencing what you believe that you are. Do you understand that? You see, you are *in* form. You are aware of that, but you are also aware that you are not form. That is the true separation [while] remaining in form. You are aware that you are moving a vehicle. You are certainly aware that you are not that vehicle. Oh, yes. You are aware that you are responsible for it. You are also aware that you are not it.

And, you see, I think what may help you the most in this constant experience of being charged, what you would understand as thrills, [is] to ask yourself the question at the time of being charged, "How much am I going—how much am I discharging?" Because, you see, you don't experience the discharge until a delayed effect.

Correct.

You see? You see, it was nowheres near as good as you had anticipated. You see, that's your awakening of the discharge that was going on anyway. Yes. Wouldn't you agree, [Student J]?

Yes, sir.

Yes. You start to think, you see. "Well, that cost me so much and that really wasn't worth that, now was it? Why did I do that?" Well, the truth was that, you see, you only did it because you believed that you were it at that moment, you see. So at that moment that if you say to yourself, "Now let's see, yes, I have established this law of need. Yes, I am considering"—if you could call it considering—"I am considering a charge. Is this going to be a quick charge? Is this going to be a slow charge? Is this going to last an hour, a minute, a week? How long is this going to last? And how much is this costing me?" You see.

You must be aware that any charge you believe you are experiencing, any charge at all, you are also discharging. You see, it's all taking place inside of you. And you believe it is a charge because you believe it is outside of you, but it's all taking place inside of you. Not only the charge, of course, the discharge also.

And, you see, it is actually happening at the same moment. You see, the thrill and the charging and the discharging is taking place simultaneously, you see. You try to understand that. You're identified with the water center in which you are experiencing a charge. You are also [discharging] the fourth and fifth centers, the air center and the electric center. Should you choose in that moment to instantly identify with the faculty of reason, you would experience your discharge that is happening simultaneous along with your, with your charge.

See, it's your perspective. You see, when you overidentify, you believe that you are the water center. Therefore, you have what you call the fullness of the thrill or the charge. Now you can, and you should, make the effort at that moment to identify with your other centers of consciousness so that at the same moment you can experience the discharge that's taking place within your being. Did that help with your question?

Yes, sir.

[The teacher laughs.] You see, in your world of form everything costs, you see. You see, a person experiencing the charge kind of gets that thinking, you know, from the water center, that thrill, that they're getting something for nothing. When that is not what's happening at all. You're paying equally. So if you have a great thrill from the charge, make the effort to identify with the center that is being discharged so that you can also experience the phenomenal exhaustion that you're having simultaneously. Because it's happening at the same time, you see. It's happening at the very same moment. Yes, [Student J].

Am I correct, then, in assuming that if we can recognize the fact that we're tempted to a possible need, that we should identify with the corresponding—

Faculty.

—faculty to the function that we're dipping into at the time?

Exactly! Absolutely! And you have all those in your text. You have all those in all the many teachings that you've received.

Because, you see, then you can balance that in consciousness. You see, there's the balance. That's where the balance is. You say, "Now let me see, I feel this *phenomenal* charge!" You see, in that moment—because that's a function you're experiencing; you experience it only because you identify with it. [If] you identify with it long enough, you believe it's you, you see? So you want to catch it as you find yourself identifying with it.

In consciousness is where it's taking place. And in the moment you find yourself identifying with it, that's the moment to move to the faculty of it, the balancing faculty, because that will take you into the Light into the center of consciousness that will balance it out. And then you say, "Look at this cost. It's phenomenal just from the temptation alone. Well, now do I want to pay that?" You see? But you will be able to make a reasonable, intelligent decision with it, you see.

Now it won't go away. Because, you see, it stays there, but your identification will move back and forth, you see? You see, you take a look and you feel tempted, you're charged—you see, those forms rise up inside of you, in that function—and you're charged, and you find that your hands are moving and everything is moving. You [have] got to stop real quick, and go right into that faculty. And what you will view in time [is] you will see what it is that's moving your hands. You won't like it, but you will see it. You will experience it. Yes. You won't like it. I know you won't like it. Because you like things that your mind judges are beautiful and nice, you see. That help you, [Student J]?

Yes, sir.

It should help everyone. Yes, [Student L].

Is it the pause that will bring you up into that faculty?

Yes, the pause that is the lion's strength. Not the pause that refreshes. You see, I find in your world two types of pauses: the one that I have shared with you and the ones your minds have created. So forget the pause that refreshes and identify with the pause of the lion's strength. Yes, the pause. You have two ways of spelling *pause*, I see: *p-a-w-s*. Perhaps you'd best consider that paws. Yes, thank you. Yes, [Student M].

Thank you. The balancing [of] the centers, is there—

You have to speak up or we'll have to turn off our waterfall.

In each of the, in each of the nine centers, is there the electro and the magnetic as a balance within each center?

Why, certainly. Because without the electromagnetic, there is no form; and therefore, that very principle of the creating of form does not exist.

And then there also is the electric and the magnetic individual centers.

Yes. You are electric—electromagnetic. You are electric and magnetic. You have identified with the magnetic in your evolution, sufficiently, to enter what you understand as a magnetic form. *[The physical form of Student M was female.]*

Yes.

Yes. Oh, then that's another whole class. It'll certainly go past this battery charge. *[The teacher laughs joyfully.]* Yes, [Student B].

When we say our affirmation, we go into the retrospin.

Yes.

What happens there to our electromagnetic?

What happens to your electromagnetic? When you go into the spin, you enter into the charge. When you go into the retrospin, you take and balance the charge with the discharge.

So it's a balance?

Yes, that's when you balance. You see, for example, you must understand when you go into a spin, you go into the involvement, you go into the overidentification with something. I've already given that to you. When you go into the retrospin, you go out of that. And when you go out of that, you bring about a balance. A balance within your own consciousness, you see? You see, you withdraw the energy and restore balance in your consciousness. You see, the faculty of reason is where the balance of the electromagnetic is in perfect balance. That's the faculty of reason. That's between the fourth and fifth center of consciousness. You understand, [Student B]?

Well, you said that we got there by identifying with it.

You get there by identifying with it. You identify with it in that which you have created within your own consciousness. Look, you see, this only exists because you have created it in mental substance. *[The teacher touches a plant in the garden, which may be the "this" he is referring to.]* That's the only way this exists. You see? You see, your little stool that you're sitting on exists for *you* because you have created it in mental substance. Now you say, "Well, all the people next to me, it exists for them." Well, they have created the same thing in keeping with the law of overidentification with limit. It does not exist. It exists only because mental substance has created it, when you identify with mental substance.

You see, the density of an obstruction is ever in keeping with your overidentification with it. *[The teacher touches that plant.]* So, for example, if you want to understand how identified you are with limit or form, then awaken to how solid this is to your senses. *[He again touches that plant.]* Then you will understand how much you have overidentified with limit. Hmm? It does not exist. Only in a mental world that one believes that they are. One believes they are a mental world for they have denied the world that they are, you see. That only exists in the world of mental substance.

You see, for example, you take the little stool or you take that board there. An object is an obstruction to the Light. An obstruction to the Light casts a shadow. That shadow is a form. When you believe, you identify with the obstruction to the Light and you believe that you are that obstruction to the Light, then you have realization of form or limit. Your eyes look at that and you say that that's a board. You have created that. You have identified. You've made it that, all right? Now what your eyes are viewing is an obstruction to the Light. As the Light moves—and it's constantly moving—that obstructs it. That obstruction is a, casts a shadow. That shadow is what you believe that you are. Yes, [Student B].

Is the Light electric? [She speaks very quietly.]

Pardon?

Is the Light electric?

The Light is the perfect neutrality. And perfect neutrality is the absolute balance between electric and the magnetic.

So is the form electric or—and is it, the form that we, the obstruction we see, is it electric or magnetic?

It's electric and magnetic. It's not in balance and that's why it's an obstruction. You see, you see, an obstruction to the Light is that which is imbalanced electromagnetically. So it could be 40 percent magnetic and it could be 60 percent electric, but that combination, whether it's in physics, in chemistry [or] in anything in your world of limit, you see, it has to be out of balance in order to be form. For if it was in perfect balance, then it is neutral. It is the Light and its full expression and, therefore, casts no shadow. Is that clear?

Yes.

Yes. So, you see, well, you see objects and you say, "Oh, that's a very dense object. That's a very light object." To your eyes. All right? And to your senses. Well, you have that which is opaque, and you take a look at it and it either casts a dense shadow or a very light shadow. And you call that light and you have that which is translucent. Well, that is dependent on the imbalance between the electric and magnetic. If the [form] contains more of the magnetic, in its imbalance, than it does the electric, then you say that it's opaque. Do you understand? And if it contains more of the electric than it does of the magnetic, then you say, well, that is translucent. Do you understand that?

Yes.

You see? You see, that's what it's all, it's all about. All the universes. It is the law, the Law of Creation. Imbalance is the Law of Creation. Imbalance is the Law of Creation.

And what is creation? [Student R]. *[After a short pause, the teacher continues.]* It is duality, isn't it? All right. Now long ago I taught you the Law of Duality or Two is the Law of Creation. Now you have moved to understand this Law of Duality, which is imbalance. It is two poles that are imbalanced. Sixty-forty. Seventy-twenty. Ninety-ten. Whatever you may want to call it. It is imbalanced. That imbalance creates that much density or obstruction to the Light. Therefore, you see that shadow and believe that it is such and such. Yes, [Student U].

In reference to an earlier class—

Yes.

—an object appears stationary as a result of its retrospin and spin.

Correct.

Now, is that the same, is that stating it in another way that an object appears in the physical, material world because of imbalance in the electric and magnetic?

That's correct. That's the only way you know it as form. That's the only way it exists as an obstruction to the Light. This is why, when you speak of balance in creation, you are speaking of something that is nonexistent. The very Law of Creation is imbalance. *[The teacher and many students laugh.]* Yes, [Student L].

Well, then . . .

You might speak of the fulfillment of need. That's greatly imbalanced. Yes.

I'm wondering if you don't have to identify with form in order—you [who are] in spirit have to identify with form in order to see these objects that we've been, that we're sitting on?

Why, certainly. You have to identify with the Law of Limit.

Well, I mean—

You have to make the effort to overidentify to the point of belief in order to experience limit.

Well, when you're not with a class such as this, you may not see these forms at all?

I see Light.

Oh.

You see what you are. You see, this—I'm so happy you asked that question. You see, you hear, you sense, you experience what you are. You see? What you believe that you are, that's what you experience. The day is beautiful or it is terrible. You are only reflecting those shadows. You see, shadow to shadow, and light to light.

Thank you.

We must grow in our understanding to that point of Light within us where we know beyond a shadow of all doubt, "All right, this is an obstruction. There's an obstruction to the Light." You see, you see, you work on that in your mind. You have a form you've created and you believe that that is you. That is an obstruction to what you are, for you are the Light. You tell yourself you need to be this; you want to be that. You're trying to be something else. You want to be a good person. You see, that's absolute, total, blatant ignorance. You *are* good. So to want to be what you already are, you never can be. You see? You cannot *be-come* what you already are. So to permit your mind to tell you, you want to *be* this and you want *be* that and you want to become something else, when you already are that—first, you must deny that you are that in order to experience the need for it. Having entered that trap, you know where you are.

So just stop doing those foolish things. Stop identifying with a realm of consciousness, the water center, that tells you, you have the need to be good, you have the need to have abundance, you have the need for this and that because you are now identifying with and believing forms you have created in mental substance. And because you have done that, you have denied what you are. You see? You see, when you already are genuine, why do you want to keep chasing counterfeit? It doesn't appear in any way, sense, or form, even to your minds, to be reasonable. Why do you want a counterfeit copy of something when you already have the genuine? You see?

So if you will understand that type of thinking is not what you are—it is something you have created with your mind that is a soulless creature, [and] that you have allowed your creation to convince you that it is you. And that's why you think like that. That's not even you that's thinking like that. That is the soulless creature that you have created that insists on its survival. So you're talking about the survival of a form that you have created. You are not speaking about the survival of what you are, for what you are isn't survival. What you are just *is*. You see.

Limit has beginning. Therefore, it has the instinct to survive. As long as you identify with limit, then you're going to do whatever your mind offers you to survive. If you believe that which you have created is you, then you trigger those instinctive survival instincts inside of you. You permit them to express themselves, and then you'll do most anything. The only thing is, who or what are you doing it for? You're doing it for something you have created that is deceiving you and telling you that you want to be this and you want to be that, so it can keep control of you. It's telling you that you want to be this and that because it first has to tell you that you are not this or that. Well, it is telling you the truth. That hollow form that's speaking through you is telling the truth in that respect. Oh, yes. It definitely wants to survive. It does not have goodness. It is not goodness. And all of those other things. You see?

And so when you permit yourself to identify with it, then you believe that you are it. And that's what you hear out of a person's mouth. Well then, you distinguish: that's that and that is that. One thing is counterfeit and the other is genuine.

Are you having difficulty this morning, cameraman there, to stay awake? Perhaps we could sit you in the sun. There's a sunny spot back there. I think the camera would still view us all right. Would you like to sit in the hot sun to stay awake?

I think I can manage it. [The cameraman responds.]

Oh, fine. Then I won't have to speak to you again, will I? *[The teacher laughs.]* You see, you see, I just want you [to] bring you back home because I don't want those hollow creatures operating that equipment. Yes. Thank you.

Then that soulless creature that's talking to you—

Oh, you have to speak up, [Student L].

That soulless creature that's talking to you then, at that time, is actually getting its charge.

That's right! And you're being discharged! *[The teacher laughs joyously.]* Yes. Some of my students almost got discharged here the other day. Yes. Yes, they did. Because they were tempted to believe that they are those hollow creatures, you see, those soulless creatures. Yes, they almost got discharged. They didn't. They're still here. Yes. Oh, yes, yes.

Thank you.

Oh, I didn't discharge them. My channel didn't discharge them. Those things they temporarily, for a moment, believe that they are and demand—the thing insist that it is the soul, oh, yes, yes, that gets discharged. Oh my, yes. Yes, indeed. Any question? Yes, [Student U].

Did form or limit exist before the fall of Lucifer?

No. No. No. That's limit—obstruction to the Light is the archangel, the fallen archangel, Lucifer's domain. That's his domain. Oh, yes, yes. Formless and free is what you are. But being formless and free, you see, there's nothing to control. You see, you try to understand that you have an experience of a need to control, then you must remember you've denied what you are and the soulless creature that you have created in mental substance certainly does have a need to control. Absolutely.

Oh, I have a question for you. Does Lucifer have a soul? [Student D] has her hand up to answer that.

Are you asking a question?

Does Lucifer have a soul?

I believe yes. He was a soul before he fell from grace, did he not?

Yes. He is a soul. Where's Lucifer's soul?

Well, that would be with God, wouldn't it?

That's right. And so now you know that all he can offer you are soulless creatures. You see, when you enter those realms, you try to understand, the soul is, what I've told you before, not at home. Soulless creatures are at home, for that's Lucifer's domain. Lucifer fell from grace: his soul is there and his form is here. You see?

Right.

So when you fall from grace, you must understand, when you allow your mind, the form, to tell you, you have need of this and need of that, which is all denial of what you are, then you must realize you have chosen to fall from the grace of Goodness, the Principle of Good, God, within your consciousness, for you are a universe, a microcosm of a macrocosm. You understand?

Yes.

And see, when you are, at those moments, identified in that way, you're identified with limit, a soulless creature, you see. A soulless creature ever chasing the universes to experience good and fulfillment. That's the Lucifer. You understand that, you see? Your soul's not in the form.

Right.

No, no, no. You see, the soulless forms is what Lucifer is. Now they are sustained by the soul, which is off into the realms of which is its true domain.

See, when Lucifer made his choice, he wanted to do with his mind, the form, what he saw or he judged—because first he judged—that God was doing. You see? See, he saw, sitting next at the right hand of God, God sustained everything. All the creatures. All the forms of all the universes. The Light, you see, which is God, sustained all of that. Sustained obstructions to the Light. In other words, God, the Principle of Good, sustained what the mind would judge is an enemy of the Light. Do you understand it?

Yes.

You see. So God sustains his own enemy. Because the principle of God is absolute neutrality. Now Lucifer, being his helper, witnessing that, Lucifer's form, mental substance, became tempted, excited, activated, and saw, well, he could control that. He was wiser than God, in his thinking. He knew more than God, in his thinking. Because, you see, he judged if he was in control, as he judged God was in control, he would not support, nor sustain, God's enemies. And so Lucifer had to leave his soul with God, fell into the realms of so-called creation, you understand—limit, mental substance, form—and began his control. He could only control the ones that he could convince that they would like to have a good life, they needed to be a good person, they wanted this, wanted that. He could only control the ones who denied what they are.

So the only time that Lucifer has control of your life is when you permit your mind to tell you that you need this, you need that, you want this, you want that, because first you must deny that you are it. The moment you deny that you are that goodness, you experience all of those needs, wants, and desires. Desire is the divine expression, formless and free, until the mind limits it. And when the mind limits it, you have this want and this need. You have your Lucifer. Yes.

Are you checking the time? *[The teacher addresses the cameraman.]* I want to keep you awake there. Yes, now you tell me how many minutes this has been going.

Forty-five.

Isn't that interesting. We have a few [minutes] more. And not many because that battery is a charge, you see, like you are. Yes. So don't fall asleep and drain the battery. We want the class to go on for a few minutes. [He] was sitting there soaking up the energy of that battery there that I'm working on charging. Yes. Yes. Yes, [Student D].

Does Lucifer also rule the other realms of form, those forms, areas?

Lucifer rules only in the bondage of belief. The higher realms of consciousness do not believe. Look, you see, your mind takes a look and says, well, here's a form; it's this and it's that. If you see a ray of light, you don't consider that form. But a ray of light is what you are, you see? So when you're in those realms, you're a ray of light. There's no nostrils. No ears. No eyes. No nose. There's a ray of light. A ray of light is what you are, you see. You're emanations of the Light. Therefore, you are a ray of light. So when you accept you are a ray of light, there is no obstruction to that.

You see, you think that light does not pass through the density of that object. *[The teacher points to an object outside the frame of the video.]* It does. But you think differently because you believe that that is a solid. You see? You believe the dense shadow that it casts, no light passes through. Because you hold it up and you look on the other side and you [say], "There's light here and there's no light there." *[The teacher gestures to suggest that he is holding a small screen in his left hand. And with his right he points to first one side of that screen and then to the other side.]* No, your judgments compare. You compare, the ribbon of comparison; you make your judgment. You look here and you see light. You look there and you don't see any light. Well, what you refuse to understand: here you see more light; there you see less light. And the less light you see, you judge that to be no light. And so you say, well, the cats and certain animals, well, they've got X-ray vision. They see in the total darkness. It is not total darkness. It is lesser light that you judge to be total darkness. There's light and lesser light.

And if you're overidentified with the shadows of life, then you have darkness. You understand that?

Yes.

You see, that's the darkness. The darkness is the lesser light beyond your judgments of light itself. And so the lions, the tigers, and the cats, they have no problem whatsoever in what you consider total darkness. Hmm? Yes.

Now we'll get close to fifty-four [minutes] and then we'll conclude this class. And so you keep your eye on that there. Because you sat there and drained almost a minute's worth of that little battery. *[The teacher again addresses the cameraman.]* Yes.

I'm wondering about people who are physically blind. If they're, if they are not in total self, can they see the lesser light?

Well, of course. But, you understand, you talk about a person that's total[ly] blind: first of all, the judgment's been made, based upon an absolute belief that they are their eyes. If you absolutely believe you are your form, that does include your eyes, you know. Includes everything. And some of the things you wish it didn't include. Yes. *[The teacher laughs.]* [Student J], where's your good sense of humor this morning?

I got time for one more question. *[The teacher looks to his wrist, but he is not wearing a wristwatch this day.]* I look here for a watch and he's got it over there. *[The teacher points toward the cameraman.]* Yes.

When did Lucifer fall from grace?

Oh, Lucifer['s] fall from grace—you see, you have in your teachings, in your Bible, what they say, "In the beginning." Correct? All right. What begins ends. Beginning and endings is a relationship to limit or form. There is no beginning or ending to formless and free, to that which is. That which is, has no beginning and no ending. Therefore, you are that which is. That is without beginning and without ending. That's why what you are is formless and free. What you deceive yourself to believe that you are is beginning and ending. So beginning and ending only exist in the realms of Lucifer. Beginnings and endings do not relate to formless and free, eternity and infinity. Yes.

So something begins for you and ends for you ever in keeping with your identification with the Law of Limit, the seeing of the shadow. Yes. So in your world this class begins and ends. Correct? So I have to consciously be aware of your world or we'll just go on all day, you see. Beginning and endings apply to your world, to apply to that little battery over there. *[The teacher points toward the camera.]* You see? They do not apply to that which is. Yes. Did that help with your question?

We're not going—no, no, no. You see, you see, we're just expanding. We're just beginning to expand a little bit. You see, you start entertaining that into your consciousness and when these forms are so limited, you will be able to expand them because you know that that is not what you are. It is subject to what you tell it to do, for you have fathered it. Do you understand that?

Yes, sir.

Oh, why, certainly. Absolutely. Time is fifty-what? *[The teacher asks the cameraman.]*

Fifty minutes.

Pardon?

Fifty-one minutes.

That's better. [We] have time for one more question here. Yes, [Student S].

Does Lucifer have an end benefit of the game?

Why, certainly. He ends and begins as you expand in consciousness. You see? As you contract in consciousness, he begins and you become more solidified in your belief you are limit. He begins to end, you understand, in consciousness, as you [demonstrate] acceptance, the Law of the Divine. Divine will is total acceptance. As you move into total acceptance, Lucifer, he starts to end. You see?

Now I did make, say, and I must repeat, that time has passed for us. You know it's almost an hour in your world. Fifty-what minutes? *[The teacher asks the cameraman.]* Isn't that nice, we have a special little counter there for him to play with. Yes.

Fifty-two.

Fifty-two minutes. Fifty-two minutes. Just think of that. Now I'll take those two minutes—do you enjoy being out here?

Yes. [Many students respond.]

Hmm? Are you comfortable?

Yes. [Many students respond.]

Do you think you maintain that sitting for one whole hour?

Yes. [Many students respond.]

You know. Well, that's nice. Yes. And isn't it lovely to see the sun? It's just beginning—too bad that you didn't get to sit right there with the sun beating into your eyes, you see. *[The teacher again addresses the cameraman.]* Yes. Fine.

Well, now I'll tell you what we're going to do. We're going to close up and for those of you who would like, we can look at this class in the dining room and have our coffee. Would you like that?

Yes. Thank you. [Many students respond.]

Would that make it too late for you?

No. [Many students respond.]

Well, that's good because I was just checking with your Lucifers. *[Many students laugh.]* Don't worry, you see, to enter here we all have to have them. Thank you. Good day. Please take care of this little microphone. Don't leave it on the bush. *[The teacher places his microphone on a bush.]* Yes.

Good day.

MAY 18, 1986

A/V Class Private 48

[This class was recorded outdoors in the garden of the temple, near the east pond with the waterfall on. The sound of the waterfall often masked the questions asked by the students.]

Good morning, students. Beautiful morning. A lovely day today.

Last week we had the, if I recall correctly, the battery class. Well, today we have the m-and-m class. Not the kind, of course, that you eat. The kind that, at times in errors of ignorance, that we serve. The microcosm and the macrocosm. I put the little before the large because that's what ignorance, at times, does.

Now you've already had, some of you, most of you, the teachings of the difference between Atlantean astrology, which, in our schools, we teach, which is based upon the nine planetary system, and the difference with Babylonian astrology, which most of you are familiar with, based upon the seven planets, in errors of ignorance, and in its so-called mysticism. So we'll speak a bit on Atlantean astrology and in what ways it is indicative and has an influence on those in their processes of awakening.

You have already been given nine centers of consciousness. The nine centers of consciousness are directly related to the nine planets in your solar system. Each time that you identify with a center of consciousness, you indebt yourself to the corresponding planet in your solar system. As the planets you view in your skies, your heavens, revolve around its central source, so do they do so within your consciousness. Therefore, the planets in their proximity to the source and in keeping with your over-identification with the center of which that planet truly is, you have varying influences.

For example, some of you are aware of our little booklet, [published] many years ago, known as "The Celestial Marriage." *[Please see the appendix for the text of that pamphlet.]* Well, we must reconsider what we're speaking about in reference to marriage made in heaven. We're not speaking about a man and a woman as you know a man and a woman. We're speaking of the celestial marriage that is the true contract between the Light and the lesser light. For you are the Light. A contract is established in order that you may experience the lesser light and, in so doing, be instruments through which the lesser light evolves, recognizes, and accepts the source which sustains it. That is the work that all beings have when they enter what you understand as creation.

Now the celestial marriage, as I have stated, is the actual, what you would understand as the contract. The sun in your solar system is the light and is the source. What you understand as the moon, that you see during times of lesser light, is an obstruction to the light itself. So when you see your moon as a half moon or a new moon or a full moon, especially a full moon, you are identifying with the full obstruction to the Light that you are. Therefore, you experience at those times, through identification to that corresponding center of consciousness, you identify and become indebted to the planet, you understand, the moon, the obstruction, that you are identifying with and is represented in that center of consciousness, which is known as the water center of consciousness.

Now it seems I'm perhaps going too fast for you this morning, so we'll pause for the questions that you may have. Such a lovely day here. I'll give you those moments to write your notes. Yes, [Student M], please.

Yes. When you say that we're indebted to the planet to which— we're identifying with a certain center—

Correct.

—corresponding with a planet.

Correct.

And we're indebted to that planet. What exactly is that debt to the planet?

Well, for exam—yes, yes. That's an excellent question. You should ask such an important question. For example, when you overidentify with a center of consciousness, you become indebted to the corresponding planet. How are you tempted to overidentify with a center of consciousness? Because you, first of all, experience in a certain center of consciousness what you would understand as receiving something that is pleasing or beneficial to your senses. Now that is the temptation. Now that is also the indebtedness because after you experience that so-called pleasure and judge that is what you want, then you are indebted to the forms that are in truth offering that sensation to you, which are the inhabitants of that planet which corresponds to the center of consciousness that, through your error of ignorance at that time, you have overidentified with. Yes. Aren't you grateful we have it on tape? *[A few students laugh.]* Yes. Yes.

Yes. Should we already know the corresponding planets to the, the nine corresponding planets to the nine centers of consciousness?

Well, through your homework and through your great spiritual efforts daily and your studies, especially in your homework, you should have some awareness of some of the planets that are represented by the center of consciousness, those centers of consciousness. Oh yes, absolutely. Definitely. I didn't want to ask you those questions today. I wanted to give you at least a week to do your homework, for you've already received all the material necessary to make a little effort and know what planet is corresponding to what center of consciousness, considering you already are quite familiar with the water center, the fire center, and the earth center. And if you only awaken to those three planets, I think you'd be doing very well. That help with your question, [Student O]?

Yes. sir.

Yes. Well, now that you've brought it up, as I say, I don't

want to ask, interrogate you on that until I've given you a week's time in your world for your homework, you see. It should have already been done. What would you think is the representation of the fire center? Which planet? There's a lovely little creature there. *[The teacher first glances; then he points upward, toward the branches of a tree.]* You already know which center is represented and what planet from the water center, don't you?

From the water center?

You already know that, don't you?

Yes.

Would you like to share it with those who think they don't know?

The water center?

Yes.

I was going to say it's the Earth.

Is that so? Oh, quite interesting. Thank you. Yes, yes. Yes, [Student P].

I'd say Mars.

Well, that's quite interesting. We're, we're—did I say the fire center?

No. [Student P responds.]

No, you said water. [Student O responds.]

Oh, I said the water center. Oh, I see. Yes, [Student M] has the answer. Thank you. She's—

The moon? [Student M responds.]

The what?

The moon. The water center.

Well, there, there's one answer there. Here's [Student U] here with another answer.

The moon. [Student U responds.]

Uh-huh. Now we have two for the moon. Be nice when we have fourteen here for the sun, won't it? Yes, yes, [Student H] has an answer here.

I was going to say the moon. [Student H responds.]

Yes. Well, now we got three for the moon. That's lovely.

All right, now it's time for your questions here this morning, because I just got through in your world spending about forty-five minutes because I can talk as fast as anyone when necessary and you got forty-five minutes worth of information there. Now it's time for you to ask some questions. Yes, [Student Y].

Is it so that— [Student Y speaks very quietly.]

Well, I'm sorry, I couldn't hear you.

I said, Is it so that the celestial marriage happens before you enter form?

Oh, yes, absolutely. It's the only way. Without the celestial marriage, without the contract, that which you are, formless and free Spirit, the Divine Light, the eternal Energy, cannot enter the bondage. Yes. That's a contract. Yes, that *is* the celestial marriage. That's the marriage born in heaven, dear. Yes. Yes, that's the contract.

You know, so many people are interested in [that] and whatever they want, they want it born in heaven. Yes. Yes, [Student B]. Thank you.

What—are the most advanced planets farthest from the source?

Well, you might consider, you might consider Saturn. Saturn.

Saturn?

Oh, absolutely. Absolutely.

And are the planets closest to the source, then, obstructions to the planet Saturn, obstructions to the Light . . . ? The moon is an obstruction to the light for Earth. [It is difficult to transcribe one word.]

Well, you see a moon. What you see is a reflection and you believe that you see it. For you are seeing its obstruction to the light, the sun, and as you see that, you believe that is the moon. Do you understand that, [Student D]?

Yes.

You do not see the moon as you think you see, and believe

you see the moon. You see the reflection of the moon's obstruction to the light. Is there anyone that doesn't understand that? So, you see, your bondage is belief in the reflections of light, you see. When you look at the moon with all of your telescopes and you look at it in an evening, what you are actually seeing is light that is reflected for it is obstructing the light of the source of the sun itself. That's what you see. You do understand that, don't you, [Student B]?

I have trouble—

The moon—Well, you have trouble accepting it because you haven't done your homework. If you do your homework, you have no trouble at all accepting it. You see, [Student B], you look at the moon and you see the various valleys and things. You cannot see that with your eyes, you understand that, unless it was obstructing the true source, the light. You see the reflection of the obstruction.

But doesn't there have to be something—

The moon in and of itself is not emanating light so that you can see it in your sky. Do you understand that?

Yes.

That's light coming from someplace. Do you understand that? There's only one place in your solar system that it comes from, and that's known to you as your sun. So what you are seeing is the moon's obstruction to the light, which offers to you the lesser light. Do you follow that, [Student B]? So you are not seeing the surface of the moon by an emanation of light from the moon itself. You are seeing the moon as it moves and obstructs the light, the sun. You are seeing that reflection of the obstruction. Now do you understand?

Thank you.

That's very, very important to—you see, seeing is believing, and believing is bondage. There's no problem with that at all, you see. You see, a person looks up at the sky and they say, "Oh, yes. Oh, isn't that a beautiful full moon there." Well, what they should be saying to themselves [is], "My, isn't that a full obstruction to the Light that I am." Now, you see, if they would start thinking that way, you see, they would no longer, in errors of ignorance, identify with that center of consciousness; they would no longer allow those forms to which they have become indebted, through overidentification with that center, that microcosm within, to tell them that what they are seeing is true. For what they are seeing, they are believing. And therefore, from that believing, they are binding themselves, for something else is telling them, as a payment for their indebtedness (what they owe) to the forms that inhabit that particular planet and tell you what you're seeing is truth.

What you're seeing cannot be truth. It is not possible to see truth. One does not see truth. One sees the opposite of truth. One sees reflection. One sees falsehood for one sees the obstruction to what is. Yes, [Student Y].

So, so our form, our very form, would be that obstruction.

That is correct.

To Light.

That is correct. Because your form is the limit, you see. So when you believe you are your form, then you're doing the same thing as looking into the heavens and believing that the obstruction to the true Light is what it is. It is not.

You see, the moon itself emanates no light. What does that mean to an intelligent person? Its light is of such a low degree you cannot perceive it. What does that reveal? *[After a short pause, he continues.]* Anyone? [Student O].

Must be of the lesser light.

What does the lesser light—what [is] the lesser light in constant, in need, in constant need of? [Student Y].

It's dependence. It's—

Energy!

Energy.

Energy! You see, the lower the light, the less the energy. Do you understand? And so a person who is a sponge and constantly absorbing, you understand, what in your world would be known, I think, more correctly as a leech, is a person who is extremely low in light and is telling you how low they are in energy because, you see, they're very low in light, you see. Now, for example, it's microcosm and macrocosm. You see, when your light of reason becomes dim, you find very little energy to move around, don't you, [Student B]?

[It is difficult to transcribe Student B's response.]

So, the dimmer becomes the Light within you, the less energy that you have, you see. Now the lessening of that Light, the lessening of that Energy is from those forms controlling your mind insisting that you believe that what you see is you. So you look in a mirror and you say, "This is me. This is me." Well, that's those forms. That is not you, you see. You are looking at the obstruction, you see?

You see, oh, how many times the prophets have taught you in so many ways: You are standing in your own Light. Well, that which stands in the way of its own Light is an obstruction to the Light that it is. Therefore, you see, [a person who] stands in [their] own light, takes a look at the shadow, and believes that's what they are. That's why you look at the moon and say, "Isn't that beautiful. Oh, such a full moon. Oh, I have this phenomenal energy." Oh, what do you think's taking place? The energy is the energy of the forms, you see. They're giving you the charge before they're give you the drain, you see. That's why I'm giving you the m-and-m class after the battery class. Yes, [Student Y].

Ah . . .

They give you a quick charge and take a long drain. You try to understand in life whatever offers a quick charge guarantees a long drain. Hmm? And also, I've taught you in other ways, you see, those who are puffivated are the fools of fools. But then there's one born every split second. Yes, [Student Y].

So could the problem be that we don't see our own Light? So that's why we believe we are the—

Correct. Because, you see, the eyes are controlled by limit. You do understand that? So that which controls limit is we all know what. So if you permit yourself to see—you see, you don't view; you see. You see things. All right. Now that is not what you are and [it] cannot be what you are. That is a contract in order to enter limit. That *is* the celestial marriage. That's why it's time for most people for divorce. *[A plane flies near the temple and its engine is heard above the noise of the waterfall.]* Yes, [Student Y].

Could you say that again . . . [The noise of the plane and the waterfall make it difficult to transcribe a few words.]

Well, I think we got one of those motors, one of those sky motors up there. We'll wait just a moment. Of course, that's part of the little payment, so microscopic, for having these classes, you know, out in nature, you see, where I've always given my classes, with the exception of this temple here, you see. And since I've been with my channel. Ah, they're going to leave us in peace now. *[The plane flies away from the temple.]* Yes, go ahead.

So I would like—could you repeat what you just said about the contract, the celestial marriage? [After a short pause, Student Y continues.] *Is it, is the celestial marriage the lesser light?*

Why, certainly. Why, certainly. In order for the Light that you are to enter bondage, there's a contract that is signed in keeping with that law so that you may be an instrument, the Light that you are, to evolve and to expand, you understand, that limit, you see. And that expansion process takes place within your consciousness. Within your mind, it takes place. So as you broaden your horizon, you expand your consciousness, you in truth evolve the limit, you see. That's the whole—that's the process. That's the entire process of the limit being expanded, you see. You take a flower. Well, the flower goes through a process of various marriages, and then you call it a hybrid. You refine it.

Is that correct? Well, that's the same thing that's taking place with the Light that enters the lesser light and the limit, you see. You see?

Yes, now [Student L] has a question [and] has been waiting.

Yes. Is that celestial marriage the contract that's signed in the Rotunda?

That is the celestial marriage.

Thank you.

That is the law. And now, for example, we're getting in quite deeply, which is going to require many hours, many, many hours of discussion. You see, your soul is evolving. All right? It has evolved through many, many forms, many planets, many solar systems. All right. Now you have in that evolution, through errors of ignorance, overidentified with certain planets in the solar system. You understand that so far?

Yes.

All right. So therefore, you enter form; you come before the Rotunda; the contract is established. You understand? Here is this evolving soul. And here is the limit and the form that [it's] to enter again. Well, you overidentified with that center of consciousness: you are weakened to that particular planet, which is corresponding to that center. And so you find yourself in form under the basic influences of that center of consciousness and of that particular planet in the solar system. Now remember, there's only influence, for you are the Light, you see. However, when you permit yourself to believe you are the obstruction to the Light, the influences of those planets, of course, have more control for you have made it so. Yes.

Do those inhabitants of those planets actually, the actual inhabitants of those places control us also or . . . just the same? [A few words are difficult to transcribe.]

They only control, those inhabitants of those planets, they only control what you have taken from them. Now if you allow yourself, what you call you're tempted by this and tempted by that and you don't consider the payment and the etc., well, you know the law is the law. You are indebted, and therefore they collect.

Thank you.

And they have no problem collecting whatsoever. And you experience that collection as your pain and suffering, you see. They do—they're wonderful collectors, you see. Oh, yes, yes. [Student O] is waiting. I'll be right with you. *[The teacher addresses a different student.]*

Yes. Those forms from, from these nine planets, do they intermingle? [Student O asks.]

Intermingle?

Yes, sir.

Well, they get along just about as well as a daisy and a rose. Not very well. Not very well. You see, you have to understand that their dedication and their duty is to that which they believe sustains them. So if you have, which you do have, you have beings which are represented by your water center; you have beings which are represented by your fire center. And tell me how well fire and water get along? Very well?

Not very well.

Well then, there's the answer to your question. Yes. However, now, water and earth get along fairly well, if they don't get out of hand and the water center tries to flood the earth center or vice versa. And so there's all of those factors involved, you see. Yes. Do you understand, [Student O]?

Yes, I understand that.

Good. Do you have another question?

Yes.

Go right ahead.

Should one—does the soul consider it as a good merit to come to Earth? Merit—

Well, the soul itself, the evolving soul, is grateful for its opportunity of expression, no matter what planet it finds itself on.

However, the limit and the form, you understand, that has all kinds of problems.

OK.

Yes. It cries, it cries the moment that it enters the bondage. And when you are aware that, what you call, that the baby is alive, the first thing you hear is a scream. If you don't hear a scream, you make sure it does scream. *[Several students laugh.]* Because you want to keep it in bondage. Don't you understand? You see? If it enters the planet and is born and there's no scream, you do whatever your mind tells you to do so you have another victim. Pardon?

Yes, sir.

Oh, yes. There's no problem there at all. Your laws guarantee it, you see. Oh, yes. Yes. Not in all civilizations, you know. When, through the divine evolution, they see that, "Well, now that is the step for this little soul. It got to be around there for about nine months. Now [it has] come out and it's going back on to its next step."

No, it isn't that I'm against evolution. Quite the contrary. I'm [in] firm acceptance of the demonstrable law. But you must understand that mental substance is doing a wonderful job in your world of interfering, the best that it can, with divine, natural evolutionary law. However, you've got to expand your consciousness and say, "All right. Well, this soul entered this particular form at this particular time of ignorance and technology." You see. I spoke to you long ago about your advancing technology far exceeds your spiritual understanding and awakening. So you're not going to put the brakes on your advancing technology because the laws have been established that won't allow you to do so. The only thing you can do is to make greater effort to awaken to the way things really are. Hmm?

Yes, sir.

Yes. Now [Student M] has been waiting with a question.

Yes. The, the forms in each, that inhabit each of these centers, these are the soulless creatures?

Now you're expanding your consciousness. Now we've spent all these years talking to you about these forms you create and these things that you serve. Now you expand your consciousness: what planets they are on and how they influence you, in keeping with the debt you owe them. Yes, [Student U].

The indebtedness that we incur by overidentification, is that . . . in addition to pain and suffering, is that being in service? [A word or two is difficult to transcribe.]

Why, certainly. Well, you consider the service the pain and suffering. Your senses consider, your senses consider that payment and that service, paying that indebtedness you've incurred; you consider that. That's what your mind tells you is pain and suffering. You see, don't you understand, you see, for example, you overidentify with a certain center. Say you overidentify with the fire center, which happens to be represented by a certain planet in your solar system. All right. Fine. And you've got all that, you know, you feel just—you think you feel wonderful and etc. And now the debt comes due. They call it in, you see. Because they gave you that. You wanted it. You asked for it, you see? You solicited it. It's known as temptation in your world. All right. So you have received it, and they've given you what you've asked for. Even though you ofttimes may not be aware that you asked for it, you did. And so they start calling in the debt. You got to pay for it.

Now what does that mean? That means they must withdraw from your universe energy, you see. You see, debts are paid in energy. All right. Now here they are, you see, siphoning this energy out of you, these forms. Because, after all, you experienced, what you call, the upliftment or the thrill or the fulfillment or the joy, whatever, whatever device your mind, they want to tell you that you've experienced. Now you feel this drain, this terrific drain. And as you're feeling that drain, [which] they're siphoning off, you, you understand, are now thinking more and more of how you feel. And you have other entities coming up and tell you you're suffering and you're in terrible pain; it just isn't worth it all. But you're the one that did it all in the first place through errors of ignorance, you see. You're paying back what you've taken.

Try to understand, [Student U], they're—something for nothing doesn't exist. You see, we hear the spoken word, it's at a cost. We breathe; we extract from the air center what you understand as air and so you continue to maintain a form of bondage. Well, there's a part of your anatomy, several parts, in fact, that must pay for that. You understand that your lungs are paying for it. All right? But then there's your heart and there's all these other various centers that have to pay that debt. Hmm? Yes. Yes, go ahead with your question.

When we see an object in creation that does not emanate its own light, we do not—

It emanates a light that's imperceptible to your seeing it, for all things do emanate some energy or they could not be things. But they emanate such a lesser light, [it is] below your ability to see them. Go ahead.

What we can see is a reflected light that does not encompass the entire light spectrum.

Correct.

Plants are green. Does that mean—

Plants aren't green. You call them green, but that's all right. Go ahead. Yes.

What is—does it mean that there are certain lights that, frequencies of light that are in rapport with a plant or an object and certain frequencies that pass through the object?

That's right. Opaque and translucent. Now you understand it. Then you say that this is this color and that is that color. It's ever in keeping to its obstruction or reflectability of the light because it is an obstruction as a form. See, all form is an obstruction to the Light. You see the shadow that is cast by the obstructions. That's what you see. You don't see what is. You see the shadow that is cast by the obstruction. Now when you believe what you see, you establish the law for your senses to feel what you see. You understand? Close your eyes. Are you touching the elephant's trunk or his tail? You see? You believe what you see. Go ahead. You have another question on that?

Then the obstruction, the form, is determined by electromagnetic—there is no form without the electromagnetic energy.

Well, no, without that, it doesn't exist as form.

Could you, please, expand on how it is that the electromagnetic energy field creates the obstruction or the forms?

Well, it is their frequency. There's high frequencies, low frequencies, midrange frequencies. And it is the movement of those, known as frequencies, that create what you understand as a particular form. For example, they're moving at a certain speed. You certainly don't understand electromagnetic energy is all moving at the same speed, do you? In the same space?

No.

All right. So they move at a different frequency. And therefore, you see that as a leaf and you see that as something else and that as a chair and etc. Depending on the density of these electromagnetic vibrations, depending upon their density is their degree of obstruction to the Light that they are. Therefore, the intensity of density is measured by acceptance. That applies to man, woman, child, dog, cat, plant, or ant. You see? So if you look at something and say, "Oh, that is so dense and so solid," well, you have to understand that that is a greater obstruction to the Light and has phenomenal density to your seeing.

You see, it's the same laws that apply to your thinking. Some thoughts you're absolutely convinced that that is you, correct?

Yes, sir.

When you understand how much energy you have directed to the formation of the thought, how much identification-attention that you have given it—the more energy you direct to that which has been created, the more energy you direct to it through attention, the more solidified it becomes as a more solid obstruction to the Light. So have a thought, direct intelligent energy to it, continue to do so, and you will be absolutely bound by your belief that it is you. The reason you believe that your thoughts are you is because you have directed so much intelligent energy to them: you have made them such an obstruction to the Light that you are. It is—to your mind, [it] tells you it's impossible to make that step. It's only because you spent your life thinking about it all the time.

So, you see, the principles of these laws are not restricted to a plant or a tree. They are universal, divine laws. And so the law that works for the plant—you understand, the more energy, intelligent energy is directed, the more atoms and electrons and molecules gather into the limit that you have created. Do you understand that?

Yes.

Consequently, you see that as a very dense, gross object. You do the same thing with your thoughts. The more intelligent energy, [the more] you identify with a thought you have created, the more solidified it becomes, the more dense it becomes, the greater obstruction to the Light that you are it becomes. Hmm? Until you're absolutely convinced that you are the shadow that the obstruction is casting and that you are seeing. All right? Did that help with your question?

Thank you. Yes.

You're welcome. And [Student M]—ah, [Student D]. [Student D] has been waiting. Yes, [Student D].

Is it our task to learn to use the view? And could you explain the difference seeing and viewing?

Yes. You see, that is the process that you are in, is moving from seeing to believing. So you have a thought in your mind. You see that thought. You don't take a look and say, "Well, my eyes see it." But you see it in what you understand as your mind's eye. Oh, you see the thought. Correct?

Yes.

And if you keep seeing the thought, you very soon find yourself believing that you are the thought. You really do believe you are that which you have created. You see, that's how you attach yourself to something. You attach yourself through a continuous, constant identification with something. Person, place, or thing, it all takes place up here. *[The teacher gestures with both hands to his temples.]* And that's where the attachment goes on. Because it takes place up here within your own mind, only in your own mind can you free yourself from it. It doesn't matter what something outside of you does or does not do. You cannot, you cannot free yourself from anything that is outside of your divine right of your own little universe . . . the microcosm of the macrocosm. *[One word is difficult to transcribe.]* And so that's how that takes place, [Student D].

Now when you view a thought, a form that you have created—now remember, you first must—it all has to take place— Excuse me. It all has to take place inside first. Now when you begin to separate what you are from what you believe you are, you are establishing that Law of Separation that you may experience the day when you view your thought and you know the difference: you know you're responsible for it; you know it is not you. And when you really know that it is not you, it will not affect you. Do you understand? That is viewing, compared to seeing.

You go out and you say, "Oh, it's so warm today," or "It's so hot today," or "It's so cold today." That is seeing. That is not viewing. You are seeing the obstruction, the shadow that the obstruction casts, because you must first do that inside of yourself. So we understand that as a person who is very self-identified. They're totally self-orientated, to such a point, you say, in your world, well, that person is terribly selfish. Well, the truth of the matter is they are constantly thinking, to the point that they now believe that they are the forms they have created and they really are convinced that the shadow that the forms they have created, which is an obstruction to the Light that they are, they really do believe that's them. Yes, [Student D].

So what would you say instead of it's cold or it's hot? What would the view words be in comparison to the seeing words?

"I am spirit, formless and free. Whatever I think, that will I be. I choose not to think that. I choose not to be cold." Now these [are] a few little words, you see, a person can work on, you see? You see? But you have to remember that you create that for you. Look, to one person it's too hot. To another person it's too cold. It only proves to you repeatedly the hot and cold is that which you have created in your mind. It's not something out there. Don't you see? It is your *seeing* something out there to the point that you really do *believe* that you are that something that is created to such a degree and an extent that it's gone beyond the seeing. It's now in the feeling and all the sensing. Did that help with your question?

Yes. Thank you.

Yes, now [Student M] is waiting there.

Yes. Is the cleansing breath and the affirmations, that brings this frequency up to a higher frequency.

Well, it does if you accept it. But, you know, there are students who say and do their cleansing breaths and when it comes to the point of a choice between the two, they go right back to revert to their bondage. So, you see, there's no cure-all, but it is given to you as a part of an entire whole process, along with your affirmations. You see, the affirmations, to anyone who is doing them and they don't work, is because they've never tried them. Oh, the forms, of course, have used the mouth and the mind, but they don't work because they've never really been used. Did that help with your question?

Yes. Thank you.

Yes. That's like levitating. You want to levitate? How can you possibly levitate when you believe you are your toes and everything else? How do you think that's possible? That's not possible. You're still in the belief and in the bondage. Bondage is controlled, of course, by gravity. Yes. Now [Student Y] has a— [Student N] has a question, please. [Student N].

How do you— [Student N speaks very quietly.]

I'm sorry. We can't hear you up here.

How do—

You're a lovely singer. Let's hear you sing out your question.

How we view?

How do we view? I think we discussed that with [Student D] a moment ago. Now when you listen to the class [tape], [Student N]—and did you not get your answer? *[The teacher addresses Student D.]*

Yes. [Student D responds.]

That answer was meant for you, too, [Student N], as well as for all the rest of us. All right? So time is passing so quickly. How fast an hour passes. I'd like to get as many questions as we can. Yes, [Student O], please.

How receptive are we to forms from other planets that we haven't even experienced yet?

Totally. Totally. You believe that you are that form you're in?

Do I believe? No, sir.

Well, perhaps, that's kind of you. *[The teacher laughs joyfully.]* That's very kind of you. You're coming along quite nicely. I would like to, you know, be diplomatic, but not at the sacrifice of the Light. No. But I do understand. I do understand. You would like not to believe you're that form. But if you didn't believe [you were] that form, then you wouldn't be able to experience that wonderful suffering that you go through periodically.

Right.
Isn't that true?
That's true.

Well, it wouldn't be possible. You see, you happen to believe that stuff, but I don't say you believe it all the time. You're certainly coming up there, though. Now what was your question?

It really was, I want to know, could we—all right, we're on the planet Earth, and we're supposed to be the planet of faith.

Well, it certainly takes a lot just to survive in that world.

Yes.

Yes.

OK. There—should we be exhibiting a predominance of faith? I mean, in other words, what I'm saying is, to my understanding, we haven't visited all the nine planets, but yet—

You haven't? [You have] spent a lot of time on them, from what my view is. Yes, go right ahead, [Student O].

OK. Well, I wondered why—there's—different individuals demonstrate a predominate of different expressions, like in the fire center . . .

Yes?

. . . the water center.

Yes. They were tempted many times in evolution to the point they're convinced that's the planet they are, you see. And when that planet is in a certain proximity to the Light, offering its greatest obstruction to the Light, they're absolutely convinced that that's them and that's when they all come in for their feeding. Now have we covered that?

Yes. I understand.

It's proximity to the Light and it's the obstruction it creates. Now I'll be right with you, ladies. [Student O] still hasn't got his question to his satisfaction.

OK. So our—even though we show or experience a predominance of another planet, even though we haven't been there, are we still destined to go to that planet, like we [are] here on Earth?

As long as you believe you're that limit, there's no escape. That help with your question?

Yes, sir.

As long as you believe you're that limit, there's no escape. The law fulfills itself beautifully. Yes. Oh, don't, don't worry and fret, because you'll get a little break, you see, before your [next incarnation]. *[The teacher makes a sound that is difficult to transcribe.]* You know.

Thank you.

Contracts have to be reviewed. That's known as your time in the Halls of Repose. You know, like in your world you say, "Oh, the lawyers got to get together and decide what they're going to do with this victim." Who's going to win out, you see. Well, that's going on all the time. *[The teacher laughs joyfully.]* But you do get a little, a little break there. You get into the Halls of Repose there, if you've merited that. Otherwise, you battle down in those other realms, you know. And then they come and they call for you; your number's up. You see? You see, you're a number, not a name, you know. We're all numbers, you see.

Right.

Yes. And woe to those number ones. Yes. Now, [Student L] had a question. Number ones seem to have so many problems. Yes, [Student L], please.

I was wondering, then, if the sun is the light in—I know that the sun is a light in our universe. Are—

No, no, no. No, no, no, no, [Student L]. The sun is not a light. The sun in your universe *is, is* light.

Is light.

Yes, indeed. Well, I think that's self-demonstrable. Yes, go right ahead.

Now are all the planets just reflections of that? Are all nine planets—

Why, certainly. Their proximity to the source creates an obstruction, a shadow, and that is their lesser light. That's their reflection. You understand that now, [Student B]?

I'm trying. [Student B responds.]

Well, you still have a problem in reference to the moon: that you see the light of the moon. Well, where do you think the light of the moon comes from?

[It is difficult to transcribe Student B's short response.]

Where does the light of the moon that you see in the sky come from?

Well, you said . . . [It is difficult to transcribe one or two words.]

No. Where do you, where do you think it comes from? I'm telling you my experiences of a long time. You can go to your books of your world, but where do you think that light comes from? [Student U], where do you—

It comes from the sun.

Well, now how do you know it comes from the sun? Because [Student B] is having a little problem here.

When we have a quarter moon or less than a full moon—

Yes, I understand that. You explain—share that.

We only see the part of the moon that's illumined by light from the sun.

Why, of course! That's the only light there is, [Student B]. The moon's light is such a low light to your perception, it doesn't emanate it so that you can see it. You have a problem with that?

Ah . . . [Student B responds.]

Even your scientists in your world will teach you that. Have you not learned that in school, [Student U]?

Yes, sir.

Yes.

I thought you were saying the moon really wasn't even there. It's just—

No, no, no, no. No, I did not say the moon does not exist. I said you do not see the moon. Only as an obstruction to the light that is the sun. You see the reflection. That's all that you see.

That's all I see, but there is a real moon there.

Oh, there's a physical—oh, definitely, because there's—oh, yes, you mustn't be upset. Because your water center is totally controlled, like everyone on Earth, their water center, emotions, are totally controlled by the inhabitants of that planet. Now I've answered that question, haven't I. Yes. Oh, yes. No, they would be very upset to be denied their existence. No, I'm the last one, in this class anyway and in the places I've been, to deny those forms their right of existence. They didn't appreciate you believing they didn't exist. *[Student B and a few other students laugh.]* Now I understand your upset. Yes, [Student S] has a question here.

Yes. You spoke— [The teacher laughs joyfully as Student S speaks.]

No, I know better than that. *[The teacher laughs again.]* I will deny nothing its right of existence. I don't want to, to be bound by it. Whatever form you deny its right of existence, you guarantee to serve it, for you are already serving it and know it not. This is why denial—be right with you—is destiny, you see. Everything you deny in life its right of existence, you are at that very moment, at that very moment you experience what you understand as a temptation; you are incurring your debt, and it shall befall all, all people. So only a fool would deny the right of existence of any form or any thought at any time in all eternity. For in that denial you direct this intelligent energy to that form, and in so doing you guarantee your service to it, your indebtedness to it until the time you become an absolute belief that you are it. No matter what you choose. Yes, go ahead with your [question].

You spoke of the time in the Halls of Repose when—

Yes.

—they're reviewing the contract.

Well, now the actual soul itself is not reviewing the contract. Oh, no, no, no, no. The contractual—well, you might want to call them magistrates. I think your world calls them lawyers and things. I prefer magistrates, myself. You know, because it always had more responsibility to it, you know. No bickering or arguing. That's the judgment. Take them away. *[Several students laugh.]* Yes, go ahead.

How much, how much time would that be in our Earth time for that to transpire?

Well, some contracts are not easily agreed upon by the lesser light. And depending on their needs, they can postpone it sometimes for many, many years. Many, many years of their attempts to negotiate. You see, they're not short of workers at that time. When they get short of workers, they don't have much of any problem of getting the contracts signed, you see. But it depends on the workers in the salt mines. If there's a shortage of the workers and there's a greater need for the salt for the work to continue, putting it graphically in that respect, then they are more ready to come to terms and get it signed and move on with things. Yes. They're very selfish that way. Yes.

And you spoke of the imbalance in the duality of creation—

Yes.

—in our last class.

Yes, indeed.

Could you please explain what you mean by the balance of nature?

You mean—are you referring to the balance of nature within your own consciousness? Because that's where it starts.

Yes.

All right. From allowing, through a lack of effort, a continuous overidentification with the forms created, you establish this imbalance law and experience all these needs. For every, for example, for every 10 percent of energy that you direct to that which you have created, if you do not direct an equal 10 percent of energy to that which you are, then you guarantee your own bondage. That's the imbalance. You see? You see, you have moments when you feel truly good inside. You have moments—and you're not in service to those things. Then you have moments of which you *think* you feel good inside, which is only that tidbit that they are offering you and your debt is due probably within a matter of hours, or at least the next day, in seventy-two [hours]. Did that help with your question?

Yes. Thank you.

That's the great imbalance. You see, I've tried to teach you, and it didn't seem to reach many of my students: you put God in it or forget it. Well, then the students say, "Well, I put God in it. Now I forgot it." No, no, no, no. No. You put God in it or forget it. You put equal energy to the corresponding faculty of the function or forget it. Because if you don't do that, your debt [is established], and then you understand that as pain and suffering and all that foolishness.

Now you keep an eye on the time there, young man. *[The teacher addresses Student R, who is responsible for recording the class.]* Yes.

Yes, let's see, [Student Y] has been waiting. I'll try to take everyone in turn here. Isn't that lovely. Daisies love the sun and how beautifully you're placed. *[The student, who was named after a flower, may have been sitting in the sun at that time. That student laughs.]* Yes. Are you comfortable?

Yes, it's all right. [The student sitting in the sun responds.]

Well, I should hope so. We have daisies here [in the garden of the temple], and I don't see them doing very well if they don't get the sun. There's some up there somewhere.

It's true.

Pardon?

It's true.

Yes. Well now they named you for a sun worshipper there. And of all of my students, I see they've placed you right there so you can get a lovely little suntan. Now I was talking to [Student Y] there. Yes.

What would we be like if, if we followed our divine, natural evolution or are we automatically following it?

Well, you are following in keeping with the laws you have established. That doesn't mean you don't change. That doesn't mean you don't have moment-by-moment opportunity to balance your functions with your faculties so you can get in balance in your evolution. You always have that opportunity. Does that help you, [Student Y]? *[After a short pause, the teacher continues.]* Well, you'd like a different answer. I know.

No, I'll accept that. I'll accept that one.

Well, you don't have to. You can deny it and become bound by it if you'd like.

No, thank you.

Yes, thank you. I know. *[The teacher addresses the cameraman.]* That's why I mentioned it to you that time was passing. An hour goes like that. *[The teacher snaps his fingers.]* Yes, [Student L], please.

In some of this conversation today, I'm wondering if the salt mines exist on many planets or on just one or two or . . .

Planets?

Do they exist on planets—

You're a microcosm of a macrocosm. That's all inclusive. They exist inside. That's how they exist outside. Nothing exists outside that doesn't first exist inside.

Thank you.

Try to be freed from that deception. Yes. Now [Student D] has a question here.

At the moment of our transition from this form into what is beyond, the center that we are in, is that the celestial marriage we will enter into in the next step?

Well, you have to go into, in order to enter expression, you understand—you see, for example, you're in expression with nine bodies. We've already gone through that. Nine bodies. Nine centers of consciousness. Nine planets. Multitudes of forms. All right? So you want to know which planet you're going to? Well, the laws have been established. And you already are aware which center of consciousness, which planet you absolutely have convinced yourself that you are.

Now I think we'll have to continue this when we're—perhaps when summer passes and we're in where we can have our blackboard and all of that, because, you see, [if] you want to know where you're going, all you have to do is say, "Where have I been?" And we all know, when we're honest inside, where we've been. I'm not talking about before you got to Earth. Just say, "Where was I yesterday? Where was I the last day? Now which planet was I on? Which center of consciousness am I convinced that I am?" You can easily understand and know which center of consciousness you send most all of your energy to. Because all you got to do is listen to your needs and find out which center they're appealing to, correct?

Yes.

Because the one they're appealing to, that's the one they're coming from and that will tell you right where you are at any moment. There's no problem at all.

Such a lovely day. And let's look up. I'm looking down to take off this little thing here [the microphone]. I won't say another word. I'll say good day. And see you next time. Thank you.

MAY 25, 1986

A/V Class Private 49

[This class was recorded outdoors in the garden of the temple, near the east pond with the waterfall on. The sound of the waterfall often masked the questions asked by the students.]

Good morning, class.

A very nice day today. And we're going to begin today's class—can you all hear me there? We're going to begin today's class with the questions that you have prepared from our last class. And so I see that [Student N] here has a question. Yes.

I was reading that Venus is considered the brightest star. Is that because of its own, it's the greatest obstruction; it doesn't emanate—does Venus emanate its own light?

Venus is known in your world as the planet of love. And I think you've just answered your question that you have. Yes. Its light is reflected. Love is the reflection in another, as I said so long ago, of the goodness in oneself. But then again, our goodness, we permit our minds to censor and judge how we will get it. And so in answer to your question, yes, of course. It shows the brighter light to the mental world. Does that help you, [Student N]?

Yes, sir.

Yes, now [Student M] has a question this morning.

Yes. Upon entering—when we have the celestial marriage before entering . . .

Yes?

. . . upon each—when we leave this particular expression on Earth and we go on to the next expression, is another celestial contract made or is there one initial at the very beginning which kind of goes throughout all the—

Yes, I feel that I understand your question. There is a marriage before there is any conception. And as far as these teachings are concerned, in reference to the celestial marriage, in reference to your incarnation into form, whenever that which you are, the formless, free Spirit, enters bondage, it enters through what is known as a marriage or the negative and positive poles of form or bondage coming together. Yes.

[It is difficult to transcribe Student M's response.]

Did you have another question on that? So the answer to your question, of course, is there is a celestial marriage prior to all incarnations, so when you leave your present form, you go through a certain process and you enter your next form as an effect of the celestial marriage or the contract that is made, ever in keeping with your evolution and the work that you have to do. Yes.

Thank you.

You're welcome. Yes, [Student B].

I've tried to figure out what centers go with what planets and I have had difficulty.

That's most understandable. You haven't had the Atlantean astrology charts yet, have you?

No.

Yes, you will be receiving those. Look forward to the fall in your world because we will give those to you on our blackboard, inside, come the fall months. During the summertime, enjoy the outside and consider, in your efforts, which planets go with which center. Once you have the Atlantean astrology, I don't feel that you'll have any problem whatsoever. Yes.

For example, you see, you do your homework and consider, as [Student N] has just said, in reference to her question on the planet Venus. Your world is already very familiar and judged the goddess Venus or the planet of love, the goddess of love. And so by doing your homework, then you will make that step in evolution and growth.

My purpose is to teach by guidance and by revelation. Not by dictation, you see. So if you do your work and then the time comes, we will reveal that to you. You will see whether your path is a little bit crooked or becoming very straight. Don't you find that most helpful?

They're very clear.

It's better, it's better to drive along a road and to stop at a detour than to ignore it and to go over the cliff. Hmm? Wouldn't you agree, [Student B]? So though your mind, in its efforts, will find many detours, if you will pay attention to the detours and you will not quit in your efforts, you will find the thoroughfare that's very straight and very narrow. But if you are not given that opportunity to drive along your highways of life, then, you see, you will not have the qualifications, known in your world as experiences, to help you to make intelligent decisions as you continue on with your study and efforts. Hmm? Yes. You see, for me to tell you prior to your efforts to awaken for yourself makes you dependent on something that is beyond your control. That is something that I spend my life making great effort that no one depends on me. For I know that if I permit them to depend on me, I have established the law of my dependence on someone else. And I've had much experience with that quite some time ago. Yes. Does that help, [Student B]?

Yes.

Yes, I'm happy to see you feeling so much better today.

Thank you.

Yes, it was too much, well, let us say, sometimes we, our mind says we're bewildered when we can't figure out something. Isn't that true? Well, the price of bewilderment, its cost, is absolute exhaustion after a time. *[Student B laughs.]* All right. Now [Student U], and I have [Student J] here.

The proximity to the source of the, the proximity of the planet to the source determines the density of the obstruction. Is that, is that correct?

Yes, that is correct in that sense. Absolutely. Yes. Go ahead.

How do you determine that proximity? Is that determined by the revolution of the planet?

Oh, that's determined by the lord of the universe. That's known as your will power. Why, certainly. Certainly. If you want your proximity, for example, if you want to identify with the water center and through the lack of effort of your will power, the lord of the universe, you want that planet in your, in your microcosm to be in a proximity where it will cast the brightest light for your own self-deception, why, certainly, your lord of the universe and your use or lack thereof will help you with that. Do you understand that, [Student U]?

Yes.

Why, certainly, yes.

How is it that the lord of our universe can respond to pleasure or pain? How is that subject to that?

How is your lord of the universe—your lord of your universe is what you use so that you can have that experience. Without the lord of the universe, you could not have that experience. So if you make a choice—[if], for example, you make a choice to have a certain experience that offers you pain and suffering, poverty and disaster, why, that's your divine right. For you, you alone are in charge of your microcosm, definitely, which is [the] direct revelation of the macrocosm.

Thank you.

Do you understand?

Yes.

Well, I do hope so because, you know, though the law reveals the 90 percent law established, you are not left without the lord of the universe, that 10 percent, to make intelligent choice based upon the proximity that, from experiences in the past, you believe that you are. Did that help you, [Student U]?

Yes.

Yes. You know, say you're going down the highways of life, you call experiences, you can take a look and you say, "Oh, now wait a minute. I think, I suspect that I have been this way before. And this was a dead end. Well, there's no sense in me going that many more miles again. I know now I've already been there before. I can vividly recall those experiences in my errors of ignorance so what is this sign that I am looking at that tells me to keep going?" So, you see, you have to use your intelligence. Yes. Now [Student J] has a question. Yes.

I believe it was stated last week, sir, that Saturn was one of the more enlightened planets.

Well, Saturn is. Yes, indeed.

Now if one is born under the Saturn influence, why would one then be destined to another planet, let's say, like, the water sign?

Oh, absolutely, you're destined to be destined to one of those functions. Absolutely. So that you can make intelligent choice and, in so doing, be an instrument of that which you truly are, the Light, to evolve the limit, the bondage, and the form. Yes. Yes, you see, you're given that opportunity. The brighter the Light, the darker the night, [Student J].

So if you have a person in their evolution, having left the planet of Saturn, of course, one of the more awakened planets, then it is absolutely in keeping with the divine law that you would have that opportunity, being such a bright light, to identify with the lesser light, you see, to be so attracted. You know, the more electric that a person is, the more attractive they become to people who are extremely magnetic, you see? You see, you take a look, even in your world, you see the birds and the bees and everything, you see. You find a real electric one, and then you find all the magnets after it. Don't you?

Yes, sir.

Well now, there you are. So when a person, an electric, [is] from an awakened planet in that respect, they have more temptation. So that they can, they can make their choices, you see, ever in keeping with their evolution, yes. So then a person says,

"Now let's see, why am I constantly tempted?" Well, then you must ask yourself, "Why am I so electric? Where's balance in my life?" Wouldn't you agree, [Student J]?

Yes, sir.

Yes, why, certainly. You are very fortunate to have such golden opportunities of temptation. I see that they're, you know, they're like a beehive. Yes, just lovely. Yes, go ahead with your question. Yes.

Well, that was one answer. Another question I had was, Why—is there a broader definition for the word marriage? *The way you're using the word* marriage—

Oh, certainly, certainly. Not this foolishness *[The teacher laughs.]* [that] you go before some priest someplace and then suddenly you're one. Well, no, no, no, no, no. You become more than two in the marriages that I see in your world. Yes, you become quite a few. *[The teacher coughs.]* Excuse me.

The celestial marriage is necessary in order to enter form, limit, or bondage, as you know form. Without that, it is not possible, you understand, for the Light to enter. Now, so this amalgamation of vibration, of your positive and your electric come together. Now, for example, you take the Divine Light, which you are. The moment it is divided, the moment the Light is divided, it conquers. What conquers? You see, the moment you have division, you have conquest. So it is a divided mind that conquers. It is a united mind that frees. So, you see, it is the house divided, of which so many often speak about. The Light that you are, in order—you see, the celestial marriage that we're speaking of, it divides. And so you have this Light that you are sustaining and supporting the lesser light. You have this Light that you are, knowing beyond a shadow of any doubt you're the formless, free Spirit. Now that's division. Would you—you do understand that, don't you?

Yes.

So one moment you find yourself in a terrible condition. You just—everything just looks terrible. Everything, all experiences are awful. And you pause for a moment and you move your identity over to this other half of you, you see. That which you truly are, those faculties. You take a look and say, "Well, this is ridiculous. Why should I put myself through all this torture and suffering. That isn't even me. That comes and goes." You do know the difference, you see. So that is the effect of the celestial marriage, you see. That is the contract.

Which side of the border will you choose at any moment? You see? Moment by moment everyone makes that choice. Now if you permit yourself to—you know, it's like, say that—I'll tell you, perhaps, in a way that you'd understand, everyone—say that you're in a concentration camp. I think you all relate to that. There's many kinds of concentration camps. You usually visualize them with barbed wire and dogs chasing you and search lights and every[thing]. Well, say you've just escaped. All right? Well, now twenty yards—you've got out, out through all that barbed wire and twenty yards away is the border. You see? Well, you look to that to freedom, you see. To all of the things that you've desired, you see. And you've been locked into this concentration camp, maybe, for many years. Now as you're looking towards that and you're running towards that border to escape, you see, all of your protective mechanisms start to relax. Do you understand that?

Beware when all seems well. Beware when you see, "Ah! Oh, freedom's at hand. I'm just about to get there." So, you see, just as you're heading towards that border, you see, all of your inner resistance and everything starts to weaken. You do understand that, don't you? Because you're filled with hope, you see. You're—you've waited so long for that escape.

Well, you get to the border, but the border isn't a line, you see, that's, maybe, three inches wide. It might be twenty yards or forty yards wide, you see? And so here you are, partway through this border to your freedom; while you're there, you are at your weakest point. You see that what you want is about to happen. You have your eye on what is about to happen, and you lose all of the protective mechanisms, you understand, that you have, available to you, that you've used to survive in the concentration camp. And by doing that, you become a wide-open victim for those guards who kept you in [that] concentration [camp], in the cell blocks, for who knows how many years. Does that help with your question?

Yes, sir.

Now that's the way—that's what you can relate to as experiences in your world. But that's the way that it is, you see. You're just about to get there. I taught you that so long ago in that just before the victory come all the hissing hounds of hell, you see. Just as you are about to enter and to cross the border, you see, into the Light, you'll have all of this after you. You cannot weaken. That's when you have to be stronger than you've ever been in the concentration camp of creation itself.

You see, it's the concentration camp of creation that you're trying to escape from. Well, you don't escape from it. That's not how you get out of the concentration camp. You accept it for what it is, and you make intelligent choice, you see? That's how you cross the border. You cross that border in consciousness. That's how you do that. You cannot afford the lower centers of consciousness. You cannot afford the earth, fire, and water centers of consciousness. Because to afford that luxury, you'll never get across the border. There's no way possible. You must learn and practice the exercise given to you known as disassociation. There's no other way to cross the border. Did that help you with that question? Yes, [Student J].

Does that mean that one should consciously abstain from the lower three centers?

Oh, no, no, no. You have a responsibility to them. You just try abstaining from them and you know what happens. You know, you see, what happens is ever in keeping with our belief that we are them, you see. That's what happens, and it's rather painful and suffering to many people. And, you know, it's like a little boy who has a need for energy because all of the energy that is available to him, [Student R], is dissipated—you are [Student R], aren't you? *[During his response to Student J, the teacher addresses the cameraman, who just moments before had panned the camera across the garden.]*

Yes, I know you're looking for the birds, but there's a bird here, too, you see. *[The teacher gestures toward himself and laughs joyously.]* A real rooster! *[The teacher laughs even louder, as do many of the students.]* Well, I didn't want to say a pheasant. Anyway, where were we? He got off into the creation. Oh, yes, we're talking about little boys, you know, you see, who have dissipated their energy, their vitality. Well, they do everything they can to create conditions and experience[s] through which they can absorb energy from someone else. Well, we have a few boys like that in school here, you know. *[The teacher laughs again.]* I've dealt with them for centuries.

And so it, of course, reveals to me that the energy available to them, which is ever in keeping with our acceptance, you see, is being totally dissipated to create fantasies; you understand them as fantasies and things and forms. And, of course, here in the school it has, to your minds, created a lot of problems over the years. [It's] not something that we're not capable of handling.

However, we want to understand how this really works. And the thing is, you see, as long as a person is permitted, like a child, is permitted to play with the available energy that they have earned and merited at any moment and they're able to dissipate that so foolishly in fantasizing and creating these forms, you see, to give them a temporal, false charge, as long as they are permitted to sponge off of someone else's energy, just because they judge, perhaps, in their little minds, that that person's got an excess and an overabundance—they're always able to get up and [etc.]. Well, you have to understand that process, you see, with people and, of course, with oneself, so we can understand it with people, and then just let them have it. You see?

Now I have, you know—in fact, my channel even said this morning to some of the ladies, well, let's see now, it's Father's Day. There'll be an anniversary. And, for the ones that survive until a couple of Sundays in your world from now, he said, well, he wasn't so worried about the women now, but perhaps [we] had better consider that some of the fathers may make it to Father's Day in this class. That's two Sundays away. And from what I viewed today, I see one that just may not make it two minutes after I have completed class today. But I have some fathers that are very, very concerned about their energy, wouldn't you say, [Student O]? So that you don't dissipate yours on some little boy?

Yes, sir. [Student O responds.]

[Student R]? Well, you'll have the job. Well, you go on there. That's part of the class, you see, to understand those things, you see. Yes, yes.

I want my students here, as my students in my other classes understand, energy is energy. It is available to all of us. You want a lot of energy? Then you must husband your energy in a sensible way. You must learn to use it wisely and not be so compassionate, as my channel has been for too many years, to simply dissipate it out for another's benefit as they turn around and just play with those forms, which take a phenomenal amount of energy. And so we've come to our timing on that, don't you see?

But understand that every experience you have is an effect of energy that you have used, you see. Now the energy for an experience that is distasteful, you see, a strong experience, is equal to the energy of this, of the same experience that is most beneficial and pleasing, you see?

So energy is energy and the more that is used by the mind to create forms, what people call thoughts and things—and I'm pleased to say that I have found, and there's something I have learned from some of you students. It's really quite interesting. It wasn't in my vocabulary, but I did put it in there. It's called mental masturbation. That didn't come from my experiences, but I'm so happy to have learned that, you see. Yes. And it is quite appropriate. But I will be honest with you in my eons of experiences with many languages, that particular terminology was not in my dictionary. But mental masturbation—and I have a few masturbators here—I have one particular, this morning, that's going to get really masturbated by my other students because I've left orders with my channel, you see. And so that's nice. So if anyone wants to see what masturbation of a little boy looks like, you're welcome to the little counseling that's going to be taking place with a couple of the men today. Hmm? Yes.

[Editor's note: this is an example of exposure. Whenever students became so overidentified with a level of consciousness that their behavior or their thought forms transgressed the rights of the Serenity Association or the rights of other students, those levels were exposed. That is, the level the student was expressing was exposed to the light of reason. The exposure typically took the form of an interrogation, often with strong, powerful language, but without any physical contact. Mr. Goodwin would usually conduct the exposures, but he often delegated that task to other students. The purpose of the exposure was to free the true being of the student from a level of consciousness and the very limited and demanding forms they were, temporarily, overidentified with to such an extent that they believed they were those thoughts and feelings. Although the exposure was often quite painful to the ego, the student who was exposed always felt much better after the exposure was completed. Indeed, it is often not

easy to free oneself from a thought pattern that has been served for a lifetime. Mr. Goodwin often used his energy to help dissipate the forms created by his students and, in so doing, helped free the true being of the student from levels that have been fed, through ignorance and through fascination, far too much energy. He was accustomed to fighting fire with fire. Often just the prospect of exposure inspired the students to make greater effort to self-control. Still, the mental forms that we have served for a lifetime do not easily bow when we begin to desire a change. Freeing students from the bondage and service to those levels and forms was one of the purposes of the Serenity Association.]

Now where were—that's very important that you understand this energy. Go ahead with your question, [Student J].

Well—

Of course, we could stand our little masturbator up here. Mental masturbation, now that's the only masturbation I'm talking about. Because I have learned that from my students right here in Serenity. It's just lovely. Such a beautiful day, you know. But I've learned that and, you know, it's come to the time—I don't like to be the kind of teacher to point a finger at someone, but I'll point my whole hand at that one because he's been masturbating before classes and was instrumental in serving those forms for our class to be a little delayed today, you see? So I'm going to stand up my students that have that need to mentally masturbate—I love that term, you see. I really do. I don't love it, but—I shouldn't say that, but I do like that term because, you see, I look and I see that this little class relates so lovely to the word. You see? And that's nice. I couldn't get my channel to use that term. *[The teacher laughs joyfully.]* But I have no problem using it. And you'll see. Enough is enough. Yes, now go right ahead, [Student J].

Well, sir—

Would you like to stay and straighten him out after [class]? I can't stay, you know.

Yes, I'll—

Oh, no, no, you have more important things to do. We'll let our good student[s] [Student O] and [Student R] and [Student U] [handle that]. And I want the, what do you call it, the fidelity of harmony full volume. Yes, now go ahead with your question. Take care of that foolishness.

In keeping with this energy conservation and, and preservation—

Yes.

—and direction, is that the reason why you've encouraged us to work and also to constantly flood our consciousness with affirmations?

Well, absolutely, because, you see, then you receive an unobstructed flow of the energy. Now, you see, the question is, What will you do intelligently with that energy, when each form, like— yes, yes, yes, that came from one of the ladies. Mental masturbation. Yes, that's it. *[The teacher laughs joyfully. He seems to really enjoy using that term.]* One of my lady students gave that to my channel. I wasted no time putting that in my dictionary. But anyway— *[The teacher laughs even more.]* You see, you have, from the flooding of your consciousness and from your proper meditations and your breathing, you become receptive to the most and the purest unadulterated energy from the source that you are, this solar system, you see: *[The teacher gestures with this hand toward his chest.]* the very source that is within your being: the microcosm of the macrocosm.

All right. Now as you look at your sky and your world out there, you look and you see, ah, the light, and you call that the sun. That's the source of the solar system. All right. Now you are a solar system. You have a sun in there, you see. Now that's the source. You become receptive to that source without all of the forms that dissipate it as it's trying to enter into your consciousness when you flood your consciousness. So that way you rejuvenate your health, your wealth, and your happiness, if you use that, if you husband that energy intelligently.

You cannot afford the luxury of what is known as daydreaming. You see, daydreaming is a lovely term for what one of my lady students taught me: mental masturbation. It's a diplomatic term; it's called daydreaming. You understand that, ladies and gentlemen? And it's a terrible, terrible weight. You see, what it does, it leaves a person feeling unfulfilled, dissatisfied, discouraged, ready to throw in—what do you call it?—the rag, the towel, I mean. Ready to throw the towel in. And to throw in anything! Anything that'll fit, you see. Just throw it in. Yes. *[Many of the students and the teacher laugh.]* Is that the way you want to live? I don't think so. *[The teacher and the students continue to laugh.]*

Well, life is beautiful. You see, I teach you that humor is the salvation of the soul. How do you think your soul is saved by humor? Because, you see, when you can feel that wonderful vibration of humor, you see, all those forms, they go phssst! They don't get any more energy. You don't feel need; you don't feel a lack of fulfillment; you don't feel all those things. You don't feel hungry for anything, you see? You don't feel all that foolishness. Well, how can you feel all that foolishness, because you now are in closer proximity—you hear?—to the center of your source, that which you are. You understand that?

Yes, sir.

So you must learn, learn how to permit that soul faculty known as humor to rise. I can assure you it is the only thing that has ever saved me in these eons of experiences: in my time in the desert; behind that terrible wall. It is the only thing, as my channel well knows, that's kept him going his short term on Earth this time. It is the only thing. It is the only thing that will rejuvenate you. The rejuvenation is your proximity to the source, that which you are. Yes.

One more brief question, sir. I'm sorry to keep you—

You're not keeping me at all. We have a long, nice, lovely, long tape in our new little picture box over there. *[The teacher refers to the video camera.]* Go right ahead.

In keeping with what you're saying, speaking for myself and I'm sure I'm speaking for other students as well, when one attempts to do the right thing, namely flood their consciousness and work hard—

Yes. Yes.

—and yet still suffer an energy drain, is there a common—

Yes, there is. There certainly is. Because, you see, the shadow of past experiences is rising high on the tide of the water center. That's, you see, you see, for example, what happens is through the Law of Association a person makes effort, and they really do make effort to make changes in their life for their own good. Do you understand?

Yes, sir.

All right. They understand that for their own good. But if they don't have the goodness for themselves, they certainly can't share it with anyone else, can they?

No, sir.

So we have to begin at home. All right. So they make great effort. And in making that great effort, they're out in the world working and etc., and they find these phenomenal energy drains, right?

Yes.

All right. Now they must look at the situation the way that it is. First off, through their changes in consciousness they have threatened the experiences of the past, the forms that had been created. They live and swim in the water center. Now a person that works very hard in making changes cannot in any way possible afford identification with the water center. There's just no way. Because if they do, they're going to face those forms from the past, you understand, you see, that had their heyday for a long time. Remember, [Student J] . . . *[A few words are difficult to transcribe.]* And the moment they identify with the water center, all of those forms grab ahold of them, you see, and they just drain them [of] every bit of energy. And they find this phenomenal exhaustion.

The, you see, the rejuvenation is in the working. It is when you permit identification with the water center that you go, "Ugh!" *[The teacher seems to collapse into his chair.]* And then you're drained completely. That's not the time to close the eyes and go into what you know as sleep. That's the time to sit. That's the time to really flood the consciousness and drift off into that [other] realm. Because [if you go to sleep while identified with the water center] at that time, you'll drown in the water center where they will just take every bit of energy that they can get. You will wake up and wonder what's happened because you didn't rejuvenate. Well, because while you were out sleeping, they were draining all of the energy, for you did not do your part before you lost conscious awareness. Hmm? Does that help you, [Student J]? Because that is exactly what happens, and not just happens to you. As you said, it is beneficial to everyone. Because that's what happens.

Now what is the benefit for those forms in the water center that way? We know they get the energy at that time. They—and then, they get their energy, and the next time you make effort to make a change, you feel discouraged; it's not worth it, and you go back to the old way. Would you not agree?

I do indeed. [Student J responds.]

Well, that's how they work, you see. So understand this: the moment you think of what you consider self, when you think of [Student J], what is offered to you at that moment is earth, fire, and water. That's offered to you, see? You want to get into the air and electric. Hmm?

Now there is a way, if you are between the air and the electric—you already know that's faith, but it's faith in something beyond that which you are used to, however. Once you're there, you can consciously make the effort to identify with the form, but you'll have an entirely different feeling considering your, concerning your form. An entirely different [feeling]. That's when you will feel it's the suit and how heavy it really is. Of course, it's very heavy, and speaking not only of weight, but of what you consider burden, you see. It's a very heavy suit. Yes. But once you get up there, you can take the moment and take a look at it, because you will see it there, and you say, "That's the suit that I'm wearing *today*. How long the day lasts, that's ever in keeping with the divine laws of evolution." You see?

But that's only one of many suits. Only one of many suits. It shows the strengths and it shows the weaknesses, ever in keeping with the uses and the abuses in the evolution of form. That's all it shows. That, of course, and its many characteristics and its functions and, and its facult[ies]. It shows what you've done, anyone, in evolution. The suit reveals it in each evolution, you see. Yes, it reveals the weakness and reveals the strengths of identifying with the suit at the expense, you understand, of that which you are, the Light. Does that help with your question?

Indeed. Thank you.

You see, you see, so people say, "Well, I have this condition. I have that condition. I have some other condition. I've had it for a long time. I've had it for the short time." You see, that's a whole open book that is showing them: these are the changes that you must make in consciousness. You must not and you cannot afford to become discouraged or any of that, because this is showing you very clearly here, right here, that you've tried before and chosen the other. You tried again and chosen the other. You see? So each time it gets, the weakness gets weaker and weaker and weaker. You see, in that respect you become more weakened when you identify with the form, with the limit, and with the suit that you wear. Yes. It's very—all pain and all suffering are registrations in those centers of consciousness through which you identified that your belief that you are the suit. You see?

You see, you talk to one of my students and they—and you tell them, well, they're leaving this world, could be any moment, and they're going to end up in the universe [and] they'll only be a thumb. Well, what are they going to do with a thumb moving around the universe, you see? That tells you, if you ask yourself that question, "I won't have no eyes, no ears, and none of those other things. What am I going to do as a thumb moving around the universe?" You see, then, within you, those forms will rise up, you see. Oh, they'll say many things, but pay attention to how you feel. That will tell you how much you believe that you are any particular part of the suit that you are temporarily wearing. And that will also, you see, it will show you, unless certain changes are made, what kind of a suit you'll be getting into. And you never know the day or the hour. Did that help, [Student J]?

Yes, sir.

Oh, my, my, yes, indeed, it does. Yes. So, you see, you don't have to have someone to tell you what your future is. Your future is revealed to you. Your future is revealed to you moment by moment. All you must do is to learn to read the signs along the highways. Hmm? That's all you have to do. You see? You see?

And I know, I know each one—I'm working with each and every one of you students each and every day. Seven days a week while you're in these private classes I'm with you. It [was] only last Sunday—I don't even think—no, you weren't here—that I worked with all of you students. We passed a new regulation. In fact, anyone who wasn't present should be aware of that new regulation: Anyone who doesn't meditate every day and do their spiritual part, their class fee will be increased three times. Three times. I think your classes now are only costing you, what, a hundred, is that all there?

Eighty-five. [A different student responds.]

Is that all? Oh, my, my, my. My, my. Well, we'll have to look into that! Eighty-five? Is that all?

Yes.

Oh, my. Well, anyway, three times that. You see? It's the first time we've had to pass that kind of regulation, you see? You see? That's the first time. But it's wonderful because you're growing, and that's most encouraging, you see. I would not consider that a temptation, to me, discouragement. My goodness sakes alive, do you know that temptation kept me on that desert for I don't know how long? I should, well—I'm not interested in discouragement. If you're interested in discouragement, go out on the desert for a few centuries and you'll lose that feeling, that temptation immediately. Yes.

Yes, did that help with the questions, [Student J]? And [Student L] here has some questions, yes.

Back to . . . celestial marriage, regarding—is that regarding the soul mate and regarding— [One word is difficult to transcribe.]

No, no, no, no, no, no, no, no. No, don't get into that terrible trap of soul mates and things. My, oh, my, you'll be spending eons looking for the right man. No, no, let's not get into that— or the right woman. No. No.

All marriage is division. *[Mr. Red, the church's dog, begins to bark.]* And you call it unity. Yes. Now, my friend, Mr. Red, that's all right. He's, he's on, he's on duty there. Can you hear me there all right? *[The teacher addresses the cameraman.]* That's fine and dandy. Yes. All marriage is division, and you're deluded and call it unity. Does everyone—does anyone not understand that? [Student N]?

Yeah, I understand it.

Oh, you do understand it. Oh, good. Well, look cheery then. There's some lovely birds in there. *[The teacher sees some birds in the tree above him.]* Did that help with your question, [Student L]?

Yes.

Yes, yes. Don't get all worried about all these teachings of all these soul mates and everything else, you know, because every desire that that lower realm wants to fulfill, it'll convince you, "That's my soul mate." How many soul mates some people have is just a really, it's a rude awakening to me. I never saw so many of them flying in the universe. Thank you. [Student Y]. Yes, that's fine. Go right ahead with your question.

Thank you. [Student L expresses.]

Lovely day today. Yes.

When you say viewing, you spoke of viewing— [Student Y begins her question.]

Yes, viewing.

Ah—

With a *v* for victory. Yes.

OK. Do you mean looking without any obstructions?

No, I mean, well, I mean viewing. Most people look. There are a few in your world who view. But most people look, you see. You see, you look, you have all of this censorship, you know. So few people look into the eyes of another. I find that in your world the house, you see, the windows are not important. It seems to be the foundation or something or the door or something. But, you see, doors, you see, let all the doors close, the light goes through the glass, through the window, see? You see? And let those doors close, because in the closing of those doors, I assure you, a window shall open. You see? So be interested in viewing, you see, you see. You can look and you'll see a door. You can view and you'll see a window. Yes. Perhaps that helps you with your question. Yes. Yes. Because everything will look there, you see, it is just a reflection bouncing back to us. We're looking at it—yes, yes, yes. *[Mr. Red walks down the stairs behind the teacher.]* No, just a moment here. Do you see this side over here? *[Mr. Red tries to pass on the teacher's right side, where there is very little room, but the teacher directs Mr. Red to the* left. *Simultaneously, the teacher picks up his glass of water. Mr. Red had a habit of knocking over the teacher's glass of water.]* Here. Here. Come over here now. You know. You know better. Yes, good boy. *[Mr. Red sits beside the teacher on his left and the teacher pets him.]*

All right. That's fine. Yes, now someone else had a question here. Yes, [Student D] has a question. [Student U], I will get to you. Thank you. Yes.

The planets closer to the sun are denser. But Saturn is the fifth from—it's not the furthest away from the sun— [Student D remarks.]

That is true; it is not the furthest away.

But it is the fifth of all the planets. [Saturn is the sixth planet from the sun.]

That is correct.

Why is there that disparity?

There's not a disparity. [Student U], I'll come to your question. Why does she see a disparity? Now, you're a student and you should know.

The density— [Student U responds.]

You heard her explanation of the teaching. Let's go—now you repeat that. To see if that's in harmony with your understanding of that particular teaching.

The density of the obstruction is ever in keeping with our acceptance. [Student U replies.]

Now. No. That's fine, [Student U]. Now [Student D] said, if I recall correctly, that Saturn was the fifth planet from the source. Isn't that what you said?

Well, Earth is the fifth. [Student D responds.]

Ah, now we're getting into a different philosophy here.

Earth is not as far from the sun as some of the planets.

You see.

Pluto is farther out.

Now listen carefully. Listen carefully, now, [Student D]. Listen carefully. Go ahead, [Student U].

The proximity of the planet to the source is determined by the lord of our universe. [Student U remarks.]

That is correct. That is correct. Now, how do you answer her question? You see, this is how we grow. Do you understand that, [Student B]? We grow through—understanding is an effect of communication. If there isn't communication, forget understanding. You see, with all your getting, get understanding. And with all your giving, give wisdom. How is that possible if there's no communication? All right. Communicate. I want to hear this. I want to hear my students' interpretation of what I have shared with you these many years. Yes. *[After a short pause, the teacher continues.]*

All right now, [Student D], you go ahead and make your statement again. Now this is important. And I will listen to [Student U]'s answer. That's known as communication. And when it's so far off that he can't perceive how far off it is, or right on, then I will speak up. Go ahead now. We're going to start growing here. A little more.

The planets closest to the sun are the greatest in density. Saturn is not as far from the sun as some of the planets, but it is the less dense of all the planets. Why is it less dense than the ones farther out? [Student D asks.]

Now have you asked [Student D]—this is important for class—have you asked [Student D] upon which teachings are the statements based? Did you—well, I think that's the first question I would ask. *[The teacher addresses Student U.]*

Upon which teachings are those statements based. [As Student U speaks, the teacher speaks as well.]

I feel good as a magistrate. It's been so many eons out of my life. Oh, it's just wonderful. Go ahead. I'm listening to . . .

I looked at a chart of the density of planets in the encyclopedia. [Student D responds.]

Yes. Well, I would like to, if I may speak, you know, I don't want to seem a partial judge in any way, or magistrate, but I do want to assure my students I am not employed by the Britannica Corporation. *[Many students laugh.]* Now please, go ahead. *[After a short pause, the teacher continues.]* This is important. Go ahead now, answer her question. She has made that effort to study what is available to her.

Now— [Student U begins.]

The Encyclopedia Britannica. Go ahead.

From our—

I'll tell you how that got started. Huh! *[The teacher spoke almost as an aside, as Student U spoke to Student D.]*

—teachings we know that Saturn is one of the most evolved planets. We also know that the density of an obstruction is ever dependent upon its acceptance. That there is a variation in planets in density does not, for me, pose any problem or question. It is an under—an expression of the law that says the density of any obstruction is measured by its acceptance.

All right. Now that's a fine answer because you're coming in from physics and she's coming in from—based [her] study upon the—what was that? Britannica?

It's one of those encyclopedias. [Student D responds.]

Yes.

I'm not sure which one.

But it's all right. Now I want to hear from [Student S]. We're going to have—we'll hold court today. Isn't that lovely? *[Many students laugh.]* Yes. [Student S], please answer her statement, ah, her question. *[After a short pause, the teacher continues.]* Would you like her to repeat it? I feel very good when I'm back in court. Yes. *[Again, many students laugh.]* Yes, you go right ahead. She would like you to, please, make the statement.

The planets closest to the sun are the most dense. [Student D begins her statement.]

I'm listening.

Saturn is not furthest from the sun, but it has less density. Why does it have less density than the ones that are farther away from the sun behind it? [Student D explains.]

Now you listen carefully. Is this all based upon the teachings received? Then please make your statement.

I'd like to ask you what you based the statement on that all planets closest to the source are the most dense. [Student S asks.]

Well, [Student U] mentioned it. And I went back over the numbers from the encyclopedia I was looking in and their numbers correspond to the closer planets are denser. Most of them. [Student D responds.]

Most of them. Now try to—remember now, I did state that I have not, nor am I at present, nor do I intend to be employed by the Britannica Corporation. Go right ahead, please.

I think that your first premise there is an error. And that's the problem with the rest of it. [Student S remarks.]

Well, that's lovely, but I don't, I don't hear any direction.

Ah . . . [Student S continues.]

I find an ending to the seeming problem, but I don't find a solution for guidance. *[Mr. Red starts to bark.]* Here. Here. Here. Now just a moment here. What is this today? Yes. What is this? Here. Here. *[The teacher addresses Mr. Red.]*

In these teachings— [Student S begins.]

You come right back here. *[The teacher again addresses Mr. Red.]*

—when there's—

Come on. Come on. You come right on. Now listen, you've always been that way in school. *[The teacher continues to address Mr. Red as Student S offers her understanding.]*

—an understanding—

Want to sit in the corner with a dunce cap? *[The teacher asks Mr. Red.]*

—you will find that it will be, it will be consistent. Where in the Earth world, when you look it up in references, if it's not

consistent with the teachings, there's a misunderstanding there. And ... [Student S explains.]

Has the class taught that the—the question I think that is plaguing [Student D] is a density-proximity problem. Is that what we're—

Yes. [Student D confirms.]

You see, so what you—in your homework for next week, study your notes and your lovely, little tapes [of the classes]. And report back, is there a teaching concerning the density and proximity that has been given to you? Do you understand that, [Student U]? You see? So that you may base the question upon class work that has been given. Do you understand? Because, you see, it is very difficult when you, when you take—you have a question and you go to sources that are not recommended. Well, it's never been asked: "What source may I investigate?" Do you understand that, you see?

You see, that makes it very difficult for any student. You see, the thing is to question and to present. "I would like to further my understanding on this particular teaching. I would like to ask if these particular books that I am considering for the furthering of my understanding would be in harmony or in keeping with the particular law that is being revealed in the classes here that I am studying." Wouldn't that be helpful?

Yes. [Student D responds.]

Yes, so, you see, all of this comes out like that. Because for me to say, "Now just a moment. This is what was said last week," you understand? And I go right down through the whole list. How is that going to benefit you? It'll only give you a crutch to lean upon. You see? And then you'll become dependent upon me because I will have established the law to become dependent upon you. And not that you aren't all lovely students, I just have no desire, nor temptation, to be dependent on form, let alone my own. Yes, go right ahead, please. Or my channel's. Yes. *[After a short pause, the teacher continues.]* Did you have anything else to say?

I didn't know if I should share it today or next— [Student S responds.]

Well, no, go right ahead. Go right ahead. We're sharing lovely today. We're finally getting there. We're holding court. Yes. Yes.

May I direct it to [Student D]? [Student S asks.]

Why, certainly. Certainly.

This morning in this class he said, it was my understanding, that humor is the salvation of the soul and helps you go in to greater proximity to your source inside.

That's true.

And that's where there is more Light. So right there that would be instrumental, I think, in understanding about the density of those planets.

Yes, [Student D].

Well, I don't know much about the planets. [Student D remarks.]

Don't you worry. Fall's coming and you're going to have the Atlantean astrology. You may not know much, but you're very interested in astrology, [Student D]. You have this, this lovely interest in that area. I know that. You know that, don't you?

Yes, I do. [Student D responds.]

Well now, so you just remember, as my student [Student S] here just said, humor is the salvation of our soul. It will move your little planet, the one you are presently identified with, that's causing confusion. From fusion. That's how confusion is caused. I want to . . . *[A few words are difficult to transcribe.]* But anyway, it will move your identification to one of those planets that's closer in proximity to the source that you are. All right? Yes, yes.

Because you're speaking of two entirely different sources, different perspectives of a teaching that we're teaching here. Do you understand that? You see? There are similarities and there're absolute contradictions. That's why I told you I have not, nor have I ever been, employed by the Britannica Corporation. Yes.

Now who else had a question here? [Student U]'s been waiting. Then I'll get to [Student M], [Student B], and [Student S]. But time's passing quickly. *[The teacher glances at his wristwatch.]* My goodness sake's. How quickly time is passing. Yes, go right ahead, [Student U].

Why is seeing so instrumental in bondage?

Well, seeing is believing. Well, it's not my fault, or is it [Student J]'s fault, that you insist on believing what you see. I teach you to view. When you view, you don't have to worry about bondage. It's when you see that you have the problem with bondage. Because, you see, when you see, then all that you're receiving is a reflection of what you're sending out. I try to teach you, to show you how to view. To stop seeing. I mean, what is it that a person would stand, day and night, in front of a mirror just looking at their reflection? Well, when you're seeing and then, of course, you're believing—why are you believing? Because you're seeing reflection of yourself. You see reflection of yourself and that is your bondage. So you must learn to view and stop learning to see. You don't have a problem learning to see. Seeing—that's no problem at all. That's why most people, they see and they have so convinced themselves, you see, they've so convinced themselves that seeing is the way that they'll come right out and say seeing is believing. Because that's what they've offered to themselves: that absolute bondage. Seeing is believing; that's why I teach you to view. I don't have to teach you to see. You have no problem seeing. Does that help with your question?

Yes.

Whatever you see is only a reflection of what you send out. That's why you can't see truth. You cannot see the Light. You view the true Light. You see reflection of yourself. That's all that you see. You think you see this lovely, lovely flower. *[The teacher gestures toward one of the flowers in the garden.]* You don't see the flower. You see your reflection in you of the flower. [If] you view the flower, it won't look like that, I assure you. No, you will not know it like that. Something far more beautiful. Did that help with your question?

Thank you.

Yes. So make some effort to stop seeing. You won't have any problem then with believing. It won't exist, you see? Yes. Now [Student M] is waiting and then [Student Y] and several others here. Yes.

Thank you. [Student M speaks.]

You're welcome.

The retrospin and the spin—

Do you have a problem with your legs that—

No.

You have a circulation problem to close your—now, you don't worry. I'm not interested in anything, if you want a little blanket or something, I'll get it for you. But crossed legs is not in your best interest in a spiritual class, unless you want to ground yourself, [Student S]. Yes, go right ahead, please. And besides, I don't see any problem here. Are these chairs too high for you? We could go get the little, little camping stools. So would that be better?

No. [Student M responds.]

Would you feel more comfortable? Yes. You see, try to understand it's more than just grounding yourself. If you would only see what you do inside of yourself, then you wouldn't be so tempted to cross those legs. Not in a spiritual class here. Yes. Go right ahead, please.

Thank you.

Yes.

With the spin and the retrospin of each of the centers, as we were taught, the clockwise and counterclockwise—

Yes, yes, yes.

—the microcosm and the macrocosm—

Yes.

—they correlate within the body, with how we had those groups of three, counter and—

Well, certainly. I have already answered that question in respect to [Student U]'s question this morning that the proximity is ever dependent on the lord of your universe and how it serves what you want it to serve. You see, we don't seem to have any problems having the lord of the universe, you know, our lord of our universe to serve anything that we believe we are for a moment. You don't have any problem, do we, [Student U]?

None. [Student U replies.]

Well, well, stop looking. Stop seeing and start viewing. You see?

Yes. [Student M responds.]

Because that's where the proximity is. Now we, as I said earlier, we will move you into Atlantean astrology that's been brought to my channel and to [some older] students many years ago. But we'll do that this, oh, this fall. Yes.

Thank you. [Student M responds.]

Yes. This fall. Yes. Because we must have the growth process take place. The mind must become satisfied with a sufficient number of detours, you see. You see, if you don't have the experience, if you don't have the experiences with doing it your way, then you cannot become qualified to accept the possibility there's some way you don't know about. You see, you must first have that opportunity to do everything your way. Do you understand that? When I say your way, I mean all of the temptations of the mental substance. You try this, you know—like one of my students said here some time ago, "Turned over every rock and every pebble and they're all the same." Well, I said, "Then why do you keep bothering—why do you make [so] much effort to keep turning them over? If you already know what's under them, then why do you keep turning them over?" Does that make intelligent sense? You see? But, you see, if you can be a little boy and sponge off of someone else's energies, well, then you've got that excess energy to keep turning over those rocks, you see, at someone else's expense. And that someone else has to wake up. Do you understand that?

Yes, I do. [Student M responds.]

See, once you've turned over every rock, what is left? You know; you see another rock? "Oh, the same as before." Because you turned them all over. See?

Yes.

Especially if you take pride that you've turned them all over. Does that help your question?

Yes.

Yes, [Student Y] has a question.

So then, could you give us a definition of viewing within this philosophy?

Well, let's see, something that you can relate to for practice. Is that correct?

Yes, sir.

The closest thing [that] at this time I can think of that you can relate to—you have already received the laws of disassociation. You already have a little proficiency with that, don't you? All right. You want to view. You want to refrain from looking. Is that correct? *[After a short pause, the teacher continues.]* Yes, yes, I'll give you an exercise. It'll just work beautifully. But you must be willing to use your lord of your universe very strongly, intelligently, to serve the Light that you are. You take a look at [Student U]. All right? Would you kindly turn to [Student U] and look at [Student U]. All right? Fine. Now you take a look at [Student S]. Do you see the two?

Yes.

Yes, you see a difference, don't you?

Yes.

When you practice—you want to view, for you've asked the question to view—and you look at [Student U] and you look at

[Student S], and there is absolutely no registration of difference in your consciousness, then you will know you are now viewing. You have freed yourself from the bondage of believing, you see. When you look and see these two—you understand that?—which for your mental world are opposites and very different. The opposites and the difference are that which you identify [with] within yourself, for they are a reflection of what you create. Do you understand that?

Yes.

They are the Light, the same as you. So you want to view instead and free yourself from the bondage of believing, you see, then you must stop seeing. And you must look, and there's no difference. I see no difference between ant and angel.

And with that I say good day. Time? *[The teacher addresses the cameraman.]* What time is it? Don't you have a counter? Well, one minute [left]? Takes me that long to take the microphone off. I'm not as young as I used to be. Thank you. I'll say good day.

JUNE 1, 1986

A/V Class Private 50

[This class was recorded outdoors in the garden of the temple, near the east pond with the waterfall on. The sound of the waterfall often masked the questions asked by the students.]

Good morning, class.

[Mr. Red, the church's dog, approaches the teacher and drinks from the teacher's glass of water.] Someone's always thirsty. There.

This morning, for our class, we'll hopefully broaden our understanding on "Be the observer and not the observed." *[This teaching was first given in Discourse 39.]* Being the observer and not the observed in no way exempts us from the Law of Progression, which is, of course, subject to participation. And on such a beautiful day we are all, of course, inspired to progress. And so this morning's class is in keeping with that law and demonstration of participation. And so I want to see [the] hands of my students this morning in their questions so they can see how well they've done on their homework this last week. Yes, [Student N], please.

Would Saturn be correlated to the electric center?

Well, as I stated last Sunday, I'm going to, this fall, with those of you who have not had the Atlantean astrology, and most of you have not, in our classes as yet had that, I will reveal that to you at that time. Yes. Do you find that you are specifically interested in being electric? *[After a short pause, the teacher continues.]* Pardon?

No.

Good. I don't want to say that it's hopeless, but it's a very slim chance in your particular incarnation at this time. Very slim chance. *(Student N is a female, which is a magnetic form. After another short pause, the teacher continues.]* Do we have any humor this morning? No. Good. [Student M]. *[The teacher and many students laugh.]*

Uhm . . . [Student M begins to speak.]

Yes, that's all right. Stay confused, it'll only—it'll pass in a moment. *[The teacher addresses Student N.]* [Student N]. It'll pass.

I can't hear you that well. [Student N remarks.]

Oh, you can't hear me. Oh, my. Can you hear me now?

Yes. Thank you.

Good. You're not confused then? *[After a short pause, the teacher repeats himself.]* You're not confused?

I don't think so. I just couldn't hear everything you said.

Oh, that's all right. You'll hear it on the little tape.

Yes. Thank you.

Yes, certainly. [Student M].

Yes. Last week [it] was spoken about conquering and divide, conquering—it was, ah, the celestial marriage and any kind of marriage was bondage. And unity was freedom. And in this conquering and division, what is the conquering of?

Well, first of all, in anything, in reference to your speaking on the celestial marriage, well, a person, a wise person, in any marriage, separates, for divorce is such a final thing. So separation, of course, is usually advisable. Many people get divorced; they, of course, experience a finality of a physical division there, of course. But they haven't separated in consciousness. So separation is the path.

Now you're speaking in reference to the celestial marriage and divide and conquer. Well, the division takes place within one's own consciousness. There are times that you believe that you're this and you believe that you're that. And that reveals abuse of the divine Law of Use. For example, when you believe that which you are responsible for sustaining is you, you abuse the divine Law of Use. And so you experience, from abuse of that law, you experience what you understand as bondage or control by something that you are responsible for controlling. You do understand that, don't you?

Yes. Yes.

So when anyone falls into that error of ignorance and they allow themselves to abuse that which, by the law, they have entered to use, then of course they experience the payment for they have incurred a debt by abusing instead of using.

Yes.

Does that help with your question?

Yes.

Now you understand that as divide and conquer. And so as you divide in consciousness that which you believe that you are, you divide or you separate yourself from, and you experience what you understand as difficulties, pain, and suffering and all of those types of experiences.

Yes.

Does that help with your question, [Student M]?

Yes.

Yes. Can you hear me in the back row back there? *[After short pause, the teacher continues.]* You can?

Yes, I can.

Yes. Good. I'm glad. Yes, [Student Y] has a question.

Does discouragement mean to divide one's courage so as to think division to form and bondage from truth and Light?

Well, yes, in the sense that discouragement is an effect of one's own abuse of the Law of Use. For example, one makes some effort or effort to accomplish something in their life. One believes that they are what they are 'tempting to accomplish. And by establishing that law they are abusing the Law of Use. And they experience discouragement when they realize, at times, that they have not accomplished what they desired to accomplish. They have not accomplished it because they believe that they were it. Yes, does that help with your question? And so then they experience what is known as discouragement, the lack of inspiration to continue to make further effort, you see. Yes. Yes, [Student D].

In our physical experiences, when we keep things that are given to us, is that, that's spin and then when we give out or surrender or meditate, which is a surrender, is that retrospin?

Well, when—if you're talking about receiving and you're relating receiving to retrospin?

Spin.

Yes, yes, of course. Because you cannot receive without establishing the Law of Involvement because if the Law of Involvement is not established, you cannot receive, you see. So if you don't spin in the consciousness in order to receive, then you cannot receive. Now many people seemingly feel that they are excellent givers; [yet] they have great difficulty in receiving in certain areas in their consciousness. Now in other areas in their consciousness, they're very poor givers and extremely, seemingly, good receivers. So, you see, we limit by our experiences that we believe that we are as we continue to abuse the Law of Use and believe we are the shadows that we have created. Did that help you, [Student D]?

[If the student verbally responded, it is difficult to transcribe her words.]

Yes. Yes, [Student U], please.

Does the separation that is different than divorce have to do with removing the forms that we have created from our water center through retrospin or how—

Well, for example—I see your point. You see, you cannot, you cannot remove experiences that are created in the water center by the little water spirits that control that center, for the water center serves its purpose of design, you see. Now what you can do, and what should be done, is to separate in consciousness: to recognize its purpose of design, you understand?

Yes, sir.

And when you enter that center in consciousness, choose wisely what you're going to service in that center. You have that conscious choice to make at any time. And so when you enter what you know as self, which exposes you in consciousness to all of those centers, and those forms that have been created call on your consciousness for you to service them, you have to make sure that you understand that they are what you have created in that particular center of consciousness. Because you have created them, you have a responsibility to them, but you are the one, in the light of reason, who makes the choice how that responsibility, or debt, shall be paid.

Now if you don't do that, of course, they very quickly, they've already made that judgment for you. Do you understand that? Separation. You see, to tempt to divorce yourself from creation, well, you won't be in creation. So you separate yourself. You don't divorce yourself. The celestial marriage, if you try to divorce yourself from the contract established, well, you're not going to be in creation. You cannot divorce yourself from it. You can separate yourself from it in consciousness. Hmm?

Thank you.

See? So when you cry, if you believe that is you, then you have abused the Law of Use, for you, believing that that is you and not what you have created, you have the full conviction that it's you and have all of the feelings that go along with it. *[After a short pause, the teacher continues.]* Progression. Yes, [Student B].

Last week you talked about the proximity of the planets to the sun.

Yes.

[Atlantean] astrology.

Yes.

Would the law of attraction and repulsion, attachment, that law, would it apply to the planets, too?

Yes, it certainly does. For example, the Law of Attraction, the water center and the magnet, if one permits themselves to believe they are that center of consciousness, well, what happens is—it's just the same [as] in the microcosm is the same as the macrocosm—then one convinces themselves that they are the shadows and under the influence of the reflection of the Light, which you know as the moon, you see.

The moon, as we stated in our last class, is such a lesser light that it is not perceived by the human eye. It is a very, very dim, dim light. The light that you see is the obstruction to the light, that reflection of that; that's known as the moon. So in that respect, you see, one, through attachment, for the moon in your world represents, in your solar system, and is, the magnet, which controls the water center of the planet on which you presently reside in physical form. So the moon affects only those people who believe they are the emotions that express through them, and the feelings. Does that help with your question, [Student B]?

So, you see, if you believe, if you have convinced yourself that you are form, if you have convinced yourself that that is what you are, then you are controlled by these various planets in their movement through your solar system, for those planets are represented, you understand, in your own little universe. Does that help with your question? In other words, for example, you have many experiences in your world where you say there's a full moon or there's a new moon and people are highly activated emotionally in the water center. Well, the only people that are highly activated in that respect are people who believe they are their form, and in so doing they are controlled by those planets in their little universe inside of them. Does that help with your question, [Student B]?

So, you see, you don't have to believe that you are your water center; you don't even have to know about a water center. All you have to do is believe that you are the physical form that you are. And in that belief, you have transgressed the Law of Use.

This is why astrology is indicative; it is not compelling. It is only compelling to those who believe they are the physical limit. Does that help? Yes. And so in that sense it's 90 percent, on your planet, accurate. Atlantean astrology is 90 percent accurate because you will find in this marriage that has taken place to enter your planet in a physical form, it's a very solid contract, but it does have 10 percent of Light in it, in the respect you always have 10 percent free will. [But if, with that] 10 percent, you can say, "Now just a moment. The moon is full. This is why I am the way I am," forget your 10 percent. You just gave it away. It doesn't matter if the moon is full or if it's a sliver or if it's a half moon. It doesn't matter. It only matters to people who believe and have convinced themselves that they are the physical form. And that their breathing and everything that they do is dependent upon them. Hmm? Yes, [Student B].

Don't we all believe we're the physical form or we wouldn't be here?

Well, in varying degrees, of course, we do. In varying degree. You see, you must enter and you must transgress that Law of Use in order to have physical expression, but what degree of transgression is dependent on the awakening of the individual. You see? You see, now some people, they can scratch their hand and they don't collapse emotionally. Would you not agree? Then you have some people who scratch their little finger and their entire day is ruined. Would you not agree? So, you see, doesn't that reveal varying degrees of belief in the bondage, by the abuse of the Law of Use, that they have established? *[After a short pause, the teacher continues.]* Pardon?

Yes.

Yes. And some people are able to experience more struggle and more suffering with less crying than others. Is that not true? Children and adults. Well, that's ever dependent upon their own bondage they insist on supporting within their consciousness. Did that help with your questions, [Student B]? Good. [Student Y], please.

Do the, do the planets that, as they move through the universe, are they affecting us in that way or do they automatically—

No, no, no. They are affecting you in that for they are affecting the physical form. And if you believe you are the physical form, then you are well affected. Yes. Yes, go ahead, [Student Y].

So if you, if you believe to a lesser degree that you are physical form, then they would still affect you because you are in form.

Correct.

But to a lesser...

A much lesser degree. Oh, yes, yes, yes, indeed. That's known as being in creation and not a part of creation, you see. That's the basic teaching, you see. Be with a thing, person, or place, never a part of the thing, person, or place keeps you separated to an extent that you can use the light of reason in all your acts, thoughts, and activities. Hmm? Yes, [Student D].

Then if you recognize that you are having difficulties and look at where the planets are, would the planet closest to the Earth be the one that is affecting you?

Well, now—

That is, if you're feeling, you know, if you're relating your—

Yes, yes. I, I want to—

... at that time. [A few words are difficult to transcribe.]

Yes. However, you may not be, in your evolution, predominantly what you understand in your world as an earth sign. You do understand that, don't you?

Yes, yes, I do.

So that all has to be considered and it has to be considered from what planet was the evolving incarnation of the soul. Do you understand? So that way you cannot say specifically. Certainly, it will affect those forms which are earth forms, you understand, and which have a predominant earth-form vibration. And that has to be considered. It has to be considered whether or not you are basically a Venusian or Saturnian or, or [have the sign of] a Jupiter or any of those other planets. That has to be considered. Then it has to be considered how overidentified are you with the form.

So you have all of these various factors that must be considered. Do you understand that? You see? So that way anyone who is looking towards the astrological implications of experiences in their life must know how attached, that is, degree-wise, that the individual is to their limited form. And it's a very rare person that will reveal that to you, even though they all know in truth. They do know. It's a very rare person that will ever reveal it because everyone wants to feel, what you say, pride when they're talking with someone. And great effort is made, of course, to put on the best image, isn't it? So does that help with your question, with all those things to be considered?

Then, really, the study of astrology is, basically, just to apply it to ourselves.

Yes. Well, Atlantean astrology is definitely for a person to help them to understand that they are the microcosm of the macrocosm and that the more they convince themselves that they are this microcosm, this limited form, the more they are affected. And they can look to the heavens and see the influences which they are experiencing ever in keeping with their belief that they are that limit, you see. Hmm? Yes, [Student L], please.

Thank you. What does it mean to be an air sign?

Well, well, I wish I could say that all of my students are air. They are at moment[s]. *[The teacher drinks from his glass of water.]* Well, I'll tell you one thing: it doesn't mean water. So, many people, you know, they say they're an air this or they're an air that. And most of it's hot air and a little of it's cool air. *[Several students laugh.]* I hope that's helped with your question. Yes, [Student U], please.

Could you speak on the division that occurs when the Spirit creates its covering known as soul?

Well, well, let's see how, perhaps, you could best experience that in consciousness. Take a breath. And hold it. Have you done that?

Yes.

No, you didn't because you just let it out. *[Some students laugh.]* Take another breath and hold it. *[After a short pause, the teacher continues.]* Have you done that?

[There seems to be no audible response from Student U.]

Fine. Let me know when you want to breathe, and in the meantime, I'll go to someone else. Yes, [Student J] here, please.

Sir—

You just speak up—excuse me, [Student J], [for interrupting]—you speak up now when you want to breathe. Don't be breathing through your nostrils either. I can see it. *[The teacher addresses Student U and then returns to address Student J.]* Yes, please go ahead.

Would you please elaborate on the statement that you made to the effect that being the observer is subject to participation?

Yes. Be the observer, not the observed does not exempt one from the Law of Progression, which is subject to the Law of Participation. Now that's very important. You see, ofttimes we are tempted—Be the observer and not the observed in order—does that mean you wish to breathe now? Excuse me, [Student J]. We'll come back to you on participation. Does that mean you want to—you already did breathe! *[Many students laugh.]* I see.

Now, we'll have to get to his question and [then] come back to yours. Now you asked a question there about the division and how there's a covering of this formless, free Spirit that you are. And I asked you to demonstrate this very question. Now you've just demonstrated it. You have demonstrated that for as long as you can hold your breath—do you understand that?—

Yes, sir. [Student U responds.]

—you are not bound by belief. But when you raise your hand to once again breathe again, that's your conviction that you are the limit. Now you think about that for a time. And after you have done that, I'll come back to you, time permitting here in your world. Now we're speaking on—really consider that now, because that's where it is.

Now we're talking on this participation. All these little things. Look how they like me here this morning. *[The teacher refers to a small cloud of mosquitoes that are focused on him.]* All these little things there. We're talking on participation, and I've got all kinds of participation around me. *[He again refers to the mosquitoes. Several students laugh.]*

Now, you see, so often, as I was saying, we are tempted by this wonderful truth: be ever the observer and not the observed. And so when it comes to responsibility or progressing, you see, which requires participation, this wonderful truth, be the observer and not the observed, rises in our consciousness. Well, what I'm trying to help you with, as students, is to understand who uses this wonderful truth in your mind at any given moment. See, the question must be asked, "Now am I using this? Or is there something else that I have tempted that's up here using it for me?"

This is very, very, very important. Because, you see, we do not want to fall into that error of permitting ourselves to be trapped by creation so that creation, in its cunningness, can convince us that it is us and use the wonderful Light that we are against ourselves. Do you understand that, [Student J]?

No, I don't.

You don't understand that. All right. Well, we'll go a little bit farther then. The letter of the law killeth is the sole domain of a mental world. Do you understand that?

Yes, sir.

The spirit of the law that giveth life is the sole domain of the very vehicle that expresses our eternal soul. That's our heart. So we must learn to discern between the letter of the law, which is the mental realm which belongs to the old boy below, and the realm of consciousness which is our heart. And not confuse our feelings as belonging to the sole domain of our heart, when so often it is the domain of the letter of the law. Do you understand that, [Student J]?

Yes, sir.

You see? You see, so if a person is guided by their feelings, they're not guided by their emotions. Oh, there's a vast difference. You see, the feelings of which I am speaking are not the feelings that can, in any way, register denial, the effect of which is need. That is the letter of law. That's the mental world that's speaking.

So participate. Now you have, in these many years, been participating more and more. You're progressing. You see? Participants progress. Non-participants do not. Hmm? You see, you take a pool of water. That which moves the water progresses. And in its progressing, so does the water. If the water is not moved, then it does not progress, you see. No. It is the moving water that is the life of your planet. It's not the still waters. It's the moving waters. Hmm?

So, as you ask a question, you see—you know, as I said earlier, just a moment ago, do not permit the awakening to be the observer to be instrumental in stifling the demonstrable law that progression is subject to participation. If you do not participate in the work that you have, the work that you have does not progress, does it?

No, sir.

Well, it's the same thing in class. The same thing. Yes, it's very, very important, [Student J]. Yes. Now all of those nice little creatures, they kind of went over there to the cameraman. *[The teacher again refers to the mosquitoes.]* That's nice. Yes, [Student M], please.

Yes. I—

I sent them over there to enjoy someone else. They had enough time feeding on me this morning. *[The teacher laughs joyfully.]* Yes, [Student M].

Yes. I would like—

Isn't that lovely.

—to know the understanding of participation.

The understanding of participation? You are participating. You just spoke.

Yes.

That is, a participation in what?

In the class when I ask you a question.

Well, it's a participation in the Law of Presence, in presence, which is the Law of Solicitation, right?

Yes.

You see, you see, a person by the Law of Presence one solicitates. But does one progress? No, one doesn't necessarily progress by presence and solicitation. One progresses by participation. Hmm? Yes.

Giving your life energy, giving the divine energy that you are, giving it forth—

Yes. Well, you—that's—what's important, [Student M] and class, is that when you speak to ask the question—

Yes.

—you have first created a form in order to move the physical body for that to happen.

Yes.

You do understand that, don't you?

Yes.

So that means there is something moving with sufficient energy in consciousness for—is your husband not feeling well this morning? *[After a short pause, the teacher continues, addressing Student M's husband, who is also a student.]* Well, it's very unusual, [Student O]: I haven't had an experience with you going to sleep in class.

No, sir. [Student O responds.]

Is the sun too—is the light too bright for you?

No.

All right, fine. Then you'll be fine.

Thank you.

Yes. Yes. Sometimes we are tempted by desire to overdo on things, aren't we? Like last night. Oh, always consider I'm right here for class Sunday mornings. Now I haven't missed.

All right now, [Student M]. Let's see, where we're we?

Ah—

Where were you?

I was talking about life-giving energy.

Well, yes. So you use energy sufficient to cause the mouth to open.

Yes.

Right?

Correct.

Well, that reveals your value for what you are receiving. So you establish the law to participate; therefore, *you* progress.

I see. Thank you.

No participation, no progression. The law reveals itself. Yes, [Student Y], please.

When one—

And we'll come to [Student O], too, with his questions because he wants to get that energy moving out of that center. Go right ahead, [Student Y].

When one is tempted to respond from the water center, what does that exactly mean?

What does that mean, when one is tempted from the water center? It simply means the forms they have created in that center of consciousness, they so convince themselves that they are those forms that they have created that those forms call them to work. Those forms require the energy so they can move around. Yes. You see? You see—and no effort is being made from the other centers of consciousness to say, "Just a moment. Now that's what I created. Do I want—No, I don't want that. That's not me." You see, the separation in consciousness must be made.

You see. You see. "Do I want to use my energy in that way? My life-giving energy."

Now, [Student O], if you'll sit up here—your spine is incorrect. You're locked into a center of consciousness. It's your spine. Your physical body. Sit up there so that your buttocks is back against the chair there, and you'll feel a differen[ce] in your energy. Now we'll give you time to formulate your question this morning, [Student O]. Yes, does someone else have a question? Yes, [Student S], please.

Yes. What part of us is actually progressing?

What part of us? No part, my dear. That which you are. The parts are that which you believe that you are, like your toe and your foot and your finger, your nose and your ear. That's the parts. What you are is what is evolving the whole being in which it is encased. That which you are is expressing. Are you interested in what part, like it's your foot or maybe your knee or something? Or what do you mean by parts? I would like to get the parts clear. You know, you see, I'm more interested in the whole, for the part of something, though it contains the essence of the whole, we're dealing with substance here, I think, in this respect. Yes.

What I meant is what—

My students don't relate to essence as well as they do substance. Yes. That is, my earthly ones. *[The teacher laughs joyfully.]*

—what we really are just is.

What you are, is.

So—

Your awakening to what you are is where the question is.

So is that the progression, the awakening to—

Why, yes. Why, certainly. As you separate truth from creation, the awakening becomes more fully expressed. Yes.

Thank you.

See? And you get yourself freed from those parts, which are subject, of course, to belief. Yes.

Thank you.
Does that help with your question?
Yes.
Yes.
How do we be the observer and still participate? [Student J asks.]

Ah, another wonderful question! And I can tell you that was given to you long, long ago and many of you [other] students that you were with that class. The lack of concern—or have you forgotten the business of common sense? *[Please see the appendix.]*

No, sir.

Then you remember that. And that tells you very clearly how you participate and be the observer. You see, you are no longer attached to the image. And therefore, by no longer being attached to the image of self, you are not concerned with someone else's attachment to the image of self that you have created. And therefore, you are successful. That's how you participate and progress. In other words, you give what you have to give and you care less what they do with it. You are free. You are what you are. Did that help you, [Student J]?

Yes, sir.

Yes. You see, you see, we are concerned with the image or how we present our self for we believe that in how we present our self, then someone else will do something else in keeping with our interests or needs, all right?

Yes, sir.

Oh, that's so far down there. You just move right on out of there. No, no, no, no, no, no. You don't need that at all. So then you will be able to participate and be the observer. You see, a person being the observer and not the observed is one who is participating, knowing full well, beyond a shadow of any doubt, that is not them: that is what they are using. Hmm? That help you, [Student J]?

Yes. Thank you.

Yes, it's the business of common sense. Now, [Student O], have you awakened this morning? Did you have your breakfast?

Yes, I did.

Did you? Good.

Thank you.

Is there anything you didn't have that you thought you needed?

I, I doubt—I, I have everything. I couldn't poss . . .

Oh, that's good, that's good. You're feeling better now?

Much better. Thank you.

Yes, yes. You got a little bit sleepy, did you?

Yes.

You ought to go to sleep at night. I didn't say to bed. I said to sleep. There is a difference, you know.

Yes, sir.

Yes. And then you would feel so good on Sunday morning. Such a beautiful day. I noticed that your wife is bright-eyed and bushy-tailed. Interesting. Well, I always did say, you know, there's a great tenacity. I think the ladies would like it known as determination in the—don't worry about being electric. You have no problem. You ladies have a very strong determination. You see how wide awake your wife is?

Yes, sir.

What happened to your energy?

I, I dissipated it on something.

Oh, you did. Oh, isn't that interesting. She didn't dissipate any of hers at all. Well, anyone else have a question this morning? Yes, [Student B]. I find that so interesting. Takes me back so many eons in time. Long, long ago. Yes, [Student B], please.

Planets have direct motion and retrograde—

Yes, you go ahead. That waterfall over there got over here. So that—could you speak your question once more? *[The teacher laughs joyfully.]* It's interesting how that waterfall moves all over. It's so nice, you know. *[The wind may have carried spray from the waterfall on to the teacher.]* Yes. Go right ahead, [Student B], with your question.

I'm wondering if the planets retrograde motion and direct motion are the same as our spin and counterspin.

They are. Spin and the retrospin or counterspin. Definitely. They are. You mean, in your solar system?

Yes.

Oh, yes, they are. Yes, yes. They are ever in keeping with the laws of attraction and repulsion.

And those planets, maybe, go into, say, retrograde for a couple of months of the year. And if we're born when it's, say—

That's correct. That's correct. They have all of those influences. Now remember, in the celestial marriage all of that contract is all written out; you see, so that the soul, your soul can only enter at a certain hour, a certain moment at a certain time. No matter, regardless of appearances, your entrance into form can only take place at a certain second, a certain time, under certain influences. Do you see? There is no other way that you could get to Earth in keeping with the contract. This is why a person, any soul—of course, the soul, it has gratitude, but the mind should awaken that whatever, whoever the person was, what they must never forget: a contract was signed in order for them to enter Earth. It was ever in keeping with that particular law. And there was no other person at no other time in no other way that could have entered their next step of evolution. You see? That was the only way possible. Hmm? For that is the law.

Yes. You entered Earth at a certain time. Do you see? A certain time. In keeping with various influences, you were destined to experience if you permitted yourself to overidentify with self. Hmm. Did that help with your question, [Student B]?

So when those planets in the solar system, you see—it's a cyclic pattern. Do you understand that? So, every so long a time, they move back into the position [they were in] at the time your soul entered form at the moment of conception. Do you understand that? So then what you experience, if you are a person overidentified with self and limit, you will experience, to the degree of your overidentification with the form, you will experience the repeat or return of the cyclic-pattern influences. You see?

Yes.

So a person goes along in their earthly life and they say, "Oh, I've been through this before. The same thing is repeating itself." Well, when you understand—first of all, you don't have to have the full impact of it, you know, as a greater awakening is made that you are using the form—and that's the Law of Use, you see, not abusing it by believing that you're it—you won't have such an impact [from] it. But those are the cyclic patterns of creation.

Now remember who controls creation. So ever in keeping, when the contract or the celestial marriage is brought about in the great, great halls in the Great Rotunda, when that has taken place, the representatives of the realms of creation are very, very well versed in the solar influences, the influences of the planets and creation—do you understand that?—so ever in keeping with that are the contracts made out between the Light and the lesser light. In keeping with what the soul, in its evolution, has accomplished and not accomplished, and the debts to be paid, and etc. Hmm? But that's not predestination for you have 10 percent free will. You see?

So you find some people in your planet, no matter what you say and no matter what you do, there is a certain influence that just seems to possess them, you see? Yes. That help with your question, [Student B]?

Thank you.

Yes. Yes, [Student H] has a question this morning.

Thank you. Is there a correlation between participation and the Law of Progression for continents and planets?

Yes.

And would this account for their progression and deterioration and stagnation?

Yes, of course, it does. Because, you see, depending upon their locations, you see—now you must understand that a solar system comes from one source. That's its birth. All right?

A part of itself—for example, you call it the sun in your solar system—a part of itself separated from itself and you have what you call the moon. All right? Now here you have, and I brought it to you in a little fable so many years ago, here you now have the celestial marriage—hmm?—revealing to you that the Light is marrying a part of itself, known as the lesser light. *[Please see the appendix for "The Celestial Marriage."]* You call that the moon. So now you have the positive and the negative; you have the father and the mother. And through that marriage, that is a reuniting of a part of itself with itself by a contract, you have the father-sun, the mother-moon and that reunification, once again, is sent out and you have the various children: you have the nine planets of your solar system. We have the mother-and-fatherance of that: your eleven; as above, so below. Given to some of you many years ago. Does that help with your question?

Thank you.

Yes. So everything returns unto itself. So the planets that you are presently experiencing, they're all in movement. They're all returning unto their source. It should take—you'll have to calculate many, many, many, many eons on your earthly experiences, but they are on their way back to the light. They're not going out from the light. They are in the returning process to. That's why your planet, your planet Earth, the fifth planet, of course, in your mental world, would be known as destroyed by fire. Well, of course, it's being destroyed by fire. It is returning to the source from whence it came out, you see. It's getting closer and closer to its source, to the sun, as all of the planets are.

And so this process takes place, I mean, you see, you study the skies, the heavens, and you can see what is the progression of all form, for it reveals the progression of all form. The rise and the fall, you see. The ascent and the descent that is the Law of Creation; it is the Law of Duality. Nothing that is created escapes that law. Everything returns unto itself. Hmm? Yes. That help with your question? Somebody else here had a question? [Student S] had a question, and [Student M]. Yes.

We place so much attention on where the planets are at the time of our birth. Should we be considering where they were at the time of conception?

No, no, no. Birth is conception. I mean, this foolishness of waiting nine months after the law has happened is ridiculous. I mean, at the moment [when] the negative and positive pole comes together it's when the soul entered. It doesn't enter nine months later. No, no, no. No. No. That's not this teaching. Certainly not. It's a teaching of ignorance. Yes, it's the letter of the law.

So then if we are interested in where the planets, what planetary influence—

Well, you must know the moment of conception.

I see. OK.

Well, that's no problem, you know. I think you people are rather concerned in your world with over populating the beautiful little planet. And why, that's no problem at all. You all have what you call those little time clocks. You set one of those clocks. The alarm goes off. You have the exact moment of conception. And there's no problem at all. Some of you—no, no, you won't. But your planet, you know, this business of children, all that foolishness, that's all taking place in your new technology: it's a test tube, you know. There's not going to be any more of that foolishness. [In] fact, they'll be raised entirely different. Yes, go ahead.

What you just said, we return the way we came. And—

Yes.

—considering—

Won't it be wonderful when you have all the test-tube ones? You just go back into a test tube. Yes, go right ahead. Thank you. Oh, it'll save you so much grief in your world. Yes. *[A few students laugh.]*

Considering that the first was Adam, with the male, I'd like to know how that relates to this progression that we seem to be in. In one of your prior classes you spoke about how the female of the species will be taking over and the male lessening.

That's true.

Becoming—

Hasn't that been happening?

—more androgynous.

Why, certainly. Well, don't you see what is happening?

Yes.

The male's in the female. The female's in the male. They've been doing it so many eons, they're making a reversal. Yes, go right ahead.

But—

Take a look at the moon and the sun.

Since it started—

Yes.

—with the male, it appears now that it's ending up with the female. Will it—

Yes.

—end the way it started, though, with the male?

Well, certainly.

How will that work?

Well, it'll just explode itself.

Oh. [The student laughs.]

Why, certainly. Why, certainly. Well, you can't go against the law and abuse the law without the law fulfilling itself, you see. You see, when you have anything in creation where you abuse the Law of Use and from abuse of that Law of Use, in what you are referring to, in the male and the female, from that, from many centuries of abuses, that which is by the law the responsibility of the male species has become and is becoming more and more the responsibility of the female. Surely you see that in your world? In many parts of your world, not in all your world. And so that is an effect and a payment of the abuses.

So in reference to—you see, you understand that the moon—[you] look up at the moon and that there is a part of the sun. As Eve is a part of Adam, the moon is a part of the sun. And shall return unto itself. Well, like I said, someday it'll explode, you see? Like a full moon.

You see, you show me people who really believe they are the limit and I'll show you people who are rather different, to say the least, on the full of the moon. They don't even have to look out and up at the sky to see if it's full or not. They're just seemingly automatically different. Would you not agree, [Student B]? Well, the laws of your land and the law enforcement, they'll all agree with no problem at all. Suddenly all these people who really believe and take great pride that they are the limited form, they go what you call berserk. Yes. Yes. Certainly.

Are you doing your part? I gave you a little job there, you know, for you to keep a look there. Are you doing that? *[The teacher may be referring to the instructions that were given to the cameraman to video the garden and the animals therein at different times during class.]*

I'm trying. [The cameraman responds.]

Oh, that's nice. Well, you're supposed to have something to do, besides—yes. Look at the birds, too. Now [Student M] is waiting, and [Student D] and [Student N]. And yes.

With progression there's always a movement of something and it seems that—

Stop at that. There's always a movement of something. What is it that can progress and does progress? What progresses?

The energy that—

No. Form progresses. Truth, the Light, doesn't progress. Progress is change. So the purpose of the Light entering form is to evolve the form, to expand it: that [is], progress it, change it, and refine it, you see. Your mind is limit. Your mind progresses. Your form is limit. Your form progresses. You all have [had] experiences in the last twenty years that your form has changed from what it was.

Yes.

Well, it's progressed.

Yes.

You may not like the progression that way and you may want it that way, but it doesn't matter. It has progressed. Go ahead, [Student M]. Go ahead.

And with this movement, like, when we talked about the frequency and the density of, you know, our senses and the planets, as this movement, like a spin, and therefore the progression speeds up as we become more what we are and less the me, from belief and faith, that progression moves . . .

Well, you, that which you are, you retrospin; therefore, you are no longer as bound by that which you are using.

Right.

You don't believe so much that you are what you are using.

Right.

That's like a person sitting down and having breakfast and they lift up a tool and they believe they're the tool. And without the tool, they wouldn't get the food, you see? So it's the same thing.

Yes.

That help you, [Student M]?

Yes, it does. Thank you.

Yes. Now [Student D] is waiting.

You—it was stated that Eve was a part of Adam.

Correct. Well, you might say, in your world, that she's even the rib. Yes, that's what they call it in your world: that she's a rib. What does a rib do? We're interested in Eve, so tell me what the rib does. Considering that she represents Adam's rib, tell me what the rib is for.
Well, it helps to protect the lungs.
What are the lungs for?
Breathing air.
And what is breathing air for?
It creates this oxygen which the body uses.
Does it use it or require it to remain in form?
Requires it for life.
Ah, good. All right. Now we know how valuable the ribs are. Go ahead.
Ah ...
Without them, man couldn't get very far, could he?
That is true.
You see, [with] no ribs there, you see, [the lungs] could easily get punctured. Right?
Right.
And then have no oxygen. So in that respect, in form, he's found himself totally dependent on what he created, right?
Right.
He created something that he's dependent on, correct?
Yes.
It only proves he created it. Go ahead. *[The teacher laughs.]*
Also, we are Spirit formless and free.
That's what you are.
Yes.
I'm not interested in you being Eve. Perhaps one of my students here might be interested.
... that is the physical plane. [Student D speaks at the same time as the teacher which makes it difficult to transcribe all of

her words. In addition to the waterfall, an airplane is also passing overhead.]

Yes.

[Student D speaks, but it is again difficult to transcribe her words.]

The physical plane?

Yes.

That's Eve. That's correct. That's where she begins and ends. Just like Adam.

Yes.

Yes. And when you're freed from that abuse of the Law of Use, there won't be any Eve because there won't be any Adam. When there's no Adam, there's no Eve. Do you understand? Don't worry about the birds and bees. Just let go of Adam and Eve. Now, yes, [Student O] has a question and I want to get to the ladies.

Yes. I'd like to ask, Is the sun stationary as we see it?

You see it stationary, yes. It's not.

It's not?

But that's the way you see it.

OK. Well, we're—

That's how you create it.

That's how we create it.

Yes, you create it. Your mind. Everyone's mind.

Well, the planets and—

You're moving right now, you see.

Yes, sir.

Around and around and around. *[The teacher gestures with his right hand making a clockwise circular motion and then makes a counterclockwise motion.]* Both directions. Do you feel it?

Oh, we're moving on the . . .

The chair you're in sitting on the Earth and the Earth that you're on is moving around that way and around that way. *[The*

teacher again gestures with his right hand forming one circle in a clockwise motion and one circle in a counterclockwise motion.]
OK, yes.
Yes. You know it's pear-shaped, don't you?
No, I didn't know it.
Well, it is. Go right ahead with your questions. It's not round at all. It's pear-shaped.
OK. Being that the planets are returning back to the, from where they returned, that would mean they're in a retrospin.
Hmm.
Is that correct?
Yes.
And, and—
They retrospin to get out. And now you want them to get back in?
OK. They retrospin to get out.
Yes, that's how you get out of something.
All right. So that—
So first of all, they were in the sun. All right, [Student O]? And through a retrospin they shot off into space. Hmm?
Right.
And so to return to the source, they would have to spin, don't they?
Right.
Oh, good. Now we've got that. All right. Be with you in a moment, [Student L].
OK. In the sun—if they're in a spin, then the sun is in a retrospin, then. Right?
[*The teacher laughs joyfully and has some difficulty speaking because of his laugher.]* Well, you—that's like, that which is, that which is the cherry of the cherry pie is telling the cherry pie what it is, when it is only a part thereof. No, that doesn't work at all. That doesn't work it all.

What is—

You see, here we have—no, no, no. We're looking through the peashooter consciousness. You see, we understand that that that shoots off from itself, like yourself, you see, your thoughts, you see, is spun off through a retrospin. It's moved out. Do you understand, [Student B]?

Now, through a spin [it] is brought to that which it shot off from. The source, in order to be the source, the very principle of the law of the source, has to be a perfect balance: spin and retrospin.

Right. [Student O speaks.]

That's known as divine neutrality, [Student O]. So you can't say that the source is spinning and you can't say the source—I understand *[The teacher acknowledges a signal from the cameraman that the tape recording the class is coming to an end.]*—is retrospinning, because the source is what is. It's spinning and retrospinning in such perfect unity, harmony, and balance it is absolutely neutral. All right?

Yes, sir. Thank you.

Hmm? Yes. Now [Student N] was waiting. We'll try to get, at least, to two more here before time is up on us in your world. Yes, [Student N].

If you're feeling uncomfortable and you're not—and you stop and you pause and you say, "This is the stuff—I'm coming—this is the thoughts that are coming from the fire center." So you distinguish—

If you are aware that it's the fire center. Could be the water. Go ahead.

Or the water center.

Yes.

And you stop and you pause and you realize that—

Yes.

—then is that the separation right there? Or—

As long as you maintain it, it is.

Oh—

And then you start and say, "Well now, that's fine. Is this what I want to do? Is this what I really want to do?" Say, "Now this is ridiculous!" And the next thing you know, you've made a change in your consciousness; you've made a little effort, and you're doing something else. Something you really want to do. You understand that?

Yes.

And what you really want to do is dependent, of course, [on] what something you went to as long as you believe you are self. You might have got up into the air center, you see. Or way down to the earth center. Try to understand that. It's very important. Hmm? As long as you feel the need, you must realize you are in service to one of the forms in one of the centers of consciousness. Because you can only feel or experience need by denial of what you are. So as long as you experience need, accept the demonstrable truth and choose wisely which forms you want to serve in what centers of consciousness. All right?

Thank you.

You see? If you do not experience need, then you can take another look and see: "Well, I will do that or I won't do that. I don't need to do it. I don't feel I particularly have to do it. I want to do it." You see? "I just want to." There's a vast difference. Yes. Discerning which is which.

[Student L], I see that our time is up here. *[The teacher glances at his wristwatch and then points to the cameraman and continues.]* You should be telling me. Yes, go right ahead.

Yes. Is the spin magnetic and the retrospin electric? [Student L asks.]

The spirit magnetic?!

No, no. Is the spin—

Oh.

—magnetic and the retrospin electric?

Yes, yes, it certainly is. It certainly is.

And so— *[The teacher receives a signal from the cameraman.]* Well, it takes me that long to drink the water that I shared with my good friend who disappeared somewhere. *[The teacher refers to the church's dog, Mr. Red.]* I will say good day. Have a nice, enjoyable afternoon. I know that you will. *[The teacher removes his microphone and lays it on the arm of his chair.]* And we look forward to seeing you on the anniversary next week here. I think you're going to find it's the anniversary. It'll be one year. One year. We'll begin our next year. *[The teacher refers to the one-year anniversary of this series of classes.]*

Thank you. And good day.

JUNE 8, 1986

APPENDIX

The Divine Healing Prayer

I accept that the Divine Healing Power
Is removing all obstructions
From my mind and body
And is restoring me
To perfect health, wealth, and happiness.
My heart is filled with gratitude
For the Divine Law of Acceptance
That is healing both present and absent ones
Who are in need of help.
Peace, the power that healeth,
Is guiding my thoughts, acts, and deeds
As God and I go hand in hand
Living a life of joyful abundance.

The Total Consideration Affirmation

I am the manifestation of Divine Intelligence. Formless and free. Whole and complete. Peace, Poise, and Power are my birthright.

The Law of Harmony is my thought and guarantees Unity in all my acts and activities, expressing perfect Rhythm and limitless flow throughout my entire being.

Without beginning or ending, eternity is my true awareness and sees the tides of creation, as a captain sees his ship.

As the Light of Truth is sustained by the faculty of Reason, I pause to think and claim my Divine right.

>   Right Thought. Right Action. Total Consideration.
>   Amen. Amen. Amen.

Divine Abundance

Thank
(Gratitude)

You
(Principle)

God
(Divine Intelligence)

I'm
(Individualizing)

Moving
(Rhythm)

In
(Unity)

Your
(Realization)

Divine
(Total)

Flow
(Consideration)

The Controlled Spiritual Environment Affirmation

You are in a controlled spiritual environment of truth and freedom
Where peace and harmony reign supreme.
Be awake, be aware, be alert.
Your purpose of being is freedom from what has been.
Thoughts of self are foreign to this environment.
Take control of your mind and experience the joy of living.

The Laws Be

Our being is the consciousness, Truth.
Holy be the identity
The joy of Life
The totality of Acceptance
In mind as it is in heart
Grant us the Light
Our daily sustenance
And forgive us our has-beens
As we forgive those has-beens who tempt to steal our joy
Free us from the romance of self-love
Deliver us from the service to the false king of shadows
For Light is the kingdom
And the power and the glory forever
Peace be, the order of Divinity

The All That Has Been Affirmation
From A/V Class Private 12

All that has been cannot be
That's not Good and I'm not free
Until I give then I be
The joy of life that sets me free.

The All That Has Been Affirmation
From a Recording of Affirmations

All that has been cannot be
That's not God and I'm not free
Until I give then I be
The joy of life that sets me free.

Oh, Love Divine

Oh, love divine, a servant be
'Til selfishness imprisons me
And warps the reason of my mind
Into the madness of the blind,
When truth cries out, "Not mine but Thine"
And frees my soul with love divine.

The Business of Common Sense

[Although the business of common sense was discussed a number of times and in particular CC 105, in A/V Class Private 43 the teacher may be referring to one of his, thus far, unpublished sayings.]

The business of common sense: It is the principle of effort that guarantees success and the principle of effort is the lack of concern.

[The following text is from the personal notes of the vice president of Serenity, a man who also served as the cameraman for these classes. This procedure is referred to in A/V Class Private 29.]

Acupressure of Circle of Logic

This procedure, as given by the Friends, is to help students restore balance in their universe, as long as effort is being made by the student who is the recipient of the procedure.

Procedure:

The student who is seeking help should sit, with back perfectly straight, on a stool or low back chair. Hands in lap, body completely relaxed.

APPENDIX 495

Student to be helped, and one who will administer the pressure, should do the cleansing breath, three times. [Note: A/V Class Private 30 also recommends that the person administering the pressure have clean hands and that their hands be rinsed with water immediately before and after the procedure.]

The student who is to administer the pressure should stand behind the seated subject. Referring to diagram, place the index finger on top of middle finger. Be sure your finger nails are short enough so they won't dig into the other student's neck. Place the middle finger on the spot, point "A" on diagram, press firmly, and rotate tip of finger in small circle to the right, clockwise, 14 revolutions. Change fingers so that the middle finger is on top of the index finger, see diagram. Press index finger firmly, on same spot and rotate counterclockwise 13 revolutions.

Find spot "B" on diagram, and repeat procedure. Rotate middle fingertip 14 clockwise, then rotate 13 counterclockwise with the index finger. That completes the procedure.

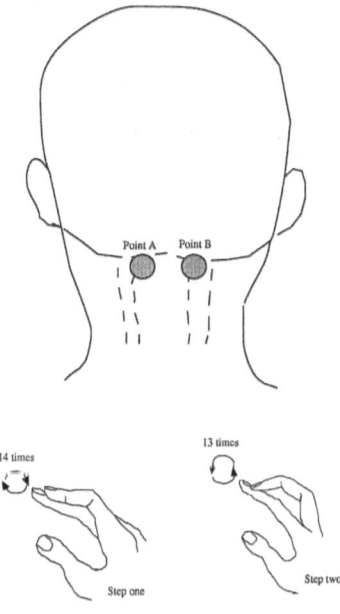

[In A/V Class Private 48, the teacher refers to a pamphlet that was published by Serenity many years earlier, entitled, "The Celestial Marriage". Here is the text of that pamphlet as it was published. An asterisk indicates a page break.]

THE CELESTIAL MARRIAGE
OR
THE DESCENT OF MAN
A FABLE
FROM
THE BOOK OF LIFE

*

GIVEN IN HUMILITY
TO ALL
HUMANITY

*

THE CELESTIAL MARRIAGE
or
THE DESCENT OF MAN

A FABLE
FROM
THE BOOK OF LIFE

*

GIVEN IN HUMILITY
TO ALL
HUMANITY

※

One day in great **ASPIRATION GOD** sent forth from itself **WILL**, and the sons of **WILL** became. Now the sons of **WILL** were of **GOD**, yea, they were **GODS** sent into form, but knew not because of form. The sons of **WILL** roamed the universes for eons and eons of time ever seeking other forms. After much searching they met to consider what they must do. For seven days and seven nights they discussed, and at the seventh hour **ILLUMINATION** fell upon them and said, "Behold, sons of **WILL**, within thyself is **COMPASSION**, know it, and unto thee shall be given." Alas, the sons of **WILL** knew **COMPASSION** and that night the daughters of **DESTINY** became.

In the morning when the daughters of **DESTINY** awoke to the sons of **WILL**, the **GODS** and **GODESSESS** of nature danced in jubilee.

Now the sons of **WILL** married the daughters of **DESTINY** and all nature wept with joy.

One day in **TRUTH** a son was born, his name was **INEVITABLE**, and the sons of **WILL** were greatly pleased. Now the daughters of **DESTINY** were quite unhappy for they **HOPED** for a daughter, and so that night in **DESIRE** a girl was born, her name was **LUST**.

Now **INEVITABLE** grew in the warmth and sunshine of the day. Oh how he loved the sun, for to him all **LIFE** was **LIGHT**.

LUST grew up to be a beautiful and lovely woman with a great fondness for the moon and darkness, for had she not been born in the night of **DESIRE**.

Time passed on, and one day **INEVITABLE** felt he would go into the night to find **LUST**, for he had heard so much about her, and had sent her many messages asking her to come into the **LIGHT** so that they may know more of each other. **INEVITABLE** went down, down into the darkness of night, and as he descended a great **FEAR** overcame him, but he found **LUST**, her face glowing so beautiful by the reflection of the sun. From the shadows where the **LIGHT** of the moon shone not, a voice spoke unto **INEVITABLE** and said, "Behold the beauty and the glory thou hast found, is it not worth the descent into our realms?" But from within, a voice spoke to **INEVITABLE** and said, "Take her to the realms of **LIGHT** that you may see more clearly in a day of **REASON**."

The senses won, and that night in **DESPAIR** a child was born, her name was **GRIEF**. The years passed and **GRIEF** could not be comforted, for she had been born of **LUST**, in the night of **DESIRE**, by the promptings of **PASSION**, and knew not of **TRUTH**.

INEVITABLE wandered on and on with the daughter **GRIEF**, hoping to return to the realms of **LIGHT**, but no, the centuries passed and only **SORROW** did they know.

Then one day a bird from the realms of **LIGHT** landed on his shoulder and sang this song, "In **SORROW** doth thou stay for self-pity knows no way."

INEVITABLE thought and thought of the meaning of those words, then he thought of his homeland **TRUTH** where he had been so very, very happy; and in **CONCENTRATION**, he found himself leaving the realms of darkness, passing through the lands of **IGNORANCE** and **EXPERIENCE** to return to his blessed land.

```
         LOVE ALL LIFE
          AND KNOW
          THE LIGHT
```

*

```
       OH MAN THINK HUMBLE
       YET WELL OF THYSELF
        FOR IN THY THINKING
             IS CREATED
         THE VEHICLE OF
            THE SOUL
```

Cover Image of 1972 Edition
of *The Living Light*

[The cover image of the 1972 edition of The Living Light *is displayed on the frontispiece of this volume. Reference to the symbolic image is discussed in excerpts from the following volumes of* The Living Light Dialogue:*]*

[Volume 2, Consciousness Class 44, pages 480-481:]
"And we'll begin with the outside of it, [The teacher refers to the cover image.] which is the snake, representative of wisdom consuming itself. Now why does the symbol of wisdom consume itself? Does anyone know? Does anyone know why wisdom is self-consuming? Because, my friends, if it's wisdom, then it can gain nothing from outside of itself: it already is wisdom. So all that wisdom is—you understand, you don't gain wisdom and neither do you give wisdom. Wisdom is self-sustaining. When you rise to a level of consciousness where wisdom expresses itself, then you will become it and it is self-sufficient unto itself. So the snake consuming itself is representative of wisdom, in comparison to what one might call knowledge. Now, knowledge is something that you gain. It's something that you put into your brain and you feed back at your discretion—but not wisdom.

"The next step is the interlaced double triangle, which is a very, very ancient symbol. It is the meeting of the spirit with matter. It is the power above that meets the forces below. And at that junction, when those two triangles meet, that's the negative and the positive poles come together in creation and the divine spark, the rays of light, life is so-called born into matter.

"Now you all know that all poles are triune. The negative pole is triune and the positive pole is triune. In fact, my friends, as we've stated before, all things that are manifest are triune and that is why three is the number of manifestation.

"Inside of the interlaced triangles you'll notice on the top of the pyramid in the rays of light is the all-seeing eye. Now the all-seeing eye is that that is not distracted, because it sees everything and so nothing gains its attention. And that is why it is the all-seeing eye. The triangle itself, the pyramid upon which all knowledge, the all-seeing eye, all wisdom, and all life rest, is the pyramid of manifestation. All things in all universes (physical, mental, or spiritual) are triune. There are three parts to all things: that is an absolute fact of physics and it is a truth of the universe."

[Volume 4, Consciousness Class 78, page 172:]
"Then, we'll be happy to share our understanding. The serpent so designed—consuming itself—is the ancient and eternal symbol of everlasting and eternal wisdom. The double triangle, with its apex downward, is the manifestation of the Divine Power and the balance of nature, its own creation. The pyramid with the all-seeing eye on the top is the eternal Light that never closes, that sees all things, that knows all things, and that ever is and ever has been."

www.ingramcontent.com/pod-product-compliance
Lightning Source LLC
Chambersburg PA
CBHW030144100526
44592CB00009B/104